Finance and Industrial Performance in a Dynamic Economy

Columbia Studies in Business, Government, and Society
Eli Noam, General Editor

Columbia Studies in Business, Government, and Society

Finance and Industrial Performance in a Dynamic Economy

Theory, Practice, and Policy

Merritt B. Fox

Columbia University Press
New York   1987

Library of Congress Cataloging-in-Publication Data

Fox, Merritt B.
  Finance and industrial performance in a dynamic
economy.

  (Columbia studies in business, government, and
society)
  Bibliography: p.
  Includes index.
  1. Corporations—United States—Finance.
2. Corporations—United States—Finance—Case studies.
3. Semiconductor industry—United States—Finance—Case
studies. I. Title. II. Series.
HG4061.F69 1987   658.1'5   86-23277
ISBN 0-231-06282-6

Columbia University Press
New York   Guildford, Surrey
Copyright © 1987 Columbia University Press

Printed in the United States of America

To William T.R. Fox
and Annette Baker Fox

Acknowledgments

This book attempts to tackle a large and complex problem: understanding the relationship between finance and industrial performance. Whatever success I have achieved in this undertaking is due in large part to the guidance and support of many other persons.

My first debt is to my teachers, who laid the intellectual foundations on which this work is built. Three of them stand out. Harold D. Lasswell taught me the importance of social science for legal scholarship and the need to study structures of authority and patterns of communication. Charles E. Lindblom taught me to examine critically the fundamental assumptions of neoclassical economics and to think creatively about possible variations from existing institutional structures. Richard R. Nelson taught me to focus on the possibilities of enhancing economic welfare by facilitating technical change and to appreciate the virtues of dynamic analysis.

I have benefited greatly from the advice of a number of scholars who have read all or parts of the manuscript at various points in its development. For their detailed reading and comment, I especially wish to thank John A. Boquist, William C. Brainard, John C. Coffee, Jr., Ann J. Gellis, Albert G. Hart, J. William Hicks, Saul X. Levmore, Richard R. Nelson, Merton J. Peck, Michael B.W. Sinclair, and Thomas S. Ulen. At an earlier stage, I received valuable research advice from John E. Tilton.

Appreciation goes to the Indiana University School of Law (Bloomington), which provided the financial support for the time needed to complete this project, and to its Library Staff, which provided prompt and untiring service. I received research assistance from a number of students at the Law School as well, and I am particularly indebted to Timothy Riffle, Rhonda Brauer, and Greg Kinkley.

Gratitude is also owed to Karen Morrow and Jennifer Watt, without whose skilled typing and other secretarial help this project would not have been possible.

A portion of chapter 6 of this book is based on material contained in a previously published article in volume 70 of the *Virginia Law Review*. I thank the publisher for permission to include a revised version of this material.

Finally my deep thanks go to Ann Gellis, my wife, for her unfailing support in all ways, and to my sons Peter and Edward, for their inspiration.

Contents

Introduction

Capital is instrumental to the production of goods and services. The institutions in each society associated with the allocation and control of capital are so important that they serve to distinguish different systems of political economy. Our society has developed over the last century and a half a variety of such institutions, including banks, institutional investors, investment advisers, corporations in their financial and investment activities, and securities markets. These institutions intermediate between the private decisions of millions of individuals to save some portion of their incomes and real investment in the concentrated amounts required by modern technology. The intermediating activities of these institutions, which I refer to as the finance process, include gathering savings, channeling them into appropriate projects, supervising management of the facilities which the savings have been used to buy, and structuring, in a variety of risk, return, and liquidity combinations, claims for receipt of any resulting proceeds. The importance of capital to the production of goods and services suggests that the behavior of these institutions would have a significant influence on the behavior of firms and industries and the consequent set of costs, mix of output, and state of technology prevailing in our economy. This book studies that influence of the finance process on industrial performance.

Increasing our understanding of the determinants of industrial performance has special relevance today. There is a general perception that the level of industrial performance of the United States economy over the last 15 years has not been as good as it could have been. This perception may exaggerate the problem: much of it is due to forces beyond our control such as increased prices for imported petroleum and a shifting national demographic mix. There is also probably an underappreciation of the many benefits, not captured by our system of national accounts, that result from industrial compliance with costly new environmental and safety regulations. Nevertheless, international comparisons of product competitiveness and temporal comparisons of the rates of GNP and productivity growth with those in the 1950s and 1960s suggest that a real problem exists. In the search for solutions, it is reasonable to ask whether there are changes in policy that would alter the operation of the finance process in a way that would have a favorable impact on industrial performance. Current proposals to encourage greater capital formation may be of relatively little help if the added capital is not well used.

Industrial performance is intimately linked to the general level of economic well-being in society and is commonly measured in terms of its contribution to that well-being. The discussion in this book will be in terms of three such measures, which taken together constitute a relatively comprehensive description of its contribution.

Production efficiency. How close does each firm, given the level of output it has chosen, come to producing its product for the least possible cost? A firm which is relatively production efficient contributes more to society's economic well-being than one which is not because it uses fewer of society's scarce resources to produce an output of the same value. A high level of production efficiency is associated with firms which assiduously pursue profits because each dollar of extra cost is a dollar less of profits.

Output choice efficiency. How close does each firm's level of output come to the level at which price and marginal cost would be equal? If each firm in the economy chooses a level of output at which price equals marginal cost, the scarce productive resources of society are used to produce an overall mix of products which best corresponds to the relative preferences of consumers. If, instead, the firms in one industry, let's say tires, choose levels of output such that the resulting price for tires exceeds the firms' marginal costs, a shift of productive resources from the manufacture of other goods to the manufacture of tires would increase the general level of economic well-being. Because the other products in the economy are produced by firms choosing output levels where price does equal marginal cost, the lost production of the other goods resulting from the shift would, at the margin, have a dollar value equal to that of the shifted resources. But the increase in production of tires would have a dollar value exceeding the dollar value of those resources. Therefore, the new mix of output would be more valued by consumers than the old mix. A high level of output choice efficiency is associated with each available product being supplied by many competing firms, all of which are assiduously pursuing profits.

Dynamic efficiency. How well does each firm in the economy search for new goods to produce and new techniques for producing goods already available in the market? When they make or become aware of such a discovery, how ready are they to commence production of the new product or implement the new technique? Increasing our understanding of dynamic efficiency is particularly important. Studies showing the dominant role played by innovation in the growth of our economy suggest that a significant improvement in dynamic efficiency would contribute more to general economic well-being than would any possible improvement in production or output choice efficiency. But much less is known about how to create an environment more conducive to dynamic efficiency than is known with respect to the other two measures of industrial performance.

No one would deny that the finance process has an important influence on industrial performance in terms of the three measures set out above. A low share price heightens managerial concern with profitability, which is related to both production and output choice efficiency. Capital availability can influence market structure and hence output choice efficiency: if only one or a few firms serving a market have access to capital, the market will have a less competitive structure than if many firms have such access. Capital availability can also significantly influence dynamic efficiency, since most innovations require new investment.

Yet, despite its importance, very little attention has been paid to the relationship between finance and industrial performance. This neglect is probably due to a general belief that the relationship is a straightforward one, conforming to a simple, widely accepted neoclassical model of finance. Most scholarly attention is instead paid to how production and output choice efficiency can be enhanced by maintenance of competition in final product markets. Correspondingly, maintenance of competition is the focus of the primary regulatory scheme concerned with industrial performance, the antitrust laws. In the few general studies of industrial performance that do not assume that the operations of the finance process conform to the simple model, the specific nonconformity is taken as given, for example capital being unavailable in amounts sufficient to establish a firm of minimum efficient scale and the consequent creation of an entry barrier. The reasons for the existence of such nonconformity are not explored. Studies specifically concerning dynamic efficiency tend to have a broader focus than more traditional studies, but they too either ignore the finance process or make assumptions concerning it (such as all investment being financed from retained earnings) that are even more restrictive than those of the simple neoclassical model.

The simplicity of the neoclassical model of finance and its relationship to industrial performance derives from the model's assumption that all participants are equally well informed and thus share uniform views concerning the probability distribution of the future events that will determine the return from each possible investment or, in the model's more sophisticated version, from the proposition that in the aggregate the finance process works as if this assumption were correct. This assumption assures that managers who fail to maximize profits will lose control of their firms, either by takeover or shareholder revolt. It also permits the allocation of capital to be treated like the allocation of any other factor of production. The price of capital, if competitively determined, represents its social opportunity cost, and it will flow, like any other commodity, to those firms which can make the best use of it. This would include firms expanding in, or entering into, markets with the prospect of above-normal profits because of lack of competition or an innovative new product or process.

But assuming equality of information results in a great loss of explanatory power. Because of its simplicity, the neoclassical model may be useful for many purposes, but it turns out to be the wrong model to use in the study of the impact of finance on industrial performance, particularly if we wish to enlarge our understanding of the environment most conducive to dynamic efficiency. Specifically because participants in the finance process in fact are not equally well informed, the core mechanisms of interaction between finance and industrial performance, the takeover threat and capital availability, do not work the way they are described in the simple model. The result is that the organization and performance of our industries are significantly different from the way they would be if the assumption of equal information were a generally correct description of reality.

This objection to the assumption of equality of information involves more than a scholarly debate as to the appropriateness of one model versus another. It has had a substantial effect on the way our legislative and administrative officials think. Accompanying the loss of explanatory power is a narrowing of policy perspective. Application of the simple neoclassical model overly restricts the range of issues considered when decisions are made concerning regulation of the finance process. Although the variety of institutions included in the finance process is large, the purposes of the respective sets of regulations under which these different institutions operate are few. Monetary policy aside, these regulations almost exclusively concern prevention of fraud on investors, protection of certain classes of investors from undue risk, and, to the extent consistent with the other two concerns, maintenance of a reasonable level of competition in financial markets. Only the last of these concerns relates to industrial performance and then only indirectly. Because capital is not an ordinary commodity and the relationship between finance and industrial performance in a dynamic world is more complex than that described in the simple model, concern solely with competition is not enough. Improving industrial performance in terms of its three measures should be, but is generally not, a conscious goal in the making of all public policy relating to the finance process.

When one looks at the influence of finance on industrial performance, differences in information should be emphasized, not assumed away. The focus should be on communications flow and the allocation of responsibility for decisions: who has what information, how has each participant obtained it, what is the range of choices available to each participant. The premise is that the behavior of each participant is a function of what he knows: he chooses among the alternative courses of action available to him in accordance with his personal expectations. The three interrelated studies that follow demonstrate how fruitful this approach can be.

The first study develops a theory of the finance process as performing a function required in all economies: to decide, taking account of information held by disparate sources, which proposed real investment projects shall receive society's scarce savings and who shall manage existing projects. Individual savers, by choosing where to place their savings and, in the case of equityholders, how to vote their shares, have the ultimate power of control over the process. They want their savings to implement real investment projects that promise the highest returns and they want existing projects to be managed by persons that will make the most of them. Since it is not obvious which proposed projects and which managers satisfy these criteria, the finance process can be viewed as one of discovery. This view makes no sense in a world of information equality, where the finance process is just a market, like any other commodity market, for the buying and selling of capital. But the view flows naturally from the "who knows what and why" approach advocated here.

Work has appeared over the last ten years recognizing that information creation, processing and diffusion has real costs which lead to information differentials among participants and that these differentials in turn substantially affect industrial performance. Information problems, however, are in large part viewed as a constraint, similar to the scarcity of some material resource. The system operates, subject to its constraints, in an optimal fashion. The regulatory implication is that the system in large part can take care of itself despite its information problems.

This study views information as too central to the mechanisms that operate the system for us automatically to assume such optimization. The finance process is an organization. Each saver has a position in this organization analogous to the head of a hierarchical organization: he wants the choices of new real investment projects and the management of existing ones to correspond to specified criteria but, at least in the first instance, he does not possess sufficient information to decide well. He deals with this problem by seeking the advice of, and delegating decisions to, more knowledgeable individuals. Like any other organization, the finance process has operating rules and feedback mechanisms that can be analyzed with the aid of organization theory to discover how well the organization is serving the goals we assign to it: promoting production, output choice and dynamic efficiency. We might ask, for example, is the organization reasonably sensitive to new opportunities arising from technical change or could its sensitivity be increased without incurring costs that exceed the prospective benefits? Does the way the organization operates enhance or diminish competition in product markets? Are there systematic biases in the way the organization executes its function, such as consistently allowing certain kinds of managerial waste, for which it seems to have no self-correcting tendencies?

The second study applies the "who knows what and why" approach to an empirical investigation of the relationship between finance and industrial performance in practice: the financing of the semiconductor industry in the first twenty-five years of its development. One of the main hopes for improving the industrial performance of our economy lies with the rapid development of industries that are based on revolutionary new technologies. The in-depth study of the financing of the semiconductor industry suggests some of the general strengths and weaknesses of the finance process as currently constituted in fostering the development of more such industries. The study also shows that there are certain peculiar, but possibly imitable, aspects of the financing of the semiconductor industry that in part account for its extraordinary performance.

The third study concerns policy: the application to questions of public choice of the general observations of the study in theory and the specific observations of the study in practice. The operating rules and feedback mechanisms which determine how well the finance process performs its organizational function are shaped by how it is structured and regulated. The study focuses on the impact of the legal structure on one component of the finance process: the dividend behavior of large corporations. Dividend behavior is very important because it determines who participates in what ways in the decisions of the finance process concerning which proposed real investment projects are implemented and which are not. The study analyzes the impact of three areas of law—securities, tax, and corporations—on the dividend behavior of large corporations and recommends certain reforms. The study is a representative example of how the application of the approach advocated in the book can lead to reforms in the regulation of the finance process that can significantly improve industrial performance.

Part I

A Study in Theory

1. The Question of Approach

This book studies the influence of the finance process on industrial performance. The finance process—the link between real investment and individuals seeking a place to hold their wealth—consists of the daily interaction of hundreds of thousands of individuals as diverse as stock market speculators, pension fund administrators, financial analysts, bank loan officers, and members of corporate capital budget committees, both among themselves and with other participants in the economy. As with any other form of social interaction, trying to understand the influence of the finance process on industrial performance by studying it as a whole would be fruitless; the interaction is too vast and complex. To think logically about the problem, one must narrow one's range of attention to a limited number of variables and rely on certain assumptions concerning their relationships.

Which variables should be chosen and what assumptions should be made? The ultimate answer is the variables and assumptions that permit the creation of a theory that, when applied to real world observations, both successfully identifies the features of our industrial system that can be attributed to particular characteristics of the finance process and also suggests changes in policy that hold the most promise for improving industrial performance. But one must develop a theory before it can be tested against these criteria. Developing a theory requires an initial choice of variables and assumptions without knowing that they are necessarily the correct ones. This chapter is concerned with making the initial choice: the problem of deciding upon the most plausible approach.*

*The reader might fairly ask why I propose to take him through the process of making the initial choice of variables and assumptions. Why not just present the

A. Identifying the Issues

1. *Finance and Industrial Peformance: The Scope of Interaction*

This book is not concerned with every aspect of the workings of the finance process, only in those which seem likely to have some kind of effect on industrial performance. The finance process is intimately connected to two types of decisions in the real economy: which proposed investment projects are implemented (project choice) and how existing productive capacity in the economy is used (production decisions).

1.1 *Project Choice*

Consider how real investment takes place. The process starts when a person or group of persons, the proponent, proposes an idea to develop the capacity to produce in a particular way a certain number of units of a good or service that will help satisfy demand in a particular market. A proposed project thus has four salient features: product market, scale, a proponent, and technology. Creating the capacity to produce normally requires the initial expenditure of an amount of money for purposes such as plant, equipment, research and development, staff, and inventory that substantially exceeds the amount (net of further day-to-day input expenditures) expected to be received in return in the near future from sales of the goods or services the production of which the capacity makes possible. Since proposed projects cannot be realized without money, the finance process stands at the gate: it decides which of the proposals are funded and which are not, either by flat interdiction or by demanding a toll (the financing terms) sufficiently onerous to turn the proponents back. These decisions, as they accumulate over time, both literally and figuratively set up the structure in which industrial activity in our

theory and test it to show that it works? As Milton Friedman and other proponents of positivism in economics point out, if a theory works, no one cares whether the approach used is plausible or not.[1] Subsequent chapters of this book will begin the process of testing the theory. But like many theories in economics and in the social sciences generally, the theory proposed here is too general to be tested conclusively within the scope of a single work. The plausibility of its approach will therefore significantly affect its attractiveness for application to questions of policy and for further testing.

economy occurs. As a consequence, they are key determinants of our economy's industrial performance.

The effect on industrial performance of a particular project succeeding or failing to pass through the gate can be seen most easily by example: a proposed project to develop the capacity to produce one million radial tires annually. First, the decision to fund the tire project instead of another proposed project, perhaps for television production, will result in a different total amount of production capacity in each industry and, through the consequent effect on marginal costs, in a different output mix in the economy. Second, the decision implies a choice of proponents, and that will affect the level of the industry's competitiveness. If the proponents are officials employed by a new entrant (a firm which just came into existence or which up until this point has not produced tires) or by a firm which currently produces tires but does not have a very big share of the market, the project will make the structure of the tire industry more competitive. The project will have the opposite effect if the proponents are officials employed by a firm which already has a dominant share of the tire market. The level of competitiveness in turn will affect firm-pricing strategies and hence, again, the mix of output in the economy. The implied choice of proponents also affects production efficiency, both directly—the question of whether the proponents are potentially good managers or poor ones—and indirectly— the effect of the choice on the level of competitiveness of the tire industry, which is positively related to production efficiency. Finally, the decision to fund a proposed tire project implies a choice of both product and process technology and is thus related to dynamic efficiency. A large portion of real investment existing in the economy at any one point does not permit much flexibility in the way it is used: it is only suited to produce one particular product in one particular way. The series of previously funded projects which together constitute the current aggregate capacity for tire production in the economy determine the level and mix of technologies prevailing in the industry. Any significant shift in technology, such as a shift from conventional to radial tires, generally requires new real investment.

Whether or not a particular project proposal receives funding is the result of the actions of one of several different possible combinations of finance process participants. The proponent may be one or a group of individuals who wish to act on an idea by setting up a new company. For the project to receive funding, financial intermediaries or savers must be willing to purchase securities from, or lend money to, the new firm. Alternatively, the proponent may be one or more managers of an existing corporation who wish to add the project to the corporation's activities. If the existing corporation is a large divisionalized corporation, the manager or managers would likely be below the very top officers in the corporation's hierarchy. They would then have to request funds for the project from the top officers. Whatever the position of the proponents in the managerial hierarchy, the project cannot be implemented unless the corporation itself has access to funds.[2] The funds might come from the net revenues of current operations that are retained instead of distributed to shareholders, from the sale of an existing real asset or, as with a proponent setting up a new firm, from financial intermediaries or savers purchasing securities from, or lending money to, the corporation.

Given such apparently dissimilar possible combinations of participants, whether or not the project idea passes through the finance process gate and receives funding may depend on which combination is actually involved (what I shall refer to as the context of the decision). Neoclassical theory suggests that there are forces at work to assure that the same decision will be made no matter what the context. But those forces may not in fact be strong enough to bring about that result within a time frame which is relevant to an analysis of the effect of project choice on industrial performance. If so, we are faced with the potentially complex task of understanding how decisions are made in each of these different contexts as well as how the legal and institutional structure of the finance process influences what portion of the economy's savings are allocated by decisions in each context. Since the proponent for any particular project usually does not have the opportunity to have his proposal considered in more than one context, these factors can be crucial in determining which projects get funded and which do not.[3]

1.2 *Production Decisions*

If a project receives funding, a unit of productive capacity is created. In terms of physical possibilities, such capacity usually permits a wide range of choice as to the level of output and, for any given level, at least some range of choice as to the combination of inputs used. The manager or managers making these production decisions can be said to control the unit of productive capacity in question. Their production decisions will directly affect the industrial performance of the economy in terms of output choice efficiency and production efficiency.

The workings of the finance process influence production decisions in two ways: provision of managerial incentives and disincentives, including threat of control reassignment; and the occasional actual reassignment of control. The structures which give rise to these aspects of the relationship between the real and the financial sectors of the economy can be primarily explained by the nature of the risks that sources of funds for investment projects undertake when they provide money to proponents. A funding source for a project (or its successor in right) has a strong stake in how production decisions are made because such decisions can affect the return on the source's investment. No source would be willing to provide funds unless it believes that the managers controlling the project will operate within a structure of incentives and disincentives, either already in place or to be put in place at the time of funding, that works to align the interests of the managers with those of the source to a reasonable degree. Nor would the source be comfortable if there were no way for control to be reassigned to another group of managers if the first group performs sufficiently badly.

The most obvious positive incentive for managers to make production decisions that serve the interests of a funding source is to give a financial reward to the managers if the outcome of their decisions is such that the source receives a good or full return on its investment.

Where the source of funds to which the proponent has appealed is share purchasers, common systems to provide such a reward include profit-sharing arrangements, stock ownership by the controlling managers, and stock options. With respect to the latter two schemes, the role of the finance process is not limited to the funding source requiring their existence as a condition for funding; at any particular time thereafter, the value to such managers of the shares or options depends on the price the market currently assigns to the shares. Share price can also provide controlling managers with incentives in the form of psychic rewards—prestige and a sense of making a score—which help align manager and share purchaser interests. The fact that controlling managers may have more projects in the future which they wish to fund from outside sources also motivates them to act in ways which would ingratiate themselves with various participants in the finance process, including those whose actions determine share price.

Where the source to which the proponent has appealed is a lender or purchaser of debt securities, the source will receive at least partial comfort from the positive incentives that provide comfort to share purchasers. Since debt service has, loosely speaking, a first claim on the cash flow generated by corporate operations and interest is deducted when profit is calculated, decisions motivated by the mechanisms that reward profit or high share prices will under most circumstances be ones that are aimed at generating a level of cash flow that will be more than sufficient to cover debt service.[4]

Where the source is top management providing funding to proponents who are managers below them, a system of positive incentives, financial and otherwise, to align the interests of the two groups can be established by administrative fiat.

Funding sources, however, generally do not view positive incentives as providing sufficient protection. First, it is difficult adequately to align the interests of the funding sources with those of the managers controlling production decisions solely through the use of positive incentives. Second, even where the interests are adequately aligned, the control group may disappoint the source that initially chose it and turn out to be incompetent. The incompetent control group's inability to make decisions in its own best interest means that it also fails to make choices that are in the best interest of the funding source. The response to these two problems is to set up mechanisms for reassigning control. Since controlling managers want to retain their jobs, the threat of reassignment of control adds a stick to the carrot of positive incentives in the effort to align the interests of the managers with those of the funding source. It also provides an escape hatch in the case of incompetent management. In the view of most observers, it is through the mechanism of control reassignment that the finance process is most likely to have a direct influence on the quality of production decisions.

Where the funding source is new share purchasers, the control reassignment mechanism involves two steps. Directors by law appoint corporate officers and possess the authority under which the corporation is operated. In most corporations, the directors may be removed at will by a majority vote of the shareholders. If the current shareholders of a corporation do not take the initiative to use this device to remove its managers, the managers may still be replaced if enough of the shareholders are induced into selling their shares to buyers who will exercise this power, i.e., effect a takeover. The range of participants in the finance process who can influence the probability of reassignment of control thus includes all those whose actions go to setting the price of the shares in the market (the lower the price, the easier to induce current shareholders to sell) and all those who might provide funding to someone attempting a takeover.

Even though this control reassignment mechanism does not allow for participation by lenders and purchasers of debt securities, it still provides them some comfort for the same reasons that they share in the benefits of the positive incentives on which new share purchasers rely. Holders of company debt also have their own mechanism of reassignment of control—bankruptcy—although it is only available under dire circumstances.* Its existence as a threat is important in cases where management has no fears of shareholder revolt or takeover,† and in circumstances where management actions which are in the best interests of shareholders are not in the best interests of lenders.

Again, where the source is top management providing funding to proponents who are managers below them, control of the project can be reassigned by administrative fiat.

---

*Institutional lenders (but not bondholders or their representatives) may also have the leverage to participate in control reassignment situations that fall short of actual bankruptcy because corporations in financial difficulties may need them as a continued source of working capital.

†Shareholders in corporations with little chance of shareholder revolt or takeover may also get some comfort from the existence of the bankruptcy threat. In a probabilistic world, risk-averse managers are unlikely to pursue a strategy serving their private interests to the extent that it drives down the expected revenues to the point just a sliver above what would throw the corporation into bankruptcy. They will leave some margin of safety so that there is a good chance they will be able to keep their jobs.

1.3 Project Choice Revisited: The Financial Role of the Management of Existing Corporations

Whenever the top management of an existing corporation decides to implement a proposed project idea, whether it is one submitted by its subordinates (as discussed earlier) or is top management's own idea, the funds must come from somewhere. In generating these funds and directing them to a particular use, top management plays a role akin to an investment company. This role can be illustrated by a hypothetical corporation whose productive capacity is solely the result of funding from shares issued at the time the corporation was founded and whose management has now decided to proceed with a second project. Consider the position of a holder of shares issued at the founding. If the second project is internally financed, the corporation is reinvesting funds generated by the corporation's original project that would otherwise be distributed to such holder. If the second project is externally financed, the holder is being required by the management to give up part of his share of the future earnings generated by existing productive capacity, which his money helped finance, in return for a share of any earnings which the second project might generate. The effect of external financing to the holder is the same as if part of his interest in the existing capacity is sold and the proceeds used to make an investment in his name in the second project.

Thus, because top managements of existing corporations have control over funds or over assets that aid in raising funds, they are participants in the project choice function of the finance process. The same mechanisms—managerial incentives and control reassignment—that work to align the interests of top management with those of shareholders when top management is playing its production decision role concerning the use of existing projects also work to align these interests when top management is playing its investment company role. But the distinction between these two roles will turn out to be very important for the analysis developed in chapter 2.

2. *Fundamental Choices in Approach and Chapter Overview*

We can see from the foregoing discussion that certain kinds of decisions made by the finance process can affect industrial performance. Inherent in the decision to fund the tire project, for example, are choices of product market, scale, proponent, and technology that will affect the production, output choice, and dynamic efficiency of the economy. Decisions made on an ongoing basis, such as security prices, also affect, directly or indirectly, all three measures of industrial performance through the part they play in the mechanisms of positive management motivation and control reassignment. We thus know the kinds of decisions on which this study should focus.

Two choices of fundamental approach are required to construct a theory of how these decisions are made and what pattern their impact will have on industrial performance:

1. *Uniformity of expectations.* Finance involves making decisions now that will have consequences later. How participants view the future is likely to be central to any description of how they make their decisions. Therefore, we must determine at the outset what, if anything, should be assumed about what each of the participants knows and the consequent degree of uniformity and accuracy of their views of the future.
2. *Static versus dynamic analysis.* A static analysis describes, for any given continuing environment, a system's final resting place—its equilibrium point. Although static analysis shows the existence of forces at work to bring the system toward that final equilibrium resting place, it does not give a detailed description of the behavior of the system at any given moment in time when the system is not at its final resting place. A dynamic analysis describes the path taken over time by the system and is therefore also concerned with the behavior of the system while in disequilibrium. Dynamic analysis sacrifices parsimony in order to describe the behavior of the system under a wider range of circumstances. With respect to the system as a whole (the one that encompasses the interaction of finance and industrial performance) and various critical subsystems (for example, securities market pricing given a particular pattern of information availability), the choice between the two modes of analysis depends on how prevalent and how critical are the circumstances under which behavior of the system or subsystem is not well described by a static analysis.

By focusing on these two fundamental choices, this chapter touches upon most of the important considerations in choosing the appropriate variables and assumptions for a useful theory of finance and industrial performance. What follows first is a statement of the neoclassical theory of finance and industrial performance, a theory that assumes uniform expectations among finance process participants and utilizes static models of the market for securities and of industrial organization. The assumption of uniform expectations is then relaxed, which causes parts of the theory—the description of how shareholders motivate firm managers and how firm managers calculate the cost of capital—to work significantly differently from the way they work in the neoclassical model. These differences would appear to require a new theory of the firm and render incorrect some of the neoclassical theory's conclusions as to the industrial performance of a competitive system. But some economists argue that substitute mechanisms exist—pressure from profit-maximizing competitors or new entrants, securities trading by the best-informed investors, and the takeover threat—which assure the validity of the neoclassical conclusions notwithstanding nonuniform expectations. A critical issue in these arguments is, with respect to various kinds of information possessed by some but not all participants in the market for securities, how quickly, if ever, the market reaches an equilibrium resembling one that would prevail if all participants knew the information. Another issue is whether the process by which various participants discover information is important. The arguments in support of resurrecting the neoclassical conclusions are not found to be wholly persuasive. The failure of these arguments to be wholly persuasive suggests that a theory that emphasizes information differences among participants and the mechanisms by which each participant obtains information would be more fruitful than a theory that assumes such differences do not exist.

This chapter then discusses static versus dynamic analysis of industrial organization. Dynamic analysis is shown to have two important advantages. First, it is more helpful in understanding technical change in the economy than is static analysis. Second, it permits construction of a theory of industrial organization which recognizes the problems, just alluded to, with the neoclassical theory of the firm that arise because of the information differences among finance process participants.

Finance is seen to be at the heart of the modus operandi of a dynamic model of industrial organization: the entry or expansion of firms utilizing innovations or more profitable operating rules and the contraction or exit of those which do not innovate or which employ less profitable operating rules.

B. The Model of Finance at the Foundation of the Neoclassical Theory of Industrial Organization

There are two versions of the neoclassical theory of finance and industrial performance: the perfect foresight model and the risk model. In the perfect foresight model all the participants, as the name implies, know the future with certainty. Because the return on any investment is certain, there is no distinction between debt and equity, concepts which relate to how a risky income stream from an investment is broken up. Capital is a single, uniform, risk-free commodity. The aggregate savings of the community are allocated among various investment projects by a perfect market with many buyers and many sellers. Buyers do not care from whom they buy, sellers do not care to whom they sell. The sellers of savings sell to the highest bidder. The buyers are profit-maximizing entrepreneurs who purchase savings as they would any other input: up until the point where the marginal revenue product of capital of each of the projects they are proposing equals the cost of the savings. A single market-clearing price is established by this process which, assuming that all the usual optimality conditions are met, reflects the social opportunity cost of capital. All investment projects with prospective rates of return greater than this price will be financed. The surplus will accrue to the entrepreneurs as profit.

This is the model of the finance process which underlies the simple textbook theory of the firm. If the model is accepted, the role of the finance process in determining firm and industry behavior is limited to project choice. The theory treats the entrepreneur and the firm as one. It assumes that the firm's behavior is based on a both subjectively and objectively rational effort to maximize profits and that all firms have available to them and are aware of the same full range of technologies. Entrepreneurs can be relied upon to operate their firms at minimum cost for whatever level of output they adopt, thus assuring production efficiency. Since capital will be provided to all proponents whose projects promise a rate of return at least equal to the price of capital, markets displaying monopoly profits will attract new entrants. In equilibrium, every industry (except a natural monopoly or oligopoly) will be composed of a sufficient number of firms that marginal revenue will equal price. Since a profit maximizer chooses output at the level where marginal cost equals marginal revenue, marginal cost pricing and thus output choice efficiency will be assured. Any innovation which promises a rate of return in excess of the price of capital will be implemented, and thus dynamic efficiency is also assured. The immediate universal awareness of any opportunity to profit from a monopolistic market structure or a new innovation makes likely a rapid adjustment to equilibrium.

The introduction of risk into the model substantially expands the role of the finance process to include management motivation and control reassignment and helps to explain the existence of a number of institutions. The finance process now not only connects savers with entrepreneurs, but also permits participants to bear different amounts of risk according to their tastes and to diversify their holdings of risky assets. The development of the modern corporation can be seen as the creation of a new financial institution. The ability to obtain capital by selling equity shares in a limited liability corporation, the return on which is related to profits, freed entrepreneurs from the unrealistic responsibility, which they held along with the right to keep for themselves any profits that a firm might earn, of shouldering the full burden of the potential losses that can result from a project of any significant size. The wide variety of intermediary institutions such as trust funds, mutual funds, and even banks can also be partially explained as ways of offering savers diversified and reasonable risk portfolios at low transaction costs.

The concept of risk employed in the model is very special: each participant, though lacking perfect foresight, knows the probability distribution of the various possible states of nature in the future. The existence of an objectively correct probability distribution—"rational expectations"—permits a definition of the social opportunity cost of capital.[5] The existence of uniform views as to the characteristics of this distribution assures the conclusion of the Modigliani and Miller theorem, that the cost of capital to a firm (i.e., the discounted value of the income stream diverted from the holders of currently outstanding shares either because earnings are retained or because income must be paid to new stockholders or new debt holders) will in a competitive market be the same whatever the source[6] and will equal the social opportunity cost of capital. Project proponents will not be prejudiced if they do not have access to all possible sources of capital.

If firms act to maximize share value, i.e., the discounted present value of the expected income stream which will accrue to the holders of currently outstanding common stock, firms will operate, as in the perfect foresight model, at minimum cost, thereby assuring production efficiency. Project choice will also operate in the same fashion as it does in the perfect foresight model, thereby assuring output choice and dynamic efficiency and rapid adjustment to equilibrium.

Because the profits of a corporation go to the holders of equity (the "owners") rather than the managers, share value maximization cannot be automatically assumed the way profit maximization is in the perfect foresight model. Separation of share ownership from control raises a potential problem. However, the assumption of uniform views as to the probability distribution of possible future states of nature permits the conclusion that the threat of control reassignment will align management's interests with those of equity holders and that the firm in fact normally will act to maximize share value. If not, the escape hatch of actual reassignment of control will work effectively. Current and potential shareholders share with management the same objectively correct view of the probability of the various consequences which might flow from each alternative possible management decision. They can detect when management makes a decision which results in an expected income stream that, discounted to present value, is less than the maximum possible. Current stockholders will vote out management whenever it appears that alternative policies could raise share value. If current stockholders nevertheless miss the opportunity, the market will price the shares at a discount, and outside investors who sense that a stock is un dervalued because of poor management of company assets will profi from purchasing the stock of the company and electing a new man agement who will pursue policies that raise the expected income stream from these assets and thus the value of the stock.

C. Assumptions Concerning the Uniformity of Expectations

The neoclassical theory of finance and industrial organization assumes that all the participants in the system—the members of management and everyone outside the firm—share the same "homogeneous" expectations concerning the future. We know that in reality each participant has his own particular collection of bits of knowledge and appraisal skills. Participants cannot be expected to share a uniform view as to the probabilities of different possible states of nature that determine the relative profitability of one management decision versus another. Two questions arise. What happens if we try to incorporate this reality into the theoretical structure? And how good a case can be made instead for ignoring reality, assuming homogeneous expectations, and continuing to use the neoclassical theory?

1. The Implications of Nonuniform Expectations

1.1 Share Value Maximization.

If the informational differences between shareholders and management are recognized, what happens to the neoclassical theory's conclusion, and all that flows from it, that all firms, even those with ownership separated from control, will act to maximize share value? The managerial and behavioral theories of the firm represent experiments with the kind of models of firm behavior that can be developed under these changed assumptions. The origin of the managerial theory of the firm is Berle and Means. They began in the 1930s to question the implication of the orthodox neoclassical model that managers are mere automatons whose values are irrelevant to the study of firm behavior.[7] Following in this tradition, Baumol, Marris, and Williamson in the 1960s each developed an explicit model of firm behavior resting on an assumption that management does not operate the firm in a way calculated to maximize share value but rather to maximize, subject to a minimum profit constraint to keep shareholders satisfied, some other measure of firm performance, such as sales or assets, that better serves their personal values.[8] Because current and potential stockholders, with their inferior level of knowledge, cannot judge with complete accuracy the wisdom of every management decision, they instead are assumed to establish certain minimum standards which management must meet or be overthrown. These standards are based on what to them would seem sensible policy, giving management some benefit of the doubt because of management's extra knowledge, and on past performance of management.

The behavioral theory of the firm[9] is based directly on empirical observation of firm behavior in many markets rather than on a logical manipulation of a set of plausible behavioral assumptions, as is the case with the neoclassical and managerial theories. The following picture emerges: out of the wide variety of possible environmental stimuli that constantly rain down upon the firm, a select subgroup are processed and evoke reaction. Reaction is characterized by stable decision rules which have been found in the past to produce results that satisfy what would appear to be the firm's performance aspiration levels. When the reaction is not sufficient to result in the attainment of these aspiration levels, a search begins for new rules of decision concerning which messages from the environment should be noted and how to react to them. If a new set of rules, when tried, allows the firm to attain its aspiration levels, the search stops and the new rules become permanent. If continued search fails to reveal a set of decision rules which will allow the firm to attain its aspiration levels, either the aspiration levels are changed or the organization disintegrates.

These results are clearly inconsistent with the share value maximizing behavior predicted by the orthodox neoclassical theory. The explanation by proponents of the behavioral theory as to what is wrong with the neoclassical theory constitutes a broad-based attack on the conceptual foundations of the neoclassical model. These proponents doubt that it is even possible to talk about individuals or organizations engaging in rational "maximizing" of anything, whether it be share value or some personal value. They suggest instead a theory of "bounded rationality." An individual or firm is aware of only a very limited selection of all the alternative courses of action open to it. The chance that it will be aware of the truly optimal course of action is slight.[10] Furthermore, they suggest, individuals are really making decisions under conditions of "uncertainty," not risk; i.e., they make decisions on the basis of their personal estimates of the probability distribution of future states of nature, not on the basis of a universally known, objectively correct distribution. In this case, it is impossible to define what rational behavior means in an objective sense because no one knows what the true probability distribution is. Rational behavior as a subjective concept must be limited to the idea of acting on the basis of rational calculations, using as "facts" the limited knowledge possessed by the decision maker and the inferences drawn from this knowledge by a process shaped by past experience and psychological makeup.[11] These proponents also observe that the communications system of an individual or organization is only capable of handling a very limited number of messages about the world around it, so that many changes in the environment to which a true maximizer would react go unnoticed.

The behavioralists do not directly comment on the role of current and potential shareholders in motivating management or in control reassignment, but their comments about how individuals and organizations make decisions and the impossibility of rational maximizing would apply to shareholders as well. The minimum level of financial performance sufficient to avoid loss of incumbent management control is therefore likely to be below the level of which management is capable. This minimum level is presumably one of the management's generally unalterable aspirations.

The managerial and behavioral theories are theories of firm behavior, not industry behavior.[12] Tracing out their implications for industry performance would require a theory which takes account not only of the relationship between shareholders and management but also the competitive interaction among firms in the industry and the role of potential entrants. At a minimum they suggest, however, that the neoclassical theory of industrial organization should not be accepted for our purposes without further scrutiny.

1.2 *The Cost of Capital*

Dropping the assumption of homogeneous expectations and recognizing the informational differences between management and participants in the finance process outside the firm may also lead to the conclusion that, notwithstanding Modigliani and Miller, the firm does not face a single cost from the different sources of capital available to it. The ease or difficulty of passing through the finance process gate may therefore depend on what source or sources a project proponent can easily turn to.

Stiglitz, in a 1972 article, demonstrates that the Modigliani and Miller conclusion requires one of four unstated sets of assumptions: (1) there are as many securities as future states of nature; (2) individuals have identical views on the means and variances of the distributions of the alternative assets, evaluation of optimal portfolios is done on the basis of only these means and variances, and there exists a perfectly safe asset infinitely elastic in supply; (3) bankruptcy is not a possible state of nature; or (4) financial intermediaries can be costlessly created or individuals can borrow with limited liability.[13] Stiglitz suggests that none of these is a realistic assumption. People do not have identical expectations because the real world is characterized not by risk, but by uncertainty, which requires individual subjective evaluation. The other three proposed assumptions, each corresponding to a special situation in which the lack of shared expectations would be unimportant, are also significantly at variance with institutional realities.

This observation opens the door to all kinds of modeling based on an assumption of nonidentical expectations. Stiglitz in the same article, for example, considers the implications of a particular systematic pattern of nonidentical expectations: the corporate borrower, because of its intimacy with the project it is championing, tends to be more optimistic than the less informed, suspicious lender. As a result, the imputed probability distribution of income outcomes corresponding to the borrower's expectations has a higher mean than the distribution corresponding to the expectations of the lender. Assuming there is a finite possibility of bankruptcy, the lenders demand a premium, which is an increasing function of the debt/equity (D/E) ratio, to cover the risk of less than full repayment of principal. The corporation (which Stiglitz equates with the holders of equity) will view the premium demanded as greater than is necessary to cover the probability, as the corporation evaluates it, that there will be less than full repayment.* The advantages of leverage in stretching the corporation's ability to invest in opportunities with above-market expected rates of return will result in the corporation borrowing up to an optimal D/E ratio above which the cost of premium demanded will outweigh the advantages of increased leverage. Thus, from positing a particular pattern of information differences, one can say something about the relative—and not equal—costs of capital obtained from debt and from equity.

---

*The borrower corporation will also view the premium demanded by the lender as greater than necessary if it is assumed that the corporation and the lender each act on the basis of its own subjective view of the probability distribution of X, the uncertain level of future corporate income (before deduction for debt service), and that the distributions imputed to the borrower and the lender have the same mean but the variance of the borrower's distribution is smaller than that of the lender. Let E(X) be

Stiglitz treats the holders of equity and the corporation as one. Consider the results that could be expected if the assumptions of the Stiglitz model were altered to account for the separation of share ownership from control in the publicly held corporation. If the entity known as a corporation has superior knowledge and predictive ability as compared with the sources from which it receives financing,

the mean of both the lender's and the corporation's imputed distributions; B be the value of X below which there will not be full repayment; and $F_L(X)$ and $F_C(X)$ be, respectively, the imputed distribution functions of the lender and the corporation. The value of the distribution function imputed to the lender will, for each possible income outcome below the mean, be greater than the value of that of the borrower, i.e., $F_L(X) > F_C(X)$ for each $X < E(X)$, where 1) $f_L(E(X)) < f_C(E(X))$ (the values of the probability density functions at the mean), 2) the distributions are each symmetrical, and 3) the slopes of the two distribution curves are each positive for all values of $X < E(X)$. Assuming $B < E(X)$, i.e., that the corporation does not propose so much borrowing that there is less than a fifty-fifty chance of full repayment, the lender's evaluation of the probability of not receiving full payment will be greater than the corporation's evaluation of such an occurrence whatever amount is borrowed, because $F_L(B) > F_C(B)$. Graphically, the area under the lender's curve to the left of B in figure 1.1 is greater than the area under the borrower's curve.

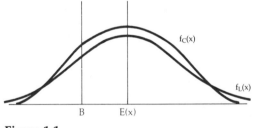

Figure 1.1

These assumptions about the imputed probability distributions of the corporation and the lender are, as a description of the average case, more realistic than Stiglitz's formulation. They are equivalent in concept to assuming that the corporation and lender each make an unbiased best guess as to the firm's level of future income, i.e., that the best guess of each is a random variable with a mean equal to the as yet unknown level of future income. Since the corporation is better informed, the variance of the distribution generating its assessment is smaller. Each knows the level of his ignorance, i.e., the variance of the distribution generating his assessment. There is no reason to think that the typical lender systematically underestimates the future incomes of the typical corporation (though it may systematically estimate the future incomes of corporations to be less than the *stated* predictions of the corporations). But because the lender is less informed than the corporation, it has less confidence in its best guess and assigns a higher probability to the possibility that its best guess is well off the mark.[14]

the component of that entity which has this superior knowledge and predictive ability is management, not the holders of equity.

In such a firm there should be a preference by management to finance investment by use of retained earnings, assuming, as the managerial theory suggests, management can survive a temporary decline in share price. If management of a firm perceives the discounted future income stream from a new investment to be higher than the investing public perceives it to be, the immediate effect of undertaking the project on the market price of the firm's shares will, using the Modigliani and Miller theorem, be the same however it is financed and will be based on the public perception of this income stream. However, in management's eyes, the ultimate effect of undertaking the project on the value of owning such a share will differ depending on the source of finance used. If the source is retained earnings, the investment will ultimately augment the value of currently outstanding shares by the full amount by which management's perception of the discounted future income stream exceeds the dollar cost of the investment. If debt or a new share issue is used, part of this excess will have to be shared with the skeptical outside suppliers of new capital.* Thus, if management is interested

---

*If, contrary to the assumptions made here, the public's perception of the firm's income stream were the same as management's, the interest rate required for debt financing and the dilution of equity required by a new share issue would, by the Modigliani and Miller theorem, in each case result in a future diversion of income from the holders of currently outstanding shares of an amount such that the value of these shares would be augmented by undertaking the investment to exactly the same extent as it would be if it were undertaken with internally generated funds. In each case, the amount of the future diversion of income will be greater if, instead, the public is less optimistic than management because the interest rate will be higher or the amount of dilution greater. Thus, if the public is less optimistic than management, the value, as perceived by management, of currently outstanding shares wi be augmented less (or even diminished) if the investment is funded externally insteac of internally.

If it is assumed, as in the immediately preceding note, that the information differences between management and outside sources of capital lead outside sources to having on average an imputed probability distribution with the same mean as that of management but with a greater variance, management would again, on average, prefer internal financing over new debt or equity even when it tries to act in the best interests of shareholders. The reasons for this, discussed in detail in chapter 2 (section C 2.41), relate to (a) the costs to the relatively ignorant shareholder, if he receives a dividend, of finding a new place to invest the funds—gathering information, delegating the investment decision to others, and taking the risk of investing in a project less rewarding than that of the firm in question—and (b) the costs to the firm of informing outside sources about its operations and plans.

in the long-run net cash flow of the firm, whether because it is truly motivated to maximize share value (as opposed to current share price) or because a high net income stream is instrumental in satisfying various other "managerial" motives, it will prefer to finance investment by retained earnings. Management will undertake investments financed by retained earnings which appear favorable to it even if they are perceived by the market to involve a diversion of income from current shareholders in excess of the discounted expected income stream resulting from the investment.

There is strong empirical evidence that firms act as though financing investment by retained earnings is significantly less costly than the use of outside sources.[15] Meyer and Kuh, in their seminal study of almost thirty years ago, question the validity of the traditional neoclassical investment theory because the level of investment in most industries (except in utilities, which are long-term and low risk) does not seem to be very much affected by changes in the interest rate. The fact that at the time of their study only 12 percent of financing for manufacturing firms came from outside sources (new equity issues, bonds, bank loans), which are the only kinds of sources that make the cost of capital explicit, adds to their suspicions.[16] A study of very large firms by Gordon Donaldson approximately contemporaneous with the Meyer and Kuh study shows that, for these firms at least, internal funds were in fact regarded by management as less expensive than external funds.[17]

Meyer and Kuh conclude on the basis of their empirical study that, in the short run, the accelerator theory best explains the level of investment during rapidly expanding economic periods and that a firm's liquidity best explains the level of its investment during stable and declining economic periods (the "residual funds" theory of investment).* Meyer and Kuh recognize an exception to the residual

---

*A general theoretical discussion of management motivation for this pattern of behavior is set out in chapter 2 (section B 3). This pattern of behavior is empirically confirmed in the study of the semiconductor industry contained in chapter 4. The influence of the liquidity constraint in periods other than those characterized by unusual expansion is not explained in the semiconductor study as a preference for retained earnings per se, but as a result of other preferences. One reason is that new shares of the firm's stock cannot be sold during a normal period for what, in the eyes of management, is a sufficient price. The incurrence of new debt, if it is available at all, may, because outside equity financing is not desirable, raise the D/E ratio above an acceptable figure or may seem spendthrift because it would make future incurrence of debt impossible if any emergency required it.

funds theory where an event occurs that pushes the marginal efficiency of investment curve way out (beyond the dogleg in the traditional textbook graphical presentation of their theory). Examples include the introduction of a revolutionary new product or of a new technology offering substantial cost savings. Meyer and Kuh found confirmation of this exception in a rank correlation between a measure of net investment and reliance on outside financing.[18]

If internal financing is in fact perceived by management as lower in cost, project choice will be distorted and industrial performance will be affected. Project proponents differ in their access to such financing. A proponent who is proposing to start a new firm or who is an employee of a firm with low earnings (relative to the number of good proposed projects within the firm) may not receive financing for a project which has prospects superior to a project proposed by an employee of a firm with high earnings relative to the number of such projects. As will be developed more fully in later discussion, proponents of the most innovative projects are often persons who are blocked from, or restricted in access to, retained earnings (see Chapter 2, sections B 2.12 and C 2.422). The lower perceived cost of internal financing, as later discussion demonstrates (Chapter 2, section C 2.43, and Chapter 5, section B), can also affect the competitiveness of market structures. One effect is that established firms will find expansion easier than a new firm trying to enter the market investing in the same type of project. A second effect is that an initial innovator may achieve long-run domination of a market because the profits that flow from the innovation mean that funds for the expansion of the innovating project by the initiator will be easier to obtain than funds for an investment by an imitator employing the innovation.

2. *The Attempt at Neoclassical Resurrection*

If, as is suggested at the beginning of this chapter, plausibility is an important criterion by which we make an initial choice of assumptions, the assumption that everyone shares the same view of the probability distribution of future possible states of nature deviates sufficiently from reality to be of serious concern, particularly in a study which primarily focuses on the relationships, in a world of rapid technical change, among project proponents, firm managers, and finance process participants outside the firm. Without the assumption of uniform views, the neoclassical model is clearly not going to work in the way described above. But is the assumption of uniform views of the future necessary to reach the conclusions of the neoclassical model? Some economists argue that substitute mechanisms exist which assure that these conclusions are correct even when views are not uniform. I find this argument unpersuasive in the last analysis, but it deserves careful review in view of the number and stature of its adherents.

2.1 *The Survival Theories*

Alchian and Friedman have each attempted to reformulate the neoclassical theory of industrial organization in a way which incorporates the idea that each individual firm is not necessarily motivated to maximize profits.[19] These examples of the so-called "survival theory" rest on the proposition that, whatever the motivations of a firm's managers are, only a firm the managers of which pursue activities that lead to "positive profits" will survive in the long run. The kind of behavior that leads to positive profits is the same as would be predicted by the traditional profit-maximizing theory.

The survival theory is unfortunately underdeveloped. Although its whole modus operandi involves the entry of one kind of firm into the market and the exit of another kind from the market, neither the mechanism of entry nor that of exit is well described. The survival theory has been subjected elsewhere to a number of cogent criticisms concerning its inadequate specification of entry and exit conditions.[20] What needs to be emphasized here is how more attention to the finance process could greatly clarify these questions.

Alchian suggests that the mechanism for entry into the market is not very important and that the mechanism for exit is obvious. He poses as an extreme case a situation where the decision rules of different firms entering the market are completely random. Over time, he suggests, some of those entering will have decision rules which correspond to what we call profit-maximizing behavior. When enough of these firms are found in the market, price (P) will drop to minimum average total cost (ATC), eliminating the opportunity for even a maximally efficient firm to generate more than zero profits (where the term "profits" is assigned the usual economist's definition: earnings above the normal return on capital). All firms which do not display profit-maximizing (and hence share value maximizing) behavior will exit because of their unviable negative profit situation.

Alchian believes that an industry characterized by random entry is the one least likely to achieve a long-run competitive equilibrium. He therefore concludes that his demonstration that such an industry will in fact achieve a long-run competitive equilibrium proves that such an equilibrium will also be achieved by industries characterized by any other pattern of entry.

In fact, a pattern of entry much less likely to result in a long-run competitive equilibrium—one which is perfectly plausible—can be proposed: systematic factors prevent any firm from entering which intends to employ what would turn out to be profit-maximizing decision rules, for example utilization of a new technology. Firms in the real world do not randomly stumble into markets: they need capital to enter. To obtain capital, particularly at an affordable cost, a new firm must persuade the decision makers in the finance process that the profit prospects of entering the market using such firm's particular proposed decision rules are good. If the finance process is systematically biased against a particular set of techniques that are in fact the optimal ones, none of the firms entering the market will have a management disposed to use these techniques. Clearly, we need to know some characteristics of the finance process before we can know about the character of the firms entering the market.*

Alchian's description of the mechanism for the exit of firms from a market is also flawed because of his failure to consider the finance process. Winter has already suggested that the presence of profit maximizers in a market may not, contrary to Alchian, eliminate the potential for other firms in that market to make more than zero profits and thus the possibility that these other firms will engage in non-maximizing behavior.[22] Equally troubling, however, is the fact that

---

*Williamson points out another factor: the potential entrant lacks a known performance record in the industry it wishes to enter. The lack of a record increases its cost of capital. This problem is aggravated by the fact that the potential entrant must raise not only enough capital to finance plant and equipment of minimum efficient scale, but also enough to cover what, given the presence of existing competition, can be considerable startup costs, such as establishing marketing channels and attracting talented managers. The existence of this financial barrier to entry is very important in industries with relatively few competitors, since that lowers the probability that at least one of the competitors will have decision rules that are profit maximizing.[21]

even if the potential to make more than zero profits is eliminated, there is a way for nonmaximizing firms to survive. A firm can, to the extent it is financed by equity rather than debt, reduce its earnings a certain amount below the level which would be a normal return on capital (i.e., earn negative profits, according to the economist's definition of the term) and continue to operate indefinitely. It is necessary only that the firm earn enough gross income after debt service to purchase the replacement of depreciated assets (i.e., earn at least zero profits according to the businessman's definition of the term) and that stockholders tolerate the use of the firm's existing real assets in a way that is less than profit maximizing or the reinvestment of the firm's cash flow in projects promising a lower rate of return than the shareholders could obtain if the funds were instead distributed to them.[23] Whether shareholders will display such tolerance is the question of whether the observed fact of shareholder ignorance will result in managerial discretion. The survival theory is an attempt to resurrect the conclusions of the neoclassical theory of industrial organization without challenging the proposition on which the managerial and behavioral theories rest, that shareholder ignorance will lead to managerial discretion. The forces of competition alone are supposed to be enough to make the conclusions right. As the preceding analysis shows, the attempt is a failure because the forces of competition alone are not enough: the exit mechanism relied upon by the survival theory requires that there be no managerial discretion. This suggests that if one wishes to resurrect the conclusions of the neoclassical theory, one must take the managerial and behavioral theories head-on and establish that the failure of the neoclassical theory's assumption of fully informed shareholders does not lead to managerial discretion.

2.2 *The Role of Investors Knowing Information Not Possessed by Others*

Is it possible that despite differences in the information possessed by the various participants in the finance process inside and outside the firm, the mechanisms by which securities are priced and by which takeovers occur are such that the conclusions of the neoclassical model concerning the elimination of managerial discretion and the cost of capital remain valid? Henry Manne provides the earliest, and perhaps still the fullest, argument that these mechanisms work in such a fashion.[24] He suggests that, among all investors, those who have the most reliable information about a firm's affairs are financially motivated to perform "a kind of arbitrage function" in the firm's stock and that in the end the price reflects only their views.[25] They will know when management is engaging in nonmaximizing behavior. Share price will be depressed accordingly, making the firm ripe for takeover. Fear of depressed stock prices will motivate management to maximize share value. If they do not, control assignment via a hostile tender offer will swiftly follow.[26]

The efficient market hypothesis permits a reformulation of Manne's thesis that is even stronger in its claims. The hypothesis is that the market price of a security "fully reflects" all information "available" at the time in question.[27] The expression "fully reflects" is not clearly defined in the relevant literature, but it appears to mean that the market acts "as if" every investor knew the available information.[28] The term "available" relates to who is aware of the information in question, and different versions of the hypothesis relate primarily to how many and which participants must be in possession of the information for it to be considered available. I will label as the "broad statement of the efficient market hypothesis" the version which considers information to be available if it is known by one or more investors outside of the management of the firm.* The hypothesis has evolved from a series of empirical studies, discussed in more detail later in this section. None of these studies specifies in any detail a model of how individual investors behave and how equilibrium prices result from that behavior,[29] but the general belief of the adherents of the hypothesis appears to be that it can be explained by a simple arbitrage model similar to the one relied upon by Manne.[30]

Manne's thesis and its efficient market reformulation each permits a neat resurrection of the conclusions of the neoclassical theory of

---

*I will avoid the conventional labels of the breadth of the hypothesis: "weak form," "semistrong form," and "strong form." The terms were originated by Fama to refer to tests of different information sets with respect to which the market might be hypothesized to be efficient, i.e., what information is considered "available," but it has been used by others with increasing imprecision. The information set contemplated by the "broad statement" differs from that contemplated by the "strong form" only in that it does not include information possessed solely by management. The focus on the "broad statement" information set is more appropriate for the issues of concern here and, as will be seen, fits the empirical tests of the hypothesis at least as well as the traditional classifications.

finance and industrial organization concerning both production decisions and project choice. Security prices are the same as if all investors had the same information and homogeneous expectations, either the expectations of the best-informed investors (Manne's original formulation) or those of a hypothetical investor knowing everything that any one or more outside participants know (the reformulation). These expectations would generally include an awareness of any nonmaximizing behavior on management's part. As noted above, the resulting depression of share price would create a high risk of takeover. Management would therefore be motivated to make the production decisions that, from the vantage point of a person having these expectations, are in the best interests of shareholders. The cost of new, externally obtained capital would also be based on these expectations and should equal management's perception of the cost of internal finance, since the expectations setting securities prices should closely resemble management's highly informed views of the future of the firm and of the projects it is considering. Thus, notwithstanding the ignorance of most investors, there would be no managerial bias in favor of inside financing, and project choice would also function in accordance with the neoclassical model.

Each of the key steps in this argument needs examination. Are there good reasons to believe that share prices reflect the views only of either the best-informed investors or, in accordance with the broad statement of the efficient market hypothesis, of a hypothetical investor knowing every piece of information held by any one or more members of the investing public? If they do, do these views capture everything that management knows? And even if both these questions are answered affirmatively, will a takeover follow automatically when share price drops in response to a management deviation from the goal of share value maximization?

2.21 *Whose Views Do Security Prices Reflect?*

2.211 *The Simple Arbitrage Model and Portfolio Choice Theory*

The first question to ask is whether there is any straightforward intuitive reason to think that the price of a security would not reflect the observably diverse views concerning its future return of the wide range of investors that might consider buying it or selling it (long or short). The simple arbitrage model is the obvious candidate for answering this question in the affirmative.[31] In one version of the model, based on Manne's original thesis, when the best-informed investor feels that there is a deviation between the price of a security and what in his informed judgment is its "intrinsic value," he will start buying or selling short the security and continue to do so until his actions, perhaps combined with the actions of other similarly well-informed traders, cause the price of the stock to move to the extent that the deviation no longer exists. In the other version, reflecting an arbitrage explanation of the efficient market hypothesis, the receipt by any investor of a piece of information that reflects positively or negatively on the future of an issuer of securities and that is not known by the other participants in the market leads the investor to believe that there is a deviation between the value of the security and the current price, since the current price does not reflect the information. He will react to the deviation in the same fashion as above. The result is that the price will always react quickly and completely to each new piece of information even if it does not become widely known immediately.

Although both versions of the arbitrage model sound plausible at first blush, the behavior required of the investor correcting the deviation is not consistent with that prescribed by the broadly accepted theory of portfolio choice.* Consider how the investor would behave according to the portfolio choice model. Like most persons, he is risk averse. He has a certain amount of wealth, W_0. He has a view of the means, variances, and covariances of the future returns of the risky securities available to him and of a rate of interest, r^*, at which he can borrow in unlimited amounts and invest in a risk-free asset. If he is a rational utility maximizer, he follows the familiar prescriptions of portfolio choice theory depicted in figure 1.2: 1) he considers

---

*Some commentators argue that the simple arbitrage model is implausible because it is inconsistent with the capital asset pricing model (CAPM).[32] The CAPM posits that a security's equilibrium price is determined by two factors—its systematic risk and its expected return—and that investors generally share homogeneous beliefs concerning each of these factors (see section C 2.23 for further discussion of CAPM). If the CAPM is correct, any given security has a large number of very close substitutes with nearly identical systematic risk/return characteristics. No conceivable amount of purchases or sales of the given security by an investor possessing special information could affect its price because the total supply of investment opportunities with the same or similar systematic risk/return characteristics is so large. It is not appropriate to use such an argument here, however, since it invokes a theory which rests on the very assumptions we seek to evaluate.

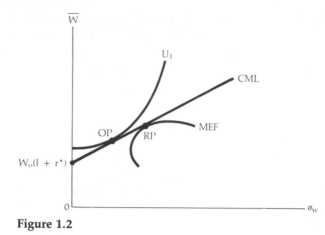

Figure 1.2

each possible combination of risky securities that can be purchased with W_o and calculates the expected return and variance from holding that combination; 2) he constructs a graph on which each of these combinations is represented by a point relating its expected return, $\overline{W}$, and standard deviation, σ_W, and from this determines the subset of these points constituting his Markowitz efficiency frontier (MEF); 3) he constructs a capital market line (CML) by drawing the line which passes through $(0, 1+r^*)$ and is tangent to the MEF, designating the point of tangency as RP (each point on his capital market line to the left of RP representing a portfolio in which some part of W_o is invested in the risk-free asset and the rest of W_o is invested in risky assets in the same proportions to each other as they are in RP; and each point to the right of RP representing a portfolio in which all of W_o and some amount of borrowed monies are invested in risky assets, again in the same proportions to each other as they are in RP); and 4) he chooses his optimal portfolio, OP, the one point on the capital market line to which an indifference curve, U_1, is just tangent.

What happens if the investor now receives a new piece of information, not yet known to any other investor, which increases his assessment of the expected return from the purchase of a share of firm i? As depicted in figure 1.3, the change of assessment will require a recalculation of the mean and variance from holding each possible combination of risky securities and will shift the location of the Markowitz efficiency frontier (depicted as MEF') and thus the

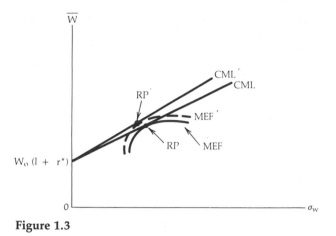

Figure 1.3

capital market line (depicted as CML'), which will be tangent to the frontier at a new point, say RP'. The shift in the capital market line changes the set of risky and the risk-free assets that constitute the investor's optimal portfolio. The new portfolio will contain more of security i (or security i will be sold short in a lesser amount).[33] However, unless the investor is absolutely certain that the return on security i will equal his assessment of its expected return (i.e., his assessment of its variance is 0),* his demand for security i will be limited. This is so despite the investor's possession of favorable information not known by other investors and his unlimited borrowing power. His demand for security i is limited because security i does not have a single "intrinsic value" to the investor; what an additional share is worth to him depends on how many shares he already holds of i and of each other security. To see why this is so involves a two-part analysis: why RP' is likely to contain other risky securities in addition to shares of i, and why there will be a limit on the total amount the investor invests in risky securities.

The goal in determining RP' is to pick a combination of risky assets that has the maximum ratio of (x) its expected second period wealth in excess of what would be received from investing W_o totally in the risk-free asset, to (y) its standard deviation, i.e., choose

---

*In such a case, if the expected rate of return exceeds $(1 + r^*)$, every dollar invested would be a sure bet, worth investing all one's wealth and all that one could borrow. If the expected rate of return were less than $(1 + r^*)$, the same would be true of selling short an infinite number of shares of i.

RP' to maximize $[\overline{W} - W_o(1 + r^*)]/\sigma_W$ (the "return/risk ratio"). This will result in the capital market line with the steepest possible slope. A capital market line with a steeper slope is always preferred to one with a shallower slope. For every point on the line with the shallower slope, there are points on the line with the steeper slope which have both a higher expected return and a lower standard deviation and thus are unambiguously preferable to a risk averse investor.

In order to conceptualize the role of security i in the composition of RP', think of a situation where there is just one additional risky security, j, and focus on

(a) the return/risk ratio of each security, i.e.,

$$R_i = \frac{\overline{P}_{1i} - (1 + r^*)P_{oi}}{\sigma_i} \quad \text{and} \quad R_j = \frac{\overline{P}_{1j} - (1 + r^*)P_{oj}}{\sigma_j}$$

where $\overline{P}_{1i}$, $\overline{P}_{1j}$, σ_i, σ_j, P_{oi}, and P_{oj} are respectively the expected values of the distributions (as perceived by the investor) of the second period prices of i and j, their standard deviations, and the current first period prices of i and j, and

(b) ρ_{ij}, the correlation coefficient with respect to the distribution of the second period prices of i and j.

Suppose after the receipt of the new information, R_i is positive and exceeds R_j, which is also positive. Suppose also, as is usually the case, $0 < \rho_{ij} < 1$. Without knowing of portfolio choice analysis, one might assume that RP' should consist entirely of i. But as a general matter that is not the case. If $R_i/R_j < 1/\rho_{ij}$, the investor should hold long some shares of j as well. This is because holding some shares of j long, despite its inferior excess return/risk ratio and positive correlation of return with i, will diversify RP' and reduce its standard deviation, σ_p, by a greater percentage than it reduces its expected return, μ_p. And the lower the correlation, the more inferior can be R_j and still be worth holding long. If $R_i/R_j > 1/\rho_{ij}$, the investor still will not want RP' to consist entirely of i: he will want to include a certain number of shares of j held short.* This is because j, despite

---

*For convenience, a margin requirement of 100% for short sales is assumed here so that it requires as much of W_o to hold short a share of a security as to hold it long. Since there is unlimited borrowing, the assumption is purely arbitrary.

offering an expected return in excess of that on the safe asset, has, relative to its correlation with i, a sufficiently inferior return/risk ratio that it can be used to hedge against i. Holding i short up to a point reduces σ_p by a greater percentage than it reduces μ_p. RP' will consist entirely of i only if $R_i/R_j = 1/\rho_{ij}$. Where there are more than two risky assets, determining the composition of RP' involves very complex mathematics but the principles are the same: because of the possibilities of diversification and hedging, it is very likely that a portfolio consisting entirely of the single security offering the best return/risk ratio will not have as good a return/risk ratio as at least some alternative possible portfolios that include one or more additional securities.

Next, consider how an investor who has determined RP' decides what the total amount he invests in risky assets will be. If the new information results in an RP' with a better return/risk ratio than RP, the investor's utility function may be such that, as illustrated in figure 1.4, he will increase the total amount invested in risky assets, either by reducing the amount of W_o invested in the safe asset or by borrowing to lever his purchase of risky assets. But again there are limits to that increase and hence to the absolute amount of security i purchased. This results from the assumption that *investors, to be willing to take on additional risk* (as measured by portfolio standard

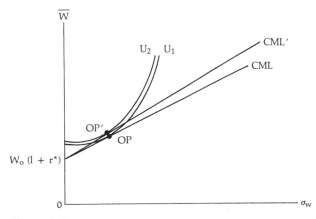

Figure 1.4

deviation), *will require more than a commensurate increase in return,* i.e., their indifference curves are concave upward.*

Portfolio choice theory does more than render meaningless the concept that a security has an intrinsic value which is best assessed only by one or more investors who have information not possessed by others and who continue to buy or sell as long as there is a deviation between their assessment of its intrinsic value and its price. It goes so far as to suggest just the opposite. Lintner has constructed a model of first period equilibrium prices in a competitive securities market where, because of different information or otherwise, investors differ in their respective assessments of the expected value and variance-covariance characteristics of the second period prices of the risky securities available to them.[34] He assumes 1) each investor has a utility function which displays a constant degree of risk aversion in the Pratt-Arrow sense, i.e., $U''(W_1)/U'(W_1)$ is constant where W_1 is the investor's second period wealth, and 2) each investor follows the prescriptions of portfolio choice theory based on his belief that the second period price of each security is normally distributed with parameters equal to his particular assessments. The model demonstrates that the price of each security reflects, with varying weights, the assessments of all participants with respect to all of the securities available.

The logic of this conclusion is that since each investor is guided by portfolio choice theory, he constructs his portfolio using the same principles as the investor in the preceding discussion. For each investor, given (a) r^*, (b) his assessments of the variance-covariance characteristics of the second period prices of all the available risky securities, and (c) his assessments of the expected value of the second period prices of all the available risky securities but security i, his demand for security i is a positive function of $(\overline{P}_{1i} - P_{oi} (1+r^*))$, i.e., his expected value assessment of the second period price of a share of i less what he would receive if he invested the same amount in the safe asset instead. For P_{oi} to be the equilibrium price, the aggregate demand of all investors at P_{oi} must equal the fixed supply of shares of i. Suppose the market for i is in equilibrium and then

---

*See appendix 1.2 for a demonstration of why the most frequent assumptions made about investor utility functions—that they display a constant degree of risk aversion or that they are quadratic—result in concave upward indifference curves.

any one investor receives favorable information that increases his $\overline{P}_{1i}$ (information which may or may not already be possessed by, and reflected in the expected value assessments of, some or all of the other investors).* If P_{oi} remains unchanged, the aggregate demand for i will exceed supply. Thus, P_{oi} will depend on every single investor's expected value assessment of the second period price of i.

2.212 *Empirical Studies Supporting the Efficient Market Hypothesis*

The foregoing analysis suggests that there is no simple intuitive model of individual investor behavior, consistent with portfolio choice theory, that would lead one to believe the proposition that security pricing occurs as if investors possess identical information and homogeneous expectations when they do not. But adherents of this proposition may fairly argue that the proposition should nevertheless be accepted if empirical evidence relating to the aggregate process of security price determination—the studies conducted to test the efficient market hypothesis—clearly supports it. There exist a large number of studies that probe at what kinds of information, if any, the market is efficient with respect to. They are reviewed below to see how good a case can be made for the broad statement of the efficient market hypothesis.

2.2121 *The "Random Walk" Studies*

The first group of empirical studies that have been used in support of the efficient market hypothesis concern the pattern of successive price changes of a security.[35] Most of the studies involve collecting a long series of periodic changes in the price of a stock, lagging the series by one or more periods, and examining the correlation between the original and lagged series. Each of the studies

___
*Implicit in this analysis is the assumption that the investor develops his view of P_{1i} independent of the current price at which the security trades. The assumption makes this analysis a "naive model" of security pricing. The investor, prior to actually receiving the information, cannot "learn" of it by deducing its existence through observation of prior changes in P_{oi} resulting from the reactions of other investors who receive it sooner. More complex models that admit the possibility of this kind of learning will be discussed later in this section.

reveals that the serial correlation is close to zero, which suggests a lack of any significant linear dependence in price changes.

These studies demonstrate that one particular type of information—the pattern of past price changes—is "fully reflected" in the current price. The lack of linear dependence revealed by the studies suggests that one cannot predict the price change in one period based on price changes in prior periods.* Since information concerning past price changes has no predictive value, a rational investor receiving it should not alter his portfolio in response to it. Further diffusion of the information will not alter demand and thus will not change current price. The price is the same "as if" everyone knew the information.

This conclusion is important to individual investors deciding whether or not to follow the advice of "chartist" advisers, whose profession is the prediction of future prices on the basis of past patterns. But the information is not the kind the reflection of which would be relevant to understanding the effects of security pricing on industrial performance.

The way to connect the random walk studies to the issues of concern here is to argue that their results are consistent with the broad statement of the efficient market hypothesis even if they do not directly establish it. Imagine that the price of a security in the current time period really does "fully reflect" every piece of information held by any one or more outside investors. Such a price would then represent as accurate a prediction of the future prospects of a security as is possible at the time. What happens to price in the next period relates to some but not all of the new information that becomes available in that period. Some of what becomes available in the next period and its implications are to some extent themselves predictable on the basis of the information available in the current period.

---

*The operative question is whether the information can be used to devise a strategy that would systematically yield returns superior to a "naive" strategy of just buying the security at the beginning of the period without the information and holding the security. Since 0 covariances, while inconsistent with linear dependence of price changes, are not necessarily inconsistent with nonlinear dependence price changes, studies have been conducted to test whether commonly advocated filter rules (strategies that call for an investor in response to certain price changes to hold cash or sell a security short instead of holding it long) can systematically outperform a naive buy and hold strategy. The filter rules are not found to be superior, a result which reinforces the conclusion that current price fully reflects the pattern of past price changes.

The price in the current period already incorporates this predictable portion of the next period information. The difference between the current and next period prices will be solely a function of the unpredictable portion of the information that becomes available in the next period. Thus, consistent with the results of the random walk studies, the security price will fluctuate randomly from one period to the next. (See appendix 1.3 for a more formal exposition of this point.)

The fact that the results of the random walk studies are consistent with the broad statement of the efficient market hypothesis is not, however, a very compelling argument that the broad statement of the hypothesis is correct. The results are also consistent with other equally plausible hypotheses that contemplate security prices not fully reflecting such a broad range of information.[36] Consider, for example, Lintner's model of security pricing discussed above, where each investor has a different assessment of the parameters of the probability distribution of a security's next period price. In the simplest case, where there is one risky security, the model shows that the security's price in one period is a function of (a) r^*, (b) a market determined measure of risk, and (c) a weighted average of the next period price expected value assessments of each investor. Assume for convenience that r^* and the measure of risk do not change from one period to the next. Assume that differences among investors in their respective expected value assessments are due to each investor's having a different set of information. Assume also that, other than dramatic information, which reaches in the same time period all active investors, each investor collects information independently of the others (i.e., the fact that a piece of information is acquired by one investor in one period has no effect on the probability of another investor acquiring that information in a subsequent period). The weighted average of the respective expected values of each investor's distribution, and hence the market price of the security, will, consistent with the random walk studies, fluctuate randomly from one period to the next as each investor acquires new information. (See appendix 1.4 for a more formal exposition of this point.)

Obviously, the assumptions in this example are not realistic. We know that certain kinds of nondramatic information known by some investors in one period diffuse in a somewhat predictable fashion to other investors in a subsequent period. But it is as reasonable to say that the random walk studies show that market pricing occurs "as if" investors collect nondramatic information independently of each other as it is to say that market pricing occurs "as if" every investor knows all available information.

2.2122 *Studies of the Reaction of Share Prices to Publicly Announced "Hard" Information*

The second group of empirical studies that have been used in support of the efficient market hypothesis concern the reaction of the market price of securities to the public announcement of specific pieces of obviously relevant information. The types of information tested include stock splits (which are generally considered precursors of increases in the amount of dividends paid), earnings announcements, dividend announcements, and press evaluations.[37] Each of the studies examines the reaction of the prices of a large number of different securities to the announcement of one of these kinds of information. The theory employed is that the market can be said to reflect fully the kind of information under study during the time period in which it is announced, if after adjustment through use of the "market model" for the normal reaction of the price of each security being observed to factors affecting securities prices generally, the data show on average that there is for that period a discrete positive price change that is not repeated in subsequent periods.

Most of the studies show that the price reactions to the announcements of these kinds of information more or less correspond to this picture. The question for us is whether these findings can legitimately be extended to apply to a wider range of information. The market may act as if the tested information is possessed by all investors soon after it is announced because it is in fact possessed within such a short period by (or by the adviser of) every investor whose decision to buy, sell, or hold the security is speculatively motivated. Investors lacking speculative motivations are irrelevant to the process of price formation because their decisions to buy, sell, or hold will not be affected by receipt of such information, whether that occurs immediately or later. If this plausible explanation of what the studies observe is correct, their results are again not very interesting in terms of whether the neoclassical theory of finance and industrial organization can be resurrected. The efficient market hypothesis becomes relevant to that issue only if it can be stated broadly enough to include the myriad of informational detail necessary to make a good prediction of the future earnings of a firm (whether generally obtainable or only obtainable by some outside investors) as well as the best analyses of this myriad of detail. The efficiency with which the market processes these types of information—information clearly not possessed by all speculative investors—is not amenable to testing by the techniques used in the public announcement studies.*

2.2123 *Mutual Fund Performance Studies*

The third group of studies used in support of the efficient market hypothesis seeks to compare the average risk-adjusted rates of return earned over a number of years by various mutual funds with the rate that would have been earned by simply buying and holding a portfolio consisting of all the different securities available in the market. Because the first two groups of studies only convincingly demonstrate the efficiency of the market in processing a relatively narrow range of information, this third group is critical to our concerns here. The best-informed mutual funds, given the resources at their disposal, are presumably as well informed concerning firms in which they invest as any outsider can be. According to economic folklore, the studies in this third group conclude that even these funds cannot outperform the market over time. This conclusion, if true, is consistent with a world in which securities are priced "as if" every investor were as well informed as the best-informed investors, since in such a world the best-informed investors would have no special advantage. That consistency is frequently cited as strong evidence that the broad statement of the efficient market hypothesis is correct.

*The studies of stock split and of earnings announcements show that, while the price of the securities shows a modest change during the month of the announcement, there were considerably larger shifts in each of the few months immediately preceding the announcement. One explanation is that the bits and pieces of detailed information that became available from time to time during these preceding months have been efficiently processed by the market so that the actual announcement provides only modest additional help in predicting the future returns of the securities in question. But this pattern of price changes is just as consistent with the theory that these bits and pieces are inefficiently processed—that it takes several months for them to be fully reflected in price—as with the theory that they are efficiently processed. Also it is hard to determine whether or not insider trading played a large part in producing the pattern.

a. *Conclusions of the mutual fund performance studies.* To start, what do these studies really conclude? The most frequently cited study in the group is an article published by Jensen in 1968.[38] He observes the extent to which the performance of each of 115 mutual funds deviated during the period observed from the performance of Standard & Poors Composite 500 stock price index, which serves as a surrogate for the performance of a portfolio consisting of all the securities in the market. The underlying question of the study is whether or not an investor can expect to be better off investing in one of the funds than simply buying and holding for the period in question a portfolio of the securities represented by the index. Because it is generally believed that investors are risk averse so that a riskier portfolio must have a higher return to leave an investor equally well off, some kind of adjustment must be made to the observed deviations in the performances of the funds from that of the index to reflect differences in the riskiness between each fund and the market portfolio. Utilizing the theory behind the capital asset pricing model (CAPM), Jensen adjusts the deviations on the basis of the systematic risk associated with the portfolios of each fund, i.e., only that portion of the total variability displayed by the fund that correlates with the variability displayed by the index. Jensen concludes:

1. The average risk-adjusted "net" annual rate of return of the funds (the actual returns less research expenses, management fees, and brokerage commissions, i.e., the amount actually available for distribution to investors) is 1.1 percent less per year than the measure of the market average.*
2. The average risk-adjusted "gross" annual return of the funds (the actual returns less only brokerage commissions) is .1 percent less per year than the measure of the market average.†
3. Thirty-nine of the 115 funds outperform the market even on a net basis; 3 of these 39 funds each have a performance that on a net basis sufficiently exceeds the market's performance that its "t" value indicates that there is less than a 5 percent probability that

*Some of the funds were in existence for the full twenty years from 1945 to 1964 and others were not, so the length of the observation period differed from one fund to the next.

†This figure is for the period 1955–1964, in which all 115 funds were observed. Jensen states that the gross returns for observation periods comparable to those used in calculating the net returns figures are distorted by problems in measuring expenses prior to 1955.

the difference is due to chance. But Jensen points out that if in fact all 115 funds had an underlying ability just to equal the performance of the market, "we would expect to find five or six funds yielding 't' values 'significant' at the 5% level."[39] From this he concludes that "there is very little evidence that any individual fund was able to do significantly better than what we expected from mere random chance."[40] Jensen refrains for a number of statistical reasons from making a similar analysis of the 60 out of 115 funds that outperform the market on a gross basis for the 1955–1964 period.

While there are other studies that come to conclusions similar to Jensen's,[41] these conclusions by no means have the support of everyone who has looked into the matter. Several studies have found that the performance of the average fund equaled or bettered the market even on a net basis. One study, commissioned by the SEC, using essentially the same methodology but a larger sample than Jensen, concludes that the average risk-adjusted net return of the funds is 1.2 percent greater per year than the measure of the market average.[42] Another study, by Mains, which uses Jensen's data but makes small modifications in his methodology by making different assumptions concerning the frequency with which each fund's capital gains and dividend distributions are reinvested and by making periodic recalculations of each fund's systematic risk, concludes the funds' average net return slightly exceeds the market return.[43] Yet other studies have come to findings similar to those of the SEC and Mains by calculating the market measure in a different fashion from Jensen[44] or making different assumptions about the probability distribution generating security returns.[45]

b. *Problems using the conclusions of the mutual fund studies to establish the broad statement of the efficient market hypothesis.* There are a number of considerations that lead to the conclusion that, taken as a whole, the mutual fund performance studies, whatever they establish for purposes of advising ordinary individual investors, do not establish sufficiently well the validity of the broad statement of the efficient market hypothesis to permit the resurrection of the neoclassical theory of finance and industrial organization.

1. *Net versus gross returns.* First, if the studies are to be used to establish the broad statement of the efficient market hypothesis, the focus should be on the funds' gross returns, not their net returns.

A finding that their gross returns exceed the market return is inconsistent with the broad statement of the hypothesis because it indicates that better-informed investors can pick portfolios that outperform the market. A finding that their net returns are not significantly different from that of the measure of the market simply suggests that the funds are capable of capturing the value of their services, which in a competitive industry would just equal their costs at the margin. Although Jensen's study shows that both the average net and average gross returns of the funds are less than the measure of the market, we have noted that several other studies find that the average net returns equal or exceed the measure of the market. In each of these studies the average gross return of the funds covered would exceed the measure of the market by a significant margin. For example, the average gross return of the funds in Mains' study is 1.07 percent greater per year than the measure of the market average. He concludes such a result does not support the broad statement of the efficient market hypothesis.

2. *Average versus individual fund performance.* Second, only conclusions relating to the performances of individual funds are relevant to proving the broad statement of the efficient market hypothesis. A conclusion that the *average* performance of the funds does not exceed that of the market is irrelevant, since the broad statement of the efficient market hypothesis is wrong if, to put it most extremely, just one fund through superior information and analysis can outperform the market. In fact, it would not be surprising if the average performance of the funds does not exceed that of the market because the trades of institutional investors generally constitute 70 percent of all trades made.[46]

Individual fund performance is the subject of the findings contained in Jensen's third conclusion, that each of three funds had a performance sufficiently exceeding that of the market to permit a rejection with 95 percent confidence that it was due to chance. At first blush, these findings appear to demonstrate that the broad statement of the efficient market hypothesis is false. But Jensen concludes that these findings are not evidence that some funds have an ability to outperform the market. He argues, as we have seen, that *if each of the 115 funds only had the ability just to equal the performance of the market*, 5 or 6 can be expected through chance to perform well enough to permit rejection of the null hypothesis with 95 percent confidence. His argument goes too far. The italicized assumption is inappropriate given his profile of fund performances. The average performance of the 115 funds is not equal to the market, it is 1.1 percent less than the market. Seventy-six funds had performances below that of the market. The observed performance of any individual fund is to some extent the result of chance, but these figures strongly suggest that a significant majority of the funds have an ability (using Jensen's measures) only to perform at a level below the market and that the average ability of members of this majority is probably more than 1.1 percent below the market. Chance is very unlikely to lift the performances of most members of this group to the level displayed by the 3 funds of concern here.* It would have been more appropriate for Jensen to have asked how many funds we would expect to see reach the level of the 3 funds if 20 to 40 firms had an ability just equal to the market and the rest had a sufficiently lower ability that chance was very unlikely to lift them to these levels. The answer is 1 or 2. All that we can really say on the basis of Jensen's findings concerning the performance of individual funds is that the performance of the 3 funds in question (and of a number of others with somewhat less impressive "t" statistics) may or may not be due to chance and that the evidence is not very strong either way.

In applying this conclusion to the question of the validity of the broad statement of the efficient market hypothesis, we should remember that we have no preconceived reason to believe the hypothesis is correct. Unlike many hypotheses in economics, the efficient market hypothesis is not the result of theory composed of behavioral propositions already shown to be valid in other contexts. And the inconsistency of the simple arbitrage model with portfolio choice theory suggests it would not be easy to come up with a simple in-

---

*Consider, for example, 1 of these 3 funds. It was studied for the full twenty-year period, displayed risk-adjusted performance that exceeded the market by 1.91%, the "t" statistic relating to the question of whether such performance was significantly better than the market was 1.89, which is just above the statistic corresponding to the 95% confidence level. If the null hypothesis was instead whether such performance was significantly better than a fund with an ability to perform at a level 1.1% below the market, the "t" statistic would have been 2.97 and the null hypothesis could be rejected with more than 99.5% confidence. Thus, there is less than 1 chance in 200 that a fund with a level of ability equal to the average observed performance of all funds would because of random factors display performance as good as that displayed by the fund in question.

tuitive theory to support the hypothesis in this fashion. Its origins are entirely the empirical studies we are reviewing, so they must affirmatively convince us of the extent to which the hypothesis is true (see note 29). The fact that some funds outperform the market is at least somewhat probative evidence that their performance is the result of superior knowledge and analysis. The conclusion we have drawn from Jensen's study is that this evidence, which if correct disproves the hypothesis, may or may not in fact be due to chance. Thus, the study does not affirmatively establish the validity of the broad statement of the efficient market hypothesis even if one regards Jensen's data and methodology as superior to those of the studies that find the funds performed better and one rejects the argument that the focus should be on gross rather than net returns.

The value of Jensen's findings concerning individual fund performance for affirmatively establishing the validity of the hypothesis is further weakened by the fact that it was very difficult for a fund to show that its superior performance was not due to chance, given the data and statistical tools used in the study.[47] One fund, for the fourteen-year period it was studied, had a risk-adjusted average annual rate of return that exceeded the average annual market rate for the period by an extraordinary 5.82 percent, but it barely achieved a "t" statistic sufficient to reject the null hypothesis with 95 percent confidence. The existence of one or more funds with the ability to outperform the market by only a fraction of this amount would provide a significant service to its investors and raise serious questions about using the efficient market hypothesis to resurrect the neoclassical theory of finance and industrial organization. Yet it is unlikely that any such fund would display a level of performance that would be statistically significant at the 95 percent level unless there were a large number of them.

3. *Problems with the CAPM.* Third, there are fundamental theoretical problems using the mutual fund studies to prove the efficient market hypothesis because of the use of the capital asset pricing model to adjust for differences in the riskiness of the funds. The CAPM assumes, *inter alia*, that investors have homogeneous expectations, but the reason we are interested in testing the validity of the efficient market hypothesis is to see if securities are priced as if investors have homogeneous expectations when we know in reality they do not. Even ignoring all the preceding discussion, this prob-

lem suggests that we should regard any evidence of market efficiency generated by the mutual fund studies with caution, since they were generated by a process that assumes the market efficiency they are being used to try to prove.[48] If in fact the market is not efficient, the CAPM is not correct, which could lead to incorrect adjustments for risk and the false impression that the market is efficient. The fact that tests of the CAPM itself show that it fits the data well, while consistent with market efficiency, is not dispositive, since the only direct test of the model would be a test of the unobservable true market portfolio, which includes human capital, "collectibles," houses, etc.[49]

There is evidence that these problems of financial theory are not just theoretical. Two recent studies of the reaction of share prices to publicly announced "hard" information (quarterly earnings, stock splits, and dividend changes) utilized the CAPM to adjust for the normal reaction of the price of each security being observed to factors affecting security prices generally.[50] Contrary to the findings of the studies of public announcements reported in the preceding section, which utilized the "market model" to make such adjustments, the new studies find that the price of the average stock continued to react to the announcement in question for several periods after the period in which it was made. One possible explanation is that the market is not efficient even with respect to publicly announced hard information. Another, more plausible explanation is that tests of market efficiency utilizing the CAPM, including studies such as Jensen's, are invalid.[51]

4. *The information employed by mutual funds.* There is one other problem with using the mutual fund studies as evidence in support of the efficient market hypothesis. Such use implicitly assumes that the funds employ their excellent information to try to maximize the fund's performance. This assumption should not be accepted uncritically. The typical fund is managed by an investment company that also manages, or advises in the management of, a number of large portfolios of individual and corporate clients. Such a firm has a number of choices concerning what to do with the information it has developed. It can share the information with the world for a price; it can use the information to make investment decisions for both the fund and the private clients; or it can restrict use of the information just to make investment decisions for the private clients. The more

dollars invested long or short in the security on the basis of the information it develops, the greater is the effect on the demand for, and hence price of, the security and the smaller is the increase resulting from the information's use in the rate of return per dollar invested.

This fact, combined with the notorious imperfections in the market for information, make the first course of action very unlikely. And it may make the second course, using the information to benefit both the fund and the private clients, relatively unattractive as well. If the information is used to benefit the private clients, its use can be described to them in a veiled fashion on a more or less confidential basis where necessary to convince them of the quality of the portfolio management or advice they are receiving and to justify a higher level of fees. If the information is also used to benefit the fund, a veiled confidential description of its use is not possible. To try would be tantamount to sharing the information with the world. Use of the information to benefit the fund can only increase the fees the firm receives for managing the fund to the extent that the firm can demonstrate resulting superior performance—something we have seen takes a long time. Use of the information to benefit the fund will reduce the amount of benefit the private clients receive from it and hence the fees they can be charged. The loss of client fees may well exceed any gain in the fee which the firm is able to charge the fund.

2.2124 *Conclusion: The Empirical Studies Do Not Convincingly Establish the Broad Statement of the Efficient Market Hypothesis.*

In the aggregate, how much do the various empirical studies reviewed here support the broad statement of the efficient market hypothesis? The random walk studies and the studies of price reaction to announcements of hard information appear to demonstrate market efficiency but only with respect to a much narrower range of information than that covered by the broad statement. The mutual fund studies constitute a test of a sort with respect to a much broader range of information, but whether or not they demonstrate market efficiency with respect to that broader range involves a number of complex, controversial issues. Given the lack of theoretical work preceding the empirical studies reviewed here, we have no preconceived reason to believe that the broad statement of the efficient market hypothesis is true. The burden of proof should be on those who, using these studies, wish to establish the hypothesis. It is highly questionable whether that burden has been met.

2.213 *More Complex Models of Security Pricing*

The evidence generated by the empirical studies reviewed here and the inadequacy of a simple arbitrage model in explaining it have stimulated considerable theoretical research in recent years that has resulted in a number of new theories of securities pricing. While these theories are much more complex than the simple arbitrage model, each is built upon one or more of three relatively straightforward paradigms. For convenience they will be labeled the "active/passive investor paradigm," the "consensus forecast paradigm," and "market-signaling paradigm." A brief consideration of each of the paradigms shows that none suggests that we should abandon our concern with who knows what among investors.

The active/passive investor paradigm has already been alluded to in the discussion of the publicly announced information studies. Stock prices adjust rapidly to publicly announced information, the paradigm suggests, because, while not every investor is immediately aware of the information, every active investor is (or is advised by someone who is).[52] Active investors speculate. They have expectations about the returns of securities based on the information in their possession and determine the composition of the portfolios on the basis of these expectations. When the information changes, their expectations change and they buy or sell securities. Passive investors, because they believe in the efficient market hypothesis or for some other reason, do not speculate. They purchase securities as a place to store their savings that on average earns a positive return, and they sell them when they need cash. Since their decisions to buy, hold, or sell are not affected by their expectations, securities prices are not affected by their eventual receipt of publicly announced information.

The active/passive investor paradigm does not by itself change the basic analysis at the conclusion of the theoretical discussion concerning the simple arbitrage model, it just focuses the inquiry on a narrower range of participants. The price of a security will depend, *inter alia*, on every single active investor's expected value assessment of the future return of that security and hence on the information possessed by each of them.

The consensus forecast paradigm relates to the way the market forms prices by aggregating the expectations of each individual investor. Each investor bases his expectations not just on dramatic information possessed as well by all other investors but also on his own particular collection of bits of nondramatic information and his own particular set of analytic skills. The suggestion is that under appropriate conditions, market prices will represent better estimates of future returns than the expectations of any individual investor.[53] The analogy is to studies that suggest that averages of the forecasts of experts in areas such as GNP growth often outperform the forecasts of any of the individual participants. Each forecast has some bias resulting from the particular information and skill utilized, but the consensus cancels out these biases and at the same time takes advantage of the diversity of information and skill not available to any single forecaster.

While conditions in the real market for securities do not closely approximate what is necessary for the price to constitute a best estimate of future returns, the consensus forecast paradigm can help explain why the risk-adjusted performance of even the best mutual funds is sufficiently close to that of the market to prevent an unambiguous conclusion that their accomplishments are the result of ability. The paradigm may also help explain why the public announcement studies often show price movement for several periods preceding the announcement. However, like the active/passive investor paradigm, this paradigm is not inconsistent with the conclusion of the prior theoretical discussion that the price of a security will depend on the particular information held by each investor. Moreover, contrary to what the efficient market hypothesis would predict, it can be shown that an improvement in the accuracy of the expectations of one investor as a result of receipt of information already possessed by another investor will increase the expected accuracy of the price as an estimate of future returns.[54]

The market-signaling paradigm rests on the proposition that each investor, knowing that the price of a security reflects the probability assessments of other investors possessing information not possessed by him, will take that fact into account in any decision to buy, sell, or hold the security. He thus indirectly learns the information possessed by others by observing the prices created by their buy, sell, and hold decisions. Some theories of price formation utilizing this paradigm show that under appropriate conditions the price of a security will be a sufficient statistic, in essence the best estimate that can be made given an information set consisting of every bit of information possessed by any one or more investors. The market will therefore be efficient with respect to all such information.[55] As complete descriptions of the process of price formation, the realism of these theories is hampered not only by the failure of the securities markets to meet the posited conditions but also by the paradox that, in a world of costly information, no one will have an incentive to collect and process information if it can be obtained cost free by simply observing prices. Grossman and Stiglitz have suggested a resolution to this paradox.[56] Securities markets are likely to have sources of uncertainty other than the uncertainty as to the future returns of securities being traded on the market. These additional sources of uncertainty create "noise" that makes it impossible for an uninformed trader to determine fully the information possessed by others. Informed traders outperform uninformed ones but must incur the costs of information gathering and processing to do so.

The market-signaling paradigm suggests the earlier discussion critiquing the simple arbitrage model is incomplete because it views prices simply as constraints, not as carriers of information. But because of the limits on the paradigm, the conclusion of that discussion is still valid. Even an active investor may use the current market price to temper his expectations concerning the future returns of a security where a deviation exists between these expectations and market price. That tempering will not, however, completely eliminate the difference, and the investor will act on the basis of the deviation that remains. Thus, we still need to be concerned with who knows what among active investors.

2.214 *The Relationship of Prices to Fundamentals*

Suppose that, despite the doubts expressed here, one is convinced by the studies reviewed above that once any piece of information, even undramatic information, is known by one or a few outside investors, it is impossible to profit by trading on it. One should not automatically jump to the conclusion that the first step of the reformulation of the Manne thesis has been established, i.e., that share prices reflect the views concerning the future performance of the firm of the hypothetical investor knowing every piece of information held by any one or more investors. To make that jump, one must assume that the way each investor makes trading profits is to detect differences between share price and the present value of the future stream of a firm's dividends (the "fundamentals") based on his assessment of the probability distribution of these dividends. If that is the case, he will focus on the information that is relevant to the level of future dividends, and evidence that he cannot make trading profits on any piece of information held by any one or more outside investors is evidence that prices are optimal forecasts of those dividends conditional on all such pieces of information.

Fundamentals, however, may not be the focus of most investors. Most investors do not hold a share for the life of the firm, the period necessary to receive the full stream of dividends. At least part—usually most—of their expected return is based on what they expect to be able to sell the shares for. If the investor thinks that the market will be "rational" in the future, focusing on future price is equivalent to focusing on fundamentals. But the investor may not believe that the market is going to be rational in the future and may focus instead on the "psychology" of the market. If enough investors share this belief over time, it is self-confirming. The investor who does not plan to keep his shares for the life of the firm but focuses solely on fundamentals will not do as well as the one that focuses on psychology because the first investor's prediction of his returns will not be as accurate.

The belief that market pricing of securities is to some extent irrational is perfectly respectable within the economics profession. Keynes, for example, made an often-cited analogy of the American stock market to a newspaper competition "in which the competitors have to pick out the six prettiest faces from a hundred photographs, the prize being awarded to the competitor whose choice most nearly corresponds to the average preferences of the competitors as a whole."[57] Other very well-known economists who see some irrationality in stock market pricing include Baumol,[58] Tobin,[59] and Modigliani.[60]

None of the studies supporting the broad statement of the efficient market hypothesis is inconsistent with this view.[61] The market may be efficient with respect to information that it would, in any case, ultimately find important, but the information which it would ultimately find important may not be information solely about fundamentals.

Shiller recently produced some startling empirical evidence supporting the view that the market is irrational.[62] Shiller looks at stock prices and dividends over the last 100 years and finds that stock price volatility "appears to be far too high—five to thirteen times too high—to be attributed to new information about future real dividends if uncertainty about future dividends is measured by the sample standard deviations of real dividends around their long-run exponential growth path." If the market is rational, stock prices should be optimal forecasts of future dividends. Optimal forecasts should be less volatile than actual outcomes, but Shiller's study shows just the opposite to be the case.

Shiller's study is controversial: there are ways of arguing that his findings are consistent with market rationality.[63] But the possibility that the market has a degree of irrationality raises further questions about the reformulated Manne thesis even before we go on to its second and third steps. If the share price of a firm is above what a rational expectation of future dividend flows would suggest, management is protected from takeover despite a certain degree of non-maximizing behavior, because the overpricing of its shares swallows up any gains that could be made from improved management after a takeover. If share prices are for a period generally below what the fundamentals suggest—as some observers think has been the case since the late 1960s—much of the takeover activity that has occurred may really be "asset plays" rather than replacement of inefficient management. The level of takeover activity in such a period creates the impression that inefficient management is more vulnerable to takeover than it really is.

2.22 *Comparing Insider and Outsider Levels of Information*

Management knows a great deal more about a corporation than even the best-informed outsider. The most important reason for management's existence is to perform a function on a full-time basis that is necessary if the firm is to act intelligently: to gather, process, and act on information both about relevant features of the environment in which the firm operates and about the firm's internal operations. It is impractical for an outsider to duplicate this gathering and processing with anything like the same intensity. Subject to certain legal obligations, once management gathers and processes the information, it controls what portion is then passed on to outsiders. For a variety of reasons, most of it is not.

One's assessments of the future should on average be more accurate if one has additional information, assuming that *ex ante* there is no reason to think the additional information is biased. Knowledge is the complement of uncertainty.[64] The accuracy of assessments by outsiders concerning the future of the firm could therefore on average be improved if they received more of the information possessed by management than they do. If the improvement would be significant, that would indicate that management motivation, control reassignment, and project choice do not work the way they are portrayed in the neoclassical model. This would be true even assuming that security prices do fully reflect the information concerning fundamentals possessed by the best-informed investors. We are confronted with two important questions: would the improvement be significant, and, if so, would the legal and institutional rearrangements necessary to make this information available be cost effective?

Some economists ignore this issue altogether, and assume that the market for corporate control works as though its participants were as fully informed as management. Other economists admit that the best-informed outsiders are not as well informed as the insiders and that this will result in a certain degree of management discretion, but that the current situation is nevertheless optimal because releasing more information—while increasing the constraints on management discretion—is not cost effective.[65] The argument is made, for example, that the market penalizes the stock of any firm which does not provide all the information that the market can make good use of. Since management wants as high a price as possible for its stock, it will provide this level of information.[66] But there are a host of issues lurking behind this simple analysis. Why, for example, does management want a high price? One important reason is job preservation. All other things being equal, a high stock price makes a hostile takeover more difficult. But other things are not always equal. Suppression of positive information may be desirable despite its potential to enhance share price if it would be useful to an outsider considering a hostile takeover. Positive information might also be suppressed because it would be useful to a competitor.[67] And where information is negative, suppression obviously helps maintain price in the short run even if it decreases it in the longer run because of damage to the firm's reputation for candidness. Management's choice as to whether to suppress or disclose such negative information therefore depends on its time horizon. This discussion suggests that it is not possible to assess the importance of the information not shared with outsiders or to consider policy alternatives without a careful examination, of the kind to be undertaken in chapter 2, into the motivational structure within which management makes the decisions concerning information release.

There is empirical evidence that the informational advantages managers have over outsiders result in more accurate assessments of a firm's future. A study by Lorie and Niederhoffer of SEC filings under Section 16(a) of the Securities Exchange Act of 1934 shows that insiders accumulate shares of their firm more intensively than usual prior to periods when their stock outperforms the market and sell such shares more intensively than usual prior to periods when their stock underperforms the market.[68] Since the study relates to purchases and sales openly undertaken by the insiders involved, the basis of their superior performance is probably just being generally better informed. Trading by an insider on the basis of a single discrete piece of material corporate information is prohibited under the SEC's Rule 10b-5 and therefore is not likely to be undertaken publicly. A study by Scholes finds that the average secondary offering causes a market-adjusted 1 to 2 percent drop in share price.[69] Since the decline is not related to the relative size of the offering, it cannot be explained by selling pressure. Instead Scholes attributes the decline to the belief by the market that if someone with a large block of shares is selling, he knows something negative the market does not know. The decline is particularly pronounced when the seller is a corporate officer. Since these sales are openly undertaken, they are again not likely to be based on a discrete piece of material inside information.

2.23 *The Degree of Vulnerability to Takeover of a Firm with Underpriced Shares*

2.231 *Theory*

Suppose that the management of a firm engages in nonmaximizing behavior, the share price reflects an assessment of the future which assumes continuation of this nonmaximizing behavior (whether the reason for the low level of projected performance—poor management—is generally understood or not), and at least one well-informed investor with unlimited borrowing power believes that the firm could be more profitable if its assets were managed differently. Will this target firm be promptly taken over? Not necessarily, suggests the discussion earlier in this chapter concerning the simple arbitrage model and portfolio choice theory (see section C 2.211). Above a certain level of holdings, each share of the target added to the investor's portfolio makes the portfolio more risky. And the amount of risk added by the marginal share is an increasing function of the number of target shares held. The portfolio in effect becomes less and less diversified. A takeover has an all or nothing aspect to it: the investor must acquire a certain minimum number of shares or he will be unable to effect the transfer of control on which his expectation of improved return depends. In the case of most investors and most firms that are targets for takeovers, that minimum number of shares constitutes a large investment relative to the size of the investor's total portfolio prior to contemplating the takeover. Altering the portfolio to include that minimum number of shares significantly adds to its riskiness. The larger the target, the greater is this problem. Unless the target is sufficiently mismanaged that the investor expects the improvement in earnings from the transfer of control to be greater than what is necessary to compensate for this added risk, the transaction will not be worthwhile for him.* This analysis holds where the investor is a firm as well as where it is an individual. (See appendix 1.5 for an analysis of this more complex problem.)

---

*Using the language of the earlier discussion of the simple arbitrage model and portfolio choice theory, given the variance-covariance characteristics of the distribution of the second period price of the target shares assuming transfer of control, the expected value of that price may not be great enough for him to want to hold as many shares in his portfolio as is necessary to effect the transfer of control.

The problem that the expectation of improved returns from better management may not compensate for the greater risk resulting from the necessarily concentrated holding of target shares is accentuated by the fact that the investor is likely to view with considerable uncertainty his assessment of the amount by which earnings can be improved from a change in management. Assessing accurately how much better he can do than current management with the target's tangible and intangible assets, new investment opportunities, and existing organizational capabilities is very difficult because it depends on a myriad of details about these assets and capabilities that are nearly impossible for an outsider to know.* The fact that this risk may be unsystematic, i.e., uncorrelated with the market as a whole, does not make it irrelevant because the concentrated ownership necessary to effect a takeover means the risk cannot be diversified away.

2.232 *Empirical Evidence*

Empirical studies of takeovers tend to confirm the conclusion that the managers of a firm must behave in a substantially suboptimal way before they risk loss of control. There have been a number of studies concerning the per share costs that must be incurred by an acquiror in a hostile tender offer compared with the price of the target's shares prevailing before the takeover. The bulk of added cost is the premium that must be paid to persuade a sufficient number of holders to sell, but there are also significant transaction costs such as the fees of investment bankers, share solicitors, and lawyers. The estimates of these costs range from 13 to 70 percent of the pretakeover price, with the more recent studies tending on the high

---

*Oliver Williamson also comes to the conclusion that the takeover threat is a relatively crude means of controlling management discretion using similar logic but posing the problem in a somewhat different way. He argues: "Given information impactedness [differences in information between corporate managers and outsiders], outsiders can usually make confident judgments that the firm is not adhering to profit maximizing standards only at great expense. The large firm is a complex organization and its performance is jointly a function of exogenous economic events, rival behavior, and internal decisions." [70] Monsen and Downs point out that outsiders have no reliable way of determining whether a firm is maximizing profits, because the only yardstick available is a comparison with other firms and no two firms are exactly alike. [71]

side of this range.[72] These figures also represent estimates of the amount by which incumbent management can underperform before it needs to worry about losing control in a hostile takeover. Assuming that the pretakeover price is the discounted aggregate expected future dividend flow if incumbent management continues to control the firm, the acquiror, for the takeover to be worthwhile, must expect that its management improvements will improve that flow by a percentage at least equal to the percentage by which the acquiror's per share costs exceed the pretakeover price.[73] In fact, incumbent management probably has even more room to underperform than these estimates suggest, since they do not include the acquiror's transition cost of bringing the target under effective control once the transfer in ownership of shares has been effected.[74]

There is also empirical evidence that the larger the corporation, the less chance of a takeover. Kuehn, in an econometric study, identifies firm size as a significant determinant of the risk of takeover.[75] Herman finds that in the period 1965–1975 not one of the largest 100 corporations by sales and only 4 of the next 100 were targets of hostile takeover attempts.[76] Of the four attempts, only one was successful. A survey by me covering the period 1976–1982 shows 2 of the largest 100 corporations were subject to hostile takeover attempts, neither of which succeeded, and 8 of the next 100 were targets of hostile takeover attempts, only one of which succeeded. For the top 500 corporations by sales during that seven-year period, the survey reveals an annual average of eleven hostile attempts and two successes.* This record suggests that the managerial constraint against nonmaximizing behavior resulting from fear of takeover is not real for the top 100 corporations, very weak for the next 100 (two successes in eighteen years), and only modest for the top 500 as a whole. This is a very important conclusion, considering the large percentage of the economy's real-level project-funding and control reassign-

---

*A change of control which starts as a hostile tender offer or proxy fight and which subsequently either turns friendly or is foiled by a merger between the target and a friendly third company (a "white knight") is counted a hostile takeover attempt, but not as one which succeeded. Any change in control which at some point receives the support of target management is one where target management receives a benefit in return for not making the change more difficult. The need for an acquiror to pay such a benefit in order to avoid continuing to incur the expenses and risk of a hostile takeover attempt gives the incumbent management of the target a margin within which they need not engage in optimizing behavior.

ment decisions which are made by these firms (see chapter 2, section B3).

2.233 *The Meaning of the Recent Takeover Boom*

The last few years have seen a substantial increase in the number of hostile tender offers for the largest 200 firms. In the period 1983–1985, 4 of the largest 100 industrial firms were targets of attempts (none successful) and 5 of the next largest 100 were such targets (3 of which succeeded).* Does this increase in offers mean that that nonmaximizing behavior by the managers of our economy's very largest firms is now constrained within certain bounds by fear of hostile takeover in the same way nonmaximizing behavior by managers of other firms has been all along? The answer to this question depends on why the increase has occurred.

The recent takeover boom has seen the introduction of two financial devices not commonly used before in connection with hostile tender offers: the two-tiered takeover and the "junk bond" (high risk, high yield publicly issued debt). It has been argued that the introduction of these devices explains in large part the sudden increase in offers for the very largest firms because they permit for the first time potential acquirors that are significantly smaller than their targets to gather sufficient funds to undertake the effort.[77] This explanation, even if valid, does not, however, automatically imply that the managers of the largest firms are now constrained in their nonmaximizing behavior. To draw this conclusion, one must assume that the increased number of offers permitted by the invention of the new financial devices involved offerors that identified target firms whose incumbent managements were engaging in nonmaximizing behavior and sought to profit by replacing these managements. The offers may in fact have been motivated by completely different factors. It is therefore helpful to explore the various possible motives for an acquiror to engage in a hostile offer. If any of these motives have increased in intensity in recent years, they themselves form explanations of the increase in offers independent of the new financial devices explanation.

---

*For the top 500 as a whole, the rate of attempts during this three-year period did not increase (an average of ten) but the rate of successes did increase somewhat (an annual average of three).

One possible motive for an acquiror to engage in a hostile offer depends, for it to be plausible, on a belief that stock prices do not necessarily reflect fundamentals, i.e., are not necessarily equal to the best estimate of the future stream of dividends discounted to present value (see section C 2.214). Under this theory of stock pricing, potential acquirors are motivated to engage in hostile tender offers when share prices become depressed well below the fundamental value of the firms they represent, as many observers believe was the case in the early 1980's. By engaging in the acquisitions, the acquiring firms perform an arbitrage function between the stock market and the asset market.[78] The sudden increase in hostile offers can be explained as the result of the invention of the new financial devices which permitted smaller potential acquirors to act on their motives to arbitrage where they had been unable to so before. This arbitrage motive can also provide an explanation of the increase in offers that is independent of the new devices because it is the sort of motive that can give rise to a speculative boom. Once some of this arbitrage based takeover activity begins to involve the very large firms at all, a larger group of potential acquirors feel the need to act quickly for fear that the targets they are considering will be plucked off by someone else or that share prices generally will increase as investors observe a higher level of takeovers. Most likely both explanations are involved. Evidence that an arbitrage motive is behind the increase in hostile offers is the large proportion involving oil companies (3 out of the 4 targets among the largest 100 were oil companies), a primary asset of which—oil reserves—is more susceptible to outside evaluation than most kinds of income earning assets. Other evidence is the development of the "bust up" takeover, whereby the target is divided into parts, some or all of which are immediately sold. The acquiror is seeking profits by buying the company in the share market and selling it piecemeal in the asset market.

A second possible motive for an offeror to engage in a hostile offer relates to the potential benefits from combining the operations of the acquiror and the target: economies of scale, a cost saving substitution of administrative for market relations between a firm and a supplier of inputs, or increased profits as the result of increased market power. While each of these benefits are obtainable by voluntary merger, the negotiations required are very complex and can fail even where terms mutually advantageous to the management of both firms could in theory be found. In that situation the management of one firm has a motive to engage in a hostile offer for the other firm. Again, the sudden increase in hostile offers can be explained as the result of the invention of new financial devices which permitted smaller potential acquirors to realize the benefits of combination where they had been unable to so before. And, again, this motive also provides an explanation of the increase independent of the new devices because the increase corresponds to a period in which government antitrust authorities eased their policies with respect to horizontal and vertical mergers. The easier policies are the result both of a change in economic philosophy and a perception that the pressures of international trade made larger U.S. firms more necessary in survival terms and less worrisome in anticompetitive terms. One would expect the increase in the number of governmentally approvable business combinations to lead to an increase not only in the number of voluntary mergers (which it has) but also in the number of hostile offers. Once the rate of business combinations, both voluntary and involuntary, begins to increase at all, speculation can again work to increase the rate further. The managements of firms A and B might each see potential gains by a combination with firm C but the first one to effect the combination gets the prize. Adding to the speculative element may be a feeling that the easier antitrust policies may be reversed at some point in the future and combinations that may have been dreamed about for decades may only be possible for a limited period of time.

A third motive for an offeror to engage in a hostile offer is the one with which we are already familiar: the identification by the offeror of a target whose incumbent management has engaged in nonmaximizing behavior. If in fact a significant portion of the recent increase in offers for the very largest firms have been so motivated, then there has been a change in the constraints imposed on the managements of these firms. Two cautionary notes should be sounded in this connection, however. First, since there is no reason to believe that there has been a sudden increase in nonmazimizing behavior, the increase in such hostile offers must be the result of the invention of new financial devices. Both the two-tiered tender offer and junk bond financing have been severely criticized, at least ostensibly for reasons unrelated to their ability to facilitate hostile offers. The use of each may be restricted or prohibited. Thus the new constraints on the managements of the very largest firms, if they exist at all, may be temporary. Second, a review of the targets of these hostile offers shows that most of them are in industries with high cash flows and real investment opportunities of diminishing quality. If non-maximizing behavior is what has motivated these offers, then, as Michael Jensen suggests, the particular behavior involved is overretention.[79] As discussed later in this book (see chapter 2, section C 2.423 and chapter 6, section C), there are other ways of increasing firm payouts. A very active market for corporate control has its disadvantages. It can divert management attention from the market for its products to concerns both about being a potential acquiror and a potential target. It can also undermine efforts to get individual managers to identify with the long run welfare of the firm by creating intense worries about job security. Thus, even if the increase in hostile offers is a sign of new constraints on nonmaximizing behavior, it may not represent the best available tool for getting at the problem they are remedying.

Ultimately, it is not yet possible to answer the question of whether the increase in hostile offers for the very largest firms means that new constraints have been imposed on the nonmaximizing behavior of their managers. The increase is such a new phenomenon that it is not possible to sort out the soundness and relative importance of the various explanations discussed here. And even if time reveals that new constraints have been imposed, we do not know whether they are permanent or temporary or even whether they are the best way of dealing with the problem.

3. *The More Promising Assumption: Different Participants Have Different Knowledge.*

What can we now say about the attempt to resurrect the neoclassical theory of finance and industrial organization in which the homogeneous expectations are those either of the best-informed investors or of a hypothetical investor knowing every bit of information that any one or more participants know? Certainly the neoclassical theory has the advantages of simple straightforward logic and a minimum of variables. Close examination, however, has shown that each step in the argument for its resurrection involves complex controversial issues which create serious doubts about the utility of its final conclusions. Despite the theory's attractions, these doubts suggest that we put it aside and see what would come from an approach which focuses on, rather than ignores, who knows what.

While the preceding critical review of the attempt at neoclassical resurrection does not provide a coherent outline for an alternative approach, it suggests the promise of such an approach by the questions it raises. Consider, for example, the fact that the ultimate source of most of the nation's savings are individual human beings, most of whom possess very little investment information. The review shows that if such an investor participates directly as a speculator in the market for corporate investment opportunities, his views will influence its prices. Where do his views come from? How does he choose his advisers and what heed does he pay them? If, as is more often the case, he delegates decisions concerning placement of his savings to a financial intermediary such as a bank, a pension or other trust fund, a mutual fund, or a venture capital firm, how does he choose that intermediary, with its influence on market prices? Behind these questions is another: how do advisers and intermediaries acquire and choose to use information? The review also highlights what a large portion of finance process decisions are made within corporations. How are these decisions made?

Consider also the tension between two other conclusions of the review. We see on the one hand that the probability of a firm's management being replaced, given any particular share price and degree of mismanagement, is an inverse function of how much outsiders understand about its operations. On the other hand, share price itself is on average a positive function of how much outsiders understand. How does management make this trade-off in choosing how much information, beyond the legal minimum, to reveal about the firm? What are the implications of this choice on the accuracy of the price of the firm's securities and on the range of managerial discretion? Does the trade-off appear different to management with regard to information concerning its finance process decisions as opposed to its "production" decisions?

Even tentative answers to these and other questions raised by the review should substantially enrich our understanding of our industrial system and provide a basis for rethinking certain aspects of the regulation of the finance process.

D. Static Versus Dynamic Models of Industrial Organization

Having explored in depth the issue of the appropriate degree of uniformity in expectations to assume, we must now face the other fundamental choice which must be made in constructing a theory of finance and industrial performance; whether we should be working with a static or dynamic model of industrial organization. Static analysis can be used to help understand any system that has a tendency to move toward equilibrium. A static analysis consists of a description of the final resting place of the system for any given continuing environment and a demonstration of the existence of forces at work to push the system, when in disequilibrium, toward that final resting place. Dynamic analysis can be used to understand any system, whether it has a tendency toward equilibrium or not. A dynamic analysis describes the position of a system at each particular moment in time, not just its position if and when it reaches equilibrium.

1. *The Neoclassical Theory*

The neoclassical theory of finance and industrial performance, as noted, utilizes a static model of industrial organization. The demonstration that a competitive system with all participants equally informed displays a high level of output choice and production efficiency is based on its behavior in equilibrium. The claim that such a system displays dynamic efficiency, to the extent it has meaning in the neoclassical scheme, is just a reaffirmation of the system's tendency, when in disequilibrium, to move toward equilibrium. Technical change is seen as a change in, or the creation of, the production function of the particular output in question. Since the set of production functions for the economy's outputs is part of the given environment, a technical change will throw into disequilibrium a system that was previously in equilibrium. The fact that the system moves over time to a new equilibrium mandated by the new set of givens shows its dynamic efficiency. The forces at work are simple. Entrepreneurs are all aware of the change and identify the kinds of projects that, given the technical change, will yield an above-normal return on investment. Investors, aware of this, will respond by supplying the needed capital. This continues until the amount of resources devoted to such projects results in a level of supply of output such that these projects earn only a competitive return.

2. *Technical Change*

A significant number of industrial organization economists today are uncomfortable with describing technical change as a shift in a production function followed by inevitable economic consequences. This discomfort can be seen as far back as the first decade of this century in the writings of Schumpeter.[80] Schumpeter's view of the everyday life of a firm is very much akin to that of the behavioralists: the firm makes all its decisions following certain simple rules developed from long experience. Schumpeter thinks that at any moment in time there are many untried ideas known to some, perhaps many, persons for what, if tried, would turn out to be a new or better product or process. The problem is the uncertainty associated with trying the new idea compared with the certainty of continuing the old ways of doing things. Innovation consists of an entrepreneur seizing such a possibility and acting on it. As others gradually become aware of the superiority of the innovation over traditional products or processes, they too change their way of doing things and diffusion occurs. Technical change, in this view, is the result of the workings of the economic system which economic theory must help explain, not a reaction to an exogenous event. The empirical literature concerning the innovation and diffusion of new technology that has built up since the 1960s on the whole confirms Schumpeter's view.[81] These studies show that inventions or other ideas that eventually become the basis for very successful changes in product or process may be around for some time before someone is bold enough to develop them to a level of commercial introduction. Even then, other firms do not always follow immediately.

Static analysis captures none of this. It does not help us understand the factors which determine where and when innovation occurs and its rate of diffusion. Yet understanding these things is very important. As pointed out at the beginning of this book, an improvement in dynamic efficiency with its attendant increase in the rate of productivity growth in the economy has much more potential for improving the general level of economic well-being than any conceivable improvement in output choice or production efficiency.

Additionally, static analysis does not recognize that innovation can alter the competitive structure of an industry in a way that may have profound effects on output choice and production efficiency, at least in the short and medium run. This problem is particularly acute in industries characterized by rapid and continuing technical change as opposed to those characterized by the more sporadic changes described by Schumpeter. As the semiconductor study in part II exemplifies, the structure of such an industry is so fluid that it is impossible to understand the output level and production method decisions in that industry by using a purely static analysis. The way to understand innovation, diffusion, and the effects of each on industry structure is by looking at the industry's "dynamic selection mechanism": the entry or expansion over time of firms utilizing the new technology and the contraction or exit over time of firms which do not switch.[82]

Finance is important in explaining an industry's dynamic selection mechanism. Neither innovation nor diffusion is generally possible without new investment.* The fact that a worthy new idea is not guaranteed finding an immediate proponent suggests that if and when it finally does, the proponent will not automatically find financial backers. The efficient market hypothesis is particularly unconvincing in this context. For example, the kind of proponent most likely to champion projects based on worthy new ideas may perhaps be someone who wishes to establish a new firm, but the kind of proponent with the easiest access to capital may perhaps be employees of a firm in an undynamic, heavy manufacturing industry. If so, the economy will not display the highest possible level of dynamic efficiency. And if an idea as it becomes known and tried eventually becomes the basis of projects proposed by a number of different

---

*In all of their studies formally modeling the Schumpeterian approach to industrial organization, Nelson and Winter assume, implicitly or explicitly, that past performance is the sole determinant of the availability of finance: investment is determined by retained earnings possibly augmented by outside sources providing capital to different firms in proportion to the profits of the immediately preceding period. They recognize this is not a serious theory of finance.[83] Some of the most important events in the history of the typical industry are the entry of a brand new firm or the implementation of a new technology requiring a large, discrete "front end" investment. These events will not involve projects financed by retained earnings or systematically augmented versions thereof.

proponents, differential access to capital can leave a strong mark on market structure.

3. *Behavior of an Industry Composed of Nonmaximizing Firms*

Even in industries where technical change is slow, the static neoclassical model of industrial organization has serious shortcomings. As we have seen, there is considerable reason to believe that managers of firms where ownership is separated from control do not need to behave in a profit-maximizing fashion. The behavioral theory of the firm suggests that firms generally act in accordance with a stable set of decision rules that have been found in the past to produce results that satisfy the firm's aspiration levels. While the effort at neoclassical resurrection concludes that these rules, even if not consciously developed to be profit-maximizing ones, will nevertheless be so, the conclusion is not entirely convincing. Stockholder ignorance hinders the workings of both the survival theory and the takeover threat, the two bases on which the neoclassical resurrection is built.

If we were looking at a very long-run equilibrium situation, such ignorance would presumably disappear and these two mechanisms would work the way proponents of the resurrection describe. But even in an industry that has not experienced major technical change in some time, there often occur other significant changes in its environment arising from shifts in the supply of inputs (for example, energy and petrochemicals over the last decade), technological changes in other industries, and changes in consumer tastes. The system's speed of adjustment, which is dependent on the dissipation of investor ignorance, may be slower than the changes in environment. An equilibrium model is not appropriate for analyzing a system in which the exogenous variables change at such a rate that the corresponding rate of change in the equilibrium values of the endogenous variables is faster than the rate at which the endogenous variables adjust toward their respective equilibrium values given a single discrete change in the values of the exogenous variables.

How can we describe the behavior of such an industry in nonequilibrium terms? At the firm level, try to determine, as I have already begun to do, the range of management behavior which does not seriously risk control reassignment. Then, to determine the prevalence at a particular time of any set of decision rules that is within that range, use the same approach as I have already considered in the discussion of technical change: the dynamic selection mechanism. Examine the entry or expansion of firms utilizing superior decision rules and the contraction or exit pattern of firms utilizing inferior ones.* Repeating what was said above, finance is obviously important in explaining the operation of this mechanism.

E. Summary

The finance process is related to industrial performance through its influence on decisions concerning which investment projects are implemented and how existing productive capacity is used. The mechanisms that link the finance process to the industrial sector are the cost of capital, the provision of managerial incentives, and control reassignment. There exists a neoclassical theory of this relationship which concludes that with competitive capital markets these mechanisms will lead to industrial performance characterized by a high level of production efficiency, output choice efficiency (assuming no natural monopolies or oligopolies), and dynamic efficiency. This theory assumes that all participants in the system share homogeneous expectations, and its predictions of efficiency relate to the industrial sector of the economy when it is in equilibrium.

The real world is characterized by participants with heterogeneous expectations. Models assuming particular patterns of heterogeneous expectations lead to the conclusion that management of existing corporations may not be motivated to make project and production choices that would maximize share value and that the cost of capital may not be the same for two proposed projects of comparable risk. But an argument can be made, utilizing the empirical efficient market hypothesis studies, that the lack of reality of the assumption of homogeneous expectations does not diminish the utility of the neoclassical theory. This argument falls well short of settling the ques-

---

*Nelson and Winter lump together decision rules concerning production techniques, the change of which may represent innovation, with all other decision rules of the firm, some of which may be known by management not to be profit maximizing. Given the role of the finance process in policing management "shirking," I think it is better here to keep the two matters separate.

tion. It should not deter us from trying to develop a theory that recognizes heterogeneous expectations because such a theory, if convincing, will be much more helpful in explaining particular features of our industrial system and providing policy-relevant advice.

The static nature of the neoclassical theory also reduces its utility. Two of the most important issues in industrial organization economics are how innovation and diffusion occur and how industries evolve where some or all of their member firms do not make optimal project choice or production decisions. The neoclassical theory does not have much to say about these issues other than that the finance process exerts forces to bring the industrial system into equilibrium and that when equilibrium is reached the issues will disappear. But there is considerable evidence that many, if not all, industries are in disequilibrium and that their environments are changing quickly enough that this is a more or less permanent state of affairs.

Ultimately the problems of heterogeneous expectations and long-term industry disequilibrium tend to merge. If the finance process worked as if every investor knew every bit of information known by any participant in the system, whether inside or outside of a firm, industries would never be in disequilibrium for long. The challenge if we reject this view of the world is to construct an alternative theory that uses differences in information among participants to explain how project choice and production decisions are made in our economy.

Appendix 1.1 The Formulation of Subjective Probability Distributions

The following is an approach to how different individuals, i and j, with different information formulate their best guesses about the value of a future event, i.e., the expected values of their respective subjective probability distributions of the event. Consider, for example, the best guesses in period T-1 by i and j of P_T, the price of a particular security in period T. Each individual receives a somewhat different set of bits of information and bases his expectation on these bits. If there is no reason to believe *ex ante* that the flow of bits that goes to either individual is going to bias that individual's expectation, i.e., that something structural in the process that determines the information received by that individual would lead him to underestimate or overestimate the probable value of P_T, each individual's best guess as to the value of P_T, $(\overline{P}_{Ti})_{T-1}$ and $(\overline{P}_{Tj})_{T-1}$, is a random variable generated by a distribution with a mean equal to the as yet unknown P_T. This way of looking at the question permits us to relate P_T to the two probably different distributions in the minds of i and j. $(\overline{P}_{Ti})_{T-1}$ and $(\overline{P}_{Tj})_{T-1}$ are each unbiased assessments of P_T. The better informed the investor, the smaller the variance of the distribution generating this assessment. The concept is roughly analogous to sampling from a very large urn containing red balls and green balls to make a best guess as to the actual ratio of the red to green balls. The ratio contained in each sample—the best guess—is a random variable with a mean equal to the actual ratio. The larger the sample is (i.e., the more information the sampler has), the smaller the variance. Each individual is assumed to know his level of ignorance, i.e., the variance of the distribution generating his best guess of P_T. Each individual makes decisions as if P_T is a random variable with a mean equal to his best guess and a variance equal to the variance of the distribution generating his best guess.

Appendix 1.2 Demonstration That a Utility Function with a Constant Degree of Risk Aversion and a Quadratic Utility Function Both Result in Concave Upward Indifference Curves

Investors are frequently assumed to have utility functions which, over the relevant range, display a constant degree of risk aversion in the Pratt-Arrow sense, i.e., $U''(W_1)/U'(W_1)$ is constant where W_1 is the investor's second period wealth. An investor's utility function can thus be depicted by the function $U(W_1) = -e^{-aW_1}$ where a is positive and is the measure of risk aversion. W_1 is a linear combination of the second period prices of each available risky security adjusted by the amount, if any, either invested in a safe asset returning r^* or borrowed at r^*. If the second period price of each risky security is normally distributed, W_1 is normally distributed. Call the mean and variance of this distribution $\overline{W}$ and σ_w^2 respectively. $-E[U(W_1)]$ is identical to the moment-generating function of the distribution of W (where the usual $t = a$). Therefore

(1) $E[U(W_1)] = -e^{-a\overline{W} + a^2\sigma_w^2/2}$.

Assuming the investor acts to maximize his expected utility, the indifference curve between risk and return for any given level of expected utility k is the depiction of the equation

(2) $k = -e^{-a\overline{W} + a^2\sigma_w^2/2}$.

This curve is also the depiction of the equation

(3) $k' = \overline{W} - a\sigma_w^2/2$.

Rearranging,

(4) $\overline{W} = k' + a\sigma_w^2/2$

(5) $\dfrac{d\overline{W}}{d\sigma_w} = a\sigma_w$

(6) $\dfrac{d^2\overline{W}}{d\sigma_w^2} = a > 0.$

Since both the first and second derivatives of equation (3) are greater than 0, the indifference curve is concave upward.

The most usual alternative assumption concerning investor utility functions is that they are quadratic,

(6) $U(W_1) = a + bW - cW^2$ (a, b, c > 0)

(7) $E[U(W_1)] = a + b\overline{W} - c^2(\overline{W})^2 - c^2\sigma_w^2.$

An indifference curve will be depicted by

(8) $k = a + b\overline{W} - c^2(\overline{W})^2 - c^2\sigma_w^2$

which, with setting $\overline{W} = f(\sigma_w)$, can be rewritten

(9) $c^2\sigma_w^2 + k = a + bf(\sigma_w) - c^2f^2(\sigma_w).$

Differentiating both sides with respect to σ_w,

(10) $2c^2\sigma_w = \dfrac{df}{d\sigma_w}[b - c^2 2f(\sigma_w)]$

or

(11) $\dfrac{df}{d\sigma_w} = \dfrac{2c^2\sigma_w}{b - c^2 2f(\sigma_w)}.$

Differentiating again,

(12) $\dfrac{d^2f}{d\sigma_w^2} = \dfrac{2c^2(b - c^2 2f(\sigma_w)) + 4c^4\sigma_w\dfrac{df}{d\sigma}}{(b - c^2 2f(\sigma_w))^2}$

(13) $\dfrac{d^2f}{d\sigma_w^2} = \dfrac{d^2\overline{W}}{d\sigma_w^2} > 0 \Leftrightarrow b > c^2 2f(\sigma_w).$

$b > c^2 2f(\sigma_w)$ throughout the range of values of $\overline{W}$ of relevance when a quadratic is used to describe an investor's utility function, which is where $\dfrac{dE[U(W)]}{\overline{W}} > 0$, i.e., where an increase in expected second period wealth, holding the variance constant, leads to an increase expected utility. Since, in this range, both the first and second derivatives of the indifference curve's equation are greater than 0, the curve is concave upward.

Appendix 1.3 Demonstration That a Random Walk Is Consistent with Efficient Market Pricing

Consider a security the only right attaching to which is the right to receive a payment, P_T, in period T. Suppose that at no point prior to period T is the value of P_T known for certain. For example, from the vantage point of all that is known in period $T-1$, P_T has a probability distribution with an expected value $E_{T-1}(P_T)$. Suppose further that because of the existence of a safe asset with a return per period of r^* and the fact that investors are risk averse, they will require an expected rate of return per period of $R > r^*$ in order to be induced to hold the number of shares of the security outstanding.

If all participants make as full use as they can of all that is known in period $T-1$ concerning P_T (a price determined in an efficient market is the same "as if" it were determined by a market where this is the case),

(1) $P_{T-1} = (1+R)^{-1} E_{T-1}(P_T)$

or otherwise one of two groups in the market, long buyers and short sellers, would have an expected gain and the other an expected loss.

By the same logic, if $E_{T-2}(P_{T-1})$ is the expected value of the distribution of P_{T-1} based on all that is known in period $T-2$,

(2) $P_{T-2} = (1+R)^{-1} E_{T-2}(P_{T-1})$.

But assuming that in period $T-2$ investors anticipate that the pricing of the security in period $T-1$ will be based on $E_{T-1}(P_T)$ and given the fact that the expected value in period $T-2$ of $E_{T-1}(P_T)$ equals $E_{T-2}(P_T)$, the expected value of the distribution of P_T from the vantage point of all that is known in period $T-2$,

(3) $P_{T-2} = (1+R)^{-2} E_{T-2}(P_T)$.

Generalizing,

(4) $P_{T-K} = (1+R)^{-K} E_{T-K}(P_T)$.

So the price each period is based on the expected value of the distribution of P_T given the information available in that period.

If the price of the security in one period is anything other than the immediately preceding period price multiplied by $(1+R)$, the deviation must be due to a change in the expected value of P_T from one period to the next. Since the distribution of P_T as viewed from the vantage point of the immediately preceding period reflected all information available in that period, the change in the expected value of P_T must be due to new information, the impact of which is inherently unpredictable, i.e., random. If this is a correct description of the pricing process and, *ex post*, we observe the prices P_{T-t}, $P_{T-(t-1)}$ . . . P_{T-1}, P_T, calculate the corresponding series of price changes, and lag the series to determine covariance, we should observe a covariance near 0.[84]

Appendix 1.4 Demonstration That a Random Walk Is Also Consistent with Inefficient Market Pricing

As in appendix 1.3, consider an economy with a single security the only right attaching to which is to receive in period T a payment, P_T, the value of which is not known for certain prior to that period. Assume that there are two price-taking investors, i and j, each of whom has a constant degree of risk aversion with a measure equal to a (see appendix 1.2), and that there are n shares of the security outstanding. Each investor, on the basis of the information known to him in period $T-1$, believes that P_T is generated by a distribution with means respectively equal to $(\overline{P}_{Ti})_{T-1}$ and $(\overline{P}_{Tj})_{T-1}$ and with variances equal respectively to v_i and v_j. If by chance they had the exact same information, they would share the same views as to the distribution generating P_T.

Lintner's model referred to earlier (see section C2.211 and notes 34 and 35) demonstrates that the market clearing price, P_{T-1}, will be a function of an average of $(\overline{P}_{Ti})_{T-1}$ and $(\overline{P}_{Tj})_{T-1}$, weighted in inverse relation to v_i and v_j. Specifically,

(1) $(1+r^*)P_{T-1} = A(\overline{P}_{Ti})_{T-1} + B(\overline{P}_{Tj})_{T-1} - Vn$

where $A = \dfrac{v_j}{v_i + v_j}$, $B = \dfrac{v_i}{v_i + v_j}$, and $V = \dfrac{v_i + v_j}{v_i v_j}$.

In the model discussed in appendix 1.3, it is assumed that, as seen from the vantage point of all that is known in period $T-1$, P_T is generated by a distribution which has an expected value of $E_{T-1}(P_T)$ and which all investors make full use of. This is equivalent in concept to assuming that $E_{T-1}(P_T)$ is an unbiased best guess of P_T based on all the information available, i.e., that the best guess is the random variable generated by a distribution with a mean equal to the as yet unknown P_T. This way of looking at the matter permits us, as detailed in appendix 1.1, to relate P_T to the probably different distributions in the minds of i and j. $(\bar{P}_{Ti})_{T-1}$ and $(\bar{P}_{Tj})_{T-1}$ are each unbiased assessments of P_T because respective distributions generating each of them has a mean equal to P_T.

Given this view of investor behavior, what can we say about P_{T-2}? Again using the Lintner model,

$$(2)\ (1+r^*)P_{T-2} = A(\bar{P}_{(T-1)i})_{T-2} + B(\bar{P}_{(T-1)j})_{T-2} - Vn$$

where $(\bar{P}_{T-1)i})_{T-2}$ and $(\bar{P}_{(T-1)j})_{T-2}$ are the best guesses of i and j of the value of P_{T-1} based on their respective collections of information in period $T-2$ and assuming, for simplicity, that v_i and v_j have the same values as above. But assuming that each investor knows that, in accordance with equation (1), P_{T-1} will be a function of a weighted average of each investor's best guess in period $T-1$ of the value of P_T, equation (2) can be rewritten

$$(3)\ (1+r^*)^2 P_{T-2} = A[AE_{(T-2)i}((\bar{P}_{Ti})_{T-1}) + BE_{(T-2)i}((\bar{P}_{Tj})_{T-1})] +$$
$$B[AE_{(T-2)j}((\bar{P}_{Ti})_{T-1}) + BE_{(T-2)j}((\bar{P}_{Tj})_{T-1})] - (2+r^*)Vn$$

where $E_{(T-2)i}$ and $E_{(T-2)j}$ are respectively the expected value operators based on what i and j each know in period $T-2$.

There is no question that $E_{(T-2)i}((\bar{P}_{Ti})_{T-1}) = (\bar{P}_{Ti})_{T-2}$, i's best guess in period $T-2$ as to the value P_T. The same can be said about $E_{(T-2)j}((\bar{P}_{Tj})_{T-1}) = (\bar{P}_{Tj})_{T-2}$.

What about $E_{(T-2)i}((\bar{P}_{Tj})_{T-1})$, i's expectation in period $T-2$ of j's expectation in period $T-1$ of the value of P_T? If we assume that, other than information that both receive in the same time period, i and j each collect information independently and that in period $T-2$ i knows nothing about what information j will possess in period $T-1$, i will anticipate that j's "sample of information" in $T-1$ will produce an unbiased assessment of P_T. Since i regards $(\bar{P}_{Ti})_{(T-2)}$ as an unbiased assessment of P_T, it will be his best guess as to the value of $(\bar{P}_{Tj})_{(T-1)}$. With the same assumptions, the same can be said about j and $E_{(T-2)j}((\bar{P}_{Ti})_{T-1})$.

We can now simplify (3) as follows.

$$(4)\ (1+r^*)^2 P_{T-2} = A(A+B)(\bar{P}_{Ti})_{T-2} + B(A+B)(\bar{P}_{Tj})_{T-2} - (2+r^*)Vn.$$

Since $A+B=1$,

(5) $(1+r^*)^2 P_{T-2} = A(\overline{P}_{Ti})_{T-2} + B(\overline{P}_{Tj})_{T-2} - (2+r^*)Vn.$

Generalizing,

(6) $(1+r)^k P_{T-k} = A(\overline{P}_{Ti})_{T-k} + B(\overline{P}_{Tj})_{T-k} - Vn \sum_{t=1}^{k} (1+r^*)^{t-1}$

where $(\overline{P}_{Ti})_{T-k}$ and $(\overline{P}_{Tj})_{T-k}$ have the equivalent meaning for period $T-k$ as $(\overline{P}_{Ti})_{T-2}$ and $(\overline{P}_{Tj})_{T-2}$ have for period $T-2$.

Under the foregoing assumptions, equation (6) implies that if the change in the price from any period $T-t$ to period $T-(t-1)$ deviates from being $r^* P_{T-t} + (1+r^*)Vn$, that deviation from the growth path will be random and that the covariances examined in the random walk studies should be near 0. This is because $(\overline{P}_{Ti})$ and $(\overline{P}_{Tj})$ will display changes from one period to the next that are independent both of past changes in their own value and also of past changes in value of the other. $(\overline{P}_{Ti})_{T-t}$ is based on all the information available to i in that period. Any difference between that value and $(\overline{P}_{Ti})_{T-(t-1)}$ must be due to the receipt by i of new information (additions to i's "sample"), the impact of which is inherently unpredictable, i.e., random. The same is true of any change in $\overline{P}_{Tj}$. The independence of changes of one from changes in a previous period of the other flows from the assumption of independent fact collecting by i and j.

Appendix 1.5 Takeover Behavior of a Corporation

In most cases, the investor contemplating a takeover is a corporation, not an individual. One way to analyze the investment behavior of an acquiror corporation is from the perspective of its managers, who have the knowledge concerning investment opportunities and actually make the decisions for the corporation. A second way is from the perspective of the acquiror's stockholders, where the corporate investment is seen in terms of its effect on the characteristics of the shareholders' portfolios of investments. In this second way, management is assumed to make decisions which shareholders would have chosen if they knew what management knows. Both perspectives will be considered in this appendix.

1. *The Perspective of the Acquiror's Manager*

The first perspective has the advantage that, unlike the second, it does not presuppose the answer to the fundamental issue that prompts this examination of the takeover mechanism: does management generally act in the shareholders' best interests? Looking at the problem from this first perspective, the firm's "portfolio" of investments, both real and financial, can be likened to the manager's personal portfolio, since his job success will be highly correlated with the success of the returns on the firm's portfolio. If the corporation is not totally diversified in its lines of business, an acquisition has the possibility of increasing the manager's utility by both increasing the portfolio's expected return and making it more diversified. The problem, as with an individual acting as an acquiror, is the all or nothing character of the choice. The expected return assessment relating to a target is predicated upon making a sufficient investment in shares of the target to wrest control of its management. That minimum amount necessary for control can easily exceed the ideal investment in terms of adding diversification, especially where the manager has considerable uncertainty about his assessment of what the expected return of the target would be under his control. The more diversified the acquiror and undiversified the target, the more serious the problem.

To illustrate this problem, consider the following highly stylized two-period model. Firm i has real assets which cost $100 to purchase in the first period. The purchase of these assets is the result of a decision of its manager to construct an optimal portfolio (according to his utility function) of firm assets given that (1) he is constrained to purchase real assets in only one kind of business, (2) in the manager's eyes, an investment in this line of business, whatever its scale, yields an expected return of 10 percent with a standard deviation of 2 percent, and (3) r^*, the rate at which the firm can invest in a risk-free financial asset or borrow in unlimited amounts, equals 8 percent. Thus, the manager's choice is limited to deciding the scale of the firm's investments in the specified kind of real assets. The level of investment in real assets, P_{oi}, is $100, and the value of these assets in the second period, P_{li}, has a distribution in the eyes of the manager with an expected value, $\overline{P}_{li}$, of $110 and a standard deviation, σ_i, of $2. This portfolio is depicted by point A, (2, 110), in figure 1.5 (which for convenience arbitrarily assumes the firm has an initial capitalization of $100). The manager's initial range of choice is depicted by the line (the "initial choice line") that commences at (0, 108) and runs through (2, 110).

This choice having already been made (as would be the case in the usual takeover situation), the manager becomes aware of firm j, which he concludes is mismanaged. Let P_{oj} be the cost of purchasing in the market n shares of firm j, the minimum number to gain control. Assume P_{oj} equals $100. Let P_{lj} be the second period value of n shares if firm i does not take over firm j. The manager assesses $\overline{P}_{lj}$, the expected value of P_{lj}, to be $110 and σ_j, the standard deviation, to be $2. He assesses ρ_{ij}, the correlation coefficient of P_{li} and P_{lj}, as .7, about average for two typical U.S. businesses. Let P'_{lj} be the second period value of n shares of firm j if firm i takes over firm j. In his eyes, $\overline{P}'_{lj}$, the expected value of P'_{lj}, is $111. Thus P'_{lj} has an ex-

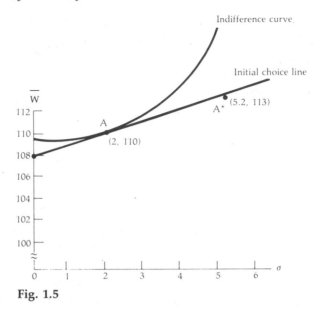

Fig. 1.5

pected rate of return significantly higher than P_{1i}, given that the firm can borrow unlimited amounts at 8 percent. Let $P'_{1j} = P_{1j} + I$ where I is a normally distributed random variable reflecting the change in the second period value of n shares of i because of the change in management. Since $\overline{P}_{1j} = \$110$ and $\overline{P}'_{1j} = \$111$, $\overline{I}$, the expected value of I, equals \$1. Assume that σ_I, the standard deviation of I, equals \$4. This relatively large number reflects the fact that it is impossible for the manager of firm i to obtain much information about j's internal operations, the nature of its staff, and its tangible and intangible assets as well as the fact that he cannot be sure of his abilities to direct the management of a different kind of business from his own. A standard deviation of \$4 means that the manager thinks that he probably can do better than j's current management and possibly much better, but he admits to himself the real possibility as well of doing worse than current management. Since the factors that lead to the manager's uncertainty as to how well he can do compared with j's current management are due to his personal ignorance and are on the whole unrelated to the factors which make it impossible to predict P_{1i} and P_{1j} with precision, assume that ρ_{1i} and ρ_{1j}, the correlation coefficients between I and P_{li} and P_{lj} respectively, both equal 0, i.e., the risk is unsystematic.*

If the manager decides not to acquire j, he will have a "portfolio" where R, the expected return of the portfolio in excess of r* divided by its standard deviation (the portfolio's "return/risk ratio"), equals $\frac{\overline{P}_{li} - (1 + r^*)P_{oi}}{\sigma_i} = 1$. If he decides to borrow \$100 at 8 percent and acquire j, he will have a portfolio, depicted by point A* at (5.2, 113), with a return/risk ratio, R*, equaling

$$\frac{\overline{P}_{li} + \overline{P}_{lj} + \overline{I} - (1 + r^*)(P_{oi} + P_{oj})}{\sqrt{\sigma_i^2 + \sigma_j^2 + \rho_{ij}\sigma_i\sigma_j + \sigma_I^2}} = \frac{5.00}{5.20}$$

A is unambiguously preferable to A* and so the takeover would not be undertaken. The slope of the manager's indifference curve at A equals 1, the slope of the initial choice line. Indifference curves relating expected return to standard deviation are normally thought to be concave upward, so an increase in risk requires more than a proportional increase in expected return to maintain the same level of utility. (See appendix 1.2.) Since the risk associated with A* is approximately \$5.20, the expected excess return would need to exceed \$5.20 by some positive amount (the size of which is determined by the degree of concavity of the manager's indifference curves) for the manager just to be indifferent between A and A*. In the example, the expected excess return is less than \$5.20.

2. The Perspective of the Acquiror's Shareholders

If we look at the question of corporate investment behavior in a takeover situation from the second perspective, it is again clear that at least in some cases a potential acquiror will need to view the target as significantly mismanaged before a takeover is judged worthwhile. Consider the following example. The manager of k corporation believes that m corporation is mismanaged. If we use the second perspective, we assume that the manager will decide to engage in

---

*Since it is very unlikely that the correlations are negative, this simplifying assumption, to the extent it deviates from reality, makes a takeover appear more likely than it really is.

the takeover only if, given his assessment of how badly m is mismanaged, the takeover is in the best interests of the holders of a majority of k's shares. Thus, to see if k will act, we need to look at the situation of an average shareholder of k, Mr. X.*

Mr. X holds what he believes to be an optimal portfolio, B, based on his assessments of the expected values and variance-covariance characteristics of the distribution of second period prices of all the available risky securities. Call B's return/risk ratio (R), based on X's assessments, R^1. As the earlier discussion of portfolio choice theory suggests, B is likely to include long or short holdings of every available security, including shares of m.†

What will the effect of the takeover be on X's portfolio? The easiest way to view this is to treat the investor's indirect holdings in m that result from the takeover as direct holdings. Assume that the shares of m that firm k acquires are supplied at P_o, the price of a share of m prior to any thought of a takeover, from all long holders of m shares (including X, if he holds m shares long) in proportion to their respective holdings of m, in exchange for cash which firm k either takes from its treasury where it was earning interest at the rate of r* or borrows at the rate of r*.‡ Countering any loss by X in direct holdings of m will be gains in indirect holdings of m which will be in proportion to his holdings of k. The combined net effect

---

*Determining whether a takeover is in the interests of the holders of a majority of shareholders by looking at the situation of an "average shareholder" is admittedly not a very rigorous approach. But any attempt to be more precise would make the problem very complex and obscure the basic considerations that management must weigh in making that determination.[85] Looking at the position of an average shareholder may also be very close to the way that a management concerned with the best interests of a majority would make the determination, since it is unrealistic to expect that management knows the portfolios and assessments of each shareholder.

†In the real world most investors do not have such a highly diversified portfolio. The assumption is made here so that the effect of the takeover on the typical shareholder as a way to profit from perceived mismanagement can be separated from the effect of further diversification of his portfolio, something he could accomplish as easily directly as indirectly.

‡This simplifying assumption works in the direction of suggesting that a takeover is more likely than it is. In fact, holders of a target must be persuaded by some kind of premium. Payment of the premium involves a transfer of wealth which benefits investors whose holdings in m represent a greater proportion of outstanding shares of m than the proportion of outstanding k shares represented by their holdings in k. The transfer harms investors in the opposite position. The second group of investors has more shares of k than the first.

on his holdings of m will be other than 0 except in the unusual situation where the investor holds the same percentage of the outstanding shares of k and m. I will call the new portfolio B*.

Under the assumptions employed in this second perspective, k will take over m only if the resulting change in the portfolio of the average shareholder such as Mr. X increases his expected utility. To determine this, I will focus on the effect of the change on the return/risk ratio of X's portfolio and assume that if the return/risk ratio is not increased, the takeover will not occur.* That leads us to examine the factors that determine whether the return/risk ratio associated with B* is greater or less than R^1.

If the R of B* were calculated on the basis of X's original parameter assessments (the ones used to construct B) and, as is likely, B* differs from B, the R would be less than R^1 (call the R calculated on this basis R'). This is because for any particular set of parameter assessments, the optimal mix of risky securities, the one with the highest return/risk ratio, is unique and B is the portfolio with that optimal mix. But the R of B* should not be calculated on the basis of X's original assessments. In the view of k's manager (which view in this second perspective should be attributed to X and thus used in the calculation of the R), the takeover is likely through the change in management to increase the second period price of a share of m. The difference between the second period price of a share of m if k takes over m and that price if k does not take over m can again be considered a random variable, I, the distribution of which, in the eyes of the manager, has an expected value, $\bar{I} > 0$, and a standard deviation, σ. It is again helpful (and not unreasonable) to assume that the distribution of I is independent of the distributions of each of the other risky securities.†

Since the takeover will (a) increase the holdings of m for the average shareholder such as Mr. X, (b) change no other holdings of Mr. X, and (c) either reduce firm k's investment in the safe asset or increase its borrowing, the takeover will increase the riskiness of X's portfolio. As we were reminded in the analysis above using the first perspective, X's indifference curves are concave upward, and the curve passing through B has a slope at that point equal to B's return/risk ratio. The rule used here—that if the R associated with the takeover exceeds R', the takeover will take place—includes cases where in fact a takeover will not increase X's expected utility and thus makes takeovers seem more probable than they are.

†To the extent that the risk in fact is systematic and there is some correlation with the distribution of the other risky securities, the correlation is likely to be positive. A

If D and V are respectively the expected return and the variance of B* calculated on the basis of X's original assessments (i.e., $R' = \dfrac{D}{\sqrt{V}}$), n equals X's net holdings of m shares in B* (n>0),* $\bar{I}_x = n\bar{I}$ and $\sigma_x = n\sigma$, then

(1) $R = \dfrac{D + \bar{I}_x}{(V + \sigma_x^2)^{1/2}}.$

The takeover will occur only if $R > R^1$. The combinations of $\bar{I}_x$ and σ_x where this would be the case are depicted by all the points above the curve commencing at Q set forth in figure 1.6.

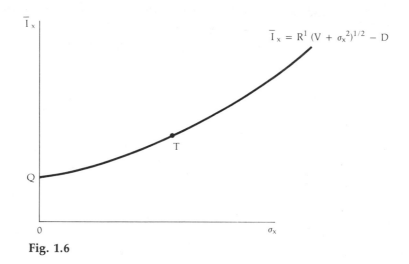

$\bar{I}_x = R^1 (V + \sigma_x^2)^{1/2} - D$

Fig. 1.6

This curve is derived by substituting R^1 for R in equation (1).

Rewriting,

(2) $\bar{I}_x = R^1 (V + \sigma_x^2)^{1/2} - D.$

Thus, Q is $(O, R^1 V^{1/2} - D)$. Since $R^1 > R'$ and $R' = D/V^{1/2}$, $(R^1 V^{1/2} - D) > 0$. Differentiating (2),

positive correlation would again work in the direction of making a takeover less attractive to X than this analysis would suggest.

*If, among all investors, the holding of k shares and m shares is not negatively correlated prior to the takeover (and there is no reason to think it would be in most cases), n>0 for the average k shareholder after the takeover.

(3) $\dfrac{d\bar{I}_x}{d\sigma_x} = R^1(V + \sigma_x^2)^{-1/2}\sigma_x$

(4) $\dfrac{d\bar{I}_x}{d\sigma_x} > 0$ since R^1, V, and σ_x are all greater than 0.

Therefore the curve is upward sloping throughout. Differentiating again,

(5) $\dfrac{d^2\bar{I}_x}{d\sigma_x^2} = R^1(V + \sigma_x^2)^{-1/2} - R^1(V + \sigma_x^2)^{-3/2}\sigma_x^2$

(6) $\dfrac{R^1(V + \sigma_x^2)^{-1/2}}{R^1(V + \sigma_x^2)^{-3/2}\sigma_x^2} = (V + \sigma_x^2)\sigma_x^{-2} = \dfrac{V}{\sigma_x^2} + 1 > 1$

(7) $\dfrac{d^2\bar{I}_x}{d\sigma_x^2} > 0$

so the curve is concave upward.

One important implication from the shape and location of this curve is that the riskier a change of m's management appears to the manager of k, the greater the expected value of the gains must be, i.e., the more mismanaged m must appear, before the takeover is considered worthwhile. This is true even though the risk, which stems from ignorance unrelated to the unpredictability of the market as a whole, is unsystematic and the manager believes his expected value assessment to be unbiased.

To see this, consider three terms: (a) $\dfrac{\sigma}{P_o}$, the measure of riskiness, in rate of return terms, of the change in second period price resulting from the change in management, (b) $\dfrac{\bar{I}}{P_o}$, the expected value, in rate of return terms, of that change, and (c) $h = nP_o$, X's dollar holdings (direct and indirect) of m shares if the takeover is effected.

(8) $\dfrac{h\sigma}{P_o} = n\sigma = \sigma_x$

(9) $\dfrac{h\bar{I}}{P_o} = n\bar{I} = \bar{I}_x.$

Therefore from (8), for a given dollar size takeover and hence given h, as $\dfrac{\sigma}{P_o}$ increases, σ_x increases. From (4), as σ_x increases, the minimum $\bar{I}_x$ that would make the takeover worthwhile increases. From (9), given h, for $\bar{I}_x$ to increase, $\dfrac{\bar{I}}{P_o}$ must increase.

2. A General Theory

The central message of chapter 1 is that if one wishes to explain the impact of finance on industrial performance, one should focus on differences in information among participants in the system. The purpose of this chapter is to develop a systematic way of looking at these differences: seeing where they come from and what their effects are through time.

A. The Basic Approach

1. *The Structure of Project Choice and Control Reassignment Decisions*

In order to get a clearer sense of the role of information, we will start the chapter by looking at five simple market economies, Worlds A, B, B', C, C', that differ only in the range of investment opportunities available to savers in any one time period.

In World A there exist no investment opportunities: all of the economy's fixed quantities of its two factors of production available in period t, labor and land, are devoted to the production of apples and nuts for consumption entirely during that period. The market will decide the total production of each output, the amount of labor and land that will be devoted to each, the method of production for each, and the allocation of each output among the individuals in society. As those familiar with general equilibrium analysis know, these decisions will be determined by the initial distribution of labor and land among individuals, the utility function of each individual, and the production function for each output. Other than prices, no participant in this decision process needs any information from anyone else. The individual just looks at his utility function and how much labor and land he owns. The producer just looks at his production function. World A is the quintessential example of the virtues of the market economy in eliminating the need for communication among participants.

In World B, part of the fixed quantities of labor and land available in period t may be devoted to two kinds of real investment opportunities, X and Y. Project choice in the economy, i.e., how much is invested in each of X and Y, is determined by the individuals in society: each can expend part of his resources on direct investments in X or Y projects instead of for current consumption of apples or nuts. By assuming that each dollar invested in X or Y represents a separate project, we can abstract away the problem of collecting savings from more than one individual for a single project. The projects require no management, and so control reassignment is not an issue. The supply of each of the two types of real investment opportunities is, as in the real world, infinitely elastic. The sole result of a saver investing in an X or Y project is his receiving a monetary return in period t + 1. All X projects will turn out to have the same return in t + 1, which will depend, *inter alia*, on the number of X projects that are implemented. The same is true of Y projects. In each case, the amount of the return associated with any given number of projects is uncertain in period t.

In World B, the saver's utility function, something inside himself, tells him the relative level of satisfaction he will receive from any particular combination of an investment portfolio, with a given expected return and level of risk, and apples and nuts of given quantities. But the expected return and risk characteristics of any particular portfolio are not known to him through experience the way the characteristics of apples and nuts are. His views of the portfolio's characteristics are based on information which he collects concerning the returns in t + 1 of X and Y. Thus, the economy's aggregate decisions—the production and allocation of apples and nuts and the amount of resources invested in X and Y—are determined by, in addition to the factors at work in World A, the information each saver possesses.

A comparison of Worlds A and B illustrates a tremendously important point. *In a world where there is real investment, each individual, in order to decide what amount of his available resources not to consume and where that amount should be invested, must look outside of himself to acquire information. Real investment opportunities are not scarce commodities that are in the first instance competitively priced.* The cost of implementing an investment opportunity is the cost of the needed real resources. The prices of these real resources are ordinarily not related to the opportunity's prospects.

This need to look outside for information not contained in prices can help explain institutions existing in the real world. Consider World 3', which includes investment advisers and financial intermediaries. It is reasonable to assume that, absent the need to decide the amount and placement of his savings, the average saver would not in the ordinary course of events acquire very much information about the prospects of X and Y. And, for reasons that will be discussed later in this chapter, it is also reasonable to assume that the market in which he can acquire information on a piece by piece basis falls far short of perfection: there are economies of scale both in the number of persons for whom it is gathered and in the amount gathered, and consumers have difficulty evaluating what is being offered them. To solve the problem of his ignorance, the saver hires someone more knowledgeable than he is. This more knowledgeable person may be an investment adviser, a person hired to give advice, or he may be the principal of a financial intermediary in which the saver invests, a more knowledgeable person that the saver in essence hires to make decisions on his behalf.

The intermediary in which the individual invests might itself not possess much information about the prospects of X or Y, and so the process of delegation might repeat itself one or more times. Thus, the saver might invest in an investment company (for example, a venture capital firm or mutual fund), the investment company in a corporation,* and the corporation would then invest the funds it receives in an X or Y project. The expertise of the investment company would be in choosing the corporation with the most expertise in

---

*Corporations are normally seen to exist for two reasons. First, the amount of capital needed for the minimum efficient scale of many projects is too large for a single individual to provide, and the corporation is a legal form which enables the proponent of such a project to gather this necessary amount from many different individuals. Second, once the investment has been made, the project must be managed for it to produce a return. World B' presents neither of these problems. It demonstrates that corporations have a third function, as intermediaries in the process of project choice.

choosing among real investment projects. The saver, the venture capital firm, and the corporation might each seek outside advice as well to make their decisions.

The position of the saver in relation to the network of persons he directly or indirectly "hires" is analogous to the head of a hierarchical organization. How much of the saver's savings is ultimately invested in X and how much ultimately in Y is equivalent to a decision of the organization. Because the head of a large hierarchical organization cannot accumulate and analyze all the information necessary for him to make sensibly all of the organization's decisions, much of his work consists of delegating the authority to make decisions on the organization's behalf to others who have accumulated more information in particular areas. The average saver is in the same position when faced with real investment decisions. Each member of the saver's network, like each member of an organization, is a decision maker in the sense that his actions to some extent influence the outcome of the whole process. But like the head of an organization being ultimately responsible for its decisions, the saver is ultimately responsible for the decision as to which real investments his savings go to because his choices dictate the structure of the rest of the process.

Worlds B and B' require no production decisions—decisions as to how existing productive capacity is to be used—and so the role of the finance process is limited to project choice. In the real world production decisions are required and the role of the finance process includes as well control reassignment, the choice of who over time makes these production decisions. Now consider World C. In period t, World C is like World B with the addition of U and V, real investment projects undertaken in period t-1 which yield returns in period t+1. Again, as in World B, each dollar invested in U or V in period t-1 represents a direct investment in a separate project. The sole result of a dollar invested by a saver in a U or V project in period t-1 is the right to receive in period t+1 an uncertain amount of money. Each U and V project requires management. In period t-1, savers have no basis to distinguish among proponents of U and V projects as to their managerial skill. Thus all U projects, depending on the total number, appear at that time to have the same prospects. The same is true for all V projects. But in fact the management skills of the various proponents of the same type project do differ, and the return in period $t+1$ on each project of the same type will vary depending on the level of that skill. In period t, partial information is available on how well each proponent is doing as manager of his project. The right to receive returns from a U or V project is accompanied by the right in period t to change the management of the project. Thus, with the addition of the U and V projects, the role of the finance process is expanded to include control reassignment.

The World C saver has a number of decisions to make in period t. As in World B, he must decide how much of his resources to expend on apples, nuts, and investments in X and Y projects. For any U or V project in which he invested in period t-1, he can keep the right to receive its returns and keep the corresponding management, keep the right to returns but change the management, or sell the right. He can expend resources in period t to purchase the right to receive the return on a U or V project from someone who invested in the project in period t-1 and wishes to sell. Such a purchase may be motivated by a desire to change project management so as to improve, in the eyes of the saver, the return in period $t+1$ over what the saver believes it would be if the current managers remain in control. Alternatively, the saver may be satisfied with current management but have a more optimistic view than the seller of what the returns in period $t+1$ will be.

Only three of these decisions are of direct interest to a study of the impact of finance on industrial performance: (a) how much, if any, to invest in X and Y projects, the new real investment opportunities; (b) whether or not to change the managers of U or V projects in which the saver has invested in period t-1 and which the saver intends to retain; and (c) whether to purchase from others any U or V projects with the intention of changing their managements. A transfer of a U or V project in period t where the buyer is satisfied with current management is simply a reallocation of existing property rights and has no real economic effect.

Now consider World C', a refinement of World C. As with B', the model is modified to permit the saver to invest in intermediaries. Assume that each dollar invested in an intermediary creates a separate entity* and that the right to receive a return on that investment

---

*This unrealistic assumption is made to simplify the exposition of the particular points developed in this model. It ignores the fact that a vital reason why a saver chooses to delegate decisions to an intermediary rather than gather and process in-

includes a right to change the management of that entity. As in World B', assume that the typical saver in period t-1 does not possess much information about the prospects of U and V projects and that in period t he does not possess much information about the prospects of X and Y projects. Also assume that in period t he would not have much information concerning the competence of U or V project managers. An intermediary can again perform the function of being a more knowledgeable person to whom to delegate the range of decisions which the saver would otherwise have to make with respect to U, V, X, and Y projects.

In recognition of the fact that multiple layers of intermediaries are likely to be used, make the further simplifying assumption that all investments made in U, V, X, and Y projects occur through two levels of intermediaries, referred to respectively as investment companies (ICs) and corporations. A saver's range of decisions in World C' in period t is his range in World C with the substitution of "new ICs" for X and Y projects and "existing ICs" (established by investments in period t-1) for U and V projects. The same is true of the range of decisions in period t for an IC, but with the substitution of "new corporations" and "existing corporations" (established by investments in period t-1) for U and V and X and Y projects respectively. A corporation has a range of decisions in period t with respect to U, V, X, and Y projects identical to that of the saver in World C. Again only those decisions which result in the funding of a new project or control reassignment of an existing project are of interest to the study of the impact of finance on industrial performance.

An analogy to a hierarchical organization can again be made. As illustrated in figure 2.1, each new project funded and each control reassignment occurring in period t is the result of a structure of decision which can be traced back to a saver. If the project choice or control reassignment decision at the real level is made by an existing corporation with management changed by command of an existing IC with unchanged management or by a new corporation created by the act of an existing IC with unchanged management, the act of the saver which structured the decision was investing in the existing IC

formation himself is that, as discussed in section B 1.1, there are economies when a single delegatee gathers and processes information in order to make investment decisions on behalf of more than one investor.

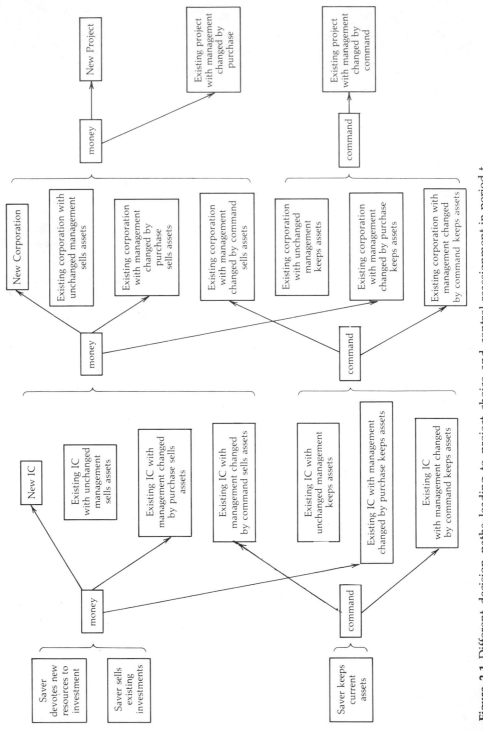

Figure 2.1 Different decision paths leading to project choice and control reassignment in period t

in period t-1. He put his faith in the management of the IC, and there have been no intervening events to take the mandate he gave them away. Otherwise, the project choice or control reassignment decision is the result of a structure established by an act of a saver taken in period t.

2. *Development of Theory*

In a world with investment yielding uncertain returns and an uneven initial distribution of information, the use of competitive markets to make the economy's decisions does not, as it does in World A, eliminate the need for each individual to collect pieces of information from, seek the advice of, or delegate decisions to other persons who possess information the individual does not. Delegation is the predominant solution to the problem, and that fact explains in significant part the existence of structures of the type identified in World C' for making project choice and control reassignment decisions at the real level. The theory of finance and industrial performance developed in this chapter is a study of these structures. It is influenced strongly by the analogy of the project choice and control reassignment decisions to the decisions of a hierarchical organization. The analogy, of course, is not perfect: it ignores the existence of economies of scale both in the production of goods and in the information gathering and processing by intermediaries. Because of these economies, corporate and financial intermediaries need to seek funds from multiple investors.* The analogy also ignores the ability of a person who is more sure of his views to magnify his influence in project choice by dividing up the income stream produced by a proposed project and offering to invest a given amount of savings in the project in return for the right to receive the riskiest portion of the stream, if others will invest in the project in return for the right to receive the less risky portions. But the analogy does serve to guide the inquiry in a useful fashion and to make important points concerning the interaction among the different levels.

The theory will be developed in two steps. The first step is a micro

---

*The scale requirements for modern industry compound the need for delegation of decision making because, even if each saver were as informed and capable as the delegatee, the coordination among a large number of savers necessary to make group decisions is impractical for most questions.

analysis: a study of the structure which determines how any particular project choice or control reassignment decision at the real level is made. The second step is a macro analysis: a study of how the finance process functions as a system and its impact on industrial performance.

The micro analysis starts at the level of a proponent seeking project funding. The messages which such a proponent emits to possible funding sources are examined. Parallel analyses are made of a manager seeking to continue to be in control of an existing project and of one seeking to have control of an existing project reassigned to him.

Next, top managements of the corporate intermediaries are analyzed. A series of questions are raised and dealt with. How does corporate management process information emitted by proponents and managers who have a stake in the project choice and control reassignment decisions which the corporate management has the power to make? What other information does corporate management look at to make these decisions? What values do corporate managers seek to satisfy, and how are the decisions they make related to these values? How are these decisions influenced by how they will appear to financial intermediaries, investor advisory services, and savers themselves? Finally, what kinds of information does top corporate management emit to such entities?

The same kind of analysis, one step up the ladder, is then made with respect to the principals of a financial intermediary.

The macro analysis starts with the proposition that every economy, whether centralized, pure market, or otherwise, needs a process which takes account of information held by disparate sources in order to decide which real investment projects shall receive society's scarce savings and who shall control existing projects. In a centralized economy, this would be a simple hierarchical organization. In a market economy, the process can also be defined as an organization, but given the millions of savers, a much more complex one. The goals which we want this organization to serve are enhancing, at reasonable cost, production, output choice, and dynamic efficiency. By seeing how the elements studied in the micro analysis aggregate and by referring to a rich body of social science literature concerning organizations as communications phenomena, some judgments will be made concerning how well the finance process in our economy is fulfilling these goals and how changes in structure might improve its performance. After the micro and macro analyses are enriched in chapters 3, 4, and 5 by the use of these analyses as a framework to study empirically the financing of the semiconductor industry, these judgments are used in the final study of the book, contained in chapter 6, to make specific recommendations concerning policy.

B. Micro Analysis

1. *Basic Conceptual Building Blocks*

Before starting a detailed look at the structure that determines any particular project-funding or control reassignment decision, it is helpful to examine two basic concepts that come up repeatedly in the analysis. The first relates to the special characteristics of information as a commodity to be bought and sold. The second relates to general principles as to how individuals and organizations process incoming information.

1.1 *Information as a Commodity*

Information is not a commodity that is bought and sold on a piece by piece basis in the ordinary fashion. This is a key reason, as suggested earlier, for the development of corporate and financial intermediaries and of information services that provide savers and intermediaries with their conclusions as to the best investments. And it also explains why the business of these interemdiaries is not significantly threatened by the potential competition of investors purchasing raw information for themselves to use in making direct investments in real investment opportunities and direct purchases of existing real projects.

One source of information's uniqueness as a commodity is that, above and beyond what must be paid the seller of a piece of information, information is costly to find and to utilize. Intermediaries and information services save the investor his own time by gathering and processing the information for him. There are enormous *economies of scale in gathering and processing the same information for multiple individuals.* An intermediary can make an investment decision for, and an information service can give advice to, thousands of investors with millions of dollars in resources using little more effort gathering and processing information than one investor acting on his own would have to exert if he wanted to make a decision of the same quality.*

The other source of its uniqueness relates to the existence of *economies of scale in the amount of information being gathered*. Since an intermediary or information service is likely to be serving many investors with aggregate resources of considerable size, it can be expected to purchase more information than an individual investor acting alone. The economies of scale derive from the fact that it can be more efficient to receive information from a source with which the recipient has an employment relationship than from a source with which the recipient must deal in the market. An employment relationship is only practical if there is a regular transmission of large amounts of information. There are three reasons why an employment relationship is, given sufficient volume, often the superior forum for transfer of information.

First, as Coase points out, there is a cost in using the price mechanism which makes it, under some circumstances, uneconomical in comparison with other forms of allocation.[1] Given the usually low value of individual bits of information, this cost can be comparatively large. The generation and transfer of information by command within an organization will avoid this cost and be more economical than use of the market.[2] The intermediary or information service gathers many bits of information from each of many sources with which it has employment relationships and then sells its services in one package, the security or the advice.

Second, an intermediary or information service is frequently in a position to provide much more incentive to information sources to produce information than is an individual investor. This relates to the public goods aspect of information: once a piece of information has been produced (discovered), the cost of transmission to other

---

*In terms of speculative profits from trading already outstanding securities, these economies are counteracted by the fact that the more broadly dispersed the information, the greater the effect on the demand and hence on the price of the security involved and the less profit that can be obtained by trading on it. But in terms of the function of the finance process steering funds to the real investment projects with the best prospects, the more broadly known the information, the more accurate the process and the greater returns it produces for investors.

people is very low. Because of the intangible nature of the commodity, once the producer has sold the piece of information to one person, it is difficult, unless the information is patentable, for the producer to have it excluded from use by others. The dilemma faced by the private producer is that he wants the knowledge used only as widely as the producer of any valuable input would want it used (to the point where MR = MC), but the sale of it to another undermines his monopoly position, since anyone who purchases it can then "produce" additional units of it himself at the same low marginal cost at which the original producer produces. If an investment idea source and an intermediary or information service have an employment relationship, they can avoid revealing the idea to others and can share the larger profit of investing or giving advice on the basis of the idea.

Third, information is hard to transfer in a market because it is hard for a user to evaluate information without learning it, at which point there is no need to pay for it.[3] Since suppliers of information are likely to demand payment or a promise to pay before revealing their information, there is an incentive for users to get their information only from suppliers who have established their trustworthiness over a long period of continued relationship. The establishment by a source of such trustworthiness is a component of what, in the language of the next section, is the "authority" of the source in the eyes of the user. As information frequently becomes just one component of an investment decision, the supplier may not be sure himself of the value of the information because such an assessment requires specialized knowledge which the user alone has. Thus, the trustworthiness of the supplier in itself is not adequate evidence that the knowledge is worth using, and the user will be reluctant in advance to pay or promise to pay for information. In such a situation, the incentive for an employment rather than a market link between them can be particularly strong.*

Even when information is transferred from a supplier to a user in what is formally a market context, this third factor may require the development of a relationship of trust through repeat transactions

---

*Oliver Williamson points out that in addition to the virtue of an employment relationship in building the authority of the information source through what he refers to as "experience ratings," it imbues the source and recipient with a sense of joint purpose which also facilitates transfer.[4]

between the same two persons, which tends to suppress competitive mechanisms and will influence the pattern of transfer in a way that as a general matter can be better explained as an employment phenomenon than as a market phenomenon. This third factor suggests that there are often economies of scale in gathering information even where as a formal matter the information is gathered through market transactions rather than from employees.

1.2 *Rules Relating to Incoming Information: Authority and Interest*

Each participant in the finance process gathers and processes information, either messages from others or physical observations about the world, in order to determine what his best course of action will be. An individual or organization is physically capable of gathering an enormous number of bits of information at quite low cost. But processing this information—absorbing it and calculating how it should influence the recipient's choice of alternatives—is costly in terms of time. Thus, the recipient needs to assign priorities to incoming messages. The higher the priority, the more likely the message will be considered seriously and influence the recipient's behavior. Priority is assigned by rules: *authority rules* and *interest rules*.

Authority rules assign priority to incoming information on the basis of its source. They relate to the recipient's opinion of the competence and trustworthiness of the source. The recipient is essentially using the source as a substitute for gathering and processing the information himself. Competence is a concern because the source is rarely just a conduit; the messages he emits are in part based on his interpretations of the information he receives. Trustworthiness is a concern because the source, in deciding what messages to emit, may have an interest in manipulating the recipient into acting in a fashion which is different from what, given the objective facts, is in the recipient's own best interests.

The degree of authority which a recipient assigns a particular source is determined by several factors. First is an analysis of the motivations of the source: does the source have any reason to transmit information in a way which would create a false or misleading impression? Second is the reputation of the source: what do other persons, who themselves have authority, say about the source? Finally, and most important, is past experience with the source. Authority rules, like other rules of information processing, are subject to feedback, and over the long run the quality of the messages from any particular source will affect the authority that the source enjoys.

Information can range from being close to raw data to being highly conclusionary. The most conclusionary information is a naked recommendation to the recipient as to what course of action he should take. The more conclusionary the information, the more important authority is in determining its priority.

Interest rules refer to rules that assign priority because of the content of information, what it is about. A recipient is concerned with only certain kinds of messages: those which analysis or experience suggest would be useful in determining the course of action that will best correspond to his particular interests. A securities analyst who is an expert in the automobile industry is valued and compensated by others for sending out very specialized kinds of messages. His interest rules would obviously be quite different from those of an analyst who is an expert in the cosmetics industry. Similarly, a mutual fund that has a declared policy of investing in blue chip stocks has very different interest rules from a venture capital firm specializing in high technology companies, but each would give relatively high priority to a much broader range of information than would either of the two securities analysts. A saver would typically have a very broad range of interests—because he is interested in knowing which among the huge variety of investment opportunities available are the best places to put his savings. But he also would usually prefer to receive information in highly conclusionary form. Thus, information from sources which are not highly authoritative does not get much priority from savers despite the breadth of savers' interests.

2. Project Proponents and Managers

2.1 Proponents

As outlined in chapter 1, the process of decision by which real investment takes place starts with a person or group of persons, the proponent, proposing an idea to develop the capacity to produce in a particular way a certain number of units of a good that will help satisfy demand in a particular market.* An idea combines bits of knowledge. It is useful to someone to whom it is proposed if it suggests a course of action that can be expected to be more beneficial than others apparently available to the recipient.

A potentially useful investment project idea might be originated by anyone. A person who thinks he has originated such an idea may want to profit from it, and that requires putting forward his idea for consideration by the finance process. There are three ways for a proponent to do so, each of which needs to be examined. The first is to sell the idea to an established firm. The second is to persuade an established firm to implement the idea with the proponent managing the project.† The third is to raise capital and start a business based on the idea.

2.11. *Sale of an Investment Project Idea*

Because of the peculiar nature of knowledge as a commodity, not many investment project ideas are likely to be implemented via a sale. It is true that some, though by no means all, scientific ideas with potential commercial applications are patentable and that rights under these patents are often sold on a royalty basis. But a patented idea is only a full-blown investment project idea in the rare situation

---

*This statement is meant to give a description of the dimensions of the problems involved in project-funding decisions. It oversimplifies the process by stating that the proposal is necessarily as specific as suggested with respect to each aspect of the project and that there is a single discrete decision to fund or not to fund the project. In fact the development of the capacity, particularly if it utilizes an innovative technology, may be the result of a sequence of decisions. The initial proposal might be for funds for the development of a prototype, and the decision might depend on fairly general descriptions of the product market, scale, and technology that would be involved. The results of the development effort would in turn be used in the making of a second decision, concerning plants and equipment, which would depend on a much more specific description of these three factors.

†Typically, the proponent is one or a group of current employees of the established firm, but there are variants. One is where the proponent is a self-employed or university-employed inventor of a scientific advance that the proposed project is intended to utilize. Another is where the proponent has previously founded a small company with outside finance which, utilizing a scientific advance, develops a modest capacity to produce a product. He proposes to sell his firm to a much larger, more established firm which will provide funding for a project, to be managed by the proponent, creating a much larger capacity to produce the product. Oliver Williamson identifies this second variant as a route which, by taking advantage of the relative strengths of both kinds of firms, permits some innovative products and processes to attain large-scale use which would not occur if only one kind of firm, new entrants or established large firms, existed in the economy.[5]

where it is fairly obvious that the idea can be transformed into a production technology and that there is sufficient demand for the product at the cost implied by that technology to make the project profitable. Where this is not the case, a project proposal must address these questions of production practicality and marketability. Ideas concerning these questions are not appropriable through a patent system and not easily transferred by a sale.*

A project idea often needs the continued input of the proponent because of the store of knowledge he has accumulated creating the proposal. In such a situation, sale is again usually not practical even if the idea has a patentable scientific component.

A project idea that has a scientific basis but one that comes from basic research is also not easily salable because not even the scientific component is appropriable through a patent. The same is true of an investment project idea that involves only market analysis and employs a known production technology. One example of this type is an idea to develop a capacity to produce a product which the market perceives as different, but which technologically is not different, such as a new clothing fashion. Another example is an idea to develop a capacity to produce an existing product, which capacity supplements or replaces current capacity in the economy that utilizes the same technology.

2.12 Implementing an Investment Project Idea Through an Existing or New Firm

2.121 Divergence of Knowledge Between Proponent and Funding Source: The Need for Authority

A proponent who proposes an investment project to a funding source is generally better qualified to predict the consequences of

---

*Arrow notes with concern that patent royalties in the aluminum, chemical, and petroleum industries usually represent a small percentage of the profits of a successful project utilizing the technology involved.[6] Williamson suggests that the reasons for this are related to the small number of existing firms which would be interested in the idea, combined with the difficulty of entry into the industries in question.[7] It seems to me that part of the answer comes as well from Schumpeter. The patented scientific idea is a necessary but not sufficient condition for real investment to occur. Substantial rewards go to the project proponent for the equally necessary production practicality and marketability components of the project proposal. These rewards are unlikely to be in the form of royalties even in the cases where the inventor of the scientific idea is also the proponent.

the investment than is the funding source, because it is the proponent's function to be an expert in such matters. This is particularly
true where the investment project involves an innovation. The proponent presents to a potential funding source what he claims to be
his predictions about the consequences of investment in the project
and a package of facts to support his position.

Ideally, for investment funds to go to the projects that promise,
on the basis of the predictions of the best-qualified observers, the
highest return, the estimate provided by the proponent should accurately reflect the proponent's views and the funding source should
believe these honest estimates. In fact, there exists an incentive for
manipulation on the part of the proponent and inherent problems
in detecting such manipulation. In the case of a project that is the
basis for the founding of a new firm, the proponent must approach
outside sources of funding. The firm will issue a given number of
shares, some will go to funding sources in return for cash, and the
rest will go to the proponent as "founding shares." What a source
is willing to pay for a share of the firm's stock is a function of the
source's expectations concerning the firm's future earnings per share
discounted to present value at a rate reflecting the source's perception of the riskiness of his expectations. The more earnings the proponent can convince the source to expect, the more cash the firm
will receive per share, the fewer shares will go to funding sources,
and the more shares will remain to go to the proponent as founding
shares. Thus, the proponent's share of the firm's earnings is directly
related to how favorable an image of the firm's future it can build in
the eyes of potential funding sources. In the case of a project being
proposed to an existing firm for its implementation, there is a similar
problem. It is in the interests of the proponent, who normally will
manage the project and receive substantial compensation if it succeeds, to persuade the firm to undertake the gamble involved even
if in fact the odds of success are not good enough to justify the
firm's doing so.

A funding source must try to calculate how much manipulation is
involved in the predictions of the proponent and try to take account
of it in the source's assessment of the distribution of possible returns
from the project. He does this by adjusting the proponent's expected return forecast by the amount of bias that he thinks exists
and by increasing his subjective measure of the riskiness of the proj-

ect because he is not sure his bias adjustment is correct. The greater the divergence in knowledge between the investor and the proponent, the greater the increase in his measure of subjective risk.

Even if the bias adjustment of a funding source is on average correct, the greater the increase in subjective risk resulting from needing to make the adjustment, the less likely it is that the source will be willing to invest in the project. New technology investments suffer in this regard compared with conventional investments because of the greater divergence of knowledge between entrepreneur and investor. Proposals based on nonappropriable ideas also suffer in the case where the proponent is trying to raise funds for a project that is the basis for the founding of a new firm because disclosure of the details of such ideas to prospective funding sources will be restricted for fear of theft. This hampers his ability to explain fully the basis of what in fact are honest predictions.

2.122 *Bases of Authority*

The degree of distortion which occurs through funding sources viewing proposals as risky because they are uncertain of the accuracy of their bias adjustments depends on the proponent's level of authority with the sources it approaches. Authority, as stated earlier, can be based on experience, reputation, or structure of incentives.

When a funding source experiences a history of the proponent making predictions relating to his investment project ideas that turn out to be relatively accurate, the proponent develops authority in the source's eyes. Obviously this takes time and frequency of contact to develop. This is a problem in the case of a proponent putting forward a project based on highly innovative technology. Many of the best such ideas are gestalt phenomena which may come from people with little previous experience or accomplishment in the area of concern. Skepticism of some relevant, broadly held scientific belief is often a precondition for original thinking.[8] Consistent with this, as the study of the semiconductor industry illustrates, the typical proponent in an industry characterized by rapid technical change is young and highly mobile, reducing the opportunities to develop experience-based authority in the eyes of funding sources (see chapter 4, section 3.1).

The reputation of a proponent in the eyes of a funding source can come from the testimony of other persons who themselves have authority of some kind and who have experienced the proponent making accurate predictions. In this regard, the typical proponent in an industry characterized by rapid technical change may have some advantages. Such industries, at least in the first most innovative stages, are typically sufficiently small that each firm's "rising stars" are known throughout the industry, and, as stated above, their personnel have a great deal of mobility. These facts increase the number of funding sources to which a proponent can appeal as well as the likelihood that a proponent will be known by any particular such source. Reputation can also come from professional credentials. The fact that industries characterized by rapid technical change are so scientifically based means that academic credentials and other "objective" measures of performance are better than usual indicators of the competence of the proponent to make predictions and to undertake the role of managing the project. The study of the semiconductor industry contains a number of examples of persons who obtained funding to start new companies on the basis of an industry-wide reputation they had developed from working at one or more firms and on the basis of their professional credentials.

A third way for a proponent to develop authority with a funding source is to vouch for his confidence in his predictions by agreeing to share in the burden of any losses that the project might incur. This may result from making an actual investment in the project (thereby providing a fund, the initial principal, to cover possible losses) or, if the proponent is or becomes an employee of an established firm that acts as a funding source, entering into an arrangement, also referred to in this discussion as an investment, which has a similar economic effect (for example, an arrangement that if the project loses money the proponent's salary will be reduced to a rate below what the proponent could earn in alternative employment).*

If the proponent did not have to worry about convincing others of the trustworthiness of his estimate, he would have no more reason to make an investment in the project he is proposing than in any of the thousands of other opportunities available (assuming he

---

*For the reasons discussed in the next section, such arrangements are rare in practice.

could find their respective proponents trustworthy). In a new firm situation, he would simply issue shares to the public in return for cash and shares to himself free of charge in a ratio sufficiently high to raise the necessary amount of capital for the project. He would pay himself a salary at the rate he could command in another company. Issuing shares in this ratio would result in the investors' expecting to receive the market rate of return (determined by reference to alternatives with risk comparable to what is perceived to be the risk of the project) on their investments, and with the proponent expected in the investors' eyes to receive, in addition to his full salary, the difference between what an amount equal to the total investment in the project would earn at the market rate and what the project is expected to earn. The possible profit from the shares issued to himself without cost would be the return for entrepreneurship (the "entrepreneurial surplus") and would be separable from the return paid to any investor for the use of the investor's scarce savings. If the project fails, the entrepreneur would lose nothing. Similarly, a proponent persuading an established firm to invest in a project he would manage could, if he were given enough latitude in negotiating the terms of his employment, work out terms with a similar payout.

The proponent, however, does in fact have the problem of convincing others of the trustworthiness of his prediction. The extreme solution to the problem would be for him to be the sole investor in the proposed project. He would then fully demonstrate his trustworthiness because he would be prepared to absorb fully the losses from failure. This extreme solution is of course impractical, since most proponents do not have the resources necessary to be sole investors (which is the same thing as saying they do not have the resources necessary to absorb the full losses in case of failure). It is also more than what is necessary for a proponent to demonstrate conviction in his predictions. An investment in the project of a large part of the proponent's total wealth may be sufficient even when his investment constitutes a relatively small percentage of the project's total requirements. Assuming that the proponent is risk averse and thus money has declining marginal utility to him, he demonstrates confidence in his predictions by choosing such an undiversified investment portfolio consisting mostly of his investment in the project. In that situation, project failure would be very painful to him.

Of course, the proponent's investment must not be such a small portion of the total investment that the entrepreneurial surplus, if the project is successful, would be large enough to make worth taking even a very high risk of failure with its accompanying substantial pain. Thus, some minimum amount of wealth is necessary even if the amount required is not as large as might appear at first blush.

A problem with a system which relies too heavily on the ability of a proponent persuading a funding source of the sincerity of his predictions by agreeing to absorb part of any potential losses is that the proponent must have at least this minimum amount of wealth with which to absorb such losses. A good investment project idea may go unheeded if its proponent has not had an opportunity to develop an experience-based or reputation-based authority relationship with a funding source or does not possess this minimum level of wealth.

2.123 *Persuading an Existing Firm*

The proponent trying to persuade an established firm to implement a project usually must rely predominantly on his experience-based and reputation-based authority with the firm's top officials. There is no practical mechanism within the corporation for the proponent to share sufficiently in the losses if he is wrong in his predictions concerning the proposed project.* The proponent can risk two forms of capital contribution to show his sincerity: his money and his time. These are difficult things to offer within a single corporate entity that has investments in several projects. Plans that involve the equity of the company, either investment of the proponent's money through a stock purchase plan or payment of part of his salary through stock options, do not accurately measure the success of the proponent's project because their value depends on all the projects of the company. A salary formula which is keyed over time to the success of the specific project would have to provide, if the project is a failure, for a salary low enough for the proponent really to "feel the pinch," and in recompense for undertaking this

---

*This is less so in the case of the variant where the proponent sells his small firm to a large established firm which will fund a new project managed by the proponent based on the business of the small firm. Payment for the purchase of the small firm can be in installments and conditioned upon performance.

risk, the formula would have to provide, if the project is a success, a salary so large that it would greatly exceed that of the top executives of the corporation. A salary much lower than what the proponent could earn elsewhere would create morale and motivation problems if the proponent stayed with the firm and enforcement problems if he tried to leave. A salary much higher than that of the top executives is something established firms do not seem bureaucratically flexible enough to permit, perhaps because it would undermine the authority of their top officials.* A salary based on project performance also prevents the proponent from taking advantage of the capital gains tax advantages of an equity form of compensation.

The semiconductor study suggests that a major reason for the relative lack of success in semiconductors of the established large electronics firms is the inability of a proponent making a proposal to such a firm to vouch for his confidence in his predictions by making a meaningful investment (see chapter 4, section 3.1). Since a proponent in a highly innovative industry is not likely to have much of an experience-based authority relationship with the firm either, he is essentially left with no tools of persuasion. Even where established firms have consciously tried to diversify into the highly innovative areas that are typically the province of venture capital firms, they have been bedeviled by these structural problems.[9]

2.124 *Persuading Sources To Fund a New Firm*

A proponent setting up a new firm is unlikely to have nearly as well developed an experience-based authority relationship with his prospective funding sources as an employee of an established firm seeking to persuade his firm to implement his project. He will have to depend much more on his own investment to convince others of the accuracy of his predictions for the success of the proposed proj-

---

*Certain star employees in the entertainment, communications, and sports industries do earn salaries far in excess of those of the top officials of their employers. However, these employees are not really part of the decision-making structure of their employers in the way proponents are. The stars' salaries, which represent rents on skills unrelated to management, are less likely to undermine the authority of top officials.

ect. Obviously, this context does not contain the impediments to demonstrating his sincerity through investment of his own time and money that are contained in the established firm context.

The semiconductor study shows that newly founded firms have done very well in the industry. The difference between their performance and that of the semiconductor divisions of the large established electronics companies appears in part to be a result of the superior ability of proponents proposing a new firm to demonstrate to funding sources the sincerity of their predictions. Lack of wealth on the part of proponents wishing to start new firms was not as serious a problem as one might have guessed, because of the relatively high salaries the proponents typically were able to command in alternative employment and the relatively low entry costs. Founders of these firms made significant investments in the form of their own cash (saved up out of the high salaries at their previous jobs) and of "sweat equity" (working for considerably less than the salary they could otherwise have been making) (see chapter 4, section 3.1). These factors are also likely to reduce the importance of individual wealth for starting new firms in other evolving science-based industries.

2.125 *Empirical Evidence Concerning Technical Innovations*

The survey type of empirical literature concerning innovations focuses more on the inventor, the person who develops the scientific idea behind investment projects involving technical innovation, than on the proponent, the person (who may or may not be the inventor) who puts together the scientific idea with an analysis of production practicality and marketability and takes the initiative to get funding for the project. Nevertheless, this literature gives us a feeling of the relative importance of different routes by which investment project ideas become implemented.

Jewkes, Sawers, and Stillerman have done a study of forty-four major inventions in the twentieth century.[10] The individuals developing the basic scientific idea relating to twenty-three of these were independent or university based. Thirteen of the twenty-three implemented their ideas by transfer to an established organization, and the other ten implemented their ideas by forming their own companies. The twenty-one not developed by independent or university-based individuals were developed by individuals employed by established corporate or governmental organizations that then implemented the ideas.

Jewkes, Sawers, and Stillerman argue that, contrary to popular impression and to the writings of Schumpeter and Galbraith,[11] highly sophisticated scientific ideas can be originated, and developed close to the point of practical production, by individuals acting alone or in small groups. Often large teams are used by established firms for reasons of speed, not because the innovation would otherwise be impossible.[12] This view corresponds with a growing consensus among industrial organization economists as to most industries and is supported by the semiconductor study there.[13] It underscores the importance for the economy's dynamic efficiency of financing being available to fund new firms.

2.2 *Project Managers*

Once a proponent gets funding for his project, the proponent usually becomes the manager of the project, and the funding source has the ongoing right of control reassignment. If the proponent has established a new firm, we can analyze the relationship between him and his funding source (a group of outside investors) in the same fashion as we would the relationship between any other corporate intermediary and its funding source, the topic of the next section. Here I will briefly focus on projects undertaken by existing firms.

A project manager's minimum goal is to maintain control of his project. How he does so is the subject of the theory of bureaucracy.[14] It is in the project manager's interest to pass on information which reflects well on him and suppress information which reflects poorly on him. Because it is not advantageous to be the bearer of bad news, the project manager may also suppress information which reflects poorly on the performance of the recipient. The recipient of the managers' information flow must try to calculate how much of these forms of manipulation is involved and adjust accordingly. This again creates uncertainty, since the recipient cannot be sure that its adjustment is correct. However, there do exist checks which keep within bounds such information distortion and the uncertainty associated with trying to correct for it: unless a project manager has a very short time horizon, he must be concerned with his authority.

In addition, corporate management (the funding source) has audit and other investigatory powers discussed in more detail in the next section.

The information emitted by potential project managers employed within the corporation who wish to replace incumbent project managers is more the subject of fictional and journalistic discussion of corporate bureaucracy than serious scholarship, since it involves communications which are likely to be kept highly confidential.

There is also not much evidence on the role, if any, that potential project managers play in the decision of one corporation to purchase a project from another corporation for the purpose of reassigning control. The fact that organizationally such transactions are typically undertaken on behalf of the purchasing corporation by financial rather than operating types of personnel* suggests that such purchases are not usually instigated by potential project managers.

3. *Corporate Management*

The top management of an existing corporation stands in the position of an intermediary in the information and decision delegation network that runs from savers to project proponents and project managers. Top management has a wide range of decisions to make. Three have direct, real economic effects: the funding of a new project, the purchase of any existing project for the purpose of reassigning its control, and reassignment by command of control of an existing project currently owned by the firm. Three are better termed financial decisions: the purchase and sale of existing projects where no control reassignment is contemplated, the making of distributions to shareholders (dividends, liquidating payments, and share repurchases), and the obtaining of outside financing. And finally, there are the decisions as to what messages to emit to financial intermediaries, investment advisers, and the general investing public.†

Each member of the top management group is, like most individ-

---

*Many large diversified corporations have a mergers and acquisitions group which reports to the chief financial officer of the corporation.

†This view of the top management of a large corporation as part of the finance process, rather than as involved in production decisions at the project level, is close to Williamson's view of the role of managements of what he calls "M-form corporations" (a corporation divisionalized along product lines) and of conglomerates.[15]

uals, assumed to be personally interested in compensation, perquisites, respect, power, affection of those around him, and a sense of rectitude. He is also assumed to have a strong desire to retain his job. Management can be expected to make decisions in the ways which it perceives best further these interests subject to the constraints within which it operates. This section will first examine the way top management receives and processes information and then the strategies it employs to make the decisions that, given its evaluation of the consequences of different actions, are the most advantageous to its personal interests.

The focus of this section is on the large, established, management-controlled corporation. This is because of the dominant role in our economy—revealed by the statistics below—that such firms play in funding the new projects and in the reassigning control of existing projects.

Of the largest 100 industrial corporations ranked by asset size, an individual, family, or financial institution directly or indirectly owns the majority of the shares of only 1 and greater than 10 percent of the shares of only 16.[16] Almost all the rest are safely classified as management controlled.[17] As one goes further down the list of large industrial corporations, management control still appears to predominate, though perhaps not to the same extent.[18]

Estimates of the percentage of the industrial sector's assets controlled by large corporations can be made on the basis of data from a number of different sources, and their results are not totally consistent. It is safe to say, however, that in the period 1976–1980, the top 100 corporations (ranked by asset size) controlled over 40 percent of the sector's assets; the top 200 controlled between 50 and 60 percent of these assets; and the top 500 controlled close to 75 percent of these assets.[19]

Exact data is also not available for the percentages of the sector's new investment that is attributable to these three groups of firms, but there is evidence that they were roughly comparable to the respective percentages of assets controlled.[20]

The dominance of the large, established, management-controlled firm is particularly important because, at least at the first level of analysis, each constitutes nearly a closed system. Clearly that is true when a firm reassigns control of an existing project which it currently owns: top management need not seek the consent of any outside party. But by and large, it is also true of its other real decisions, new project funding and control reassignment by purchase of an existing project, since such a firm relies for investment so heavily on internal sources of finance. In the period 1976–1980, close to 90 percent of all capital expenditures of all United States corporations were internally funded.[21] There are no readily available figures on what percentage of the capital expenditures of the largest 100, 200, and 500 corporations are internally funded, but there is evidence that they are comparable to the percentage for all corporations (which is hardly surprising, considering what a large percentage of all new investments they are responsible for).[22] And as we have seen in chapter 1 (section C 2.23), these largest corporations have, at least until recently, been the targets of relatively few successful hostile takeovers.

3.1 *The Processing of Information for and by Corporate Managers*

Ideas relating to the real and financial decisions of top management may have their origins inside or outside the firm. Either way, they are likely to be processed as they make their way toward the top managers of a firm. The processing has two functions: (a) to make available to the managers the expertise of other members of the organization so that managers can best estimate the probability distribution of possible outcomes from implementation of each idea, and (b) to reduce, by eliminating those least critical to the managers' decisions, the total number of information bits reaching top managers to a number they can handle. Ultimately, the managers want to choose from among a list of alternative ideas, each accompanied with as good an estimate as can be made of the probability distribution of possible outcomes from implementation of the idea.[23] And, without being overwhelmed with more bits of information than they can handle, they want information to help them judge the reliability of each such estimate. The information may include not only justifications for the conclusions of the staff, but also evidence concerning the competence of, and manipulation by, the staff members.

Top management is motivated to make this information collection and processing system work as well as is possible for any given level of cost. The better it works, the better the chance will be that the decisions they make will be in their own best interests. But motivation may not guarantee results. (See section C 2.421 for a general discussion of communications-based organization theory.)

It has already been suggested that project proponents and managers are motivated in many situations to emit information different from that which would be the most helpful to its recipient. It is a matter of organizational skill how successful managers are in reducing incentives for this behavior and taking what remains into account when the information received is processed. A certain residual amount of uncertainty is inevitable at each level. Williamson and Monsen and Downs[24] have made the point that the larger the firm, the more levels through which information will be processed and the greater the uncertainty by the time the information reaches the top.*

For a firm with a given level of organizational skill, the seriousness of the uncertainty generated by the possibility of manipulative information depends on the nature of the idea the information concerns. A typical firm tends to specialize in certain areas. This specialization is reflected in the training and job histories of its personnel. And within its areas of specialty, it develops experience as to what has and has not worked in the past. This experience helps determine the firm's interest rules: which information gets attention and which does not. Thus, even within its areas of specialty, a firm tends to tolerate only a narrow range of ideas. Burton Klein, for example, concludes that this tendency explains why, when he looked at the histories of a number of industries, he found that a precondition for a period of rapid innovation was a minimum of four to eight firms accounting for 50 percent of the market.[25]

This combination of specialization and experience makes the firm highly sensitive to the possibilities of certain ideas. But the trade-off is that it is relatively insensitive to the possibilities of many others.

A firm's narrowness is likely to take on a conservative shade as both its authority and interest rules ossify over time and block the types of information that result in innovative investment. Anthony Downs suggests as a matter of organizational theory that the older

---

*Williamson and Monsen and Downs would refer to this problem as "distortion" rather than "uncertainty," but they are referring to the same phenomenon. The assumption here is that a recipient, aware of the possibility of distortion, must guess at what the true state of affairs is. His guesses will not systematically be biased, but any one is not likely to be completely accurate.

the organization, the less receptive it is to innovative ideas.[26] Organizations develop rigid rules on the basis of experience and become prisoners of their past successes. Ruth Mack comes to a similar conclusion using a somewhat more complete theory. She suggests that human beings have an intolerance (irrational from an *ex post* point of view) for actions involving what she terms "ambiguity": actions the riskiness of which is difficult to evaluate.[27] Because established organizations have past experience which enables them to evaluate very capably the risks associated with certain kinds of actions, intolerance of ambiguity leads them to favor such actions over innovative actions, with which by definition they have no experience.

When all the factors are added up, it is clear that established firms vary in their ability to find good investment ideas. Meyer and Kuh, for example, find that contrary to what would be predicted by the simple application of neoclassical investment theory, firms with machinery of high average age invest at a lower rate than ones with newer machinery.[28] Part of the reason for this is luck: they are specialized in an area in which possibilities are developing rapidly, either because of basic research that is occurring in the area or because of a fast-growing demand for a particular type of product. By reason of circumstance their managements each receive a strong flow of promising investment ideas. Carter and Williams have reported, for example, that firms in technologically fast-advancing industries require a higher minimum expected rate of return before they will invest in a project because they have so many more opportunities in which to invest.[29] Part of the reason for the Meyer and Kuh findings may, as the above analysis would suggest, be the age of the firm: there is empirical evidence, discussed in more detail later, suggesting that older firms are unable to find projects in which to reinvest their earnings which are as profitable as those found by newer firms.[30] But there is also reason to believe that some firms do better than others as a result of conscious effort, both in terms of improving the flow of promising ideas and their organizational skill in reducing the uncertainty associated with such ideas.

Firms making an effort to improve the flow of promising ideas are described by Marris as "transcendent firms."[31] An important element of being a transcendent firm is devoting considerable resources to research and development. The semiconductor study showed, for example, a strong relationship between R & D expenditures and firm growth (see chapter 4, section 1.33). The theory being developed here would suggest that such expenditures would be helpful because, all other things being equal, ideas generated within the firm are more likely to get favorable attention as a result of the existence of well-established lines of communication (efficiency-inducing use of secondary symbols that develop from frequent contact) and the inevitably greater authority of a well-known internal idea source. Also, appropriability problems may mean that the firm does not even get a chance to consider ideas developed outside.

The organizational skill of reducing uncertainty associated with investment ideas involves the simple recognition of the importance of a good information-processing system. This requires a variety of techniques of good administration, including the recruitment of good personnel, continuing intelligence on the quality of their work to assure that behavior which serves their interests serves the intersts of the firm, use of competing sources of information in order to eliminate blind spots and check the motivations of different staff members, and separation of operations from information-processing functions so that information processors are not trying to cover past mistakes.[32]

3.2 *Decision-making by Top Corporate Managers*

A top manager of an established firm, as stated earlier, is personally interested in compensation (salary, bonus, stock options, stock appreciation rights, and fringe benefits), luxury perquisites on the job, respect, power, affection of those around him, and a sense of rectitude. It is assumed that having climbed the difficult road to the top and possessing much of their human capital in firm specific form, the typical manager is not willing to add significantly to the risks of losing his job just to obtain more of any of these rewards than the generous amount he receives without taking such risks. All the decisions top management makes have the potential, directly or indirectly, of affecting the level of these rewards to its members. At least some of the decisions which would further some or all these values are ones which are not in the best interests of shareholders. To the extent that managers can resolve such conflicts in their own favor without significantly increasing the likelihood of the only threats to the jobs of the group—bankruptcy and hostile takeover—they will do so. A resolution of conflict in management's favor, if detected with reasonable assurance by an outsider, may demonstrate the possibility of a profitable takeover and become the basis of an attack on management. Thus, management should, in making real and financial decisions which pose such a conflict, resolve them in their favor only where detection is unlikely. Information should be emitted in a fashion which maximizes the percentage of decisions involving a conflict with shareholder interests that can be resolved without detection in management's favor.

What follows is a plausible decision strategy for the top management of a large management-controlled firm. First the strategy itself is laid out. Each of the elements represents beneficial behavior *ceteris paribus*. Then there is an extended discussion concerning the strategy, which includes consideration of the trade-offs among the elements and citation to a variety of empirical studies suggesting that the managements of large management-controlled firms in fact behave as if they follow the strategy set out here.

3.21 *A Strategy Advancing Management Interests in the Management-Controlled Corporation*

1. Keep the debt/equity ratio low. Bankruptcy occurs when debt service payments exceed net operating revenues (gross revenues less cost of inputs).* A lower debt/equity ratio means lower debt service payments for any given level of capital base from which net operating revenues are produced. Net operating revenues are inevitably somewhat uncertain in amount from year to year. The lower the debt/equity ratio, the lower the probability that net revenues will dip below the required level of debt service in any given year.

2. Have the best information-generating and -processing functions possible for any given level of cost in order to identify the best new investment project ideas, existing projects worth buying or selling because of differences in opinion between top management and another party as to their prospects, existing projects which are worth buying to reassign control, and existing projects currently owned by the firm that need reassignment of control.

---

*Debt service includes both principal and interest payments. A firm will not be able to "roll over" its debts as they come due when it approaches the point of bankruptcy.

3. Use the predictions derived from the firm's information functions to command control reassignments of existing projects owned by the firm where such reassignment is expected to increase the discounted income stream from the project.

4. Use the predictions derived from the firm's information functions to identify a list of the best investment opportunities that can be found—new projects, existing projects owned by others where control reassignment is contemplated, and ones where it is not—according to expected rates of return adjusted for systematic risk. Refinance any existing debt as it becomes due to the extent necessary to prevent firm shrinkage. Retain as high a percentage of cash flow (after payment of interest and unrefinanced principal owing on existing debt) as shareholder pressure will permit, and make investments going down the list of opportunities as far as the money retained will take the firm. Do this even if the risk-adjusted expected rate of return on some or all of these projects is less than the stockholders' rate of return ("SROR"), i.e., the risk-adjusted rate which shareholders on average could earn on the money if returned to them and reinvested.*

---

*The comparison between the risk-adjusted expected rate of return and SROR is best understood by first examining the question at a very abstract level. Imagine a corporation with just one shareholder, X. A corporation whose management decides whether or not to invest in a proposed project on the basis of its effect on shareholder welfare must compare X's expected utility from his portfolio if the corporation invests in the project with X's expected utility from his portfolio if instead the corporation pays out in dividends the amount the project would have required and X reinvests the money. Management starts by using its subjective probability distribution of the possible returns from the project to calculate the effect of investment in the project on X's Markowitz efficiency frontier and hence the position of X's capital market line. This calculation should be made assuming that X will retain his shares, since the effect of the investment, if not felt by X, will be passed on to another investor. Then the Markowitz efficiency frontier and the position of the capital market line (again assuming retention by X of the corporations's shares) must be calculated where X receives the dividend and reinvests. In each case the level initial wealth position available for investment must be adjusted for the transaction costs associated with any portfolio changes occurring as a result of the corporation's decision (For a discussion of the mechanics of this kind of analysis, see Chapter 1, section C 2.211, and appendix 1.5.) This analysis may show that the capital market line associated with one decision dominates the one associated with the other or the two lines may cross. If they cross, the corporation must also know something about X's utility function and resulting indifference curves to make the decision that is better for X.

This is, of course, an unrealistic description of what a public corporation is able to do. It has thousands of shareholders and has little information concerning each share-

5. Minimize the variability in the firm's total cash flow by avoiding investments which might add significantly to this variability (for example, a project which is large compared with the size of the whole firm and which has a high degree of either systematic or unsystematic risk associated with it) and by seeking diversity in investments.

6. To the extent shareholder pressure permits, do not sell any project even if its sale would yield proceeds that, if returned to shareholders, would permit them to reinvest the funds and receive risk-adjusted returns that exceed the amount the project earns in the hands of the firm.* In other words, avoid partial or total liquidation.

7. As we will see, some of the elements of this strategy are in the best interests of shareholders and some, at least under certain circumstances, are not. The following steps should be undertaken to minimize, for any given level of corporate performance, the chance of takeover and thus maximize the extent to which the elements of the strategy which are not in the best interests of shareholders can be safely pursued.

  a. Issue predictions concerning future shareholder income that are as accurate as possible but in highly conclusionary form (i.e., without giving the facts on which the predictions are based).
  b. Issue as little other information about the corporation as possible. As part of this, avoid outside financing other than refinancing existing debt, especially publicly issued equity, unless it would permit the firm to invest in an opportunity with a rate of return above SROR.

---

holder's expectations (needed to construct his efficiency frontier) and concerning his utility function. The best the corporation can do in most circumstances may be to adopt the approach recommended in standard corporation finance texts, which is based on the capital asset pricing model and hence assumes homogeneous expectations.[33] Management uses its subjective distribution functions of the project's possible returns and of the possible returns of the market as a whole to calculate the project's expected return and its systematic risk. The expected return is adjusted by what appears from historical data to be the market price of systematic risk. That figure is compared with the expected return from an investment in the market of risky securities as a whole.

*An exception exists where there is an investment opportunity on the firm's list which is below the project reached on the list through investment of retained funds but which has an expected rate of return higher than the project which the firm currently owns (calculated in terms of its expected earnings and its potential sales price).

c. Maintain the firm's market share in each market in which it participates.

d. Do everything else possible to boost top management's authority.

3.22 *The Strategy Considered*

3.221 *Top Management and Shareholders: Convergences and Divergences in Interest*

a. *Convergences.* Maintaining a low debt/equity ratio, the first element of the strategy, is, at least according to the Modigliani and Miller theorem, a matter of indifference to shareholders. Any shareholder who prefers a higher ratio can engage, to the extent permitted by law, in "homemade leverage":* buying on margin in what in practice amounts to a nonrecourse basis.† The second element, having a good information function, is clearly in the shareholders' best interests: information collection and processing is the raison d'être of all intermediaries between the savers and real investment. The third element of the strategy, commanding control reassignments of

---

*As discussed elsewhere in this book (chapter 6, sections B2.1 and C3.14), there are a variety of other considerations not accounted for in the Modigliani and Miller theorem as to what, if anything, constitutes an optimal debt/equity ratio from the point of view of shareholders. These considerations include agency costs, "signaling," "bonding," bankruptcy costs, taxes, and the transaction cost economies of firms providing for clienteles with different risk preferences securities to fit these preferences. The combination is sufficiently complex that perhaps the best that can be said is that, consistent with the Modigliani and Miller theorem, there are no clear reasons for believing that a managerial desire to have a low debt/equity ratio to reduce the possibility of bankruptcy is, absent any motivational effects on management, harmful to shareholder interests.

There is one factor which, *ceteris paribus*, unambiguously makes shareholders have an interest in a high debt/equity ratio. A high debt/equity ratio increases the dispersion of possible returns after subtraction for debt service. This permits the shareholders to enjoy the increased possibility of large upside gains while saddling creditors with the increased possibility of large downside losses. However, things are not *ceteris paribus*, because a creditor at the time it makes its loan will, in determining the rate it will charge, assess the existing debt/equity ratio and try to anticipate any changes which might occur during the life of the loan. Thus in fact neither the initial ratio nor, assuming the creditor's estimate is unbiased, subsequent changes in that ratio will on average transfer wealth from creditors to shareholders.

†Margin shares are normally pledged to the lender and are sold by the lender to satisfy the debt if the share price drops below a level which provides the lender with a certain cushion of security. The Federal Reserve places limits on the percentage of the share price which may be borrowed to finance its purchase.

existing projects owned by the firm where a change in project management would result in increased income, is also in the best interests of shareholders. The strategy suggests that top management wants the manager of each existing project—an existing unit of productive capacity—to make the most efficient possible production decisions, the ongoing operating decisions concerning the combinations of inputs used by the project and the project's level of output. Thus, short-run sales maximizing would be avoided where a project could earn a higher operating profit from lower sales. Similarly, for any given level of output, the firm would choose the most efficient method of production from among those known to it to be permitted by the existing unit of capacity.

b. *Divergences.* Investment and financial policy is where there is a potential divergence of interest between top management and shareholders. Management is interested, as an instrument for serving its personal values, in the size of the flow of cash that is available each year for dividends, internally funded investment, and management compensation and expenses. Specifically, the goal of management implied by the suggested strategy is, subject to the constraint that firm size should not shrink, to maximize the firm's aggregate available cash flow ("AACF"), i.e., its aggregate future earnings, before deductions for depreciation and management compensation and expenses, discounted to present value at a rate reflecting management's time preference and risk aversion. Elements 4, 5, and 6 of the strategy all reflect this instrumental goal. Retaining a dollar to invest in a project with a rate of return that is less than SROR but greater than zero increases AACF but is not in the best interest of shareholders. Thus, elements 4, 5, and 6 of the strategy, at least if carried to their full extreme, are not in the best interests of shareholders, unless a firm is in the position such that: (i) if it makes no distribution to shareholders and invests, going down its list of opportunities, all of its available cash flow, no project has a rate of return lower than SROR; and (ii) it currently owns no existing project the income from which, when compared with the amount for which the project could be sold, represents a rate of return lower than SROR. There is substantial evidence that a significant portion of large industrial firms retain and reinvest more of their cash flow than can be justified in terms of shareholder interests. (See appendix 2.1 for a general discussion of this evidence.) It is impossible to demonstrate empirically that such firms also hold on to projects when it would be in the shareholders' best interest to sell the project and distribute the proceeds, because the potential sale price of any particular project is generally unknown. But just because of this difficulty of detection, a firm is at least as likely to engage in such behavior as it is to retain and reinvest too much of its cash flow.

c. *Rationale of the strategy.* The proposition that top management strives to make the firm's AACF as large as possible reflects first the concept that the larger the available cash flow, the greater the capacity of the firm over time to satisfy interests of each of the top managers: compensation, luxury perquisites, respect, power, affection of those around him, and a sense of rectitude. A "diversion" of a certain amount from the available cash flow in any one period to pay greater compensation and provide more perquisites than is competitively necessary is a smaller percentage of a large available cash flow than of a small one and thus harder to detect.* The same is true of a diversion of a given amount to engage in an activity which gives top management a sense of rectitude for "doing good" but which does not contribute to firm profitability. Striving to make AACF as large as possible also implies, after deduction for management compensation and expenses, the largest possible growth in firm assets (subject, of course, to the constraint that each project invested in is not expected to lose money). The larger the assets, the greater the respect and power which attaches to a top management job.[34] The greater the rate of growth of the assets, the more opportunities for promotion, thereby improving the relations between top managers and those directly below them.[35] The constraint of refinancing existing debt to prevent firm shrinkage may run counter to maxmizing AACF if the cost of the new debt exceeds rate of return on the most marginal new project, but avoiding shrinkage now, with its severe damage to organizational morale, is likely to be preferred even if it means smaller available cash flows in the future since they can be adjusted to over time.

*A number of economists have studied the relationship between large firm management compensation and various measures of firm behavior such as profits, share value, and sales. The purpose of these studies is to see what kind of decisions would best serve management's interest in compensation. On the whole, their results are consistent with the proposition that management will strive to make AACF as large as possible, although they provide little direct support. See appendix 2.2 for a discussion of evidence concerning the determinants of managerial compensation.

d. *Management time preference and risk aversion*. AACF is a function not only of the aggregate expected available cash flow but also of top management's time preference and degree of risk aversion, the two factors which go into the rate of discount. If top management differs from shareholders in either of these respects, that also raises the possibility of conflict of interest.

Consider first time preference. There has been much discussion about the tendency of top management of large American corporations to have a very short time horizon and to be concerned with profits in the very near term.[36] The empirical evidence given in support of this proposition tends to be anecdotal. One supposition behind the proposition is that because the average chief executive will only have his job a few years, he will not care what happens after he leaves. This supposition greatly underestimates the ability of top management as a team to operate as a self-perpetuating institution with long-term goals.* The time when top managers are most likely to adopt a short time horizon is in a period of crisis: long-run damage to business is of little concern to them if the alternative is a loss of their jobs through bankruptcy or takeover.

A second supposition behind the proposition is that stock price based compensation schemes focus top management's attention on profits in the near term because decisions that increase current profits have a more favorable effect on share price than decisions that improve the firm's long-run profitability. The idea that concern with stock price leads to a managerial tendency to favor current profits too much at the expense of future profits ultimately turns out to be a more elaborate version of the general proposition that top management itself has a short time horizon. Current profits are undoubtedly used by the market as a measure of future profitability and thus influence the firm's stock price. But if current profits are earned at

---

*A good example of such an institution is a large corporate law firm. The more senior members of the firm have no long-term stake in the profitability of the firm because they do not own stock and will only remain partners a limited number of additional years. Yet they cooperate in a system of rewards and sanctions for members of the organization that focus on such long-term concerns as the reputation of the quality of the firm's work, cementing relationships with clients, and recruiting high-quality young lawyers. An explanation may be that long-run profitability of the firm is what makes promotion within the group desirable. The more desirable promotion is, the more powerful those who control promotion decisions—the senior members—feel. This feeling of power can be a significant source of utility.

the expense of future profits, then current stock price will be earned at the expense of future stock price. If management as a team has a long time horizon in terms of what it wishes to get out of the corporation, the trade of current share price for future share price is not worth making because the firm is likely to continue to use share price based compensation schemes. Even if, for the sake of argument, we posit that top management's time horizon in terms of what it wishes to get out of the corporation is only a few years, stock price based compensation schemes should on the whole increase, not decrease, management's concern with long-term profitability. Share prices are affected by beliefs concerning the long-run profitability of the corporation derived from information other than this year's profits. There is no reason to think that the market's assessment of the future prospects of a firm should be systematically biased. Over time the market should be able to discern the relationship between a firm's current and future profitability. Management could "fool" the market by an undisclosed change in policy that changes the relationship the market has discerned, but this is not a trick that can be used repeatedly, and it undermines top management authority.

Risk aversion presents a more serious problem. Management is concerned with the variability of the return on the firm's investments, whether that variability stems from systematic or unsystematic risk. For a given debt/equity ratio, the more variable the return, the greater the chance of very low cash flow in some period and thus of top management job loss through bankruptcy. Stability of cash flow may be helpful as well in reducing the risk of hostile takeover. And to the extent that a manager's compensation is related to firm earnings, the manager has an additional stake in their stability. The more variable the earnings, the more variable his compensation. Since his compensation is likely to be a large portion of his total income, he will be concerned with the unsystematic as well as the systematic component of this risk. The typical shareholder, on the other hand, is ultimately concerned with the variability of earnings from his entire portfolio, not that of each of the shares composing it.* The unsystematic component of any particular firm's

*There is a long history to the proposition that management in management-controlled firms makes decisions which reflect greater aversion to variability than is in the best interests of shareholders. William Fellner pointed out in the late 1940s that there is an asymmetry in possible gains and losses from risk taking by corporate

earnings are of little concern to him because he can construct a portfolio deriving income from a diverse set of investment projects by owning shares in a variety of firms.

Management's preference for a low variability of return motivates it to seek a diverse set of investment projects in order to achieve stability by reducing unsystematic risk, the component of variability with which the shareholder is not usually concerned.[42] This seeking of diversity is frequently not in the shareholders' best interests because management is not expert in new areas in which it invests. Motivated by these concerns, top management will also tend to avoid any high-risk project which would constitute a significant portion of the firm's assets even if the risk is unsystematic and the project has a high expected return. (For an analytical treatment of the consequences of the difference in attitude toward unsystematic risk on the part of management and shareholders in the context of the decisions as to whether or not to attempt a takeover of another firm, see appendix 1.5.) This tendency will produce a bias against large innovative investment.

e. *Comparison with managerial theories of the firm.* Before going on

---

managers. A sharp increase in earnings may lead to an increase in a manager's compensation (though small compared with the total corporate gain), but a sharp drop in earnings may lead to a loss of his job. The chance of the positive outcome is not likely to compensate for the risk of the negative.[37] Gordon and Monsen and Downs have approached the issue in a similar fashion.[38]

The empirical evidence is mixed concerning the risk characteristics of returns on the investments of management-controlled firms. Boudreux looks at the standard deviation of the rate of profit of 36 management-controlled firms and 36 owner-controlled firms.[39] He finds that the management-controlled firms have a smaller average standard deviation, indicating a general aversion to variability on the part of their managers. Management that shies away from variability would presumably, contrary to the best interests of shareholders, shy away from unsystematic risk as well as systematic risk. However, other studies, which attempt to control for rate of return or leverage, show no significant difference in variability between the two groups, at least for the largest 375 industrial firms.[40] A study by McEachern shows that management-controlled firms display greater systematic riskiness of share price than "externally controlled" firms (a control bloc of shares exists, but the owners are not managers).[41] It is not reported whether management-controlled firms displayed less unsystematic risk (as a combination of the results of the McEachern study with the Boudreux study would suggest). The problem with drawing conclusions about the welfare of shareholders of management-controlled firms from studies which compare management-controlled firms with firms not controlled by management is that the risk preferences of the two shareholder groups with respect to the income derived from shares of the firms in question may be very different.

with a further examination of the strategy set out here, this is an appropriate place to explore how the strategy compares with the "managerial" theories of firm behavior of Baumol, Marris, and Williamson discussed briefly in chapter 1. Baumol in his first edition of *Business Behavior, Value, and Growth* develops a static one-period model in which managers strive to maximize sales subject to a minimum profit constraint to prevent takeover.[43] Clearly, as noted earlier, that implies behavior different from what the strategy set out here implies. In the revised edition of the book, the model becomes dynamic and the firm seeks to maximize the growth of sales.[44] In this theory, a minimum level of profits must be obtained in any given period in order to attract the necessary outside finance to permit future expansion. This second model appears to deal with a situation which is not of interest here: the firm has sufficiently attractive investment opportunities that it would seek outside finance.

Marris' model is much closer to the one set out here: management strives, subject to a minimum stock price constraint, to maximize asset growth by retaining earnings and investing in projects even if their rates of return are below the cost of capital.[45] The problem with the Marris model is its focus on growth as an end in itself. He is not very convincing as to why the greater the rate of growth, the higher the level of each manager's utility. In the approach used here, too high a rate of growth of assets is disadvantageous because it will reduce AACF, which will negatively affect not only the ability to keep shareholders happy with dividends but also the funds available for management salaries and expenses.

Williamson's theory suffers from the opposite problem.[46] His description of the managerial utility function, which is close to the one set out here, is reasonably convincing. But his theory, like Baumol's first edition theory, is based on a static one-period model (though he makes some useful hints as to its dynamic implications).

More important are differences between the purposes for which my theory has been developed and the purposes for which the Baumol, Marris, and Williamson theories have been developed. The managerial models are used to determine firm output and growth rate responses to shifts in demand, to the imposition of lump sum taxes, and to the imposition of proportional taxes on firm profits or on firm market value. The implication of the theories that firms will retain more earnings than would be predicted by neoclassical theory is noted but its consequences are not explored. The determinants of the level of the stockholder constraint on the minimum level of profits, dividends, or firm value which must be maintained are not explored at all. The emphasis here is on finance and investment: who has the mandate to make investment decisions in our economy and what are the consequences in terms of the ability of the system to identify the most promising projects and in terms of market structure? The analysis includes a consideration of the determinants of the level of stockholder constraint and their effect on managerial behavior.

3.222 Management Techniques for Pursuing Greater Available Cash Flow Than Is Shareholders' Best Interests

The farther top management can pursue elements 1 through 6, the more successfully over the long run they can use the firm to satisfy their personal interests. But for a significant portion of large management-controlled firms, pursuing elements 4, 5, and 6 beyond a certain point is not in the best interests of shareholders, and that presents a risk to management of job loss through hostile takeover. How far top management can safely pursue these elements depends on how they act to counter this risk.

An analysis of the probability of a hostile takeover by a particular potential acquiror rests on looking at each possible actor in the process and comparing (a) the actor's subjective probability distribution concerning the dividends and other distributions (collectively referred to in this discussion as "dividends") which a share of the firm's stock would yield in each future time period assuming management remains in control, and (b) the actor's subjective distribution concerning future dividends assuming that the acquiror obtains control. In the case of a takeover through a proxy fight, the relevant actors are the acquiror and current shareholders of the firm, the persons whose votes are needed to replace management.* In the case

---

*In theory, the perspectives of other investors could be relevant also. If an investor who does not own shares of the firm associates a more favorable distribution with the acquiror than with management and he believes that the acquiror will win the proxy contest, he might, if the price were low enough, buy shares and vote them in favor of the acquiror.

of a hostile tender offer, the acquiror alone is the primary actor, but the acquiror's shareholders or its financial sources may play a part as well.*

The way for incumbent management to avoid a takeover is to be sure that, for each person who is a relevant actor in any possible takeover threat, the subjective distribution concerning dividends which he associates with incumbent management has a more favorable combination of risk and return parameters than that which he associates with the potential acquiror. There is no reason to believe that there should be a systematic bias in the actor's best guesses as to level of future dividends that could be expected with incumbent management (the mean of the distribution associated with incumbent management) or in his corresponding best guess associated with the potential acquiror. This poses a problem for any incumbent management that, by pursuing elements 4–6 of the strategy with vigor, is not acting in the shareholders' best interests. On average, the mean of the subjective distribution which the actor associates with incumbent management will be below that he would associate with the acquiror if the acquiror is truly interested in shareholder welfare (for example, one considering wholly owning the target firm). Thus, in-

---

*The implication here is that none of the target firm's current shareholders makes a comparison between the subjective distribution that he associates with incumbent management and that he associates with the acquiror. That implication is correct in the case of a shareholder who is facing an offering where the price is high enough that, given the distribution he associates with incumbent management, he wants to sell all his shares, and the acquiror has agreed to purchase all the shares offered to it if it purchases any of them. In such a case the shareholder has no reason to be concerned with how the acquiror might manage the company. But where one or both of these factors are missing, the shareholder will in theory want to make a comparison between the distributions. A shareholder in this situation who associates with the incumbent a more favorable distribution than he associates with the acquiror faces a dilemma because, if the tender offer succeeds, he may continue to own some of the firm's shares. If he responds to the tender offer, he increases the probability that the acquiror will succeed in gaining control of the firm, making his remaining shares worth less in his eyes. But if he does not respond to the offer, he loses the opportunity to sell some of his shares at what he believes to be a favorable price. Although concern with this dilemma is the primary justification for the offerer disclosure requirements under the Williams Act,[47] it is of little practical importance to the average shareholder because of the "free rider" problem. The average shareholder will not wish to give up the opportunity of a favorable financial transaction for the small chance that his response would make the difference in whether or not the acquiror obtains control.

cumbent management, to make the subjective distribution that the actor associates with it more attractive than the one he associates with the acquiror, must make it less risky than the other. This is the object of element 7 of the strategy.

Compare this strategy with the conventional wisdom that a high current share price is the best takeover protection. A high share price represents current and potential stockholder confidence that management can be expected to produce a good future dividend stream. A high share price can also easily make any acquisition too expensive to be profitable even if the potential acquiring company is confident it can increase the income stream. However, it is hard over the long run to maintain the highest possible share price unless management resolves in the stockholder's favor all conflicts between its own interest and those of stockholders. In contrast, management can follow in perpetuity the strategy, set out in this discussion, of fending off takeovers by maximizing the risk differential, as perceived by the relevant actors, between the income stream prospects of incumbent management and that of each possible acquiror while resolving such conflicts at least to some extent in its own favor.

How does an incumbent management go about maximizing this risk differential? As element 7 of the strategy suggests, part of the answer relates to information management should release and information management should not release. Management should release predictions, which are as accurate as possible, concerning future income to shareholders: statements which are, or by common rules of inference can be translated into, something roughly akin to management's announcement of what it believes is the probability distribution of future dividends. Generally, predictions over anything more than a very short time period are more likely to be made concerning earnings than dividends. But, as we shall see shortly, the number which is given as earnings is not necessarily the same as the amount which an economist would calculate as the earnings of the firm's current assets. For the typical corporation, its dividends, at least in the medium and long range, tend to be a rather stable fraction of its announced earnings.[48] Thus, the prediction of earnings becomes an indirect, but relatively dependable, prediction of dividends. Management's predictions should be conclusionary: as little information as possible to which management has special access should accompany the predictions by way of explanation.* As a general matter, as little information internal to the corporation as possible should be released.

Why this approach to the release of information? Each relevant actor in any potential takeover attempt must establish in its mind its subjective probability distribution associated with incumbent management. The degree to which the subjective distribution is formed from the management's prediction (the probability distribution of dividends that management announces) depends on the authority of the management in the actor's eyes. Authority in this situation is likely to be primarily experience based: how close was the firm's actual performance in each past period to that which would have been expected if management's announced probability distribution relating to the period was correct? Reputation-based authority shaped by other information the actor may have concerning the competency and integrity of the management may also be a factor.

Because processing information is costly, management's authority is very important in determining how risky the actor's subjective distribution will be. If management has great authority, the announced distribution will be highly credible and the actor's subjective distribution will closely resemble it. If management does not have much authority, the actor's subjective distribution will be relatively more risky because it will have to be based on limited alternative bits of information generally unanalyzed by anyone with the expertise of management.

Releasing as little hard information as possible about the operations and management policies of the firm obviously makes management's announced distribution less credible than it might be. But it does more damage to the distribution which each relevant actor associates with any potential acquiror. Consider the various possible relevant actors. As demonstrated in chapter 1 (section C 2.23), the less confident a potential acquiror feels about its assessment that it can increase the profitability of a target firm, the less likely it will engage in a hostile tender offer. The less information the acquiror has about the firm, the less confident it will feel about that assess-

---

*A prediction would still be conclusionary if it is predicated upon information about which the actor has as good an ability to guess as top management has, for example next year's interest rates or the growth of the economy over the next decade.

ment.* Having little information about the firm also makes it difficult for an acquiror considering a hostile tender offer to marshal facts to convince, if necessary, financial sources or its own shareholders that the takeover is wise. For the unusual acquiror considering a proxy fight, the problem of convincing the target firm's shareholders is even more difficult because they are likely to be suspicious that the acquiror's motives are opportunistic.

Ideally, incumbent management would want the firm to be considered a black box that produces dividends each period. Each period the firm announces a joint probability distribution relating to the dividends in subsequent periods. As the passage of time permits the repeated testing of these announced distributions, they are seen to bear a reasonable relation to actual results. The stockholder, unaware of elements 4, 5, and 6 of the firm's investment strategy, values the security on the basis of the latest announced probability distribution, which he tends to trust because of the authority that management has built up by the dependability of its previous announcements. The security in effect is discounted once and for all for the negative effects of elements 4–6 of the strategy, and thereafter its performance will appear to be comparable with other securities in the market. The initial current assets are more valuable than admitted, and the extra unadmitted earnings form a fund the income from which subsidizes the strategy.

Because firms need to conform with securities laws and keep good relations with their shareholders, they cannot conform perfectly to the "black box" ideal. In particular, publicly held companies must regularly report their aggregate earnings and provide a very limited breakdown of the sources of these earnings.† If these were reported

---

*An empirical confirmation of the logic of this statement comes from the behavior of acquirors in the case of friendly takeovers, where they have full access to internal information about the target. The acquiror normally takes advantage of this opportunity and scrutinizes the target intensely before it binds itself irrevocably to going through with the transaction.[49] Even then an acquiror sometimes fails to discover important facts known by the management of the target.[50]

†Since 1978 the Securities and Exchange Commission (SEC) has required each public company to report annually for each of the company's "significant industry segments" the amount of revenue, operating profit or loss, and identifiable assets attributable to that segment. An industry segment is a component of a company which provides a product or a group of related products primarily to unaffiliated customers. An industry segment is significant if its revenues, operating profit, or identifiable

in accordance with what an economist would say were the earnings of the current assets of the firm, it might become obvious over time that the firm was engaging in an investment strategy which was not in the shareholders' best interest. Whatever portion of earnings is not paid out in dividends must be considered investment, and after a period it would become apparent that too much investment was going on and too much emphasis was being put on the stability of firm income. Fortunately for incumbent management, they can take advantage of the flexibility of accounting rules[52] and the orientation of these rules toward antifraud considerations.* These rules seriously impede attempts to overstate income because of the fear that such overstatement will be extrapolated into the future and encourage potential stockholders to overvalue the shares. They impose almost no barriers to understating income by treating as expenses what is really investment or by creating unnecessarily large reserves. This flexibility permits confusion as to how much investment is being made and how much current assets are worth. Stockholders thus tend to look upon earnings as nothing more than a predictor of dividends, the focus of attention that a firm pursuing a "black box" policy wishes to encourage.

Accounting rules also present the possibility of "smoothing" announced earnings through the establishment of reserves over which firms have considerable discretion as to size and through flexibility as to which period to assign certain kinds of costs and revenues.[53] Although use of smoothing cannot improve the accuracy of incumbent management's long-run predictions, it can improve the accuracy of short-term predictions by eliminating extreme deviations on

assets constitute 10% or more of the corresponding amounts for the whole enterprise. The breakdown of a company into significant industry segments is undertaken in the first instance by the company itself, and it is allowed considerable discretion in this determination. Disclosure may be avoided by dividing very finely, resulting in a group of segments none of which is significant. It can also be avoided by dividing very coarsely, resulting in a large portion of the business being placed in one segment. The SEC will not condone divisions that have no sensible basis, but, within the zone of discretion available to a company, the use of these two techniques can minimize the amount of useful disclosure. The result is that even the largest, most diversified industrial companies rarely report on more than three of four industry segments.[51]

*The use of this flexibility to make nonmaximizing behavior hard to detect with assurance is, as indicated, a separate question from whether analysts can make unbiased estimates of future dividend flow on the basis of the information released, which there is no reason to believe they cannot.

either side of the prediction. A record of relatively accurate short-term earnings forecasts and of dividends which are stable in absolute amount in the short run and stable as percentage of announced earnings in the medium and long run establishes an image of dependability. Establishing such an image reduces the need to make disclosures concerning operations of the firm for purposes of shareholder relations.

Another technique for minimizing shareholder demands for information concerning the firm is to maintain the firm's share of the market. Because the exogenous influences on firm performance are presumably felt by all the members of the industry, market share is an indication of how management has been able to perform given the general business environment in which it must operate. A management which is anxious to create the impression that it is doing as well as it can given its external environment will be anxious to maintain its share of the market.[54]

Avoiding outside financing, particularly by means of a public offering of equity securities, is another way to eliminate unnecessary disclosure. The process of generating a registration statement necessary for engaging in a public offering inevitably results in disclosure concerning both the financial status and the expected environment of a corporation. Although all public corporations are required by the Securities Exchange Act of 1934 to make periodic disclosure through filings and statements sent to stockholders, the disclosure process connected with a registered public offering is, as discussed in more detail in chapter 6, likely to require more disclosure. The corporation and its officers and directors face considerably greater potential liability for misstatements and failing to disclose material facts when the corporation is selling securities than when it is making required periodic disclosure. Moreover, most public offerings involve an underwriter, which, in order to avoid the same liability, must engage in an investigation of the corporation and insist on disclosure of all material information which it finds (see chapter 6, section B 1). Less undesirable, but still better to avoid from the point of view of disclosure minimization, are private placements of securities and loans from banks or other financial institutions. Any source of one of these types of financing would want to know a great deal about the firm before committing itself. Although the specific pieces of information such a source receives would be given to it in confidence, the impressions which the source gains and at least some of the pieces of information it receives inevitably make their way into the financial community at large.*

In addition to announcing as accurate predictions as possible, there

---

*Frank Easterbrook makes a similar observation that the review of a firm's affairs by an investment bank or other financial intermediary that accompanies the request for outside financing is likely to force management to act more in the investors' best interests than does the management of a firm not subjected to such scrutiny.[55] Easterbrook makes this observation in connection with an effort to explain the existence of firms that both utilize outside finance and pay dividends, behavior which at first blush seems paradoxical given that the amount of outside finance sought and its accompanying transaction costs could be reduced if the dividends were eliminated. He suggests that such firms pay dividends because the consequent need to seek additional outside finance introduces an agency cost reducing monitor of management behavior.

Easterbrook's suggestion that there is a set of firms whose managements have incentives to pay dividends is not necessarily inconsistent with the analysis set out here that there is a set of firms whose managements have incentives not to pay dividends. This is easiest to see in an all equity world. If we assume that the sole instrumental goal of management is to maximize AACF, there exist firms that the analysis above suggests would seek external funds: those with project lists sufficiently good that if they paid 0 dividends they would still have unfunded projects with expected returns in excess of the cost (defined in terms of effect on AACF) of such external funds. Such firms will not invest in projects with expected returns less than the cost (so defined) of external funds because AACF is greater if the firm foregoes such investments and raises commensurately less external funds. Thus their managements have no overinvestment to hide (assuming that the cost of external funds is at least SROR, which it would be if investors make unbiased estimates of future dividends) and therefore less to fear from the additional scrutiny that seeking outside funds triggers. And such firms may well decide, as Easterbrook suggests, that they can reduce in the long run their costs of external funds by establishing a pattern of paying more than 0 dividends thereby increasing the amounts of external funds needed and creating the expectation of more regular monitoring by external funding sources.[56] The main focus of the above analysis is on a different set of firms, ones from among those that would not seek external funds. These firms have project lists such that if they paid 0 dividends they would be funding projects with expected returns below SROR. They are the ones that have managements with incentives not to pay dividends. Seeking external funds would both lower AACF and attract unwelcome scrutiny.

If we introduce debt, the situation becomes more complex. It is suggested in the analysis above that firms in this second group, in order to avoid shrinkage in the level of real assets of the firm, might choose to refinance existing debt as it becomes due even if that reduces AACF. While Easterbrook's theory would suggest that this behavior would be self-defeating because the resulting scrutiny would prevent management from continuing to put its own interests ahead of the shareholders, this is unlikely, particularly if the debt is not publicly offered. The source of such funds will not find an extensive investigation of the firm to be cost effective if, as is often likely to be the case, an initial investigation indicates a high assurance of sufficient cash flow to cover a firm's debt service obligations. Thus seeking debt funding to maintain a debt level successfully sustained by the firm in the past offers much less monitoring potential than seeking substantial amounts of new equity where the characteristics of the full probability range of the firm's future cash flow must be examined.

are other steps which incumbent management of a firm may undertake to enhance its authority. One, which is at odds with the goal
of maximizing AACF, is a refusal to admit past mistakes. It may be
in the management's best interest to continue a project that is not,
using rational economic criteria, worth finishing. Its financial results
after completion can be buried among other statistics.[57] A discontin-
uance would be an authority-diminishing admission of mistake. A
portion of future costs may be allocated elsewhere, and the exaggerated future net revenues of the losing project may be used to "justify" costs already incurred.*

There are also techniques directly aimed at increasing management authority, which are not costly and may be at least marginally
helpful.[58] One technique is to get well-known businessmen to be on
the board of directors who are too busy and too friendly truly to
scrutinize the way the company is run (although this technique has
become more difficult because of increasing fear of director's liability). Maintenance of good personal relations with financial analysts
and with columnists who write on financial matters is also valuable.[59]

3.3 *The Firm as a Nexus of Contracts—a Comparison*

Before proceeding to the next step, financial intermediaries, it is
useful to digress briefly to compare the foregoing description of top
management decision making with a different, more traditional approach to the question of managerial behavior where some or most
of the shares of the corporation are held by persons other than management. Developed over the last ten years, this approach has been
variously labeled the "contractual," "agency," and "property rights"
theory of corporations.[60] The approach views the corporation "as a
nexus for a set of contracting relationships among individuals" who
supply the various factors of production such as labor, capital, and
managerial skills.[61] If these contracts could be costlessly written to

---

*A public refusal to admit past mistakes by discontinuing a project may be rein-
forced by the easy self-deception on the part of the top management which accompanies an attitude of denying mistakes to the public. An example of this dual problem
may have been General Dynamic's decision to continue the Convair 880 project despite indications that it was going to be a financial disaster of ever-growing proportions.

cover all contingencies and costlessly enforced, the behavior of these individuals, including managers, would be as predicted in the neoclassical model. Adherents of the approach realize, however, that such an assumption is unrealistic. Instead the system incurs certain "agency costs" that are not present in the neoclassical model. These include the expenditure of resources for writing, monitoring, and enforcing the contracts; expenditures of resources by the promisor (the agent) to give the promisee (the principal) a degree of assurance that the promisor will not deviate from his promised performance ("bonding costs"); and the "residual loss" to the promisee resulting from the remaining deviation in the behavior of the promisor from what it would be if the assumption of costless contracting were correct (i.e., the deviation from what would be predicted by the neoclassical model).[62]

In its analysis of management behavior, the contractual approach has some things in common both with the managerial theories of firm and with the preceding discussion. Its adherents acknowledge that because management does not feel the full effects of its actions and shareholders are not fully informed, management will not act to maximize share value. And for the portion of firms that dominate the industrial sector, where share ownership and control are separate, at least one adherent, Fama, recognizes that "Manne's approach, in which control of management relies primarily on the expensive mechanism of an outside takeover, offers little comfort [to those concerned with the incentive problems caused by such separation]."[63] Unlike the preceding discussion, however, the contractual approach, at least in the way it has been applied to issues of public policy, exhibits a general prejudice that, beyond enforcement of a literal interpretation of the terms of these contracts, efficiency is harmed by legal intervention in the relations among their parties. According to the approach, the system will work to minimize total agency costs. Pareto optimality does not require that these costs be eliminated, only minimized, since some agency costs are the inevitable result of utilizing the advantages of having separate persons specialize in risk bearing (shareholders) and in management.[64] The faith that agency costs will be minimized arises from an analysis of a number of forces that supplement the hostile takeover threat as constraints on managerial behavior. A quick review of these forces suggests the case that agency costs are minimized is unconvincing, at least with respect to the kinds of deviations that were the focus of the preceding discussion: retention of earnings for inferior investments and a pattern of disclosure that makes such behavior difficult to discover.* That discussion suggested that such deviations are committed by the managements of a significant portion of the type of firms that dominate the industrial sector—large firms where share ownership and control are separate.

a. *Articles of incorporation.* Jensen and Meckling proposed that when the entrepreneur who established a corporation sells shares to outsiders, he has an incentive to include provisions in his contract with them (the articles of incorporation) which, to the extent cost effective, constrain his ability to deviate from share value maximization. This proposition rests on their demonstration of two points. First, the entrepreneur's utility gain from any deviation, whatever its extent, is not as great as what his utility loss would be if his wealth position were diminished by the full amount that the deviation decreases the value of the firm. Second, at the time of the sale of shares to outsiders, the entrepreneur's wealth position will in fact diminish by the full amount of the decline in firm value that would result from the extent of deviation that would be expected given the terms of the contract. This is because potential shareholders have rational expectations and discount fully for such an expected deviation when they determine what they are willing to pay for the shares.[65]

Jensen and Meckling's model is of an entrepreneurial firm where management continues to hold a significant portion of the shares of the firm. Although their conclusions have been used indiscriminately by some commentators to make policy recommendations relating to corporations of the type covered by the preceding discussion as well as to entrepreneurial firms,[66] Jensen and Meckling concede that they have not worked out the application of their analysis "to the very large modern corporation whose managers own little or no equity."[67] Fama states that the Jensen and Meckling model is "not

---

*These two deviations are, it will be remembered, undertaken to further the instrumental goal of maximizing AACF. Maximizing AACF serves the personal goals of management both directly (by increasing top management prestige, power, and, through increasing promotion opportunities, the affection of those below them) and indirectly (by permitting greater salaries and perquisites before the point is reached where detection is easy and a hostile takeover becomes a serious risk).

likely to allay the fears of those concerned with the apparent incentive problems" of the management of such firms.[68]

Most of the corporations that dominate the industrial sector issued the bulk of their publicly held stock between 50 and 100 years ago and have financed their enormous expansion predominantly through retained earnings and debt. It is not believable that the provisions of their articles of incorporation, whatever their agency-cost-minimizing attributes at the time the corporations went public, represent the agency-cost-minimizing way of controlling managerial behavior today. It is not really possible to draft long-term contracts of this type with terms that continue to be effective in the face of such changing circumstances. The company is a very different company operating in a very different world in terms of general financial understanding, business culture, regulation, taxes, and the size and efficiency of the outside sector of the finance process. The provisions of the contract at the time the corporation went public are unlikely to be the provisions that would result if management had to renegotiate them today in order to retain its equity. The articles of incorporation have probably been amended from time to time since the stock was issued but not as a result of pressures that would reshape them into the document that would come out of such a total renegotiation.

b. *Discipline of the external managerial labor market.* Fama believes that for corporations where share ownership is separate from management, the primary disciplining of managers comes through managerial labor markets.[69] In his formal model, Fama lumps together the external market and what he calls the "internal market" and assumes that the manager's next period wage would be the same in each.[70] This wage is determined by the expected value of his marginal product for the period, an arrangement that will be optimal for risk-neutral shareholders and, assuming long-term contracts are not available, for the manager as well (even if they are risk averse). This expected value is an unbiased estimate of what his marginal product will at the end of the period be measured to have been. The noise—the difference between the expected and measured product—results from errors in measuring the manager's contribution to team production, the genuinely uncertain consequences of a given amount of effort by the manager, and stochastic changes in the manager's skills and tastes for leisure and perquisites. Since the wage is set in advance, the noise is absorbed by the shareholders. However, in the manner of Muth's rational expectation hypothesis, the expected value of the manager's marginal product, and hence his wage, for each period in the future, is revised on the basis of the difference between the current period's expected marginal product and what the marginal product is measured to be at the end of the period. If the manager stays in the market an infinite number of periods, the aggregate effect of these wage revisions will exactly equal his current period deviation. If the interest rate is zero, this wage revision process will represent a full *ex post* settling up for any deviations from the contributions to share value that were expected of him when he entered into the contract. If he stays in the market less than an infinite number of periods but the noise is not sufficiently large (compared with shifts in his expected marginal product owing to stochastic changes in skills and tastes for leisure and perquisites), "the manager's current marginal product is 'very nearly' fully absorbed by the stream of wages over his future working life."[71] If a manager of a corporation where share ownership and control are separate has to pay very nearly fully for his deviations, he is essentially no different from an owner manager and the agency cost problem disappears.

The Fama model formalizes the important insight that a manager cannot be oblivious to his future wages when he considers how to behave on the job in the current period. Even assuming, however, that the wage-setting process internally and externally is as described, differences between the model's other assumptions and reality cast doubt on the labor market's effectiveness as a control mechanism. Top managers are usually no more than ten or fifteen years from retirement, and they often have multiple-year contracts. Stochastic shifts in skills and tastes at this point in their careers are probably small compared both with measurement errors of their marginal product, particularly by the poorly informed external labor market, and with uncertainties in each contract period as to what a given level of skill and effort by the manager will produce. Thus, the number of periods is small and the relative amount of noise is large. Furthermore, the interest rate is greater than zero. And since the noise will have a systematic element because of the effect of economy-wide factors on managerial marginal products, shareholders will not be risk neutral.

Equally important, the description of the wage-setting process seems wrong. Consider first the internal process and ignore for a moment any effect of the external labor market. Management is a team. Under some circumstances, as suggested in the preceding discussion, the interests of the team deviate from those of shareholders. In the process by which management as a team sets the salaries of its individual members, rewards will be given out for behavior that serves team interests whether or not it also serves shareholder interests. Any gains that the team achieves as a result of deviations from shareholder interests will be distributed among members of the team in some sort of political fashion.

What does the existence of an external labor market do to the analysis? One pressure, according to Fama, is the continuing need for the firm to hire new managers. Potential recruits will be interested in the responsiveness of the firm wages to managerial performance. But there seems no reason why a potential recruit would shy away from joining a team that rewards managers according to their contribution to the team's interests rather than to the interests of shareholders. Another pressure from the external market is the threat that the best team members will leave unless their performance is properly rewarded. For this to be a significant pressure, Fama's assumption that the internal and external wage will be equal is essential. This generally is not the case, since managers tend over time to develop firm-specific assets—the ability to get things done within the organization in which they have worked for many years—and their value to the firm and thus internal wage is augmented by the presence of this asset. Also, after a number of years of employment, a manager may, through seniority-based increases, receive an internal wage that exceeds his marginal product. The logic of such a wage structure is that it represents a way for the firm and the manager to share the costs and returns of on-the-job training. The manager's wage in the early years is reduced below his marginal product to pay for some of his training costs in early years, even though the training represents an investment by the firm, and he receives some of the firm's returns on this training in later years.[72] Also, job change involves considerable disruption and uncertainty for the manager who undertakes it. Empirically, most managers by the time they reach the top level are not a very mobile group.[73]

In any case, to the extent executive defection does put pressures on the internal wage-setting process and hence behavior, it is not clear that the pressures force behavior that favors shareholder over team interests. Most of the hirers in the external market are also teams whose interests under some circumstances deviate from those of their shareholders. Whether or not they are engaging in such deviations at the moment, such hirers would not penalize potential hirees if the hirees behave in their existing jobs in ways that deviate from shareholder best interests in the ways discussed. Fama does suggest one factor that might influence the external wage-setting process to reward behavior that favors shareholder over team interests: the share price of the potential hiree's current firm will be used as an indicator of what his marginal product would be working for the hirer.[74] The market for managers would piggyback on the information-processing capabilities of the stock market. Because of differences in the degree of individual responsibility for group performance, stock price performance would presumably be most influential in the case of a potential hiree who is a chief executive and least influential in the case of the lowest members of top management. Counterbalancing this, however, is the fact that in the political process that distributes to individual managers the gains to the team from deviations, the highest executives would get the biggest share.

c. *Internal monitoring and the board of directors.* Fama also suggests that internal monitoring by managers of those below them, lateral to them, and above them will, through its influence on the wage-setting process, reduce deviations from share value maximizing behavior.[75] While it is very believable that managers make very well-informed monitors of each other and that this can work laterally and above, not just below, there still remains the question of the criteria by which performance is judged. Again, where there is a conflict between the interests of management as a team and those of shareholders, the criteria will be to reward behavior that serves team interests. The only counter to this is the argument that the firm's share price affects the individual manager's external opportunity wage and that concern with his external wage influences the criteria by which he judges the performance of other team members. We have just seen that both links in the chain of this argument are weak.

Fama and Jensen develop a much more sophisticated model of how internal monitoring can relieve the problems of separation of share ownership and control. They suggest that in complex organizations such as large corporations, specific information (i.e., information knowledge of which is difficult to transfer across agents) is diffused among agents at all levels of the organization. Diffusion of information makes diffusion of "decision management" (initiation and implementation of decisions) economical. To reduce the agency cost associated with such management decision diffusion, "decision control" (ratification and monitoring) is separated from decision management.[76] In large corporations where shareholders are also diffused, there is commonly "nearly complete separation and specialization of decision control and residual risk bearing."[77] Fama and Jensen conclude that "separation and diffusion of decision management and decision control—in effect, the absence of a classical entrepreneurial decisionmaker—limits the power of individual decision agents to expropriate the interests of the residual claimants [the shareholders]."[78] The use of the word "individual" is important. It is not clear how separation of decision control and decision management in corporations where share ownership is diffuse stops expropriation that serves the interests of management as a group. The only thing that they point to is the outside members of the board of directors. While suggesting that the board's most influential members are appropriately insiders and that outsiders are appropriately nominated by insiders,* they nevertheless believe that outside directors "can carry out tasks that involve serious agency problems between internal managers and residual claimants."[80] The outside directors have sufficient incentives not to "collude with managers and expropriate residual claimants" because the value of their human capital, which is important to them in other employment, depends on their reputations as experts in decision control.[81] Such capital is supposed to suffer substantial devaluation when a hostile takeover

---

*These principles of board composition are derived from the proposition that "since the takeover market provides an external court of last resort for protection of residual claimants, a corporate board can be in the hands of agents who are decision experts."[79] Internal managers should be on the board because they have much specific information about the firm. They should also nominate the outsiders because they know the kinds of complementary knowledge that would be useful for the outsiders to possess.

occurs, thereby signaling that the outsiders failed and internal control broke down. Thus the analysis oddly comes back again to the efficacy of the market for corporate control.

Given that the market for corporate control grants management a wide band of discretion, a point established in chapter 1 and seemingly conceded by Fama in his article focusing on the managerial labor market, it is implausible that the consequences of a takeover to an external director are going to be so dire that, out of fear of one, he will constrain management to operate significantly further inside that band than it otherwise would.* Even if there exist potential outside directors who are predisposed to play the aggressive role Fama and Jensen foresee, why would internal managers wish to nominate such individuals in preference to more docile candidates? Fama suggests that the presence of such directors is agency cost decreasing because it reduces the need for resort to the high-cost hostile takeover.[82] But other than the slow-acting forces of evolution, discussed below, there seems no reason why the managers of established large corporations would wish to reduce agency costs in such a fashion. Most empirical studies of board behavior are also at odds with the Fama and Jensen hypothesis. They suggest that while minority outside directors appointed by, and serving on a board dominated by, insiders may be some help in uncovering specific acts of managerial wrongdoing or blatant overreaching, they are not an effective check on management discretion in such fundamental policy areas as investment and disclosure.[83]

d. *Survival*. The respective articles by Fama and by Fama and Jensen discussed above each state that its purpose is to explain the survival of the modern corporation with diffuse security ownership. The underlying assumption is that the survival of these corporations operating as they currently do shows that they represent an efficient organization form. Citing Alchian's survival theory of the firm, Fama and Jensen begin their joint article with the statement "Absent fiat, the form of organization that survives in an activity is the one that

*Firms operating inside this band may sometimes become targets of hostile takeovers either because the market for corporate control, in seeking out poorly managed firms, has a stochastic element to it or because hostile takeovers are motivated by factors other than poor target management. But the more probable are takeovers of firms within this band, the less of a signal they are that the outside directors have failed.

delivers the product demanded by customers at the lowest price while covering cost."[84] Competition, Fama states, "forces evolution of devices for effficiently monitoring the performance of the entire team [the factors tied together by a set of contracts that make up the firm] and of its individual members."[85]

The problems with the survival theory have already been discussed in chapter 1 (section C 2.1). It was demonstrated there that, if shareholders tolerate the situation, a firm can, to the extent that it is financed by equity rather than debt, reduce its earnings below the level which would be a normal return on capital (i.e., earn negative profits using the economist's definition of the term) and continue to operate indefinitely. It is necessary only that the firm earns enough gross income after debt service to purchase the replacement of depreciated assets (i.e., earn at least zero profits according to the businessman's definition of the term). In other words, product competition will not eliminate to a significant degree inefficiency in organizational form and practices. The problem is not cost of production but continuing expropriation of shareholders. Hostile takeover, despite the latitude it gives management, is likely to be more effective at combating such inefficiency than the forces relied on by the survival theory, i.e., product competition and bankruptcy.

As suggested in chapter 1 (section D), evolutionary theories become much more useful when they are made dynamic. Clearly, in an economy dominated by established firms that rely primarily on internal finance, firms that have inferior project lists relative to their cash flows and that retain their cash flows to invest in projects with expected returns below SROR grow more slowly than firms that have relatively superior project lists and that, using either internal or external funds, only invest in projects with expected rates of return of SROR or greater. This is because the higher-earning investments will generate more funds for future investments. Ironically, however, any firms with relatively inferior project lists that, contrary to the predictions of the preceding discussion, choose to return cash flow to shareholders rather than invest in below-SROR projects grow more slowly than either of the other two classes of firms or even shrink and disappear. Thus, among firms with relatively inferior project lists, behavior that maximizes share value is maladaptive. Notwithstanding this perverse feature of the system, if we look at all the established firms in the economy and assume that each will maintain the same status in terms of the quality of its project list relative to its cash flow, the percentage of investment undertaken by established firms which do not implement below-SROR projects will grow over the long run. And new firms, at least when they start, also will not engage in below-SROR investments. But even the conclusion that the system will gradually evolve toward one dominated by firms investing only in SROR and above projects needs to be qualified because the assumption that each firm will maintain its status may be incorrect. There are both theoretical and empirical reasons to believe that on average the capacity of firms to come up with good ideas declines with age.

The point of this discussion concerning survival is that the mere fact that the industrial sector is dominated by large established firms that rely primarily on internal finance and that face no significant legal restrictions on their dividend and investment policies does not prove that such an arrangement is optimal. As just noted, forces exist to increase the role of firms with efficient operating rules. If these were allowed to operate unimpeded for long enough without exogenous changes, the system would approach some kind of optimal equilibrium. But the current structure is not necessarily near that equilibrium. It is more likely the cumulation of reactions to a rapid series of momentous technological and social changes that have occurred over the last 100 years. The forces for efficiency are slow moving, and there are cross-currents opposing them (see section C 2.5). Empirical and theoretical analysis may suggest changes in the legal structure in which firms operate that would increase the level of the economy's industrial performance to a level that would, if ever, only be reached after a much longer time period without such legal changes.

4. Financial Intermediaries and Investment Informers

The next layer in the network of information and decision delegation that runs from savers to project proponents and managers is occupied by financial intermediaries and investment informers. Financial intermediaries include investment banks, mutual funds, venture capital firms, commercial banks, insurance companies, and pension and other trust funds. Investment informers include consultants, financial news sources, and brokers who tie giving advice with the sale of transaction services. The bulk of the discussion concerning this layer of the network is devoted to financial intermediaries because imperfections in the market for information make them of greater importance to this study than investment informers.

Looked at sufficiently abstractly, financial intermediaries might appear redundant to an economy dominated by corporations divisionalized along product lines. The principals of financial intermediaries appear to make the same kind of decisions, one level higher, that top corporate managers of divisionalized corporations do: funding new investment opportunities which they will not directly manage, participating in command decisions to change the management of existing investments that the entity currently owns, buying existing investments from others with the goal of changing their managements, and speculation (buying and selling existing investments not because of a plan to change their management, but because of a different view of their future prospects under existing management from the view of the other party to the transaction). One can imagine a world in which the decisions currently made by financial intermediaries would be made within superconglomerates which would face savers directly. But this is not the way the economy has developed: in 1980 financial intermediaries held 36 percent measured by market value, of the domestically held equity of United States nonfinancial corporations,[86] and projections suggest their share will continue to grow.[87] Given the dominant role of insurance companies, pension funds, and banks in debt financing, the share of the debt of nonfinancial corporations held by financial intermediaries must be even greater. The discussion which follows suggests that the reason for the importance of financial intermediaries is that they have a role to play which cannot be performed by the nonfinancial firm.

The distinguishing characteristic of a financial intermediary is that its long-term investments in firms are not of the size and nature that would give it control.[88] The financial intermediary is thus largely limited to two specialties: providing funds for new investment opportunities offered by new and existing firms (an indispensable function, since firms almost never receive new funds from savers directly) and speculating in existing investments. The role of the financial intermediary in control reassignment is at most indirect (except for "special situation" investment companies, which, with the aim of short-term gain, buy a control block of a relatively small firm's shares in order to improve management and then resell the shares at a higher price).[89]

The persons who make a financial intermediary's important decisions, its "principals," are assumed to be personally interested in the same values as a top corporate manager. Again, their decisions will reflect what they perceive will best further these values subject to the constraints within which they operate. To explain the behavior of financial intermediaries we must, as in the study of top corporate management, examine both the information on which they base their perceptions and the structure of incentives in which they operate.

4.1 *Information Processing by Financial Intermediaries*

The key determinations which the principals of an intermediary must make are the prospects of the various investment opportunities available to the intermediary. The more accurately they do so, the better the chances are that the investment decisions which they make will turn out to be in their own best interests.[90]

In order to determine the prospects of a particular investment opportunity, the principals of an intermediary cause their organization to gather both publicly available and private information. As previously discussed (section B 1.1), the nature of information as a commodity means that there are significant economies of scale both in gathering information and in providing services based on it. So the intermediary will gather far more publicly available information in making a determination than the typical saver would do if he were making the same determination himself without an adviser. And the intermediary will have more time, resources, and experience than the typical saver to devote to analyzing the publicly available information it gathers. An intermediary also gathers information not available to the typical saver through special relationships which it develops with existing firms. The intermediary may insist on disclosure of such information before extending financing to a firm, and the firm may agree only on the condition that it be kept confidential. Confidential information may also be received as a result of a more long-term arrangement: a flow of special bits of information in return for easier access to credit at some time in the future.[91] Such an arrangement may be institutionalized in the form of representatives of the intermediary serving on the firm's board of directors.

A financial intermediary faces two kinds of applicants for new funds: a proponent of a project that is to become the basis of a new firm and the top management of an existing firm.* As we have seen, the intermediary's advantages over the typical saver derive from the intermediary's greater ability to gather and analyze public information and, in the case of existing firms, access to confidential information. But, given the range of opportunities an intermediary must survey, it cannot as a matter of economic practicality possess all of the knowledge of the proponent or top management. The challenge to the financial intermediary is, for any given level of expenditure on gathering and processing information, to produce the best predictions it can as to the prospects of the opportunities before it.

Earlier in this chapter, we considered the problem of the proponent seeking to persuade a financial intermediary to provide funds for a new project which is to be the basis of a new firm. It will be remembered that because of the divergence in knowledge between the intermediary and the proponent, the proponent must have authority in the eyes of the intermediary if the investment opportunity that the proponent is offering is not to be regarded as hopelessly risky (see section B 2.124). Such a proponent is unlikely to have authority stemming from the intermediary's past experience with him, but he may have authority based on his reputation in the industry, his scientific credentials, and his own investment in the project.† What needs to be added is that the problem of a proponent's authority is not just one for the proponent. If the intermediary is going to have a chance at funding what objectively are the projects with the best prospects, it must be sensitive to the features and actions of the proponent that should create authority in the intermediary's eyes. A venture capital firm, for example, often includes within its

---

*Where an existing firm seeks funds for a project which would constitute a substantial portion of its total assets, its management will be treated in this discussion as akin to a proponent proposing to set up a new firm.

†The study of the semiconductor industry shows that financial intermediaries are at least as concerned with the personal characteristics of a project's proponent as with the ideas on which the project is based. There is evidence that this is true with respect to projects in other high technology areas as well.[92]

ranks persons who were formerly executives or high-level engineers in the industries in which they consider investing. These persons not only have technical skills, but they also can give the intermediary guidance concerning the reputation of a proponent within his industry. In the case of most industries, however, there are only a limited number of intermediaries that have a high level of such sensitivity. Thus, unlike in the neoclassical world, a proponent's investment idea is often of interest to only a limited number of reviewers.[93]

The situation where an established firm seeks funds from an intermediary is significantly different. The return on the investment opportunity being offered the intermediary will be based on the performance of the firm as a whole, not just on the project for which it is seeking funds. The information divergence between an intermediary and the management of an established firm offering an opportunity is even greater than between an intermediary and a proponent starting a new firm. In directing the operations of the firm, the management automatically acquires, with respect to a possibly diverse set of existing projects, large amounts of information concerning markets, technology, and the firm's own organizational capabilities. Management's authority in the eyes of the intermediary is thus potentially even more important than in the case of a proponent starting a new firm.*

The position of the management of an established firm seeking funds from an intermediary is similar in many respects to that of a proponent trying to persuade an established firm of which he is an employee to implement a project. The management must rely predominantly on the authority it builds up in the eyes of the intermediary based on prior dealings and general reputation rather than on the structure of incentives. Because an established firm is likely to

---

*Since the past performance of existing projects gives some guidance as to future performance of the firm, investment opportunities offered by established firms have less "residual risk" (risk that would remain if the divergence in information between funding source and proponent were eliminated) than those offered by a new firm. But that divergence does exist. Thus, authority is important in that there is still the need to determine how a particular opportunity offered by one established firm compares both with opportunities offered by other such firms and with opportunities offered by new firms (adding whatever premium, if any, is necessary to compensate for their greater residual risk).

be much larger than a new firm and infusions of outside financing may be required repeatedly, it is less likely that each time the firm seeks outside financing the top managers can make enough of an investment to demonstrate the sincerity of their predictions by absorbing part of the losses if they are wrong.*

Again, the problem of the management's authority is one for the intermediary as well as for management. This leads the intermediary to want to develop special relationships with the managements of a certain number of established firms in order to permit experience-based authority to develop more fully. A manifestation of these relationships is the channels of confidential information from firms to intermediaries alluded to above. Typically, an existing firm will have well-developed experience-based authority relationships with only a few intermediaries.[95] While this will not bar it from seeking funding from other intermediaries, the terms the others offer are likely to be somewhat less favorable. Thus, any new project idea faces a higher hurdle if it does not meet with the approval of one of the limited

---

*A manager's existing shareholdings may constitute some measure of sincerity as well, but this measure has shortcomings, even in the case of a new equity financing. First, the fact that the manager holds a certain number of shares of his firm only has significance if it reflects a willing choice not to sell his shares at the price at which the new issue of shares is sold. Only then do the holdings show that the valuation he puts on the shares given what he knows at least equals the new issue price. But often the manager does not have a meaningful option of selling his shares at that price. There may be no active market for the shares or the market may be too thin to absorb many of the shares at the new issue price. Even if a market exists which can absorb all his shares at the new issue price, the manager may not wish to sell them because of tax considerations, a requirement to return profits under Section 16(b) of the Securities Exchange Act of 1934, or the need to hold the shares in order to maintain control of the firm. Second, if the investment of the proceeds of the new issue is motivated by the benefits which the manager expects to receive from the investment as a result of his status as a manager even though it harms shareholder welfare, the new issue will dilute his ownership percentage and reduce the negative impact of the investment on him as a result of his status as a shareholder.

A high debt/equity ratio is another instrument available to the management of existing firms to enhance their authority in a structure of incentives fashion. Along the lines of the "signaling theory" of Stephen Ross, one can argue that a high ratio signals that management is confident in its optimistic predictions of firm income because, if they did not believe their predictions, they would be taking a high risk of bankruptcy, which is for them a very undesirable state of affairs.[94] Given the variety of factors that over time cumulate to determine what the debt/equity ratio of a firm is, there is some question as to how strong a signal the ratio is at the point that any given financing from outside sources is sought.

number of reviewers that have a special relationship with the firm. Again, this is a difference from the neoclassical world.*

To the extent that a financial intermediary is guided in its speculation in existing investments by looking for discrepancies between a security's "fundamental value" and its price, the intermediary will be seeking the same kind of information as it does when seeking opportunities to extend new funding. Because of the preference of firm top managers for avoiding disclosure, the intermediary is not likely to obtain as much confidential information from a firm the securities of which it only speculates in as from one to which it regularly provides new funding. However, up to a point, the interest of management in share price may outweigh the value to it of avoiding disclosure. It is widely believed that a firm's share price is enhanced by having a "following" of analysts who take an interest in the shares and that a certain amount of disclosure is necessary to attract and retain such a following.[96]

4.2 *The Incentive Structure for Financial Intermediary Principals*

Financial intermediaries are a varied group. Analysis suggests, however, that the structures of incentives within which their respective principals operate are such that all intermediaries behave in the same general fashion. Assuming the principals of an intermediary are properly regulated to prevent their other business and financial interests from corrupting the decisions they make on behalf of the intermediary, the intermediary can be expected to try to find the best possible investment opportunities of the types in which it deals and not to invest funds in ones which have expected returns less than SROR. To see why the investment behavior of intermediaries differs from what has been suggested is the investment behavior of firms, I will first look at the incentives of the principals in a stylized

---

*This is not meant to suggest that there is not considerable competition to supply an established firm with funds or that such a firm would only on the rarest occasions give business to a source outside of the small group that knows it best. Sources outside this group are always glad to develop new relationships and may even sometimes offer a little "loss leader" incentive to do so. The firm would be foolish to spurn all such advances because it must guard against its traditional sources attempting to exploit a monopoly or oligopoly position. Nevertheless, the traditional sources do perceive the cost of lending to the firm to be lower than the outsider does, and this cost difference should generally result in a price difference that leads to repeat business.

model of an open-end investment company. Then, by taking this model as a starting point and adding a degree of institutional detail, the incentive structures of the principals of each of the major types of financial intermediaries will be explored.

4.21 *A Model of an Open-End Investment Company*

An open-end investment company, commonly known as a mutual fund, is a corporation which permits a shareholder to redeem his shares at any time for an amount equal to his pro-rata share of the value of the assets of the fund at that time. Each time a shareholder avails himself of this right, the company is partially liquidated. In addition, all interest and dividends are typically passed on to investors, and so the principals cannot increase the company's equity by retaining earnings.[97] The easiest way to depict the redemption and no retained earnings features of a mutual fund is to treat the fund as if at the end of each period it liquidates all of its investments and returns the proceeds to its shareholders and starts afresh at the beginning of the next period raising all the funds which it will invest during that period.

A mutual fund is initially organized by an investment management company (an existing investment bank or broker or a new company) which then enters into an investment advisory contract with the fund to make the fund's investment decisions. The managers of the management company are thus the fund's principals. The contract typically provides that the management company be given a fee each period which is equal to a stated percentage of assets under management at the beginning of the period and thus not related to the success of investments made during the period. The net revenues of the management company are these fees less the costs of gathering and analyzing information in order to find good opportunities.* The goal of the fund's principals is to maximize

---

*Typically, the management company also underwrites the shares of the fund. This formulation of net income assumes that any "sales load" (a one-time amount paid to the management company at the time a share is purchased) associated with the fund is roughly equal to the sales expenses which the management company incurs. In the 1950s and 1960s many funds had load fees as great as 8% and engaged in massive sales efforts. This gave the impression that the way to make money managing a mutual fund was to be good at selling the fund's shares, not at finding promising investment opportunities. Today most funds have no load fee, and casual empiricism suggests that there has been an accompanying decline in selling efforts.

the management company's net revenues over the long run, all or a significant portion of which they typically keep.

Let Q be the amount of assets under management (the number of dollars the fund receives from the sale of its shares at the beginning of the period), F be the management fee per dollar of assets under management, and I be the total cost of information gathering and analysis expended to find opportunities in which to invest the amount of funds received from savers. The management company's net revenues will equal $QF - I$. For convenience, assume that the risk characteristics of the fund's portfolio are given. For any given F, one technique for increasing Q and hence net revenues for the period is to persuade savers to expect that the fund's portfolio will have a rate of return greater than the rate that the principal expects. But such a technique would be harmful over the long run because it would deprive the principal of authority. A better long-run strategy is to announce the return that the principal honestly expects given the investment opportunities he thinks he can find. A management company without a track record starting a new fund will be viewed by savers with suspicion because of the fear that the fund is claiming a higher expected return on its portfolio than it really expects. Their subjective evaluation of what the return will be will consist of the claimed return adjusted to reflect this fear. But if the management company follows the strategy suggested here, its announcements of the return it expects on its portfolio will become increasingly credible over time, and the subjective evaluation of what the return will be will come closer and closer to the claimed rate. The management company will be able to charge a higher management fee or attract more savings than another management company with a comparable ability to find investment opportunities but with less authority.

This discussion suggests that the management company should try to maximize its net revenues in each period, subject to the constraint that the rate of return it expects from investing the amount of savings it attracts equals R, the announced expected rate of return. For a given level of authority and a given ability to use resources effectively to find good investment opportunities (neither of which the company has control over within any one time period), the problem each period is determining the optimal level of savings to attract (the "quantity" of service to provide), which in turn is a problem of the level at which to set F (the "price" it charges for its services).

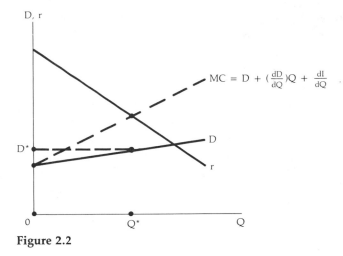

$$MC = D + (\tfrac{dD}{dQ})Q + \tfrac{dI}{dQ}$$

Figure 2.2

Analytically, this problem can be treated with the aid of figure 2.2 as follows. Each share is sold for a dollar and that money is invested. The number of shares demanded, Q, is a function of the announced expected net dividend. D = R − F (which, because of the constraint of honest projections, equals the dividend the fund expects to pay out).* DQ is the total amount the firm must pay out to shareholders if it sells Q shares and in fact earns an average of R on its investments. I, the information-gathering and analysis cost to find investment opportunities for the fund, is also a function of Q. The curve relating D + (dD/dQ)Q + dI/dQ to Q is the marginal cost curve. Gross revenue is the return on the investments which the firm makes. And r, a function of Q, is the expected return on investment of the Qth dollar. The marginal expected revenue curve is thus just the curve relating r to Q.† Q* is the number of shares at which MR = MC. Expected net revenues are maximized at Q*. D* is the expected div-

---

*Demand is not infinitely elastic because, even if the company has a diversified portfolio of securities, the typical saver will want to diversify among investment companies so as to avoid the risks associated with relying too heavily on the skills of any one such company. To be willing to place more funds with the company, the saver will need to be compensated for the resulting risks of a reduction in diversification of skills (see chapter 1, section C 2.211).

†The element dI/dQ is treated as part of the marginal cost curve so as not to stray too far from the traditional method of presenting the problem of firm profit maximization; dI/dQ is the additional expenditure for information gathering and analysis necessary to find an investment opportunity for the Qth dollar that has an expected return of r. It might be more appropriate, however, not to treat dI/dQ as part of the marginal revenue curve but rather to have an adjusted marginal revenue curve equal to

idend corresponding thereto. The company calculates its expected average return on investment (the area under the marginal revenue curve from O to Q* divided by Q*) and announces that number as R. F, the management fee, should be set to equal $R - D*$.

This analysis suggests that the principals of the fund have two incentives in order to maximize net revenues over the long run. One is to find the best investment opportunities for any given cost of search, thereby moving the marginal revenue curve up. The other is to increase authority by being consistently honest in its projection of D, thereby moving the demand curve for shares (the curve relating Q to D) to the right.

4.22 *Application of the Model*

There are a variety of types of financial intermediaries, the respective holdings of which are set out in table 2.1. Considering the complex of contractual and regulatory constraints within which each type acts, and the conflicts among the customers or beneficiaries of each, developing a thorough understanding of their impact on the functioning of the finance process would be a very extensive project. Nevertheless, this simple model is a useful starting point for looking at the most general features of the structure of incentives for principals of each major type of intermediary.

Mutual funds. A mutual fund does not in fact announce a specific expected rate of return, but it resembles the model sufficiently closely to give it plausibility. Through the fund's communication with investment informers and promotional messages aimed at savers, which are usually interpretations of past performance, the prospective shareholder does develop a perception of the risk and return the fund is suggesting he should expect. Differences in the demand for the shares of one fund compared with that for another are a result of these perceptions. One legitimate concern with the model is whether the principals of a fund will be concerned with maximizing long-run net revenues through creation and maintenance of reputation when it takes so long to establish whether good or bad perfor-

---

$r(Q) - dI/dQ$. As Q increases, the company has a choice of spending more and more to find additional high-quality opportunities or facing declining expected returns on its investment opportunities. Either way, marginal revenue would decline as Q increased.

Table 2.1 Market Value of Stockholdings of Institutional Investors and Others in 1980

Type of Holder	Billions of Dollars, End of Year	Percentage of Domestically Held Stock Outstanding
1. Private Noninsured Pension Funds	175.8	12
2. Open-End Investment Companies	44.5	3
3. Other Investment Companies	2.3	—
4. Life Insurance Companies	52.9	4
5. Property Liability Insurance Companies	32.3	2
6. Personal Trust Funds	132.9	9
7. Mutual Saving Banks	4.2	—
8. State and Local Retirement Funds	44.3	3
9. Foundations	32.9	2
10. Educational Endowments	10.4	2
11. Subtotal	532.5	37
12. Less: Institutional Holdings of Investment Company Shares	12.6	1
13. Total Institutional Investors	519.9	36
14. Other Domestic Investors	938.9	64
15. Total Domestically Held Stock Outstanding	1458.8	100

Source: Securities Exchange Commission, *Monthly Statistical Bulletin* (August 1981), 40:8.

mance is due to anything but chance. Savers, however, do not need to wait until they can reject at the 95 or 99 percent confidence level the null hypothesis that the relatively good or bad performance of any particular fund is due to chance. The capacity to reject the hypothesis at a much lower level of confidence, which requires fewer years of observation, still serves as a useful guide to investment choice. Thus, while some principals may pursue large short-run profits through fraud or just gimmickry, strong incentives for a long-run strategy of looking for the best investment opportunities and honest communication with prospective shareholders do exist as a way of assuring a consistently high management fee rate or consistently large amounts of assets under management.[98]

Venture capital firms. A closed-end investment company, often referred to as a venture capital firm, is a financial intermediary which, like an ordinary corporation, does not grant its shareholders a right of redemption. Typically, a venture capital firm invests in minority blocks of shares of companies which are not publicly traded. This makes venture capital firms important in the financing of new companies. Investments of this kind are not practical for a mutual fund because of the right of redemption granted its shareholders. To be able to grant such a right, it is necessary that the value of the investment company's assets be unambiguously determinable at any point in time and that these assets can be sold off on a piecemeal basis. Large blocks of shares of nonpublic companies have neither of these characteristics.

As with a mutual fund, a venture capital firm is initially organized by an investment management company that enters into an investment advisory contract with the firm. Again the managers of the management company are the principals of the venture capital firm. And again the management company's compensation is a given percentage of assets under management. It might appear that without the redemption feature, principals of a venture capital firm have the same incentives to overinvest as have the top management of industrial firms. There are significant differences, however. The principals typically own 20 percent or more of the shares of the venture capital firm. The firm usually has a limited life span, for example fifteen years. Many do permit redemption, once a year during the latter portion of the company's life, though at a discount and limited in amount. And often the management company will start one or more additional venture capital firms if the original is proving successful. Its ability to obtain funds for new firms depends on the reputation it develops with the original one.

Commercial banks. In one sense the top management of a large commercial bank and that of a large industrial firm are in very similar positions. Each heads a large organization where ownership is usually separated from control. One might wonder whether a strategy similar to the one set out for the industrial management would be in the best interests of the bank top management as well. But there is an important brake on bank overinvestment. The bulk of the funds lent out by large commercial banks is received from the issuance of certificates of deposit of relatively short duration, not from federally insured savings and checking accounts or from shareholders' equity. This places the commercial bank in a similar situation to the open-end investment company in terms of raising funds. The bank must repeatedly return to the market to raise funds, and its reputation governs how much it can raise at a given interest rate.[99]

Investment banks. An investment bank engages in a variety of activities including trading on its own account, investing in shares of nonpublic companies, underwriting public offerings of securities, and brokering major transactions (private placements of securities and loans and mergers and acquisitions). Since the principals of such an investment bank typically have a claim on a significant portion of its profits, the first two activities can be analyzed in the same fashion as the activities of a closed-end investment company. The remaining two need more comment.

With the exception of certain large utilities, any firm which wishes to raise funds through a public sale of a new issue of securities uses an investment bank as an underwriter. The underwriter purchases the securities as a block for a negotiated price and resells them through a network of dealers to the public. This nearly universal practice results from the fact that the value of the issue of securities is uncertain: the fact that the firm has decided to make the investment may change the income prospects of the company in the eyes of the investors, and the large dollar size of the newly offered obligations means that they cannot be instantaneously absorbed by the market at the maximum possible price (i.e., they are illiquid). Thus the market price of the firm's currently outstanding publicly traded securities, if any, is not a sure guide to what the public will pay for the new issue. The firm is in doubt because it has difficulty guessing what the reaction of the outside members of the finance process will be to its actions. This uncertainty presents a problem for the firm because the firm wants to know what the cost of capital will be before it makes its decision to raise and spend it. Because of the underwriter's specialized knowledge of the market for securities, it can guarantee financing at a certain price and absorb the risk of an uncertain market reaction.

Since the underwriter usually intends to resell all of the securities immediately, its specialty of knowing the market is not really related to our concerns: it does not depend on the information it has gathered and analyzed concerning the issuing firm. But the underwriter also plays additional, less obvious roles, which are related to our concerns. First, as mentioned earlier, the underwriter is in essence a guarantor of the contents of the registration statement (which includes the prospectus distributed to prospective security purchasers). Any material false or misleading statement or omission of which the underwriter is aware, or would have become aware if it had engaged in a "reasonable investigation" of the issuer, can give rise to underwriter liability under Section 11 of the Securities Act of 1933 (see chapter 6, section B 1). The existence of this potential liability creates an incentive for the underwriter to investigate the issuer and insist on disclosures which the issuer, though also liable, might choose not to make. But the incentive goes beyond legal liability because the underwriter connects its reputation with the issue. The purchaser of the security cares very much who is selling it and assumes that an underwriter with a good reputation knows the issuer reasonably well and will not be selling securities which the underwriter believes are more likely to fall than rise in value as the future unfolds.[100] This endorsement is particularly valuable in the case of new issuers, which are not well known in the market. The value to the underwriter of this reputation as an aid in selling securities makes it worth creating and preserving. Thus, it can be expected that an underwriter has an incentive to employ care in choosing which issuers to underwrite and at what prices to sell their securities. These same concerns are present, perhaps to a lesser extent, in an investment bank's brokering activities.

Insurance companies. An insurance company is a financial intermediary as a result of both of the services it provides: risk management and money management. In performing its risk management function, the company needs to accumulate reserves because, although it pools risk by issuing policies to a large number of persons, the occurrence of the contingency which requires payment to one policyholder is often not independent of the occurrence of the contingency which requires payment to one or more others. The return on the investment of these accumulated funds is a way of reducing the cost of providing insurance services. As in the case of the industrial firm, it is in the interests of the top management of an insurance company to operate its business at minimum cost. Thus, it will seek to find in a cost-effective fashion the best investment opportunities in which to invest its reserves. This does not assure that the reserves are as well invested as savings which are given to intermediaries specifically for the purpose of investment. The amount of funds which any particular insurance company accumulates is the result of not just its investment acumen, but of its whole operations, including the costs of the activities directly related to insurance and the effectiveness of its marketing. A firm with a short list of good investment opportunities may have more funds to invest than one with a longer list. But unlike the management of an industrial corporation, which may gain from retaining funds which could be more profitably invested elsewhere, the management of an insurance company, to the extent it appreciates its limitations, will pass funds for reinvestment on to other financial intermediaries with better opportunities.

An insurance company is also a money manager. Whole life insurance is really two products tied together in one package: life insurance and a program of savings accumulation managed by the company. Traditionally the typical purchaser of whole life insurance did not make a careful comparison between buying the two services as a package and buying them separately. To the extent that they are still insensitive to the comparison, then as with reserves, a firm with a short list of good investment opportunities may nevertheless have more funds to invest than one with a longer list. The motivational structure for top management is also the same. Inflation, high interest rates, and increasing financial sophistication among the general public may have made purchasers much more sensitive to the comparison between buying the services separately and together. If they are, then the money management function of an insurance company, because of its redemption features, can be analyzed in the same fashion as that of a mutual fund.

Pension fund. A pension fund for the employees of a company can be administered in a number of different ways. The most common arrangement is for the fund to have an administrator, which is usually the company itself or officials thereof, and an investment adviser, who is hired and can be fired by the administrator. The administrator, to assure avoidance of liability for breach of its fiduciary duties, almost always follows the investment advice of the adviser.* The adviser is compensated on the basis of an agreed percentage of the assets under management. If an administrator is likened to a saver, principals of the adviser can be considered as the principals of the fund. The problem can then be analyzed in the same fashion as the open-end investment company in terms of the volume of dollars entrusted to any particular adviser by one or more funds and the decisions as to how to deploy them.

*Often the assets of a fund will be broken up into several pieces with a different adviser responsible for the management of each piece.

How apt is the analogy of the administrator to a saver? The answer depends to an extent on the type of fund. Pension funds are divided into two categories: defined benefit plans and defined contribution plans. In the first, each employee is promised a defined benefit at retirement, and the employer must make contributions over time to assure that there is money available to make these payments. With such a plan, the administrator is likely to act like a saver; the better invested the early contributions are, the smaller the later contributions need to be to assure funds to make the payments. With a defined contribution plan, the employer contributes a defined amount each year for each employee, and the employee receives at retirement an amount based on how well the investments made by the fund have worked out. The administrator has an economic interest in the contributions being well invested, but it may not be as energetic in pursuing its goal as it would be with a defined benefit plan. The pension benefits are part of the compensation package for employees. The general perception on the employees' part that contributions are being well invested and will yield significant benefits at retirement should reduce the salary expenditures needed to attract and retain a given quality of work force. But one may question whether employees, particularly younger ones, behave like rational economic actors in this regard.

Personal and common trusts. Personal and common trusts are administered by a trustee, which is typically one or a group of individuals or a bank. In some cases, particularly where the trustee is a bank, the trustee will make the investment decisions. Often, however, the bank or individual trustee will instead hire an investment adviser, who will effectively make the decisions since, as with pension funds, the adviser's advice will almost always be followed. Such an adviser is typically compensated on the basis of a given percentage of assets under management. The adviser can be replaced at any time. If the trustee in fact represents the interests of the beneficiaries, the arrangement can again be analyzed in the same fashion as the open-end investment company, with the principals of the adviser analogized to the principals of the investment company. Beyond the minimum standards set by a trustee's fiduciary duties, the extent to which it is likely to act vigorously in the best interests of its beneficiaries depends in large measure on the ease with which it can be replaced. Trusts vary a great deal in the provisions for replacement of a trustee.

4.3 *Investment Informers*

Investment informers—pure consultants, brokers who give advice, and financial news services—do not require extensive comment. Investment informers have two roles. One is in competition with financial intermediaries: to identify for savers good investment opportunities at the firm level. The other is to identify for savers good financial intermediaries in which to invest their savings. In comparison with financial intermediaries, investment informers, to one extent or another, labor under the difficulties discussed earlier associated with transferring information by means of market sales. Further, an informer is less likely to establish authority because savers make the final choices and consequently no one automatically keeps careful track of the value of the information that the informer gives. Reputation generally comes more from personality, convincing presentation, and image-building advertising.[101] In addition, informers who are brokers are involved in a conflict of interest, since they tie giving advice to providing transaction services. A broker will profit from a saver making frequent purchases and sales of securities whether or not such "in and out" transactions are really in the saver's best interests.

Investment informers do have one distinct advantage in the competition with financial intermediaries: independence from investment decision making. Like top management of the firm, the principals of a financial intermediary are motivated to obtain the most accurate possible evaluations of investment opportunities. But, as with the firm, there is a tendency for information flow within a decision-making organization to be distorted on its way up the hierarchy because at each level the information is used to justify the decisions of the emitter and to please or manipulate the recipient. Although this is a less severe problem in most financial intermediary organizations than in industrial firms, because they are typically smaller and the ultimate consequences of decisions are more easily measured, some such distortion is inevitable in any decision-making organization.[102] And because of the relationships which form between intermediaries and firms, resulting in a quasi-organizational whole, the problems of linking decision making and information emitting together may occur not only within the firm and financial intermediary organizations but also between the two. Investment informers in performing their role as competitors with intermediaries serve to help keep the system honest.

The second role, to advise savers in their choice of financial intermediaries, is one for which there is no substitute. Notwithstanding all the burdens under which they operate, investment informers performing this role make a positive contribution in the operation of the finance process if their advice is anything better than random.

C. Macro Analysis

1. *Overview of the Macro Analysis: The Cybernetic Approach*

Every economy needs a process that, taking account of information and analytic abilities possessed by disparate persons, decides which proposed real investment projects shall receive society's scarce savings and who shall manage existing projects. Looking at our economy's finance process from this highly aggregative point of view, one can see that it is just as much a social decision-making process as the savings and investment decision process of a "centralized" socialist economy consisting of a single large bureaucracy. Because no one individual possesses sufficient information to make all finance process decisions himself, in the socialist system, just as in ours, the decisions must be made by many different individuals, each with his own mandate.[103] The principal difference is that the mandate-defining framework in which participants in the socialist economy operate is a simple hierarchy structured according to the legislature or executive fiat, while the framework in which participants in our economy operate is determined ultimately by all of the savers in the economy through their power to choose where to place their savings and, in the case of equity holders, how to vote their shares.

In the socialist system and in ours the finance process is an organization: a group of persons who communicate to each other in a structured way to produce decisions. Given the millions of savers involved, our finance process cannot be analyzed as a simple hierarchy. But, as the introduction to this chapter illustrates, unlike a world where there is no investment and all decisions concern the production and distribution of goods for current consumption, the finance process cannot be analyzed as a simple market phenomenon either. Although markets are involved, the need for participants to gather information and expert conclusions from others and the heavy use of delegation give the finance process a flavor which has something in common with hierarchial organizations as well. The preceding micro analysis investigated how any particular project choice or control reassignment decision is made by looking at how the various parts of the system operate. The question before us now is how to analyze the workings of the process as a whole.

The reason for this study's interest in the finance process is because of its impact on industrial performance. Implicit in such an interest is a goal for the process: enhancing at reasonable cost the production, output choice, and dynamic efficiency of the economy. The purpose of analyzing the process as a whole is to evaluate how effectively the finance process as currently constituted promotes these goals and what changes, if any, could be made to increase its effectiveness. The primary focus will be on project choice rather than reassignment of control of existing projects, since the micro analysis suggests that project choice is where the system may have serious problems. While the top managements of large, established corporations are motivated to cause project-level managers to make production decisions in a manner consistent with our goals for the finance process, they are not necessarily motivated to make project choice decisions in the same manner.

The project choice function of the finance process is discovery. Which proposed projects most enhance industrial performance are not obvious. We live in a world where technological possibilities and consumer tastes change with each passing time period and are difficult fully to comprehend. The extent, if any, of monopoly profits in each industry is also not immediately apparent. The finance process must ascertain, by gathering information concerning these matters from disparate sources, how promising each proposed project is and rank them accordingly.

Cybernetics is a developing field of study which regards an organization as a communications phenomenon and analyzes its behavior on that basis. Despite the increasing interest by economists in information, the profession has paid relatively little attention to cybernetics.[104] Karl Deutsch has employed cybernetics to develop a very enlightening theory of politics based on communications, and I have found his particular approach very helpful in analyzing the equally diffuse organization that is the subject of this book.[105] Deutsch's basic construct is to conceive of an organization as a "self-modifying communications network" or a "learning net." The focus of inquiry is how well the organization "steers" itself toward the attainment of the goal which has been assigned to it.

The modus operandi of a learning net is "feedback": the monitoring of the results of current action in order to plan future action.* This is necessitated by a lack of perfect information about how the world works and changes. The motive is to reduce the distance between actual performance and the goal.

To see how we would apply this construct to the finance process, consider what we have learned in the micro analysis of a project choice decision. We saw a chain of command. Always involved are a saver at the top and the proponent of the proposed project at the bottom. There may also be a corporate manager and the principal of a financial intermediary between the saver and the proponent. What decision is made depends on the *personal motivations* of each actor involved, the *structure of incentives* within which he works, the *information which he receives* from the level below and from independent sources, *how he processes the information* he receives, and the *information which he emits* to the level above. Personal motivations among actors tend to be similar and predictable. Incentives depend on what is known about the acts of the actor. Thus, *in the end, what decision is ultimately made is determined by how the system handles information.*

The way the system handles information can be characterized as a set of rules. A feedback system measures the efficacy of these rules and indicates when alterations are in order, either because total performance is not adequate or because particular rules have failed. This is how the system "learns." Learning capacity is the ability to make changes in rules easily and sensibly in response to a changing environment.

---

*Describing a system in terms of its feedback mechanism is an alternative to describing it in terms of its equilibrium resting place. The advantage of using feedback as the theoretical construct for analyzing a dynamic system is that, unlike an equilibrium model, feedback helps explain the system's speed and path of adjustment.[106]

Organizational theorists have identified a variety of pathologies that commonly afflict simple hierarchical organizations.[107] Most of these pathologies can be classified as aspects of what we might call "communications rigidity." Communications rigidity is the result of an overemphasis on efficiency of communication rather than the efficiency of the organizational performance as a whole. Efficiency of communication requires the minimum number of bits of information being passed from one participant to another and the minimum amount of original input on the part of each participant (thus, by this definition, an organization which has much routine passing of paper from one participant to another might still be called communications efficient).

There seems to be a natural tendency for an organization to acquire communications rigidity to the extent that there are not forces to prevent it. The system fails to react to changes in environment, including good new ideas, because the organization uses routine communications methods. Such methods employ highly selective authority and interest rules and highly information-digestive symbols. As a result they screen out information concerning changes in the environment or prevent such information from reaching those persons who could most appreciate it.[108] If the system does not have an adequate feedback process, these failures are not recognized and corrected.

The following macro analysis concludes that there is good reason to believe that the finance process in our economy displays such communications rigidity. The system is very communications efficient. It uses a smaller amount of real resources for information gathering, processing, and transmission than alternatively structured systems might use. In an economy that displays little technical or other change, such communications efficiency might be ideal. The savings in real resources devoted to information would not come at an undue cost in terms of other measures of organizational performance. But in an economy such as ours, which displays much technical and other change and has the potential for more, the high level of communications efficiency presents serious problems. The system's feedback process, given the legal and cultural environment in which it now operates, may not work effectively to correct this rigidity. *The issue addressed in reaching these conclusions is not whether or not the institution used for making project choice decisions will be the market* (which is defined here to mean a process involving the interaction of a large number of individuals in nongovernmental settings each pursuing his own private interests). *That is assumed. The issue is whether or not the existing rules within which the market operates, for example with respect to the dividend and disclosure practices of large corporations, best promote industrial performance.*

The method of analysis used to reach the conclusions of the macro analysis has both the kind of mixed positive and normative character and the kind of mixed theoretical and empirical character that typifies much work in economics. It states goals—enhancing at reasonable cost the production, output choice, and dynamic efficiency of the economy—and is oriented at evaluating how effectively the finance process as currently constituted promotes these goals. Because effectiveness at promoting these goals is not directly measurable, the evaluation is in terms of an analysis of structure. First the structure of the system is ascertained. Then the effectiveness of the system at promoting these goals is determined by looking at the decisions that one would expect would be produced by a system with such a structure. This expectation is based on a logical manipulation of plausible assumptions combined with as much empirical verification of particular steps in the reasoning as can be found.*

---

*The study of the role of competition in industrial organization is an example of a body of scholarship in economics which has this kind of mixed positive and normative character. The theoretical backdrop to the discussion is the demonstration that an economy in which factor and final product markets are perfectly competitive will, given certain other assumptions, make pareto optimal decisions. That theory sets up a structural ideal. Decisions made by rational utility or profit-maximizing participants acting within such a structure are shown as a matter of logic to reach this result. No one suggests that we should test empirically whether there is some other structure which would result in decisions such that some persons would be better off and no one worse off than under the ideal. Most industrial organization literature, whether theoretical or empirical, focuses on particular deviations from the structural ideal: how important the deviations are and what, if anything, can be done about them.

Ruth Mack provides an explanation of why so much literature in economics has this character. She makes the point, in her study of organizational decisions under uncertainty, that normative judgments about the quality of particular decisions are almost impossible given the complexity of the world. Most are within a range such that reasonable men could differ as to their wisdom, at least until they have the benefit of hindsight. Rational analysis of decision structure is more likely to come to normative conclusions which command broad-based support.[109]

2. *Evaluation of the Finance Process*

2.1 *The Patterns of Decision*

We have already learned a great deal about where and under what circumstances decisions are made concerning which new projects get funded and who manages existing projects. To start with, consider some of the hard factual data discussed earlier (section B 3):

1. The largest 200 industrial corporations control over half the industrial sector's assets and make over half of the new real investment decisions; the largest 500 control almost three-fourths of the sector's assets. This data suggests that the bulk of real level project choice and control reassignment decisions in our economy are made by the top managements of a few hundred very large corporations. Most of these corporations are management controlled.
2. Most new real investment undertaken by existing firms is financed by internal cash flow rather than outside finance.
3. The typical corporation does not release, and interested persons have no legal right to obtain, much of the information within the corporation's possession concerning its operations.

Thus, most of the real-level decisions of the finance process are made by corporate managers who do not seek much outside finance, who limit the amount of information available about their firms, and who have a certain amount of discretion to make decisions that suit their needs even when the decisions are not in the best interests of shareholders. The picture that emerges is one of a closed system.

The system described is highly communications efficient. Consider the way the bulk of real-level project choice decisions are made. Information concerning any particular proposed or existing project goes from the proponents to just one recipient: top management of the relevant corporation. Because of the opportunity of top management to establish close ongoing relationships with their employees at the operating level, top management can often rely on summary messages from these employees as a basis for making decisions. Relatively little of the information in the hands of top management leaves the firm, in part because management desires to prevent takeovers or other interferences in its autonomy. Management is not interested in emitting any more information to the outside finance process than the pressures on it require. The heavy reliance on inside finance eliminates a significant potential source of such pressure. Pressure is further reduced to the extent that management follows a policy of releasing highly dependable earnings and dividends forecasts.

2.2 *Potential System Failures*

What does this pattern mean? Is it good or bad? Can it be improved upon? These are really questions of how well suited the process is to meeting goals assigned to it. The finance process shares with all other organizations at least four potentials for failure in terms of the way it handles information. In subsequent sections, this typology of potential organizational failures will be used to evaluate the effectiveness of the finance process in meeting our posited goals, first in a hypothetical world of slow change and then in the real world of fast change.

1. *Failure to use the best available evaluations.* A system may be structured such that its decision whether or not to undertake any particular action does not correspond to what is suggested, given the system's goals, by the best evaluation being made in the system concerning the consequences of the action. For an example within the context of the finance process, consider two project-funding proposals, A and B. Information concerning the prospects of A goes to Mr. Y, who by way of background is the person more capable of evaluating its prospects than anyone else receiving the information and who evaluates its expected rate of return as 6 percent. Information concerning Project B goes to Mr. Z, who has the same status with respect to Project B. Mr. Z rates the expected rate of return of Project B at 12 percent. Y and Z evaluate their respective projects as equally risky. Project A is funded and Project B is not. A failure of this type is understandable in terms of static efficiency analysis. The problem is output choice efficiency. Scarce productive resources are not being used to produce an overall mix of product that, given known production functions, best corresponds to the relative preferences of consumers.

2. *Failure to make as good evaluations as possible.* A system may be structured such that information relevant as to whether or not to undertake a particular action fails to reach the persons capable of

making the best evaluation of the consequences of undertaking the action. As an example, consider a proposal to fund Project C, which is evaluated only by Mr. W. Mr. W evaluates the project's expected return and riskiness as sufficiently unattractive to suggest that, given the evaluations of all the other proposed projects in the economy made by those responsible for evaluating them, Project C should not be funded. As a result, Project C is not funded. However, if the proposal had been evaluated by Mr. X, who is better qualified by way of background than Mr. W. to evaluate its prospects, X's assessments of its rate of return and riskiness would have made the proposal sufficiently attractive compared with the evaluations of the other proposals proposed to suggest that the project should receive funding. A failure of this type is better understood in dynamic rather than static efficiency terms. Production functions relating to possible new products and processes are not well understood. Finance is part of the process of discovery. The structure of information flow may be such that this process of discovery does not work as well as it could, thereby retarding technical change.

3. *Failure to account for secondary effects on system goals.* The pattern of information—which evaluators receive information and whose evaluations are heeded—can have secondary effects that run counter to the goals assigned the system. For example, in the case of the finance process, it often happens that several different proponents propose nearly identical projects. The pattern of information processing might work consistently to give a better hearing to a particular proponent's project proposals over projects based on the same good ideas proposed by the others. In such a situation, the favored proponent's proposals might always be funded and the others denied funding. Assuming that an omniscient observer would conclude that the idea behind each funded proposal is worth implementing but that there is only enough demand to require implementation of one of the proposed projects based on the idea, we would conclude that the finance process had in this case avoided the first two types of organizational failure. But the cumulative effect over time of the same proponent each time being the only one to get a good hearing is to increase concentration in the industry in which it operates.

4. *Costs in excess of benefits.* The information-processing system of an organization requires real resources. There will be a point at which

the cost of improving the system's performance exceeds the benefits.

2.3 *Effectiveness of the Finance Process in a Hypothetical World of Slow Change*

A good way to get a sense of how the finance process as currently structured works in our fast-changing world is to start by asking how it would work in a hypothetical slow-changing world and then see what fast change does to our conclusions. The communications efficiency of the system as currently structured means that, as noted earlier, it requires less real resources than alternative structures would require. There is little chance that the system is failing the cost criterion. The key issue is whether these savings are a false economy because the structure's handling of information fails in one or more of the other three possible ways I have identified.

a. *Failure to use best available evaluations.* First, does the system heed the best possible evaluations of proposed projects? Most project proposals considered by the finance process as it is currently structured are generated by employees of large established firms and proposed solely to the top management of their employers. The evaluation of such a project by top management is usually, by default, the best one being made in the system because no one else makes an evaluation. The only other possible persons to evaluate such a project would be one or more outsiders who, though not receiving direct information concerning the proposal, might try to second-guess management. There is a vast difference in information levels between top management and any such outsider, both because management is closer to the proposed project than is the outsider and because it will usually pass on very little information concerning the proposal outside of the firm. Top management's superior level of information normally makes its evaluation more accurate. It knows better than anyone else whether the project is relatively promising.

The micro analysis provides reason for concern that the proposed projects determined most promising according to these evaluations are not the ones that are consistently funded. It suggests that the typical management of such a firm has the ability and inclination to withhold from shareholders, and to reinvest, a large part of the firm's cash flow whether or not that can be justified given the quality of the potential investment projects on the firm's list. But, in a world of slow change, that concern is probably unwarranted. Consider the kind of new project that is likely to be proposed: a replacement of, or an addition to, a similar project already existing in the economy. Changes in demand and factor supplies are gradual. Product or process improvements are minor because that is all the rate of scientific advance permits. A replacement of or extension to a project already existing in the economy is most likely to be proposed by an employee to the top management of the firm holding the existing project. A firm that operates in a market with a gradually increasing demand or which has a superior record of figuring out minor product or process improvements both will have a list of projects which are superior to those of a firm with the opposite characteristics and will be more profitable. Thus, in a world of slow change the distribution of profits anticipates the evaluator's evaluations. The most funds automatically go to the evaluators who are being presented the most promising projects to evaluate.

b. *Failure to make the best evaluations possible.* Second, would the system send information concerning whether or not to undertake a particular action to the persons capable of making the best evaluation of the consequences? Certainly one has reason to wonder. We have seen that in the case of most project proposals, information concerning the project goes, already highly summarized, to just one recipient—the top management of the employer of its proponent—and very little of what is received by top management is passed on to finance process participants outside the firm. However, organization theory suggests that such a parsimonious pattern of information handling is perfectly appropriate in a world of slow change. In such a world, the questions that need to be answered are well defined. Decisions can be based on a program relating stimuli to appropriate response which feedback processes have shown to have worked well in the past. The communications system can employ well-recognized symbols that incorporate a great deal of information. Authority rules will allow participants in the system to be very selective in the information to which they pay attention, because it is easy to assume the competence and integrity of an information source in the current situation if they have been demonstrated many times before in similar past situations. The same is true for interest rules because experience tells the participant that it is safe to ignore messages of many kinds of content.[110]

The small number of people to which information goes with respect to any project are in fact the ones who in a world of slow change are likely to be the best able to use it. Remember that the typical proposed project will be an extension in some sense of an existing project in the economy and will be proposed to the top management of the firm holding the existing project. The persons best qualified by way of background to evaluate the proposal would be the top managers of that firm, and these are just the persons to which information concerning the proposal is sent. They know the nature of the proposed project, and since demand, factor supplies, and technology change slowly, they know as well the environment in which it would operate. The organizational winnowing of information before it reaches the top managers is likely to be rational for the same reasons that past experience will be highly relevant to the current situation.

The finance process as currently structured handles information in a way very similar to that of Burton Klein's ideal form for an organization trying to achieve success in an environment of slow change. The range of decisions which must be made is divided into narrowly specific categories, and a specialist is assigned to each of these categories to make the decisions arising in it.[111] Relatively few bits of information flow to savers, the final decision makers of the organization.

c. *Failure to account for secondary effects.* As to the third kind of potential failure, there is no reason to think that the way the system would operate in a world of slow change would have negative secondary effects on the goals assigned to it.

To conclude, in a world of slow change the currently structured finance process would not only be economical to operate, but also would assure that proposed projects would be evaluated by those most qualified to do so and that the proposals evaluated as most promising would be the ones to get funded. In fact, a more elaborate and expensive system would be dysfunctional because, as Karl Deutsch points out, the more cohesive the group within which information is transmitted, the less the distortion and admixture of irrelevant information.[112]

2.4 *Effectiveness of Finance Process in a Fast-Changing World.*

What about the effectiveness of the finance process as currently structured in an economy such as ours, where the rate of scientific advance is rapid and where there are sudden changes in tastes and in the supply of vital factors of production?

We can still say that the communications efficiency of the system saves real resources. But can we say that the system also still successfully avoids the other potential failures that can beset organizations in the way they handle information? The analysis that follows suggests we cannot. The system fails to heed the best evaluations currently made: some projects that receive funding have been evaluated as inferior to some projects that do not. The system fails to make evaluations as well as it could: the flow of information and assignment of decision making in the finance process makes it less sensitive to the potentialities of innovative investment than would be the case with a more open system. And the system works in a way that has secondary negative effects on the goals assigned to it: innovation in a world dominated by internal finance tends to promote concentration.

2.41 *Failure To Use the Best Available Evaluations*

We have seen that most project proposals considered by the finance process as it is currently structured are generated by employees of large established firms and proposed solely to the top management of their employers. The resulting evaluations are by default the best ones available. A high level of industrial performance requires that the finance process heed these evaluations and fund the proposed projects that the evaluations suggest have the best prospects.* This will not happen unless the finance process has the capacity intelligently to move funds from one firm to another. There is no mechanism in the world of fast change akin to the one in the world of slow change where the profits of a firm anticipate the quality of its list of proposed projects. In particular, there is no reason to believe that a firm which has a good idea that is innovative will have corresponding profits to finance the idea internally. Several empirical studies support the proposition that rapidly innovating companies are more likely to require outside financing. Meyer and Kuh state so explicitly for the United States,[113] as do Carter and Wil-

---

*The evaluation of an evaluator is the conclusion he reaches for himself, which is not necessarily the same as what he tells others is his conclusion. The question of how well the system uses an evaluator's evaluation goes in part to the motivational structure in which the evaluator operates and to the effect of that structure on what he does and says given any particular evaluation.

liams for Britain.[114] Implicit support comes as well from the finding of Mansfield that on average the innovating firms in each of the industries he studied grew at twice the rate of the industry's non-innovating firms of equal size.[115] This means that unless there was a dramatic difference as well in their rate of return on current investments, the innovating firms were more likely to need outside financing.[116]

In an ideal world the movement of funds among established firms in the economy would be such that no proposed project of any established firm that received funding would have prospects inferior to any proposed project of any other established firm that did not receive funding. In the real world the transfer of funds is costly because of divided knowledge among system participants. We therefore must have the more modest goal of funding projects in rank order of their evaluated prospects to the extent that the gains from moving funds from one firm to another to further the ideal justifies the costs.

2.411 *A Stylized Example of the Costs and Benefits of Moving Funds Between Firms*

To see why the process of moving funds involves costs, consider the following highly stylized example. Firm C is an established firm. The marginal investment project on its list would cost $100. C's management knows for certain that the rate of return on the project is 10 percent. Firm C has sufficient internal funds to finance the project if it chooses to implement the project rather than pay out the $100 as a dividend to its sole shareholder, Mr. X. Firms D and E are each seeking $100 in financing for the only two other project proposals in the economy. The managements of D and E know for certain that their projects have rates of return of 11 percent and 6 percent respectively.* D and E have no current assets, income, or shareholders.† X has the low level of knowledge of the average saver.

---

*The analysis would not change if we assumed that the rates of return are the expected rates in the eyes of the three managements rather than the certain rates, the managements of C, D, and E are respectively as competent as anyone to evaluate the prospects of their proposed projects, and the three projects are judged by their respective evaluators as equally risky.

†On the basis of reasoning akin to that of the Modigliani and Miller theorem, we can say that the analysis would not change if D and E were ongoing firms and their

If C does not invest in its marginal project and instead pays the dividend, X will invest the $100 either solely in D or solely in E, depending on which he assesses to have a higher rate of return.* Consistent with my practice elsewhere in this book, I assume here that saver X's information set is such that his assessments of the rates of return of D and E, though uncertain, are unbiased and that he knows the joint probability distribution that generates the deviations between his assessments of the rates of return of D and E and their actual values. In other words, the way he generally receives information in each case makes his assessments as likely to be above as below the actual value, and he has a sense of his degree of ignorance, i.e., how likely it is that his assessment will be relatively accurate. (See appendix 1.1 for a more analytic description of the process by which X generates assessments.)

An omniscient observer who combines the knowledge of C, D, and E would know that efficiency would require C foregoing the investment in its marginal project and the funds being used to finance D's project. But here there is no such observer, just X and the managements of C, D, and E, each with their own information sets.

Payment of the dividend is a transfer of funds from someone who is well informed with respect to the prospects of at least one project to someone who is well informed with respect to the prospects of none. X's assessments of the prospects of D and E, though unbiased, are highly risky because of his relative ignorance. There is a possibility that X will assess E as having a higher rate of return than D and invest accordingly. This possibility means that the expected return (based on the actual rates of return for D and E and the probability distributions generating X's assessments of these two rates) from X's reinvesting the $100 will clearly be less than 11 percent even assuming that the managements of D and E were both prepared to offer terms, which because of transaction costs they would

managements acted in the best interests of their current shareholders. The focus would then be on X's ability to evaluate not only the prospects of the two proposed projects but also that of the firms' existing projects.

*The example also avoids the possibility that X uses the dividend to purchase securities already outstanding; but again recognition of that possibility would not change the analysis. Such a purchase is a financial transaction with no direct real effects. Assuming that payment of the dividend does not increase aggregate consumption in the economy, ultimately the $100 will end up in the hands of someone who must choose between D and E.

not be, that would pass on the whole earnings of their projects. Depending on the joint probability distribution generating his assessments of D and E, the expected return from reinvestment could even be less than 10 percent. Payment of the dividend converts X's situation from one where he is sure (perhaps unbeknownst to him) to receive 10 percent to one where, depending on his choice, he will receive either 11 or 6 percent.

Obtaining advice or services from a better-informed person can reduce X's possibility of misinvestment (i.e., choosing E because his probabilistically determined assessments of D and E suggest E is the better investment) and increase the expected return from reinvestment (based on the actual rates of return of D and E and the probability distributions generating X's assessments of these two rates). The more information is obtained to guide the reinvestment, either by the saver or by the intermediary whose services are retained, the greater the reduction in the probability of misevaluation and hence misinvestment, but also the greater the cost. X, aware of the extent to which each added piece of information reduces the variances of the distributions generating his assessments of D and E, will directly or indirectly obtain information up to the point where the marginal cost of obtaining more information starts to exceed the marginal gain to X from the resulting increased expected return.

X would be better off with C retaining the $100 unless the terms offered by D and E are such that, after obtaining this level of information, the expected rate of return (based again on the same factors) from his reinvestment of the dividend is sufficiently greater than 10 percent to cover the costs of obtaining the information and any brokerage fees that reinvestment requires.* The terms offered by D and

---

*In the context of this example, therefore, SROR is X's expected rate of return (based on our perspective) from reinvestment of the dividend less the cost of obtaining information and brokerage services. It includes the possibility of misinvestment. There is no way that in any one situation the management of C could know this expected rate of return and hence SROR. C is ignorant both of the actual returns on D and E and of X's ability to discern which is the better investment. But, as discussed more rigorously when the concept of SROR was first introduced (section B 3.21), C might properly assume that the average shareholder will earn about the same risk-adjusted return if he is given a dividend to reinvest as shareholders on average have done historically (adjusted to reflect current projections of future business conditions generally), i.e., adopt the approach recommended in standard corporate finance texts

E will not provide respectively the 11 percent and 6 percent rates of return that their projects could earn, because D and E must take account of their expenses in informing X of the prospects of their projects.

We can conclude from this stylized example that even if C restricted itself to retaining earnings only when it is in its shareholder's best interests to do so, it is quite possible that C's project will be funded and D's will not be, despite the findings of the respective evaluators of C and D that the certain rate of return of D's project is 1 percent higher than that of C. This is the consequence of divided knowledge, not perversity on C's part. If X, who acts to bridge the knowledge of C, D, and E, devoted more resources to increasing his knowledge, that act would increase the chance that the evaluation made by the three managements would be heeded by the system and D's project would be funded. But the gain may not be worth the cost.

for determining the cost of capital, which is based on the capital asset pricing model. This projected return would then be compared with that of the project C is considering.

This analysis leaves out consideration of the effect on the riskiness of X's portfolio of receiving and reinvesting a dividend. The projects being considered by C, D, and E each have the same variability—none—in the eyes of the persons that respectively know them best. If C uses the $100 for its project, X's return on the $100 will be a certain 10%. Payment of the dividend creates uncertainty: there is a particular probability that X's assessments will be such that he will invest in D and receive an 11% return and a particular probability that they will be such that instead he will invest in E and receive a 6% return. Which course of action he takes depends on the particular information set he possesses, and the composition of his information set is determined probabilistically. If X is risk averse because money has diminishing marginal utility to him and his only investment is in C stock, the uncertainty resulting from the payment of the dividend is a cost to him.

If the model were expanded to provide for the possibility of X's holding a variety of stocks each paying dividends that are reinvested and X in fact chooses to have a diversified portfolio, the effects of this uncertainty associated with each dividend payment would cancel out. Relative ignorance would lower his expected return because of the chance of misinvestment but would not increase the variability of his portfolio as a whole. Of course X might choose not to have a diversified portfolio, and it is even possible that he and the functioning of the price system are better off if he does not, but those possibilities involve a host of issues that take us too far astray from the point of this exercise. We can at least say that in an economy with many corporations paying dividends and many corporations seeking external finance, payment of dividends does not add to the aggregate variability of return on all investment even though they pass through persons like X who are relatively ignorant.

The possibility that the dividend money will be misinvested in E would not be eliminated by broadening the model to assume thousands of C shareholders and millions of potential investors in D and E and introducing the mechanisms discussed in chapter 1 that increase market efficiency. As long as the managements of D and E, because of information known only by them, have more accurate assessments of the prospects of their respective proposed projects than do any participants in the market, misinvestment is possible.

2.412 *The Costs and Benefits of Moving Funds Between Firms: The Empirical Record*

Appendix 2.1 discusses a number of empirical studies relating to whether different groups of firms have different rates of return on their marginal projects. Although each of the studies is open to one kind of methodological criticism or another, they are, taken together, relatively convincing that the marginal project of the average established firm with sufficient internal funds relative to its list of investment opportunities so as not to seek outside finance, particularly equity, has an annual rate of return which is less than the annual rate of return of the marginal project of the average established firm with insufficient internal funds compared with its list of opportunities. The difference—what I will call the "internal finance differential"—is hard to quantify precisely, but the overall impression from the review of studies in appendix 2.1 is that it probably is at least 2 or 3 percent and possibly much greater. Can the internal finance differential be explained as the result of the firms that do not seek outside finance taking note of the cost of moving funds and deciding it is in the best interests of their shareholders to retain their cash flow to invest in their marginal projects rather than to pay a larger dividend? The stylized example above suggests that a shareholder of such a firm is worse off with the last dollar retained for the marginal project of the firm instead of paid out to him as a dividend if the rate of return he would have been able to earn from reinvestment of the additional dollar of dividend would have on average exceeded the rate on the marginal project by an amount more than the sum of (a) the cost (spread over the life of the real investment project which the reinvested money would ultimately fund)* of obtaining information or services to aid in finding where to place the money, and (b) the cost (similarly spread) of any brokerage fees necessary to affect the reinvestment. I will call this sum the "savers' costs" of moving funds between firms. The stylized example also suggests that for a potential recipient of this money to find it worthwhile to seek the money, the marginal real investment project on its list must have an expected rate of return which exceeds the expected rate of return it must offer to obtain the money from its source by an amount (spread over the life of the project) equal to the firm's transaction costs (most of which directly or indirectly involve informing the source concerning the prospects of the recipient firm). I will refer to these transaction costs as the "recipient's costs" of moving funds between firms. The total cost of moving funds from one firm to another is the sum of the saver's costs and the recipient's costs.† If the total cost of moving funds equals or exceeds the internal finance differential, the system is working well. But if the sum of these costs is less than the internal finance differential, a greater movement of funds between firms could be a cost effective way of improving industrial performance. We have a feeling of the magnitude of the internal finance differential. To compare, we need to get a feeling as well of the magnitude of the saver's costs and recipient's costs of moving funds.

First let us look at the saver's costs. Consider a saver who during a given time period receives from his various shareholdings dividends aggregating $1,000. Assuming he wants to stay an equity investor, one option is to consult a broker who gives advice and brokerage services as a package. A survey of such brokers reveals that the fee would be 2–3 percent for reinvesting the $1,000 (and much less for larger amounts). If we assume that the project which the funds ultimately finance has a life of fifteen years, this would amount to about .30 percent per year (taking account of the time

---

*If the shareholder sells the security purchased with the dividend money before the end of the life of the project, the higher rate of return that the security will pay if it meets this test will increase the sale price of the security and the shareholder will still be fully compensated for this cost.

†The mechanical cost of a firm's sending out a larger dividend is not considered because it is trivial or nonexistent.

value of money). Another option is to invest in a mutual fund or venture capital firm, which today typically have little or no load fee but have management fees that range from .25 to .50 percent per year. These numbers give us a feel for the brokerage cost and costs of information or services needed by the saver to find an appropriate new place to put his funds.

Now let us look at the recipient's costs. Consider the typical firm making a public offering of its shares. The firm must pay underwriters' commissions, legal and other expert fees, printing expenses, and registration fees. A registration statement under the Securities Act of 1933 for a primary public offering for cash requires that these costs of issuance be itemized.[117] A survey of such registration statements reveals considerable variation in the total of these costs as a percentage of the proceeds of the issue, but the figure rarely exceeds 4 percent for issues of the type of issuers involved in the appendix 2.1 studies and is often half that. These numbers do not include the value of executive time involved, but, given the large absolute size of the offerings, adding in the value of executive time will not dramatically change the results. Assuming again a fifteen-year project, the costs of effecting the sale of the shares would generally be in the range of .20 to .40 percent per year.

These figures show that the recipient's costs and the saver's costs add up to something probably in the range of .50–.90 percent per year over the life of the typical project receiving funds. Thus, from what we know about the magnitude of the internal finance differential, it appears larger, perhaps much larger, than the cost of moving funds between established firms through outside capital markets. This suggests that a greater movement of such funds through capital markets would be a cost effective way of increasing the chance that the most promising project proposals considered by these firms are the ones to get funded. (The costs and benefits of practical proposals to increase this movement of funds are considered in chapter 6, section C.)

2.42 *Failure To Make Good Evaluations: Insensitivity to the Potentialities of Innovative Investment Proposals*

The second question to be addressed is whether the system is structured such that information relevant to the prospects of a proposed project is reaching the persons capable of making the best evaluation of those prospects. In a world of fast change, this question translates to the question of whether the flow of information and assignment of decision making in the finance process as currently structured makes the system's evaluations of innovative investment proposals as sensitive to their potentialities as they might be. The difficulty of studying the sensitivity of the system using conventional static efficiency analysis is an important reason to approach the finance process as an organization rather than as a simple market phenomenon. I will first discuss what communications theory tells us about the characteristics of innovative organizations generally and then, in the light of this discussion, take a look at the characteristics of the finance process.

2.421 *The Characteristics of Innovative Organizations*

a. *What makes an organization innovative.* Let us start with some very abstract observations. Innovation involves the search for alternatives and evaluation of their expected consequences if pursued. The capacity of an organization to innovate relates to its ability to rearrange items of information into new patterns and identify the occasions when a particular rearrangement would be useful.[118] The fewer and more aggregated the pieces of information that flow through the system, the fewer are the possible rearrangements. For new ideas to make it through the communications channels, the symbols used must aggregate less information and the authority and interest rules must be less selective. A large portion of the participants who have significant impact on the organization's decisions should themselves be sensitive to new ideas, i.e., their internal information-processing structures should have characteristics resembling those which are desirable for innovative organizations.[119] The environment in which they operate should encourage this sensitivity. And rather than just one, a number of persons, with differing backgrounds, personal information-processing structures, and tastes for risk, should have the opportunity to act on the basis of the same idea.

b. *Structural characteristics of innovative organizations.* These abstract observations have several important implications about how an organization should be structured in order to have innovative capacity.

1. *Staffing and allocation of assignments.* Burton Klein suggests that persons of responsibility in the organization should not be narrow experts, not all be from the same background, and not be given rigidly defined roles.[120] These rules give each person of responsibility practice in dealing with the new ideas. And when one member misses the promise of a good idea, another may pick up on it.

Klein's ideas are similar in many ways to those of Harold Wilensky. Wilensky suggests that a large organization should have a group of highly professional persons devoted to broad-scale intelligence for major decisions and that the group should be relatively independent of those responsible for day-to-day operations.[121]

Wilensky's proposal stems from his observation that the vast information networks that large organizations develop are often dysfunctional. Decisions made by creative people who, because they had to bypass the traditional network as a result of crisis, have relatively little information are observed frequently to be of higher quality than decisions made on the basis of information that has come through the full network.[122] He gives as an example a comparison between the decision-making process in the Bay of Pigs invasion and the one in the Cuban missile crisis. In the former, he portrays the decision process as bureaucratic and following proper channels. The result was that the intelligence which reached the final decision makers was faulty (reflecting the prejudices of the participants and of the structure) and promising alternatives were not presented. In the latter, the decision was made by a small group of top decision makers who because of the time constraints and the need for secrecy were basically on their own. Because they avoided the barriers to good communication caused by hierarchy and culture, they in the end came up with a much more accurate estimate of the situation and a more creative solution to the problem than did the bureaucracy in the Bay of Pigs case.[123] Another example given by Wilensky of dysfunctional behavior by the information network of a large organization is the American Express salad oil scandal, in which mounting evidence of fraud was ignored by the relevant officials because traditional procedures indicated that everything was in good order. The results was a loss of hundreds of millions of dollars. Wilensky also points in support of his contention to the often-stated observation that new government agencies make better decisions than old ones.[124]

Wilensky argues that his proposal for a separate intelligence group is a way of avoiding the causes of these failures. Its smallness relative to the organization as a whole prevents the establishment of rigid routines. Its professional orientation and independence prevents the use of communication for purposes of intraorganizational manipulation instead of for furthering organizational goals.

2. *Uncertain environment.* Where an organization, or the subgroups or persons constituting it, operate in an uncertain environment, the organization will have a greater capacity for innovation. Stress arising from the uncertainty leads to the active questioning of old truths that would otherwise act as a barrier to the discovery of new ways of doing things. This proposition flows neatly from behavioral theory: a person, or group, searches for new ways of doing things when the current way of doing things does not result in performance that satisfies its aspiration levels (see chapter 1, section C 1.1). Uncertainty means that the current way of doing things is less likely to result in a satisfactory level of performance. Shielding an individual or group from such uncertainty blocks the flow of negative feedback.[125] The need to cope with an uncertain environment forces a group to appoint to positions of responsibility persons who are sensitive to new ideas and to reward those who take risks and act on them. And the authority and interest rules of viable organizations in an environment of uncertainty will not as a general matter be as selective as those of one in a certain environment.

3. *Low Autonomy.* For an organization to be innovative, none of the groups that make it up should have a high degree of autonomy: each should be forced to look outside itself to seek the assistance of a continuously changing list of others in order to undertake the acts that will meet its goals. In the case of an industry, autonomy would in part be a function of the degree of vertical integration of the firms composing it and in part the degree of horizontal competition both within and among these firms. In support of this conclusion Klein suggests, for example, that measures of the capability of an industry for innovation are the amount of interaction between each firm in the industry and universities, the amount of subcontracting each firm engages in, and how often each changes subcontractors.[126] He argues, citing the relatively slow rate of productivity growth in Germany between 1900 and 1945, that cartelized industries, where each firm has the autonomy stemming from a guaranteed market share, are slow to change.[127] He also argues that the unusual firm, such as

IBM in recent decades and Ford up until 1920, that promotes internal competition by encouraging several groups or individuals to pursue parallel paths toward the achievement of the same objective is more innovative.[128]

Communications theory suggests a number of reasons why autonomy can be expected to be inversely related to capability for innovation. Through habit, autonomous groups tend to overvalue parochial or internal sources of information. They block out information from sources with wider ranges of experience, since nothing forces them to have contact with such sources.[129] As a general matter, groups have a bias to let things stay as they are because it is easier to agree to let things stay as they are than to agree to institute one of several possible changes.[130] Autonomy reinforces this tendency because there are fewer possible constraints that prevent the solution currently in use from continuing to be workable.

Advancement within an autonomous group is more likely to go to an "organization man" who focuses inwardly on the existing internal rules of the group and on how to use them to his advantage rather than to a person who focuses on establishing his worth by taking actions that result, directly or indirectly, in reactions by persons outside the group that benefit the group. A person with the first focus will have much less use for new ideas than one with the second. This is especially true if the rules of the group, as is typical, take more notice of mistakes than of good results.[131]

Finally, the external constraints that lack of autonomy implies force a group to collect and process information better—to be more "intelligent"—than it would otherwise have to be in order to accomplish its goals. It must substitute brains for brawn. The group would prefer, other things being equal, not to have to rely on the assistance of others any more than necessary because outside assistance comes at a price. Maximizing the impact of the group's limited internal resources requires maximizing the group's foresight concerning changes in its external environment and its speed of response to them. Deutsch, for example, applies this last point to his theory of politics. He suggests that in an ever-changing world, governments with little power must compensate by increasing their foresight and speed of response. Using formal cybernetic terms, they must make up their low capacity for "gain"—the size of their response to change—by increasing their "lead" and cutting down on their "lag."[132]

c. *Innovative and noninnovative behaviors are each self-reinforcing.* One further point can be gleaned from the discussion concerning what makes an organization innovative. Both high and low levels of innovative behavior by an organization are self-reinforcing. If an organization undergoes only slow change for a period of time, the components that succeed are ones which are well adapted to slow change, i.e., those that display a high level of information efficiency. Ones which are well adapted for fast change, which are the likely sources of future innovation, have information-processing systems that are too costly to survive. Those that remain have a vested interest in maintaining slow change. Conversely, if an organization undergoes fast change for a period of time, the components that succeed are the ones which are well adapted to fast change so there will be many sources of future innovation. Each component will be operating in an environment of uncertainty, and each is likely to have limited autonomy. *Therefore, an organization's level of innovativeness may be more a product of its past than of outside forces that move it toward some optimal trade-off between innovativeness and communications efficiency.*

2.422 *Application to the Finance Process*

Now let us look at the organization that is the subject of this study, the finance process. We have seen that most new investment is undertaken by an existing firm and is financed by internal cash flow. The proponent, with only occasional exceptions, is an employee of the firm. The firm releases to the outside world only a small portion of the information it possesses concerning itself and the project. In the case of a large firm, the type that makes the bulk of real investment decisions, management has considerable discretion in which way to decide. There exist outside capital markets, including a market for venture capital which serves as a source of funds for new and small, rapidly growing firms, but a relatively small portion of real-level investment is the product of a decision process that involves outside capital markets. This concentration of communications within individual firms is communications efficient, but it is not a structure which is likely to be very sensitive to new ideas.

We saw earlier (section B 3.1) that the system of information gathering and evaluation used by the top management of any one firm is usually specialized in certain areas of investment proposals, narrow in the range of ideas it will tolerate, and tends over time to develop a conservative bias. If, typically, the proponent trying to persuade such a firm to implement an innovative proposal is one of its employees, he may at least have some experience-based authority in the eyes of the top management of the firm. But the firm will not be sensitive to the possibilities of his idea if, as is often the case, it is either outside any of the firm's areas of specialization or inside such an area but outside of the generally conservative range of ideas which the firm will tolerate.

It is rare for a proponent to approach an established firm of which he is not an employee because such a proponent faces a very difficult fight even if one of the approached firm's areas of specialty covers his proposal. The chance of success is usually too low to justify the cost of trying. This is especially true where the proponent is an employee of another firm, since such an attempt would be viewed with displeasure by his current employer. Difficulties exist by whatever route a nonemployee proponent chooses to approach an established firm. We have already seen that the sale of an investment idea is rarely a practical route to implementation (section B 2.11). The alternative for a nonemployee is to approach a firm and suggest that the firm hire him and implement his proposal. Such a suggestion will have trouble getting a proper hearing because the proponent lacks experience-based authority in the eyes of the firm. And even where he overcomes this barrier, if the firms specialized in the area of the proposal are well established, the conservative cast to the range of ideas they will tolerate prejudices the chances that a truly innovative idea will be implemented by any of them.*

An example from the semiconductor study is revealing with respect to employee proponents trying to persuade their employers and other firms specialized in electronics to fund innovative investment proposals. In the 1950s most of the important ideas relating to semiconductors were coming out of the R & D laboratories of the large established electronics firms. The primary business of these firms was manufacturing electronic tubes and products, such as radios and televisions, that wired these tubes together to perform a

---

*Since there is not complete overlap, the larger the number of such firms, the better the proponent's chances.

particular function. Top management in these firms thought of semi-conductors only as one for one replacements for individual tubes in existing products. They blocked implementation of projects to produce components useful in new electronic configurations (new products and old products made new ways) which took better advantage of the potential functions semiconductors could perform (see chapter 4, section 2.12).

The other way a new idea can be implemented is for a proponent to approach one or more of the sources that constitute the "outside sector" of the finance process—financial intermediaries and wealthy individuals—to seek financing for setting up a new firm* to implement his proposal (see section B 2.124). Members of the outside sector are not as likely to reject a proposal because the proponent lacks experience-based authority, and, as will be argued in a moment, they are less likely to have a conservative bias. But the outside sector is relatively small as the finance process is currently structured, and, as we will see, that smallness limits its effectiveness in making the system more sensitive to innovative ideas.

2.423 *An Alternative Structure*

Suppose that the finance process were restructured so that large established firms would distribute to shareholders more, perhaps even all, of their available cash flow. The communications analysis that follows suggests that such a restructuring, which would increase funds in the hands of the outside sector, would increase the sensitivity of the system to the potentialities of innovative investment ideas. To start, the number of proposals to finance new firms considered by the outside process would likely increase. This is important because an evaluation by an outside source of the investment idea behind a new firm proposal is less likely to display a conservative bias than would an evaluation by an established firm of a comparable idea proposed to it by an employee. The favorable effect from the increase in the number of new firm proposals considered is reinforced by the fact that the more such proposals the outside sector considers, the higher the quality of its evaluations. Finally, the restruc-

---

*As earlier, the case of a small firm seeking outside funding for a project of such size that the whole nature of the firm will be changed if the project is implemented is treated here as equivalent to a proponent seeking funding to start a new firm.

turing would alter the environment in which established firms make their evaluations of project proposals in a way that would increase their openness to new ideas.

a. *Evaluation of new firm proposals by the outside sector.*

1. *Likely increase in proposals evaluated.* To see why an increase in funds received by the outside sector is likely to increase the number of new firm proposals given serious evaluation, we need to consider the incentives facing the typical outside sector funding source.

Each additional request for funds that the source evaluates, whether from a new firm proponent or from an established firm, will on average improve the quality of the request or requests it finally chooses to fund because it increases the chances that one of the requests being considered is an unusually good investment. But each request evaluation is costly. The amount of funds a source controls limits the number of requests it can fund. The benefits from evaluating an additional request display diminishing returns because the more requests that are evaluated, the less chance that any given one will lead to a funding decision. For any given amount of funds under its control, there will therefore be an optimal number of requests for a source to evaluate. The larger the amount of funds, the greater the optimal number. An increase in funds received by the outside sector as a whole will probably increase both the number of sources and the amount of funds each controls. Thus, there will be an increase in the total number of evaluations made by outside sources.

With the increase in funds received by the outside sector will come an increase in the number of requests for external finance from established firms. There is no absolute guarantee that the change in structure, though leading to an increase in evaluations of requests for funds generally, will lead to an increase in the number of evaluations of requests for funds to start new firms. However, an increase in the number of evaluations of new firm requests is very likely, since the change gives such proposals a chance to be considered to receive some of this increase in funds, and some of them should look good enough to succeed. Without the change in structure, all of the additional funds received by the outside sources as a result of the change would instead have stayed within established firms and for certain funded their projects.

2. *Greater sensitivity to innovative proposals.* The method by which an outside finance source evaluates the investment idea behind a

proposal to fund a new firm, as we saw earlier (section B 4.1), is distinctly different from the method a firm uses to evaluate a project proposal by one of its own employees. Experience-based authority is less important; general personal reputation and incentive structure authority are more important. There is no well-established information network as there is within the firm. Because the communications channels involved get much less frequent use, the authority and interest rules which govern the gathering and processing of information for the principals of an intermediary (or for a wealthy individual investor) are not as selective and the symbols used not as information digestive. Corresponding to the criteria of Klein and Wilensky, those who staff financial intermediaries are not on the average as narrow experts as those who staff corporate bureaucracies. Financial intermediary organizations tend to be much smaller and involve less hierarchy. Unlike corporate officials, they are separated from the operations of the firms the project choice decisions of which they participate in. And there are multiple sources to which a proponent can turn, which means both that a single proposal may receive multiple evaluations and that the persons making the evaluations are operating in an environment of competition.

Obviously there are costs to funding a new project externally to become the basis of a new firm compared with funding a new project internally to become part of an existing firm. At the time the proposal is made, the persons making the internal decision are likely to know both the proponent and the industry into which the project falls much better than an outside source that is approached. The outside sources can, to the extent they wish, make up for this deficit by collecting information after the proposal is made. That, however, involves the expenditure of real resources that internal sources need not incur. Some of this collection of information will probably occur, but in the end the typical outside source is likely to make an evaluation on the basis of less information than is an internal source. A system which makes investments on the basis of less-informed evaluations is more likely to make errors and invest in projects which do not turn out well. But the advantage to external evaluation is that it is less likely to have a blind spot that rules out an innovative proposal.

The study of the financing of the semiconductor industry that follows shows a pattern: at the time of each major technological jump, the breakthrough investment opportunity was proposed internally to one or more large established firms and rejected. The proponents then obtained outside financing to start a new firm based on the same idea. This finding is consistent with the findings of case studies of numerous other industries to the effect that new entrants are very important sources of innovation and contribute a disproportionately high share of truly revolutionary advances.[133] It is also consistent with W. S. Comanor's finding that industries with only moderate entry barriers have a higher level of R & D intensity (measured by ratio of R & D employment to firm size) than industries with high entry barriers,[134] because it suggests the existence of an expectation that new entries will be innovative which forces established members to be innovative as well in order to compete.*

3. *Reinforcing tendency of increase in proposals evaluated.* An increase in the amount of funds controlled by outside sources is not only likely to increase the number of new firm proposals evaluated by the sector, but it is also likely to increase the sensitivity to the potential of innovative ideas of this already more sensitive context for funding decisions. Part of the reason is that a larger outside sector would be likely to increase the number of potential reviewers of any given proposal. This improves the chances that the proponent of a good innovative idea will be able to find the evaluator that by its particular background and experience would naturally appreciate the proposal. There is also evidence that a sufficient flow of innovative proposals to the outside sector changes its attitude about such proposals. Consider the fact that certain metropolitan areas have attracted a large number of technologically based industries and others have not. A U.S. Department of Commerce Advisory Committee on Technology and Innovation report attributes much of this to differences between the areas in the attitudes of bankers and other fi-

---

*Unlike the semiconductor study that follows, the conclusions based on the other case studies and the Comanor study do not differentiate between new entries that are new firms and new entries that are established firms in other industries. An established firm considering an investment proposal outside its area of specialty would not be as likely to display as conservative a bias as one already in the industry because it would not be the prisoner of its past successes. The difference between the information-processing capabilities of such a firm and that of a participant in the outside sector source is that the firm displays a conservative bias evaluating some proposals (those within its areas of specialty) and not others, while the outside sector participant is unlikely to display such a bias with respect to any proposals.

nanciers toward new ideas and in the attitudes of scientists and pro-
fessors with regard to commercial exploitation of their ideas.[135] There
seems to be a cumulative gain of experience in dealing with innovation financing so that participants which have been involved before are more willing to be involved again than those who have not
been involved previously.

4. *Empirical record of new firm performance.* While research reveals
no study that would come close to settling the matter definitively,
there is some evidence that, despite many failures, the average rate
of return on long-term (ten or fifteen years) equity investments in
new firms founded for the purpose of implementing innovative
projects exceeds equity investments in established firms. That in turn
suggests that such new firms make better use of the funds made
available to them than do established firms.

Two studies of innovative new firm performance show very high
rates of return but are of only limited help because they show no
self-consciousness of their obvious methodological problems. One,
which finds an annual average rate of return between 30 and 40
percent, has as its empirical basis interviews with "authoritative
sources."[136] The other, which finds an average annual return of
slightly above 30 percent, is based on data provided by *Venture Capital Journal* and provides no information concerning how the firms
included were selected, how the rate of return calculations were made
or the time period covered.[137]

A third study, by Huntsman and Hoban, does deal seriously with
the methodological issues involved.[138] Their sample is the 110 equity
investments in new innovative firms made between 1960 and 1968
by three venture capital firms. They find that as of 1975 the annualized rate of return of this composite portfolio to be 18.9 percent
(net of management costs of 4 percent). They find it is not possible
to make any kind of risk adjustment to this figure because there is
not available reliable data of the kind needed to make alpha and beta
estimates. For most of the investments, price information is inter-
mittent and not indicative of the valuation that would be made of
the same security if continuously traded in large volume. The price
information is also hard to collect, since none of the firms were publicly traded for the full period of the study and many of them never
were so traded. There is also some question about whether the 110
firms in the sample are representative of all innovative new firms,

since they were ones chosen by three successful venture capital firms.

Because of the lack of risk adjustment and possible sample bias, we must be cautious in any conclusions we draw from a comparison between the 18.9 percent figure and the average annual rate of return of 4.3 percent that investors received during the period 1960–1974 from investments in common stocks generally.[139] But the inherent nature of the subject under study makes these methodological problems difficult or impossible to overcome, and we should not completely ignore the best evidence we have concerning the average returns on the real investments of innovative new firms compared with those made by existing firms.

b. *Evaluation by established firms of internally generated proposals.* Even if established firms were to pay out all of their available cash flow in shareholder distributions, such firms would still be expected to undertake much of the real investment occurring in the economy. A large portion of potential proponents are employed by such firms, and proposing projects to the top managements of their own firms still would have the advantage of an experienced-based authority relationship. Although the increase in funds to the outside sector makes proposing a project to an outside source more inviting, many such employees still would not have sufficient wealth or potentially sacrificeable future income to establish incentive structure authority in the eyes of an outside source. Many also may not have the taste for the risks and change of work style implied by setting up their own firms. In getting funds from the outside sector to finance a real investment project, an established firm would also still have an advantage over a proponent proposing to start a new firm. When an existing firm incurs debt or issues equity, the supplier of finance can look to existing profitable projects as a source of future cash flow to help provide a return on his investment (see chapter 1, section A 1.3). The firm may also have a proven record of having chosen good new projects in the past which would be evidence of the quality of the project it is currently seeking funds to implement.

Thus, it is important to ask what the effect would be of restructuring the finance process to increase distributions to shareholders on the evaluative process of established firms. The first thing to note is that if an established firm distributes more of its available cash flow to shareholders, its autonomy is reduced. It must "subcontract" more of its financing requirements. The preceding discussion concerning the characteristics of innovative organizations applies neatly to this situation. The need to seek outside finance forces the firm to answer hard questions posed by the outside sources and to engage in an exchange of ideas. This in turn forces it to ask hard questions of itself, the questioning of old truths that is essential to innovation. This questioning is reinforced by the real pressures that the lack of a captive source of financing forces upon the firm. The reduction in elbow room means that more often continuing to do things the same way as before will not be a viable course of action, and a search for a new way of doing things will be necessary.

The comparison of the investment behavior of new semiconductor firms with that of the established diversified electronics firms in the study that follows lends empirical support to the conclusion of the communications analysis that a change in structure increasing shareholder distributions would increase the innovativeness of established firms. The picture that emerges has a David and Goliath flavor. The new firm is small with only limited resources at its disposal. It makes up for this limitation by finding an investment project incorporating a frontier idea just at the earliest practical moment of implementation. The initial market for such an innovation is small, so that large-scale investment is not necessary. As the innovation proves a success, expansion is funded by the high profits of the initial project. The established firm, which has more resources at its disposal, invests on a much larger scale, but its timing is less precise. The effect is often wasted because it gets into the market a little too late. Like the small power in Deutsch's cybernetic theory of politics, the small firm makes up for its lack of gain by having low lag and good lead. In the process it is using society's scarce resources more productively. If large established firms were more restricted in the internal resources at their disposal, they might be forced to improve their lags and leads also.

The conclusion of the communications analysis also gains indirect empirical support from certain studies relating to the relationship between market structure and innovation.[140] To see how requires a brief detour to consider three well-recognized *a priori* theories concerning this relationship. The first theory stems from the behavioral theory of the firm. A moderate level of competition in an industry is viewed as conducive to innovation because the stress it puts on the firms encourages the search for new solutions. The second theory stresses the relationships between innovation and the size of the resulting profits. Here, a certain degree of monopoly power is viewed as conducive to innovation because such power lessens the prospects that the innovation will be immediately copied, thereby resulting in the gains that would otherwise accrue to the innovator being shared with others or competed away. The third theory stresses the need for a certain amount of discretionary funds and organizational slack if a firm is to engage in research and development and innovative investment. Under the third theory, again a degree of monopoly power is conducive to innovation. The second and third theories together form the basis of Schumpeter's argument that large firms operating in concentrated industries are the key to innovation.[141]

Evidence supporting the first theory clearly supports the conclusion of communications analysis concerning the effect of restructuring of the finance process to increase shareholder distributions. Evidence supporting the second theory neither supports nor contradicts this conclusion. Competition may result in stress, which stimulates innovation, and a fear of profit erosion from imitation, which stifles innovation. Even if the second effect dominates the first, that would be no reason not to put stress on firms through payment of larger shareholder distributions. Evidence supporting the third theory is clearly inconsistent with the conclusion of the communications analysis.

If one surveys the experiences since 1900 of the full range of industries in the United States economy, one sees many examples of highly innovative industries that are moderately competitive and many examples of highly innovative industries that are concentrated. The existence of the competitive examples is evidence of the first theory, which is reinforced by a number of case studies that suggest that the mechanisms relied on in the theory are in fact at work.[142] The existence of the highly concentrated examples could be taken as evidence of the second or the third theory. It is important for our purposes to know which one (or whether it is evidence of both). Scherer suggests an approach that jibes with the first and second theories to explain the existence of the concentrated examples of innovativeness side by side with the moderately competitive examples of innovativeness, and that does so in a way that does not require reliance on the third theory.[143] Simplifying somewhat, Scherer says that in an industry where the knowledge base is growing rapidly so that the potential profit to the industry as a whole for a given amount of development effort is large, it will be worthwhile for a firm to undertake the development even though the profit will in time need to be shared with a number of imitators. Up to the maximum tolerable number of firms with which to share, the more firms in the industry the greater the number of centers of initiative and the faster innovation will occur. Where the base is growing slowly so that the profit to the industry as a whole from a given amount of development effort would be less, the effort would not be worthwhile unless the number of firms with which the profit would eventually have to be shared is small. This approach is consistent with empirical studies that show a positive relation between R & D effort and concentration in industries with slow-growing knowledge bases and a negative relation in industries with fast-growing knowledge bases.

2.43 *Secondary Effects of a Finance System Dominated by Internal Funding: Innovation-Induced Concentration.*

The third question to be answered is whether the existing structure of the finance process—which evaluators receive information and whose evaluations are heeded—has among its secondary effects tendencies that run contrary to one or more of the goals of production, output choice and dynamic efficiency. The dominance of internal financing is likely to make industries displaying rapid technical change more concentrated than they would be otherwise. The first firm to adopt a new cost-saving technique or new product will tend to monopolize the use of innovation and expand (or, in the case of a significantly differentiated new product, continue) to dominate the market, and other firms in the market will face difficulties copying the technique or product.[144] Because most innovations require new investment, diffusion is closely connected to the inclination and ability to invest. In a neoclassical model, diffusion occurs rapidly because the implementation of an innovation by one firm would immediately result in the incorporation of the idea in the production functions of all other firms in the industry and would raise their marginal efficiency of investment curves. Being profit maximizers, they would then invest in the new technique. It is not as simple in a system dominated by internal financing because the amount of investment is partially dependent on the level of profits. Profits of the initially innovating firm will increase, while profits of competing firms will normally decrease. In a system in which internal funds are the preferred source for investment, there will be a substantial difference between the effect of a rise in the perceived marginal efficiency of investment curve on the level of investment undertaken by firms experiencing a gain in internal funds (from increased profits) and the effect of such a rise on the level of investment undertaken by firms experiencing a fall in internal funds (from decreased profits). In chapter 5 (section B) it is demonstrated, given plausible assumptions, that if an innovation results in a sufficient shift in the marginal efficiency of investment curve of the firms in an industry, the initial implementers of the innovation will grow relative to, and in some cases may grow in terms of absolute size at the expense of, their actual competitors and that initial implementers have substantial advantages over potential competitors as well. The chapter concludes that this phenomenon is the single best explanation of the level of concentration that has existed in many product lines of the semiconductor industry.

The problem is aggravated by the fact that the use by an innovating firm of internal finance sends off fewer signals to the outside world concerning the profitability of the innovative investment. This makes imitation riskier and slows diffusion.

The tendency of the finance process to encourage concentration is a secondary effect of the way it selects which investment opportunities to fund* and obviously runs contrary to the goals of production efficiency and output choice efficiency, each of which are encouraged by competition. It may also run contrary to the goal of dynamic efficiency if, as we have seen some economists maintain, a moderate degree of competition encourages innovation. If they are correct, innovation in an economy dominated by internal finance, rather than being self-sustaining, would tend to destroy the circumstances that initially encourage it.[145]

2.5 *The Ineffectiveness of Feedback*

The preceding evaluation of the finance process suggests that it exhibits each of the three possible types of system failures I have

---

*Implicit in this analysis is the assumption that the finance process is relatively slow in responding to project proposals intended to gain a share of monopoly profits in an industry.

identified, and so, at least in theory, there is room for improvement in system performance. In chapter 6 I will explore whether there are practical changes in policy that would help alleviate these failures and investigate in a rough empirical fashion whether such changes would be cost effective. The issue addressed here is why the system does not have within it sufficient forces for self-correction that we should assume without such further investigation either that current performance is optimal (i.e., no cost-effective reduction in the system failures is possible) or that the system is moving toward such an optimal point at such a rate that policy changes, with their inevitably uncertain results, are inadvisable. In communications theory terms, the issue addressed is how well does the feedback mechanism work in the system as currently structured.

All three of the system failures are attributable to the domination of internal finance. We have seen from the micro analysis that the problem of internal finance domination is in part due to the fact that managers often retain earnings under cicumstances where shareholders would increase the dividend payout if they knew what the managers knew and had the power to do so. The earlier review of the contractual approach to the study of firm behavior (section B 3.23) suggests that, even if this pattern of managerial behavior remains unchanged, forces exist that will reduce over time its negative consequences. If there are two groups of firms in the economy—those that only invest in projects with expected returns equal to or in excess of SROR and those that invest in below-SROR projects as well—the percentage of new real investment undertaken by the first group will grow over the long run because the investments they make in one period will generate greater earnings in future periods and thus make more funds available for investments in those periods. The following stylized example, which utilizes plausible parameters, demonstrates, however, how slow moving these forces are and how counterforces may eliminate their effectiveness.

Suppose that investment is made only by established firms. Firms generating half the cash flow of the industrial sector, Group A, have sufficiently good project lists that they do not invest in any projects with expected returns below SROR. The average real rate of return on Group A new investments is 10 percent. Firms generating the other half of the cash flow, Group B, have poorer lists and do invest in projects with expected rates of return less than SROR. The average real rate of return on Group B new investments is 8 percent.

Group A firms are assumed, because of their better investment opportunities, to retain 80 percent of their internally generated cash flow for new investment (as compared with the actual average retention rate for all U.S. corporations of 67 percent); Group A firms are also assumed to be responsible for all of the 10 percent of investment in the economy that is externally funded (corresponding to the actual percentage of investment by nonfinancial corporations that is externally funded).[146] Group B firms, reflecting a certain degree of shareholder pressure, retain only 55 percent of their internally generated cash flow for new investment and engage in no external finance. Altogether, then, in the current period Group A firms are responsible for 63 percent of all investment and Group B firms are responsible for 37 percent.

Assuming that all Group A firms and all Group B firms maintain these same characteristics over time, what is the situation after twenty years? Group A firms would have only increased the share of investment for which they are responsible from 63 to 77 percent, and Group B firms would have only decreased their share from 37 to 23 percent. Thus the forces for efficiency—stockholder pressure and the automatically increasing mandate to managements making better investments—have in twenty years only reduced the share of investment made by firms that invest in below-SROR projects from a bit more than a third to a bit less than a quarter.

The stylized example does not take account of the creation and rise of new firms, which when they would start would only invest in SROR or above projects. But it also does not take account of the fact that, twenty years older, some of the Group A firms may take on the characteristics of Group B firms. As explored in earlier discussion, there are good theoretical and empirical reasons for thinking that such transformations will occur (and will dominate any going in the other direction).[147] Thus one can imagine a sort of steady state developing with a fixed percentage of firms always investing in below-SROR projects.

The problem with the existing dominance of internal finance goes beyond the inability of shareholders, individually or as a group, to obtain their pro-rata shares of the firm's cash flow when management does not want to pay it out. If shareholders gained that power, the failure of the system to heed the best evaluations being made would be significantly reduced: more cash would flow out of established firms that invest in projects with expected returns below SROR and into established firms that have more promising project lists. But the domination of retained earnings financing might be only partially reduced, and the resulting trade-off between communications efficiency and sensitivity to innovative project proposals might still not be optimal.

To see why this is so, we have to remember the analogy, set out in the beginning of this chapter, between the finance process and a hierarchical organization. Real investment opportunities are not scarce commodities that are allocated by the price mechanism; they are places to put scarce real resources. These places are found by a process ultimately under the control of individual savers that, like a hierarchical organization, relies on the advice of, and the delegation of decisions to, more knowledgeable individuals. Savers have very little idea what real investment projects their savings would best be used to implement; they rely on this process. Organization theory teaches us that both innovative and noninnovative organizational behavior is self-reinforcing. As we saw earlier, an innovative component in an otherwise noninnovative organization is badly adapted; the component's information-processing system is too costly to survive (see section C2.421). Thus, even if shareholders had new powers to increase the role of the outside finance process and such an increase would be desirable, it might not occur. Savers might not seek greater dividend payouts because they would not be aware of the innovative new firm opportunities that are being missed. The number of financial intermediaries who can perform the function of finding good innovative new firm possibilities may be well adapted to the current level of dividend payout. Potential new intermediaries will have difficulty persuading investors that they can find additional opportunities. The operations of such intermediaries are expensive, making their services high priced, and it may take a decade for them to be able to demonstrate the full dimensions of the rate of return being realized on any initial investments they are able to gather funds to implement.[148] Reliance on individual investors to take the initiative to enlarge the outside sector runs into the additional problem discussed earlier (section C2.423), that there are system-wide learning economies from an increase in the funding of innovative new firms. It is also unlikely that shareholders of an individual firm will impose on the firm the innovation-inducing pressures of lower available internal funds, since the immediate effect of such action would be to raise the firm's costs compared with its competitors. Yet the preceding analysis suggests that if all established firms operated under these pressures, the benefits from the increase in innovation might well outweigh the increased costs.

3. Williamson's M-Form Hypothesis and the Role of the Conglomerate in the Finance Process

This macro analysis provides a framework for analysis of, and can be further illuminated by comparison with, Oliver Williamson's theory of the "M-form" corporation.[149] Of particular interest to us are his conclusions concerning the role of the M-form conglomerate in the finance process. M-form firms contain a number of semi-autonomous divisions organized along product, brand, or geographic lines. The operating decisions (what we have referred to here as the production decisions) of each division are made by the managers of the division with relatively little involvement by the top managers of the corporation. Top corporate management (the "general office") engages in strategic planning and resource allocation (what we have referred to as project choice), establishes incentive structures for division managers, and monitors the results of their operations.

In what constitutes a major transformation over the last fifty years, most large U.S. corporations today utilize the M-form.[150] The development of the M-form, Williamson suggests, in turn permitted the development of the M-form conglomerate firm in which now a significant portion of all business activity occurs. The M-form conglomerate consists of a diversified set of operating units whose joinder cannot be explained in terms of the ordinary technological or organizational advantages of vertical or horizontal integration.[151] Williamson makes two key propositions concerning the effects of these developments on industrial performance: (a) the significant alleviation of the problem of the separation of share ownership from control originally identified by Berle and Means and later more formally analyzed by managerial economists including himself,[152] and (b) the creation of a superior substitute to external capital markets as a means for allocating funds generated by existing operations to implement the proposed projects in the economy with the most promising prospects.[153]

Williamson starts his analysis, as we have here, with the assumption that human beings have bounded rationality (limited knowledge, diffused heterogeneously, and limited computational ability) and behave opportunistically. From this, he concludes that organization theory has important contributions to make in the study of economics. He also shares the doubts expressed here concerning the effectiveness of the takeover threat and product competition as checks on managerial discretion.[154] Yet both of his key propositions are, to some extent at least, at odds with the conclusions reached here. The micro analysis of management behavior in large firms, on which the macro analysis is in part built, suggests that the separation share of ownership from control leads to significant deviations from what neoclassical theory would predict (see section B3.2). The macro analysis of a world of fast change suggests that allocating by external markets the cash flow generated by existing operations, while costly, has significant advantages and that the existing system may not be at the optimal point in the trade-off between these advantages and the lower operating costs of a finance process dominated by internal funding (see sections C2.42 and 2.5). It is thus worthwhile looking at his two key propositions to determine what differences really exist and, to the extent they do, why.

The discussion below suggests that Williamson exaggerates to the extent that he claims that the M-form in and of itself has systems-level consequences as opposed to being just an efficiency-enhancing reform internal to each firm that adopts it. However, he makes a subtle and important point that the M-form conglomerate is a historically new and special entity that requires separate analysis from that of the ordinary firm in order for us to have a full understanding of the effect of the finance process on industrial performance. Because the conglomerate straddles the positions of being a firm and being a systems-level alternative to the market, the analysis of the conglomerate has been postponed until the point, now reached, where the tools for analyzing the system as whole have been laid out.

3.1 *The M-Form Hypothesis*

The starting point for a discussion of Williamson's theory is his analysis of the historical origins of the M-form corporation. Relying on Chandler's histories of American business,[155] Williamson suggests that the development of the M-form firm was preceded in the late nineteenth century by the development of the U-form corporation, a large single product enterprise organized along functional lines with divisions such as sales, finance, and manufacturing. Enterprises of such large size became an efficient way to produce certain goods both because of innovations leading to technological economies of scale and because of changes leading to organizational economies—factors that made a hierarchical organization a more economical governance structure for making allocation decisions than a set of smaller firms performing in the aggregate the same work and linked by markets. Organization along functional lines permitted an efficient division of labor. As U-form firms continued to grow, however, the higher hierarchical levels tended to lose control over their lower ones (because of difficulties in specifying goals for the functional divisions in terms of overall enterprise objectives and because of difficulties in the coordination of the complex interactions among large functional divisions). Top managers became so overwhelmed by the supervision of operational decisions that they could not attend to long-run strategic entrepreneurial decisions.[156]

The first firms to convert to M-form organization were General Motors and Du Pont in the 1920s. The M-form effected a decomposition of corporate activity in a way that permitted the subunits to operate more independently of each other. Each unit became a profit center. Top management did not need nearly as much information to monitor effectively operating divisions. Much less coordination among divisions was needed, thereby further freeing up top management. The imposition of appropriate incentive structure caused the division managers to identify with a goal (maximizing divisional profits) which was more consistent with firm goals than was the case with the U-form, where division managers simply wanted to maximize the size of their division.

Williamson sees the creation of this new form as having revolutionary consequences for the operation of the finance process. Top managers act like agents of the shareholders because, without operating responsibilities, they are more likely to identify with the firm-wide goal of profits as opposed to the various organizational subgoals associated with the various operating units.[157] Williamson recognizes, as I do in chapter 1 (section A1), that firm management can perform both finance process functions: project choice and, through control reassignment and the creation of incentives, the structuring of existing project production decisions. In his terms, the M-form is like a miniature capital market but with the functions being performed administratively by the general office rather than by an actual market.[158]

Compared with the real market, Williamson believes that unless the M-form "diversif[ies] to excess," the administrative substitute performs these functions better.[159] It monitors more effectively because of its intimate knowledge and its insider status; it can reassign control of existing projects with the ease of an executive fiat instead of a cumbersome hostile tender offer or proxy fight; it prevents cash flow from automatically returning to its source for reinvestment and instead exposes the proposed projects of each unit to internal competition judged by top management, which has more in-depth knowledge than the outside capital market.

While the M-form first appeared as a method of reorganizing existing U-form firms, its creation ultimately led to the development of a new kind of firm, the M-form conglomerate. M-form conglomerates arose both out of new, more diversified real investment by previously undiversified M-form firms and out of mergers, acquisitions, and hostile tender offers. Williamson hypothesizes that the M-form provides an answer to the puzzle as to why conglomerates, which have no obvious reason for existence in terms of any need for interaction among their operating units, have nevertheless arisen. A large portion of conglomerate firms exist, in his view, simply because of the ability of the general office to perform in a superior fashion functions that would otherwise be performed by the external capital market. But for the development of the M-form, the individual operating units of M-form conglomerates would be independent firms.

3.2 *The M-Form and the Problems Arising from Separation of Share Ownership from Control*

The question of whether the M-form has really significantly alleviated the problems arising from the separation of share ownership from control is best answered by asking it first with respect to transformed U-form firms and then with respect to M-form conglomerates.

3.21 *Transformed U-Form firms*

Williamson makes a strong case that when undiversified U-form firms reorganized into M-form firms, the outcomes of the firm decision-making process were ones more in line with shareholder interests. And if you define the class of persons that constitute "management" broadly enough, some of the changes came at the expense of management. It is harder to argue, however, that the M-form is a reform that alleviates the particular problems that occur because share ownership is separated from control. Compare a chief executive of one U-form firm who is also a control shareholder and the chief executive of another U-form firm where control and share ownership are separate. The micro analysis suggests, it will be seen, that the personal interests of each chief executive are equally damaged by managers that head up his firm's functional divisions pursuing parochial rather than shareholder interests. It also suggests that the conversion to M-form should be equally helpful to each. Interestingly, as Williamson himself notes, the pioneer M-form conversions, General Motors and Du Pont, were not firms where share ownership was separated from control.[160]

The highest level of management of a U-form, the level to which shareholders have directly delegated decision making, are above the level of managers heading up functions (even if the functional managers in the U-form participate in central decision making). If the micro analysis is correct, the instrumental goal that best serves the highest-level management (what we refer to as top management) of a U-form firm where share ownership and control are separate will be maximization of AACF (aggregate available cash flow for the life of the firm discounted to present value; see section B3.2). The transformation to M-form serves this top management goal as much as it does the interests of shareholders. AACF is increased when cash flow from existing operations is allocated to the proposed investment projects with the highest yields and when the firm's production decisions maximize the cash flow generated by existing productive capacity. Equally important, the transformation to the M-form does nothing to correct what the micro analysis identifies as a primary deviation between actual management behavior when share ownership is separated from control and what is predicted by the neoclassical model: the desire, when the supply of internally generated funds exceeds the needs of proposed projects with expected returns greater than or equal to SROR (what shareholders could earn if they received dividends and reinvested them), to utilize the funds to invest in proposed projects with expected returns less than SROR.

3.22 *M-Form Conglomerates*

We are still left with the question of whether the rise of M-form conglomerates, another phenomenon permitted by the development of the M-form, alleviates separation of share ownership from control problems. The M-form conglomerate involves a genuine change in the interface between shareholders and an operating unit. With U-form firms that were transformed into M-form firms, the functions of capital allocation, control reassignment, and incentive structuring with respect to each of the multiple operating units were already being made within a single firm (though perhaps not as well as after the transformation). With an M-form conglomerate, the individual operating units, before joinder, each constituted an independent firm, and these functions were performed by the external capital market interacting with their respective managements. The M-form involves the substitution of an administrative mechanism to perform these functions.

Although Williamson sees one advantage of interposing the conglomerate general office between the operating units and external capital markets to be an increase in the effectiveness of the monitoring of unit managers, the micro analysis suggests that such improved monitoring is unnecessary as far as production decisions by unit managers are concerned. If the unit managers were instead the top management of independent firms seeking to maximize AACF, they would be self-motivated to make production decisions (the inputs and outputs of existing productive capacity) identical to the ones that are in the best interests of shareholders. Maximum share value and maximum AACF each requires existing capacity to be used in a way that maximizes its cash flow.*

---

*The micro analysis does not include top management compensation and expenses as an input expense. AACF is the source of funds out of which these are paid (as well as out of which dividends and internally funded new investment is paid). In part because of the separation of share ownership and control, top management compensation and expenses include a managerial surplus in the sense that they are greater

Project choice is another matter. In management-controlled firms, project choice involves aspects of congruence between management and shareholder interests and aspects of divergence. The congruence is that both share value and AACF are enhanced when the firm uses internally generated funds for investment in proposed projects with better prospects in preference to those with worse prospects. Thus, in that aspect, there is again no problem of separation of share ownership from control to be alleviated by interposing the general office of the M-form conglomerate. The divergence, as noted above, is the desire, when internal funds are in sufficient supply relative to the firm's list of proposed projects, to use them to invest in projects with expected returns less than SROR.

There is no reason to believe that this divergence of interests is any less in the case of top management of an M-form conglomerate and its shareholders than in the case of the top management of an operating unit maintained as an independent firm and its shareholders. First, the micro analysis would suggest that maximizing AACF is an instrumental goal that serves the personal values of conglomerate managers as well as it does managers of independent operating unit firms. Conglomerate top management should not identify any more closely with shareholder interests in this regard than managers of individual firms.* Chandler, whose managerial firms serve

---

than would be competitively necessary to retain the existing management team. A conglomerate central office may be able to reduce or eliminate the managerial surplus that managers of the operating units would enjoy if they headed independent firms. There is no *a priori* reason to believe, however, that the managerial surplus of the top management of the conglomerate, an enterprise equal in size to the aggregate of its operating units, would not be at least as great as the aggregate of the managerial surpluses of each of the units if run as independent firms.

*Concerning this question, Williamson says: "The M-form conglomerate can be thought of as substituting an administrative relation between an operating division and stockholders where a market relation had existed previously. . . . The substitution can have beneficial effects in goal pursuit. . . . The advantage to goal pursuit is that which accrues to M-form organizations in general: since the general management of an M-form conglomerate is disengaged from operating matters, a presumption that the general office favors profits over functional goals is warranted."[161]

There seems to be no reason why the very top managers of an independent operating unit firm, who are above any managers with specific functional concerns, would be any more inclined to identify with particular functions over profits than the top managers of a conglomerate. By using the term "profit," Williamson unfortunately masks the key conflict between the goal of shareholders—share value maximization—and the instrumental goal of the managements of both independent operating units and conglomerates—maximization of the available cash flow of the firm over time.

as Williamson's model for the M-form, sees the tendency to retain and reinvest more than shareholders would wish to be one of the hallmarks of the economy's transition to managerial capitalism. Managers in such firms think of themselves as members of a group dedicated to the profession of managing operating units and are therefore always looking for objects on which to exercise their professional skills. Second, it is unlikely that shareholder constraints on the extent to which management can deviate from shareholder interests by investment in below-SROR projects will be greater in the case of conglomerates than in the case of independent operating unit firms. In fact, the constraints may be less in the case of conglomerates because of their greater complexity and size. Complexity makes deviations harder for outsiders to detect and size makes firms more difficult to take over.[162]

Compared with managers of the individual units operating as independent firms, then, conglomerate managers are as likely to invest internal funds in inferior projects when better ones are not available and are subject to no greater shareholder constraints on making such investments. Nevertheless, the rise in M-form conglomerates does reduce the importance of these factors by reducing the number of situations which trigger this behavior. As is illustrated in the next section, unless any two or more operating units are in identical positions in terms of their supplies of internal funds relative to the quality of their proposed project lists, their joinder into one conglomerate is likely to reduce the number of below-SROR projects, if any, that are implemented.

The joinder of any two or more operating units that results in a reduction in the number of below-SROR projects implemented will create an entity with an increased aggregate AACF. Thus, there exist financial incentives for the managers of such units to merge and, where the managers of the units cannot agree, for the managers of one to attempt hostile takeovers of the others. In addition, one of the most interesting ideas to flow out of Williamson's M-form hypothesis is that the principal explanation for the increase in hostile tender offers is the development of a group of potential acquirors, the M-form conglomerates, whose managements have the skills to run a diversified set of operations and thus can easily digest their targets.[163]

In theory, these factors could lead to a series of joinders such that below-SROR investments are completely eliminated from the econ-omy. Industry would consist of a set of conglomerates each of which would be an optimal pool of operating units matching the surplus internal funds of some with the shortage of others, thereby render-ing irrelevant our concerns about overretention. In fact, the degree and pattern of joinder is likely to fall well short of this ideal. To start, fighting against the financial incentives for merger are man-agers' personal desires for autonomy and job security. Second, a merger requires some kind of understanding concerning how the managerial advantages of the combined firm will be divided be-tween the two constituent management groups. The parties to a po-tentially advantageous voluntary merger may not be able to reach such an understanding because each party is risk averse and does not possess as much information as the other concerning the poten-tial of the other to contribute to the AACF of the joint enterprise. The other alternative, a hostile tender offer, is significantly impeded by the informational problems discussed in chapter 1 (section C2.23) and the strategies discussed the micro analysis (section B3.222). Fi-nally, the ability of top management teams to successfully run highly diversified sets of operating units, a precondition for both voluntary mergers and hostile tender offers, appears to have been overopti-mistically assessed in the 1960s and early 1970s. This is suggested by the recent "de-diversification movement" among large firms,[164] by the poor long-run share price performance of the most diversified conglomerates that were formed during the earlier period,[165] and by case studies of the ultimate success of diversified acquisitions.[166]

3.3 *The M-Form Conglomerate as Substitute for the Market in Reallocating Cash Flow.*

Williamson's second key proposition is that the wide adoption of the M-form has created a superior substitute to the use of external markets as a means of allocating cash flow generated by existing operations to implement new investment projects. He is presumably referring here to the M-form conglomerate, since U-form firms were already performing this reallocation function internally before their transformations to M-form. Williamson's proposition is based on two distinct premises. One is that cash flows "are not automatically re-turned to their sources [the operating units]" for reinvestment but instead are exposed to internal competition and assigned to those projects proposed to the general office from all over the firm possessing what the general office believes to be the best prospects.[167] The other premise recognizes the possibility that if the operating units were independent firms, they might not retain all of their cash flow for reinvestment. In comparing the ability of the general office of a conglomerate to find places to reinvest these funds with that of the market, the general office "trade[s] off breadth for depth" in terms of information concerning possible investment projects.[168] As long as the conglomerate does not diversify to excess, the gains from depth outweigh the losses in breadth.[169]

In essence, Williamson's second key proposition is that the rise of the conglomerate constitutes a change in the structure of the finance process that improves the way it engages in project choice. The proposition can be examined in terms of the criteria developed in the macro analysis: to what extent does the change help or hurt in terms of the potentials for failure in the way the system handles information? Does the change increase or reduce the extent to which the system heeds the best available evaluations of the projects being proposed in the economy? Does the change aid in sending information to the persons best able to evaluate their prospects? Does conglomeration increase or decrease the cost of operating the finance process, and how does any alteration in costs compare with any improvement or decline in system performance in terms of the other two criteria?*

3.31 *Effect of M-Form Conglomeration on the Extent to Which the System Heeds the Best Evaluations Available*

The top managements of large firms, to whom are proposed most of the projects in the economy, have the inclination and ability to withhold from shareholders, and to reinvest, a large portion of the firms' cash flows whether or not justified by the quality of the firms' proposed project lists. The preceding macro analysis, which took no account of the special role of the conglomerate firm, suggests that in a world of fast change such as ours, this inclination on the part of

---

*Whether or not conglomeration has effects on competition and hence a secondary effect on system goals is a much debated and complex question outside of the scope of this book.

top management leads to a considerable deviation between the proposed projects actually implemented and the ones that ought to be implemented given the best evaluations available (see section C2.41). This is because firms that have the best ideas do not necessarily have the internal funds to implement them, and the inclination to retain by the managements of other firms with less good ideas impedes the needed movement of funds from one group to the other.

3.311 *Considerations of Retention and External Finance Behavior*

What does the rise of conglomerates do to this picture? To start to determine this, we obviously need to know something about what is the retention and the external finance behavior of a typical conglomerate, and what would be the corresponding behavior of its operating units if they instead were independent firms. Williamson says nothing explicit about this matter. However, his first premise, quoted above, with its reference to cash flows that absent conglomeration "automatically return to their source," seems to imply that all firms retain for reinvestment some similar fixed percentage of their cash flows. While analysis will suggest that the M-form conglomerate does in fact aid the system in heeding the best available evaluations, this implied assumption of a fixed rate of retention exaggerates the effect of conglomeration compared with more realistic assumptions concerning firm retention and external finance behavior.

To see the importance of assumptions concerning retention and external finance on the effect of conglomeration, first assume that (1) each of the operating units of a conglomerate would have the same retention rate (whether 100 percent or less) if they were independent firms, (2) the conglomerate would also have the same rate, and (3) neither the operating units as operating firms nor the conglomerate would raise funds externally. Also assume for the moment that the general office of the conglomerate makes its decisions on the same (and therefore equally accurate) evaluation of the prospects of each proposed project as the managers of the operating units and that the general office makes these evaluations costlessly. Under these assumptions, unless each of the operating units generates a cash flow precisely in proportion to its list of proposed projects, the conglomerate would enhance the extent to which the best projects are chosen. The general office could take funds from a unit with an inferior list that would have been invested within the unit if it were separate and give it to the unit with a superior list to fund a project that the unit with the superior list would have skipped if it were separate. This point can be easily seen by the stylized example set out in table 2.2. The example involves three operating units, A, B, and C, each of which has a list of four proposed projects with expected rates of return as set out in the table. Each of the twelve projects requires the same amount of funds for implementation and is equally risky. Each of the operating units has a cash flow equal to the amount needed to implement two projects. Scenario I portrays a situation where each operating unit is an independent firm, each

Table 2.2

| | | *Scenario I* | |
	Unit A	*Unit B*	*Unit C*
Rates of Return	.01	.04	.07
on Proposed	.02	.05	.08
Projects	**.03**	**.06**	**.09**
	.04	**.07**	**.10**
		Scenarios II, III, and IV	
	Unit A	*Unit B*	*Unit C*
Rates of Return	.01	.04	**.07**
on Proposed	.02	.05	**.08**
Projects	.03	**.06**	**.09**
	.04	**.07**	**.10**
		Scenario V	
	Unit A	*Unit B*	*Unit C*
Rates of Return	.01	.04	.065
on Proposed	.02	.05	**.07**
Projects	.03	**.06**	**.08**
	.04	**.07**	**.09**
			.10
		Scenario VI	
	Unit A	*Unit B*	*Unit C*
Rates of Return	.01	.04	**.065**
on Proposed	.02	.05	**.07**
Projects	.03	.06	**.08**
	.04	**.07**	**.09**
			.10

retains 100 percent of its cash flow, and none resort to external funds. The projects implemented are in boldface and their average expected rate of return is 6½ percent. Scenario II portrays a situation where the three operating units are joined in a single conglomerate firm which retains 100 percent of its cash flow and does not resort to external funds. The projects implemented are again in boldface. The general office has moved the funds generated by unit A and used them to implement two projects of unit C that had gone unfunded in Scenario I. The average expected rate of return is 7⅝ percent.

These assumptions concerning retention and use of external finance are not, however, very realistic. Shareholder pressure is not totally ineffective, so firms with inferior proposed project lists relative to their cash flows should retain less than firms with relatively superior lists. Firms are not likely to avoid outside finance if their project lists are sufficiently good. Thus, we might more plausibly expect firms with relatively inferior lists to retain sufficient cash flow to fund projects with expected returns a certain margin (the "discretionary margin") below SROR and distribute the rest. Similarly, firms with relatively superior lists would be willing to engage in external finance if after utilizing all of their cash flow (or all that is available after payment of some level of dividend that they feel is necessary for other reasons) to fund projects on their list, they have remaining unfunded projects with an expected rate of return in excess of SROR plus "total external finance cost", i.e., "recipient's costs" (the firm's transaction cost of obtaining outside finance) and "saver's cost" (the saver's cost of finding a place of new investment) (see section C2.41 for an elaboration of these concepts).* This retention and external finance behavior would be predicted by the micro analysis, which posits that managers maximize AACF subject to a shareholder constraint.

With these changes, the conglomerate has a reduced role in aiding the system to implement projects which the best available evaluations indicate have the highest prospects. The focus is now a smaller group of projects, those with expected rates of return in the range ("the internal funding only range"):

---

*For savers to be willing to purchase the firm's securities, the expected return of the security must exceed SROR by an amount at least equal to saver's cost. The saver's net return would then at least equal SROR.

(SROR - the discretionary margin) ↔ (SROR + total external finance cost)

Whether the operating units are independent firms or are joined in a conglomerate, all projects with expected returns above this range will be implemented, and all projects with expected returns below the range will not be implemented. If the units are independent, each firm will fund projects within the range to the extent that there are internal funds remaining to do so. Conglomeration pools the projects on the list of each unit and the funds generated by each unit. After first funding projects on the pooled list with expected returns exceeding the internal funding only range, the internal funds, if any, remaining are used to fund the best of the projects within the range on this pooled list. Conglomeration would result in an improvement in the projects chosen only when one unit has one or more projects within the range that would otherwise go unfunded and that are superior to the projects of another unit within the range that otherwise would be funded.*

Two more examples, Scenarios III and IV (where conglomeration has no effect) and Scenarios V and VI (where it does), illustrate these points. Throughout, we assume that for each unit as an independent firm and for the conglomerate as a single firm, SROR is 6¼ percent, the discretionary margin is 1 percent, and total costs of external finance are ½ percent. Thus, the internal funding only range in which conglomeration has the potential of altering the projects implemented is 5¼ to 6¾ percent.

In Scenario III the three units are independent firms. Unit A implements no projects, since all fall below the range. Unit B implements its two most promising projects, using up all of its internal funds. Unit C implements all four projects. The funds for two are raised externally, since its internally generated funds have been ex-

---

*Because of its partial equilibrium nature, this analysis leaves out one potential beneficial effect of conglomeration on project choice. Suppose there were two units where, if they were independent, one unit would fund a project in the internal funding only range and the other unit would fund no such projects and need to seek external funding for a project above that range. Joinder would result in the funds for the first project going instead to the second, and between them the two units would fund one less project. Demand for external funds would be reduced, thereby lowering SROR and permitting some other firm to implement a project with an expected return that previously was in the internal funding only range and that was not implemented because of insufficient internal funds.

hausted implementing its two most promising projects, and its two remaining ones, the 7 percent and 8 percent ones, have expected returns above the external finance threshold. In Scenario IV, the three units are joined in a conglomerate. The same six projects are implemented. The conglomerate firm has internal funds sufficient for six projects, and there are only six projects above or within the internal funding only range. Consequently, the issue of external finance does not arise. The reason conglomeration has no effect on the projects implemented is that the pool of projects within the range is simply unit B's 6 percent project, and so unit C does not contribute a superior project within the range that would go unfunded if C were independent.

Scenario V differs from III and Scenario VI differs from IV only in that unit C has a fifth proposed project on its list. Now the projects implemented by the units as independent firms, Scenario V, are different from those implemented by a single conglomerate of the units, Scenario VI. This is because the pool of projects within the range now includes C's 6½ percent project as well as B's 6 percent project, and as independent firms the 6 percent project would be funded and the 6½ percent one would not be.

3.312 *Considerations of General Office Evaluations and Cost*

The discussion so far concerning the effect of conglomerates on the extent to which the finance process heeds the best available evaluations assumes away two important interrelated considerations. The first consideration concerns the project evaluations on which the general office makes its investment decisions. These evaluations, though unbiased, are not on average as accurate as those of the managers of the operating units proposing the projects, who are closer to the facts. We know from the micro analysis that a project proponent may have an interest in persuading the funding source to implement the project when it is not in the source's interest to do so (see section B2.121). The top manager of the operating unit is either the proponent himself or is put in a position akin to a proponent *vis-à-vis* the general office when he seeks project funding. He may be opportunistic and communicate to the general office a more optimistic projection of the project's prospects than he truly believes to be the case. The general office can try to correct for this bias, but the uncertainty associated with the correction makes the general office evaluation less accurate.

The lesser accuracy of general office evaluations means that, unlike what the analysis so far would suggest, if conglomeration results in a change in the projects selected for implementation, the change is not necessarily an improvement as judged by the best available evaluations. The general office might incorrectly believe one project superior to another, where the more accurate unit manager evaluations suggest the reverse. An inferior project might then be funded in preference to a superior one, where the opposite result would have occurred if the units had been independent firms.

The other consideration assumed away in the preceding section concerns the changes in the costs of information gathering and processing caused by conglomeration. Conglomeration, it turns out, has both negative and positive cost effects. The negative effect relates to projects which in the eyes of unit managers have expected returns within the internal funding only range. The costs of the general office evaluation of proposed projects come on top of those incurred by unit managers in the making of their evaluations. In the case of proposed projects within the internal funding only range, no costs evaluating the proposals beyond those of the unit managers would be incurred if the operating units were independent firms. Thus, with respect to these projects, any improvement that conglomeration brings in the extent to which the projects chosen correspond to what is suggested by the best available evaluations comes at the price of an increase in the cost of operating the finance process.

The likely positive cost effect concerns projects which in the eyes of unit managers have expected returns above the internal funding only range. These are projects which, other than in the case of an overly erroneous negative general office evaluation,* will be implemented whether there is conglomeration or not. If internal funds are insufficient, funds will be obtained externally. Conglomeration reduces the number of instances where external funds are needed. For example, in each of Scenarios III, IV, V, and VI, unit C's 7 percent and 8 percent projects are implemented. But in III and V, the proj-

---

*SROR, the rate of return, net of shareholder cost of reinvestment, that shareholders can expect to receive if they receive dividends and reinvest them, is already in essence discounted for the probable error rate (measured against the best evaluations available) that external finance entails.

ects are funded with external funds, whereas in IV and VI, where the operating units are joined in a conglomerate, no external funds are needed. This is because with the independent firms, the cash flow of unit A is paid out to the external finance process in the form of dividends, but with conglomeration that cash flow is captured internally and directed to the unit C projects. External finance involves system costs—the sum of recipient's cost and saver's cost. To the extent that conglomeration reduces external finance, it eliminates these costs. If the costs of the general office evaluation is less than the total cost of external finance, then, with respect to the projects that convert from being externally funded to being internally funded, conglomeration reduces the cost of operating the finance process.

The critical issue arising from these two interrelated additional considerations is whether the rise of the M-form conglomerate has made a net contribution when we weigh against each other the two criteria so far considered—the extent to which the system heeds the best available evaluations and cost—and without yet factoring into the analysis our third criterion, i.e., the ability of the system to make good evaluations. In the case of proposed projects that unit manager evaluations put within the internal funding only range, we need to know whether the improvements in the system heeding the best evaluations we originally identified (when we assumed the general office used the same evaluations as unit managers) survive when we recognize that the general office will decide on the basis of unbiased but less accurate evaluations. And assuming some of these gains survive, are they worth the increased cost of information processing that the extra layer of evaluation involves? In the case of proposed projects that unit manager evaluations put above the internal funding only range, where conglomeration substitutes internal for external funding, we need to know whether the cost of general office evaluation is less than the cost of external finance. If so, are the savings worth the decrease in accuracy of evaluation which leads to the failure to implement some worthwhile projects that would have been funded with independent firm-operating units?

At the heart of all these questions is the ability of the conglomerate general office to come, at reasonably low cost, to evaluations close to those of their unit managers. In the economy there almost certainly exist some sets consisting of a management group prepared to act as a general office and two or more operating units where 1) the unit manager evaluations would suggest a benefit in transferring funds generated by one unit to fund a project proposed by another unit, and 2) the general office can cheaply (both absolutely and compared with the costs of external finance) come to evaluations that are very close to those of the operating unit managers. The existence of sets with these two characteristics means that there are potential conglomerations which, weighing the two criteria considered so far, would yield net system gains. The existence of sets possessing the first characteristic is the inevitable result of differences among operating units in their supplies of internally generated funds relative to the quality of their project lists. Some of these sets should also possess the second characteristic. Unit managers of conglomerate divisions have a better chance to develop experience-based authority with the general office than do managers of independent firm-operating units with participants in the outside finance process. A general office, because of its ongoing management of the operating unit, may, prior to receiving the project proposal, have an abundance of knowledge not likely to be possessed by any outside finance process participant concerning the technology and market relevant to the proposal and the ability of the operating unit as an organization to carry it out. This knowledge permits the general office to second-guess the professed evaluation of the unit managers without great cost. All of this is the "depth" to which Williamson refers.

Any conglomeration of a set of a management team and two or more operating units that has these two characteristics will create an entity with an AACF greater than the aggregate AACF of its constituent parts as independent firms. As discussed earlier, this creates financial incentives for both voluntary mergers and hostile tender offers. Therefore in terms of the two criteria considered so far— heeding the best available evaluations and cost—we can see not only potential system gains from some conglomeration but also the existence of forces to achieve this conglomeration. Assuming, however, as Williamson does, that at some point the gains from breadth are overwhelmed by the corresponding loss of depth, there can be such a thing as too much conglomeration. If the only force for conglomeration is the financial incentives just discussed, we obviously need not worry about too much conglomeration in terms of the two considered criteria because the incentives for voluntary merger or hostile tender offer would disappear at that point. On the contrary, as also developed in the earlier discussion, the existence of a variety of impediments to voluntary mergers and hostile tender offers means that in some instances conglomeration will not occur despite the existence of such incentives, and so system gains will be missed.

This conclusion that, in terms of the two considered criteria, the rise of conglomeration has yielded system gains is nevertheless tentative. Conglomeration may occur for other reasons such as subtle anticompetitive designs, the accumulation of political power, or managerial aggrandizement. If these factors are sufficiently important, the amount of conglomeration that has occurred may have exceeded the optimal trade-off point and may have led to system losses as measured by the two considered criteria. A definitive conclusion as to whether there are system gains or losses as measured by such criteria ultimately requires a fuller understanding of the managerial motives behind conglomerate mergers than is possible within the scope of this book.

3.32 *Effect of M-Form Conglomeration on the Extent to Which the System Sends Information to the Best Evaluators*

A full assessment of the effects of the rise of conglomerates on the finance process cannot stop at a weighing of the criteria I have considered so far—heeding the best available evaluations and cost—but must also include an examination of what that change in structure does in terms of information reaching the persons capable of making the best evaluations of projects. Specifically, in a world of fast change, do the changes in information flow and decision-making assignment from conglomeration enhance or diminish the system's sensitivity to the potential of innovative investment proposals?

The finance process is an organization. As developed in the macro analysis, if we look at the question of what makes an organization innovative, several general principles emerge: persons of responsibility within it should not be narrow experts but should have overlapping roles; persons playing intelligence roles should be different from those involved in everyday operations; and persons and subgroups constituting the organization should operate in an uncertain environment and with a low degree of autonomy (see section C2.42). The finance process as currently structured, with its high degree of reliance on internal funding, does not fare very well under these measures. It appears highly communications efficient but not very sensitive to new ideas. A restructuring in which firms would pay out more or even all available cash flow is seen as an antidote. Such a restructuring would increase the number of new firm project proposals evaluated by the outside sector, a context for evaluation that is more sensitive to innovative ideas than established firms considering proposals of their own employees. The need, with such a restructuring, for established firms themselves to seek outside funds also increases the innovation sensitivity of the primary other context for evaluation—top management of such firms reviewing proposals of their own employees—because the restructuring reduces autonomy and increases stress.

Assuming for the moment no restructuring to increase payouts generally, inclusion into the analysis of an intermediate-level organization, the M-form conglomerate, has two effects on innovation sensitivity that work in opposite directions. To the extent that the operating units, if independent firms, would finance their investments internally, joinder in a conglomerate adds stress and reduces the autonomy of operating unit managers. For the same reasons that forcing established firms to seek outside funds increases their sensitivity, this added stress and reduced autonomy should make the unit managers, when formulating their project lists, more sensitive to innovative proposals coming from proponents within their own units. On the other hand, to the extent that operating units, if independent firms, would finance their projects externally, joinder in a conglomerate reduces the sensitivity of the system to innovative investment proposals because, as we have seen, conglomeration, by substituting internal for external transfers of funds, reduces the dividends paid out to the outside sector of the finance process. Reduction of the role of the outside sector has three negative effects. First, the very factors that make this substitution of general office-directed intrafirm transfer for external finance lower in cost—the presence of well-established interest and authority rules employed by the general office when dealing with unit managers—makes the funding sources less open to innovative ideas.* Second, the unit manager can appeal to only one source rather than to a group of different sources with a diversity of viewpoints. Third, the reduction in funds entering the outside sector reduces the number of new firm project proposals that will be considered by the system.

It is not possible at a theoretical level to determine how these factors balance out. However, the comparison in the semiconductor study of the semiconductor investments of the large diversified electronics firms with both those of the established firms predominantly devoted to semiconductor manufacture, which because they were growing rapidly frequently sought external funds, and those of new firms founded to implement a project does not reflect well on the diversified firms in terms of innovation. The more specialized established firms tended to make more innovative investments, though not as innovative as brand-new firms. The weakness of the diversified firms appears to stem from the unremitting pressure that the general office puts on its divisions to produce maximum accounting earnings. This makes unattractive the most innovative investments, which tend to have a significant period of negative earnings (reflecting noncapitalizable investment expenditures) but hold out the possibility of large positive earnings in later periods. The findings of the case study concerning general office impatience are consistent with

---

*As discussed in the micro analysis of financial intermediaries, the managers of an established firm seeking funds from an external source, the comparative alternative to a manager of an operating unit division seeking funds from a general office, also rely primarily on experience-based authority as opposed to structure of incentive-based authority, reliance on which does not create as much bias against innovation (see section B4.1). The problem with the conglomerate context for innovation is the very ease with which divisional managers in a conglomerate establish such an authority relationship with general office personnel. Both contexts for project evaluation provide some room for structure of incentive-based authority, but neither provides nearly as much room as does the new firm/external source context. In establishing incentive-based authority, the divisional manager has one advantage and one disadvantage compared with the manager of an independent operating unit firm seeking external funds. The advantage is that the general office can easily and flexibly build relevant incentives into the employment arrangement with the division managers. The disadvantage is that the division manager, unlike the manager of the independent firm, cannot own stock in the unit he manages. As is discussed in the earlier section, continued holding by the manager of an established independent firm of the firm's shares constitutes under some, but not all, circumstances a solid basis for structure of incentive authority.

a number of postmortems of the generally unsuccessful "corporate venturing" efforts that were undertaken by established diversified corporations in the 1970s across a wide range of new technologies.[170]

It is possible to develop an information-based explanation of the impatience of the general office of a diversified firm and the resulting bias against innovation relative even to the established, more specialized firms. It is not as easy for investors to understand what is going on within large diversified corporations as it is with more specialized firms. This leads to greater reliance in evaluating a firm on current accounting numbers and recent trends. With a less complex firm, investors may be willing to use softer information and determine share value by capitalizing potential future earnings that do not yet have precursors in the form of favorable current accounting earnings or trends.*

3.4 *Conclusion: M-Form Conglomeration and Forced Dividend Payout*

Conglomeration is a method of facilitating the transfer of funds generated by certain operating units so that they are invested in projects other than those on the proposed lists of the units generating funds. The preceding analysis comes to two conclusions concerning whether the rise of conglomerates has, by providing this method, improved project choice. First, unless there are strong managerial motives for conglomerate mergers beyond the advantages discussed here, the degree of conglomeration that has occurred in the economy is one that yields net system gains as measured in terms of heeding the best available evaluations and cost. Second, the effect of conglomeration on the capacity to make good evaluations, specifically on its sensitivity to the potential of innovative investment proposals, is probably negative.

---

*As discussed in the micro analysis of firm management behavior (section B3.221), the plausibility of this sort of an evaluation depends on the time horizons of top management. If the inability of investors to understand the future earnings potential of an innovative investment leads to a lower current share price when such investment is undertaken and management, out of concern for current share price, avoids such investment, it is doing so at the cost of future share price. Even if conglomerate top management has a long-run time horizon, however, it may act irrationally. If the investment community is always asking accounting-earning questions, this may become the focus of the general office and shape the pressures they put on operating unit managers. Lower current share price may also make acquisitions more difficult.

These conclusions are not highly definitive and they cut in opposite directions without providing guidance as to how one can be weighed against the other. Certainly they do not form the basis of a call for direct regulation of conglomerate mergers under a theory that such mergers alter the finance process in a way unambiguously harmful to industrial performance. Nevertheless, the preceding analysis has important applications informing a variety of other policy choices.

To start, the preceding analysis suggests that Williamson's outright enthusiasm for the M-form conglomerate (unless "too diversified") needs to be dampened. While his insight as to the special subtitute capital market role of conglomerates is crucial, he does not pursue it very far. A harder look suggests that the potential is more limited than he implies for conglomerates to alter for the better (given the best available evaluations) which of the proposed projects in the economy are chosen for implementation. At least as important a force for promoting conglomerate mergers is the cost savings in information gathering and processing which result from substituting internal for external finance of projects that would be implemented with or without conglomeration. Unfortunately these cost savings, while desirable considered in isolation, are associated with a change in finance process structure that is likely to make it less sensitive to the potentialities of innovative investment proposals.

The more balanced view of conglomerates that comes out of the analysis is relevant in weighing the pros and cons of certain antitrust, tax, and securities law provisions that, among their various consequences, affect the climate for conglomerate mergers. In this connection, the analysis suggests some fruitful lines of empirical research that would add to our understanding of the desirability of conglomerates. One, along the lines of the studies reported in appendix 2.1, would be a comparison of the tendency of diversified versus undiversified firms to overretain. Such a study would give us a better sense of how much conglomerates help in this regard. Another would be further study comparing conglomerates and less diversified firms in their proclivity for undertaking innovative investment (though such a study would not capture the negative effect of conglomeration on innovation that occurs through the resulting reduction of funds in the external sector of the finance process available for starting new firms).

The analysis also helps inform a more fundamental policy choice that is further considered in chapter 6. So far the discussion has been in terms of whether project choice functions better with or without conglomeration assuming that corporate managers, conglomerate and otherwise, retain their wide discretion in determining distributions to shareholders. The macro analysis suggests that it is useful to think about how project choice would work if the system were restructured so that large established firms would distribute more, perhaps even all, of their available cash flow. Such a fundamental reform is another method of facilitating the transfer of funds that can be viewed as an alternative to conglomeration. That raises the question whether, assuming conglomeration is better then nothing, project choice is better off relying on conglomeration or forced payout as the method for facilitating transfer. It also raises the question of whether conglomerates would still have a role to play if some kind of universal payout rule were adopted.

A restructuring to increase payout, at least in its most extreme form, would completely rob the conglomerate of its internal transfer function because all of the cash flow of the operating units would have to be paid out to shareholders for transfer in the market. Compared with conglomeration, forced payout as a mechanism of transfer has the advantage of being more comprehensive. As we have seen, a conglomerate, depending on the cash flows and project lists of its constituent operating units, may still invest in projects with expected returns below SROR. Furthermore, impediments to voluntary mergers and hostile takeovers mean that there remain in the economy independent firm-operating units that invest in projects with rates of return below SROR. The empirical evidence discussed in appendix 2.1 suggests that such investments constitute a substantial problem. Although the data relates in large part to a period preceding the conglomerate merger boom of the 1970s, it covers a period when diversified corporations were already common. The universal payout rule would eliminate all funding of projects with returns less than SROR.

In addition to the advantage of completely eliminating below-SROR investments, the increase in the use of the external sector would have one other big advantage, an increase in the sensitivity of the process to the potentialities of innovative investment, and one big disadvantage, higher systems costs. A general weighing of these factors will be postponed until chapter 6, but some specific comments should be made now concerning transfers among operating units that, absent a universal payout rule, would be effected by conglomerate general offices. At first blush it would appear that a universal payout rule would cause the disappearance of conglomerates since it would eliminate the main forces for their creation—increased AACF through transfers that would not occur without the conglomerate (or the rule) and information-gathering and -processing cost savings. The universal payout rule would appear to substitute a more expensive method of transfer for a cheaper one. A closer look suggests that conglomerates might not disappear and that the extra costs for these transfers may not be so significant. The conglomerate could serve as a special kind of financial intermediary, differing from the traditional intermediary because of a formal organizational relationship with operating unit managers, but offering its investors the same kind of service as do traditional intermediaries: searching for good investment opportunities. The formal organizational relationship should again provide depth versus the breadth advantages of traditional intermediaries. Conglomerates could increase profits not only by finding good opportunities but also by establishing a reputation for candid projection of shareholder returns, which would significantly lower their costs of external finance.

D. Summary

Every industrialized economy must have a finance process: a way for deciding at the real level which proposed investment projects should receive society's scarce savings and who should manage the projects already in existence. In our economy, the decisions made are ultimately traceable to all the individual savers through their choices of where to place their savings and, in the case of equity holders, how to vote their shares. But savers rarely have enough information to make the real-level decisions directly themselves. Like the head of a hierarchical organization, the typical saver obtains the services of persons more knowledgeable than he who either provide him with information or make decisions on his behalf.

The second part of this chapter—the macro analysis—focuses primarily on project choice decisions because the micro analysis that precedes it suggests that project choice decisions are more likely to display problems. These decisions are shaped by how the system handles information, information concerning both the prospects of proposed projects and the behavior of the more knowledgeable individuals and institutions—financial intermediaries, investment informers, and top corporate management—that stand between the saver and the real-level decisions. A conventional economic analysis of the way the system handles information has certain shortcomings that arise from the pervasive imperfections in the market for information. A cybernetic approach, utilizing the partial analogy of the finance process to a hierarchical organization, is an alternative that offers significant insights into the relationship between finance and industrial performance.

The finance process as currently structured is very communications efficient: it uses relatively little resources. The bulk of all project proposals are made by employees of existing large corporations to the top managements of the corporations for which they work. Information concerning such a proposal thus goes to only one recipient, and often, because of the close working relationship between top management and proponents, it is in highly summarized form. Relatively little such information subsequently leaves the firm, particularly in the case of the large number of firms that engage in no significant external financing.

The low cost of operation of the system as currently structured would, if other things were equal, be desirable, but other things are not equal in a world of fast change such as ours. To start, there are substantial theoretical and empirical reasons to believe that the proposals made to established firms that the system chooses to fund are not consistently the ones that the best evaluations being made suggest have the most promise. The projects of firms that do not seek new equity finance are on average historically inferior to those that do. The firms that do not seek equity finance should be investing in fewer projects so as to make available through the payment of dividends more funds in the capital markets to implement currently unfunded projects of the firms that do seek equity finance. Second, the closed system nature of most project choice decisions in the finance process makes the process less sensitive to the potential of innovative project proposals than would be the case if a smaller percentage of projects were internally funded. Finally, the internal finance bias of the system in the presence of technical change encourages concentration in product markets.

Whether or not practical changes in policy can be found that would ameliorate these problems at acceptable cost will be addressed in chapter 6. The cybernetic analysis makes clear, however, that there is no reason to assume that the current system necessarily represents an optimal trade-off between communications efficiency and serving the goals of output choice, production, and dynamic efficiency.

Appendix 2.1 Evidence Concerning Large Firm Investments Financed by Internal Funds

1. *Donaldson*

The earliest empirical evidence concerning investments by large firms financed by internal funds comes from interviews conducted by Donaldson for his study of corporate debt capacity published in 1961.[171] Donaldson chose twenty large corporations from five industries for intensive examination. He found that an overwhelming percentage of their total funds required for investment, dividends, and additions to working capital were internally generated and that, as a general matter, the firms had high earnings retention rates.[172] Interviews with the financial officers of the corporations involved suggested that the reason for this pattern was an undue preoccupation on their part with maintaining and increasing earnings per share.[173] Unlike obtaining a dollar from an external source to invest in a project, a dollar retained from the firm's cash flow and so invested will always increase earnings per share, as long as the project has a positive rate of return, no matter how low. The financial officers had a difficult time identifying with the concept that there is an opportunity cost to shareholders from such a policy in the form of the lost return from reinvestment of dividends not received.

These findings would suggest that a firm with an ample internal cash flow compared with the quality of its list of investment opportunities would, contrary to the best interests of shareholders, invest in projects with a risk-adjusted rate of return less than SROR.

In order to update Donaldson's findings, I chose at random twenty firms from the list of the *Fortune* 500 and examined their published financials for the five years 1977–1981. As a measure of the independence from the outside finance process of each of the firms in the sample, I calculated the ratio of the firm's Internally Generated Funds to Uses of Funds for each year. Internally Generated Funds were defined as Net Income + Deferred Taxes + Depreciation + Proceeds from Disposition of Property Plant and Equipment + Extraordinary Losses + Decrease (or − Increase) in Liquid Assets − Undistributed Earnings of Unconsolidated Subsidiaries. Uses of Funds were defined as Additions to Property, Plant, and Equipment + Increase (or − Decrease) in Inventory + Dividends + Repurchase of Firm Shares + Dividends to Minority Shareholders of Consolidated Subsidiaries. In essence, Internally Generated Funds is a redefinition of Net Income to approximate cash flow into the firm other than externally raised capital, and Uses of Funds is intended to reflect cash flow out of the firm (other than interest, which is already deducted from Net Income and not added back in, and repayment of debt principal, which is generally refinanced).

The ratios of each firm for the five years were averaged. Of the twenty firms, nine had ratios greater than one, four had ratios between 1.0 and .8, five had ratios between .8 and .6, and one had a ratio between .5 and .6. Thus, almost half the firms had the capacity to be completely independent of outside capital markets (other than for debt refinancings), four had the capacity to be relatively independent, and six had substantial needs for net external infusions of cash.

2. *Baumol, Heim, Malkiel, and Quandt*

The first scholars to study quantitatively the effectiveness with which large U.S. industrial firms use internal funds were Baumol, Heim, Malkiel, and Quandt ("BHMQ").[174] They looked at the growth in the earnings from 1946 to 1966 of the 900 industrial firms on the Standard and Poor's Compustat tape. They ran regressions to see how much of this growth could be explained by investment financed by "ploughback" (earnings + depreciation − dividends), how much by debt, and how much by new equity. Out of these came estimates of the rate of return on investments funded by each of these sources of finance. Depending on the definition of earnings and the assumed lag between the time of investment and the commencement of returns, the return on ploughback ranges from 3.0 to 4.6 percent, on debt from 4.2 to 14 percent, and on newly issued equity from 14 to 21 percent. These startling results were the subjects of a number of methodological criticisms. [175] BHMQ produced a second study redesigning their tests in ways that they felt were responsive to some of these criticisms.[176] Out of this second study comes the finding that the return on ploughback for firms which issue more than negligible amounts of new equity is in the same range as the return on equity and on debt. But for firms which issued no significant amount of new equity, the average rate of return on ploughback is in the neighborhood of 0.

If correct, this estimate of the average rate of return on investments for firms in the second group is very important. It suggests that the typical firm that does not seek equity capital ploughs back too much of its cash flow given the quality of its list of investment opportunities and should pay larger dividends instead. The rate of return on the most marginal project in which such a firm invests is likely to be less than 0 if the average is in the neighborhood of 0. Yet SROR is surely greater than 0.

How serious the misallocation is depends on how much SROR exceeds the rate of return on the most marginal project of the typical firm not seeking equity capital. One way of calculating this difference is to take the average annual return of 12.6 percent which investors received during the 1946–1966 period from investments in common stocks[177] as the best measure of SROR and subtract from this the below-0 marginal rate implied by the BHMQ second study. This might be criticized as calculating a difference from noncomparable numbers: one set of numbers has been derived through econometric testing of a controversial model which might introduce significant biases, the other set involves a simple average of observed facts. Nevertheless, the spread between the two sets of numbers is large enough to cover a significant amount of bias and still suggest a problem.

Another way of calculating the difference is to compare the two sets of numbers that come out of the same process—the 14–21 percent average rate of return of the first group and the near-0 average rate for the second group—and make some educated guesses about what those figures imply about the marginal rates for each of the two groups of firms. If the marginal rates of the first group are higher than those of the second group, it would suggest the second group is investing in projects with expected rates of return less than SROR.*

It can be argued that the fact that the average of the first group is higher than that of the second does not prove that the marginal rates of the two groups are different. Consider two firms, A and B, with the same amount of available cash flow and with marginal projects that have identical rates of return. Firm A issues equity and firm B does not. Since equity financing involves costs that ploughback does not, it is likely that A ploughed back most or all of its available cash flow before resorting to equity finance. This implies that the total amount which A invests is greater than the total B invests. A must have a list of projects which permits it to go farther down the list before hitting the marginal project than firm B can with its list. Thus, the average project on A's list above the marginal one must be better than the average project on B's list above the marginal one. The problem with this argument is that, intuitively, the observed difference in average rates of return between the two groups—14 to 21 percent—is too great to be explained solely by the superior quality of the top projects of the first group. This observation is reinforced by the fact that the difference in the total amount of investment between the two may not be as great as suggested by the argument. As suggested in this chapter (section C2.412), the extra costs associated with equity issues (the "recipient's costs" plus "saver's costs") compared with inside finance are conservatively estimated to be only .5–.9 percent per year. Therefore firms may not plough back all available cash flow before resorting to equity. There is empirical evidence that firms that issue equity regularly in fact feel a need to pay dividends.[178]

3. Grabowski and Mueller

Grabowski and Mueller have produced somewhat more indirect evidence that firms with fewer good investment opportunities overinvest.[179] They divided the firms on the Compustat tape into two groups, mature firms (those which were in existence before World War II and produce predominantly products in existence before World War II) and nonmature firms (the rest). They assume that nonma-

---

*A small difference would be expected because of the cost of moving funds from a firm in the second group to the first. See section C2.412.

ture firms have more investment opportunities than mature firms. They try to calculate the average rate of return on investment for firms in each category. Depending on the period studied, the difference in the average return of the nonmature firms exceeds that of the mature firms by 4 to 17 percent. Again this is a large difference to be solely the result of the higher quality of projects on the top of the nonmature firms' lists and suggests there is a difference in the marginal rates as well. By regressing stock prices on dividends, retained earnings, and depreciation, Grabowski and Mueller found that the market, in the case of the typical mature firm, would prefer a lower rate of earnings retention but, in the case of the typical nonmature firm, would not prefer a lower rate.

4. *Williamson*

There is at least one other kind of evidence that is consistent with the hypothesis that large, management-controlled industrial firms retain too much available cash flow. Almost every study that has been completed shows that these firms have a lower return on investment than firms where ownership and control are not separated.[180] Yet Williamson has shown that firms with a higher percentage of managers on the board (a measure of separation of ownership from control) retain a higher percentage of earnings.[181]

Appendix 2.2 Evidence Concerning the Determinants of Management Compensation

The earliest study in the area, by McGuire, Chiu, and Elbing ("MCE"), suggests that sales, not profits, are the main determinant of executive salaries and bonuses.[182] This conclusion is the result of a cross-section study of forty-five large industrial corporations regressing salary plus bonus of the top executives of each on sales and on profits. For five of the seven years studied, a significant relationship between compensation and sales is shown, while a significant relationship between compensation and profits is not shown in any year.

The MCE study, which fits neatly into the sales maximization hypothesis of Baumol, is criticized by Lewellen and Huntsman because of the high collinearity between sales and profits and because the error terms in the equations were heteroscedastic.[183] To correct for these problems, Lewellen and Huntsman divide through the MCE equation by the book value of the assets of each firm. By doing this, they find a positive relationship between executive compensation (both defined to include just salary and bonus and defined to include stock price based components as well) and profits. Little or no relationship is found between executive compensation and sales. They also regress each of these measures of executive compensation on the market value of the firm (each divided by the book value of the firm's assets) and find a positive relationship as well.

In any one year, the firm striving for a large AACF would make production decisions which make the most profitable possible use of its existing assets regardless of the level of sales, just as predicted by the Lewellen and Huntsman study. Over the long run, if the study is correct about the relationship between profits and compensation, the strategy suggested in this chapter of striving for a large

AACF would in one respect contribute to higher compensation than would seeking to maximize shareholder welfare and in another respect contribute to lower compensation. Compensation is closely tied to the size of a firm's assets.[184] The more dollars that are retained for reinvestment, the more is added to the book value of the firm's assets even if the amount retained exceeds what is in the shareholders' best interests. The Lewellen and Huntsman study abstracts this factor out in order to correct for the collinearity and heteroscedascity problems. On the other hand, the ratio of earnings to assets will be lower if earnings are retained beyond the point which is in shareholders' best interests. Thus, for any given level of assets, the firm which gets to that level having overretained earnings would have lower management compensation than the one which gets there having retained only as much each year as would maximize shareholder welfare. Nothing in the study suggests that the second factor dominates the first, however. The same analysis can be applied to the relationship found in the study between compensation and market value of the firm, each divided by the book value of the firm's assets.

Robert Masson points out that none of these studies focuses on management motivation within the firm because they use cross-section analysis.[185] He performs a times series analysis regressing for each of thirty-nine firms the annual change in a broadly defined measure of the firm's after-tax executive compensation on the firm's annual change in sales, change in earnings, and change in "stock value." The firms were selected from the electronics, chemical, and aerospace industries. The coefficients for individual firms relating to each of these factors turn out not to be significantly different from 0 because of lack of degrees of freedom in the estimating equation. But he notes that thirty of the thirty-nine firms had a positive coefficient relating to change in stock value, which permits him to reject at the .999 percent confidence level that the coefficient in each case equals 0 and that the result was due to chance. If, as appears to be the case, his measure of change in stock value does not include any dividend payments during the year, the results of his study are again consistent with the strategy of striving for a large AACF. Each dollar of earnings retained for reinvestment in a project with an expected rate of return greater than 0 increases the future cash flow to the firm and hence the value of each share, even if the rate of return is less than SROR and hence not in the best interests of the shareholders. And assuming the firm is already engaging in a regular practice of overretention (perhaps because it serves other management values) so that the market expects a level of future dividends reflecting a continuation of the practice (whether the reason for the level of dividends expected is understood by the market or not), the effect of the increased future cash flow is the only effect on share value resulting from the overretention.

In any event, the Masson study is not very helpful in determining whether overretention helps or hurts management compensation because the three industries from which the thirty-nine firms were chosen are all technologically progressive. Presumably most of their members have enviable lists of investment opportunities so that overretention is not possible. Grabowski and Mueller's study of the "life cycle" differences in investment opportunities among industries confirms this, since, unlike with firms in the "mature industries" in their study, there is no indication that the market would value the shares of firms in any of these three industries more highly if they increased their dividend payout.[186]

Part II

*A Study of the Financing of the
Semiconductor Industry*

Introduction to Part II

We now have in hand an information-based theory of the role of finance in industrial performance. The conclusions of the theory are that, judged by the standards of encouraging production, output choice, and dynamic efficiency, the finance process makes sound decisions with respect to control of existing real-level projects but does not do as well with respect to real-level project choice. Specifically, three types of failure have been identified. First, the group of projects which are chosen by the finance process to be funded are not consistent with the ranking of proposals made to established firms that would be implied by the evaluations of the respective managements evaluating them. Second, because the current structure of the finance process concentrates project proposal evaluation within established firms with substantial internal resources, the system is not as sensitive to the possibilities of innovative project proposals as it could be. Finally, when several proponents propose projects all based on a similar idea, as would usually happen during the diffusion of an innovation, the way the finance process chooses which projects to fund contributes to industry concentration.

Existing studies comparing the rates of return on projects of firms which do and do not use outside finance provide direct empirical support for the proposition that the first type of failure is a real problem. Existing empirical work lends some support as well to the theory's conclusions that the system displays the second and third types of failure. No study, however, addresses these conclusions directly. The following case study of the financing of the semiconductor industry in the first twenty-five years of its development is intended to fill this void by looking at the process of decision from the bottom up. It examines where the industry's innovative project proposals come from and how they are evaluated and decided upon in each of the contexts in which they are likely to be considered. It also considers what the pattern of resulting decision implies about the extent to which the economy takes advantage of the opportunities created by scientific advance and about the impact of innovation on market structure.

The manufacture of semiconductors is a high technology industry which developed from infancy to multibillion-dollar maturity in twenty-five years. A wide range of products can be classified as semiconductors, but all these products share the basic characteristic that they are solid state electronic components which alter the flow of electrical current. Current-altering components form the heart of the electronic devices ranging from television to computers that so characterize our modern age. The commercial introduction in 1950 of the first semiconductor product, the point contact transistor, and the subsequent introduction of ever more sophisticated semiconductor components since that time have revolutionized the electronics industry because of the cost, reliability, and size advantages of these solid state components over the vacuum tube components that previously performed similar current-altering functions. Total United States semiconductor sales in 1974, the last year of the period under study, exceeded $1.8 billion.

The case study covers three chapters. Chapter 3 is a general description of the industry and its history. Chapter 4 is an examination of how the economic system during the period studied determined the aggregate level of investment devoted to different products and processes within the industry. In a dynamic industry such as semiconductors, this examination really concerns the role of investment decisions in innovation and diffusion. Chapter 5 concerns the role of finance in determining the level of concentration in the semiconductor industry.

The findings of the case study generally support the conclusions of the theory I have developed. Evaluation by established firms of internally generated innovative proposals is found not to be as sensitive to their possibilities as outside sector evaluation of proposals that would be the basis of new firms. The internal-funding bias of the finance process is found to be the best explanation for the relatively high level of concentration in most of the industry's product lines. Equally important, the study demonstrates the efficacy as a guide to empirical investigation of the "who knows what and why" approach on which the theory is built. A rich picture emerges of the process of investment decision making in an innovative industry that enhances our understanding of the role of finance in industrial performance in ways that go beyond confirming or denying particular theoretical conclusions.

There are three sources of information for the case study: interviews, publicly released accounting data of firms in the industry, and published material concerning the industry. The interviews were conducted in late 1973 and early 1974. The study speaks as of the period of the interviews and constitutes a history of the financing of a new high technology industry during its first twenty-five years of development.

The interviews were conducted with the chief financial officer or chief executive of nine major firms in the industry and with officials of two venture capital groups which were associated respectively with the creation of two of these firms.[1] Together the nine firms interviewed were responsible in dollar volume for over 70 percent of all the semiconductors manufactured in the United States.[2] The list includes three of the top four firms in the market as of 1974 and six or seven of the top nine. They represented a cross-section of the kinds of firms in the industry at that time: two were less than five years old, while several others were far older than the industry itself; for some of the firms semiconductors constituted 100 percent of their business, and for others it was less than 10 percent. Interviewees were questioned about their internal processes for evaluating the prospects of, and choosing among, different investment opportunities; the pressures, if any, to avoid outside financing; how the choice is made among retained earnings, debt, and equity; their attitude toward vertical integration and diversification; how much the effect on their firm's stock price is taken into account when investment decisions are made; and other factors related to investment.

Accounting data and other statistics concerning the nine firms interviewed and other firms of interest in the industry can be found in their annual reports, SEC filings, and new issue registration statements. Unfortunately, multidivisional companies have not generally broken out statistics with respect to their semiconductor divisions, but some officials were willing to give some aid in interpreting their company-wide statements so as to provide more information concerning their semiconductor operations.

The growth and revolutionary impact of the semiconductor industry on other parts of the economy have been so spectacular that the industry has been the subject of innumerable articles in general business and specific trade journals which provide a large number of statistics about firms and quotes from industry leaders. There are a number of semi-scholarly reports by consulting firms and government agencies that are also helpful. The industry has attracted some serious scholarly comment as well.[3]

3. The Semiconductor Industry: A General Description

Understanding the role of finance in the semiconductor industry requires some background on the nature and development of the industry. The technology has developed from the simple point contact transistor to the large-scale integrated circuit. The history of the industry has been one of steadily declining prices and constantly improved product performance. Semiconductor firms have both invaded existing markets previously served by conventional components and created new markets by making possible products which were not technically or economically feasible before. The result has been dramatic growth. During this period of growth, the structure of the industry—the pattern of entry-expansion, contraction-exit, and pricing—has also changed in interesting ways.

A. The Technology: Principles and Development[1]

Active electronic components modify electrical signals in ways such as amplification, modulation, and switching. Active components have been the primary focus of electronic research and development in this century, and the success achieved has permitted the wide range of electronic products available today. The active component which propelled the world into the electronic age was the electron or vacuum tube, which was invented in the early 1900s and became commercially available about 1920. Competition for the tube did not arrive until 1948 with the invention of the point contact transistor, the first discrete semiconductor. The integrated circuit, which combines more than one electronic function into a single semiconductor device, first became available in 1960.

Semiconductor components are made of a solid semiconductor substance such as germanium or silicon. Such substances have a limited ability to conduct electricity. If impurities full of extra free electrons or holes are added to a piece of semiconductor material at strategic places, the piece of material can act as a conductor when certain electrical charges are applied to it. For example, the bipolar transistor has three leads coming out of it that hook into three separate deposits of impurities. The lead on one end is an emitter of electrons, and the lead on the other is a collector. The piece of material making up a bipolar transistor will conduct electricity from the emitter to the collector through the middle impurity deposit if a small electrical charge is applied to the middle lead. The level of conductivity will correspond to the level of electrical charge applied to the middle so that the component can act as an amplifier. To oversimplify slightly, the active components in a radio receive the weak electromagnetic signal from the airwaves which is circuited into the middle lead. This controls the level of a much stronger current going from a power source into the emitter, across the base, and out the collector into the speaker. A device using the same principles also can obviously perform the simpler on-off switching function that is the heart of the electronic computer.

Semiconductors have several advantages over tubes: they use far less power, generate almost no damaging heat, are more reliable and long lasting, are far smaller and lighter, and in more recent years have become much cheaper for most functions. The development of semiconductors is divisible into two distinct stages: improvement of the discrete semiconductor and the invention and improvement of the integrated circuit. The different process and product developments for discrete semiconductors were directed at a number of goals: lower cost, greater reliability, greater correspondence between labeled and actual characteristics of performance, a wider range of performance characteristics, and a wider range of possible operating conditions. Integrated circuit development was aimed both at these same goals and at combining a greater and greater number of functions in a single device. Each increase in the number of functions per device allowed greater size and space savings, greater reliability (by eliminating hand-soldered interconnections between devices and

by allowing testing for the several functions and their interconnections at one time) and eventually, after the product matured, lower
cost per function.

Progress in semiconductor technology has involved a number of
discrete jumps. Among the most important developments were the
silicon transistor, which replaced the temperature-sensitive germanium transistor; the diffusion method of introducing impurities into
the semiconductor material, which permitted more precise control
and batch processing; the integrated circuit; and the metal-oxide-
semiconductor (MOS), which required fewer processing steps and
less power to operate. Each jump has provided commerical opportunities for particular firms to profit and grow by being the first to
produce the better or cheaper products the new technology permits.
Between the jumps have been a large number of small advances,
many of them learned in the process of production, that have also
in the aggregate significantly improved the technology.

The trend in semiconductor innovations has been from breakthroughs based on theoretical knowledge in physics, metallurgy, and
chemistry to breakthroughs based on more practical knowledge in
geometry, mechanics, electronic circuits, and production skills.[2] This
is of importance to diffusion of the technology because discoveries
based on theoretical knowledge, once made, can be passed on to,
and hence exploited by, others more easily than those based on skills
built up through experience, which are generally only exploitable by
those with similar experience. The trend in these innovations has
also been toward greater capital intensity and larger minimum efficient scale (see chapter 4, section 3.22).

B. Sales, Quantity, and Price—The Importance of the Industry to Economy as a Whole

1. *Quantity and Price Trends*

The semiconductor industry developed from nothing into an important factor in the total economy over its first twenty-five years. Table
3.1 shows that sales of the industry grew from a substantial $90 mil-
lion in 1956, when the industry was already well established, to $1.8
billion in 1973, an annual compound growth rate of 17 percent.

The very substantial growth in dollar sales greatly underestimates

Table 3.1 United States Production of Semiconductors in Terms of Value

Year	Production in Billions of Dollars	Year	Production in Billions of Dollars
1956	.09	1965	.86
1957	.15	1966	1.10
1958	.21	1967	1.08
1959	.41	1968	1.16
1960	.56	1969	1.40
1961	.57	1970	1.28
1962	.59	1971	1.15
1963	.60	1972	1.56
1964	.71	1973	1.80

Source: *Electronics Market Data Handbook, 1975* (Washington, D.C.: Electronic Industries Association, 1975).

the growth in the value of the goods produced for the benefit of the economy as a whole. Table 3.2 shows that from 1957 to 1972, the number of semiconductor units sold increased 35-fold, an annual compound growth rate of 27 percent. The number of individual electronic functions or "bits" provided by all the items sold increased 750-fold, an annual compound growth rate of 56 percent. To put this figure in context, compare the growth in the total number of electronic functions for the seventeen-year period from 1939 to 1956, when active electronic functions were provided almost exclusively by electron tubes, with such growth in the sixteen-year period from 1956 to 1972, when semiconductors came into their own and overtook tube production. In the earlier period, the number of electronic functions increased 5-fold. In the latter period, the number of functions (tubes and semiconductors combined) increased 175-fold. Electronic functions form the heart of all electronic products from television to computers. The increase in functions over the second sixteen-year period shows the incredible growth in the number and sophistication of electronic products provided to the economy and the importance of semiconductors in this growth.

The two middle columns of table 3.3 provide the price trends for transistors and integrated circuits. These indicate a substantial decline in prices for each. On a price per function basis, the cost of the average bit decreased from $.83 to $.01 from 1964 to 1973, which is equivalent to a 43 percent decline per year.

Table 3.2 Number of Tubes, Semiconductor Units, and Electronic Functions Produced in the United States (in millions)[c]

Year	Number of Transistors	Number of Semiconductor Rectifiers	Total Number of Discrete Semiconductor Units	Number of Integrated Circuits	Total Number of Electronic Functions	Number of Tubes
1954	1.3	n.a.				
1955	3.6	n.a.				
1956	12.8	n.a.				
1957	28.7	55	84		84	456
1958	47.1	72	119		119	397
1959	82.3	120	202		202	432
1960	127.9	185	313		313	393
1961	190.9	278	459		459	372
1962	240.3	354	595		595	361
1963	300.0	439	739	.5[a]	745[b]	395
1964	406.9	626	1033	2.2[a]	1059[b]	368
1965	608.1	912	1520	9.5		396
1966	856	1330	2186	29.4		442
1967	759	1305	2064	68.6		323
1968	883	1543	2426	133.9		301
1969	1143	1977	3120	253.6		280
1970	922	1732	2654	300.0		231
1971	891	1398	2289	363.0		223
1972	1278	1812	3090	603.6	63,390[d]	199

[a]"The Changing Face of the West," *Electronics* (August 9, 1965), 38:72.
[b]Estimate based on assumption that the average integrated circuit of that period has 12 functions.
[c]Except as otherwise indicated, the source of these materials was *Electronics Market Data Handbook, 1975* (Washington, D.C.: Electronic Industries Association, 1975).
[d]Estimate based on assumption that average integrated circuit has 100 functions.

Table 3.3 Average Prices for Transistors, Integrated Circuits, and per Function

Year	Average Transistor Price ($)	Average IC Price ($)	Average Price per Function ($)
1953	8.00[a]		8.00
1954	3.87		3.87
1955	3.36		3.36
1956	2.91		2.91
1957	2.43		2.43
1958	2.40		2.40
1959	2.70		2.70
1960	2.36		2.36
1961	1.57	20.00[b]	1.57
1962	1.21	50.00[c]	1.21
1963	1.02	30.00[d]	1.02
1964	.83	18.50[a]	.83
1965	.66	8.33[a]	.66
1966	.56	5.05	
1967	.53	3.32	
1968	.43	2.33	
1969	.37	1.67	
1970	.38	1.49	
1971	.34	1.27	
1972	.28	1.03	
1973 (est.)			.01[e]

Sources (unless otherwise noted): Tilton, *International Diffusion of Technology: The Case of Semiconductors* (Washington, D.C.: Brookings Institution, 1971), p. 91; *Electronics Market Data Handbook, 1973* (Washington, D.C.: Electronic Industries Association, 1973).

[a]"Transistors: Growing Up Fast," *Business Week*, February 5, 1955, p. 86.

[b]"Next Step Beyond the Transistor," *Business Week*, October 28, 1961.

[c]"The Changing Face of the West," *Electronics*, August 9, 1965, p. 72.

[d]"Circuit in a Nutshell," *Business Week*, December 8, 1962, p. 86.

[e]W. C. Hittinger, "Metal-Oxide Semiconductor Technology," *Scientific American*, August 1973, pp. 48–57. This is the price of a single function in a middle-scale integrated circuit of 200 or more functions.

2. *Explanation of the Trends*

The data show a strong inverse relationship over time between price and quantity of semiconductor bits sold. Comparative statics would suggest that this could be the result of a downward-sloping supply curve accompanied by a shift out in the demand curve, a downward-sloping demand curve accompanied by a shift down in the supply curve, or both. While the trend data alone cannot reveal the slopes and the shifts over time of the supply and demand curves, such data combined with other information about the industry can allow us to develop a picture of what has happened.

A downward-sloping industry supply curve can exist in a disequilibrium industry as the simple result of the aggregation of the downward-sloping supply curves of individual firms each enjoying economies of scale. The firms can coexist in the short run without one firm expanding to dominate the market if institutional factors exist to limit the market share available to each particular firm. This seems to characterize the semiconductor industry. The technology, particularly as it has developed since 1960 with the batch processing made possible using diffusion techniques, is one involving substantial economies of scale. The production process has been described as the most complicated high-volume process ever developed by man, involving 80–100 steps and 1,000 variables.[3] But in sufficient volume the process is a low-cost one because tens of thousands of transistors or thousands of integrated circuits can be processed on a single silicon wafer, and as many as 100 wafers can be processed simultaneously. Initial development costs which become part of overhead are also an important part of total cost and contribute to economies of scale. Even more important than these static economies of scale is the existence of dynamic economies of scale, i.e., learning economies. These learning economies can either be pictured as part of downward slope of a supply curve for the relatively brief life of the product or as movement downward during the period of a very short-run supply curve. For the purposes of this discussion, the first interpretation is more appropriate. (See chapter 4, section 3.22, for a discussion of static economies of scale; dynamic economies of scale are treated as a moving of the cost curves in chapter 5.) Factors which would allow several firms with such downward-sloping supply curves to coexist include established customer-supplier relationships (not irrational in the electronics industry because of the value to a customer for planning purposes of being able to trust a supplier to deliver on schedule goods of consistent quality), product differentiation, and information imperfections. The long run consists of a series of these disequilibrium situations because of the disruptions from periodic jumps in technical change.

The contribution of a downward-sloping industry supply curve to the explanation of these price quantity trends is limited, however. While there has probably been a gradual shift outward in the demand curve over time because of increases in population and in the relative cost of products and services with a higher labor content, this would not be enough of a shift along a downward-sloping supply curve to explain most of what we have seen.

It is the shift of the supply curve downward accompanying each jump in technology that has likely accounted for most of the extraordinary decline in price and increase in quantity documented above. This can be seen by the pattern of substitutions and the introduction of new end products that have occurred with each technological advance. There have been sudden conversions from tubes to semiconductors for particular functions in traditional products such as television and radio, just at the point in time when the semiconductor becomes the less costly way to provide such functions. There have been a series of new products marketed that were technically conceivable using earlier models of semiconductors or, in some cases, tubes, but were economically infeasible until the price per function declined. Such products include large-scale computers, electronic calculators, electronic timepieces, and antiskid computers in automobiles. And in each of these cases, further declines in the price per function of semiconductors have dramatically reduced the price of the final products in which they are used and increased the derivative amount demanded of semiconductor functions. The transistor radio and the pocket calculator are prime examples.

The development of the semiconductor over its first twenty-five years was, in simple partial equilibrium terms, one of enormously increasing surplus value resulting from the downward shift in the supply curve. The industry is a prime example of gains to society from technological change. Understanding the role that the finance process plays in bringing about this technological change is important.

C. Market Organization of the Semiconductor Industry

The semiconductor industry has throughout its history had some distinct organizational characteristics that are the result of the rapid pace of technological change and relatively low entry barriers. It is valuable, before proceeding with the more detailed and focused analysis of the financing of the semiconductor industry, to take a look over time at the firm composition of the industry and its profitability.

1. *Firm Composition of the Industry Over Time*

The transistor was first made commercially available in 1951 by Western Electric, three years after its invention by that company's research arm, Bell Labs. The first companies to enter the industry were the major manufacturers of tubes, which in general were large diversified electronics companies. Raytheon, General Electric, and Sylvania had commercial transistors on the market by the middle of 1951,[4] and by 1953 all of the major tube manufacturers were manufacturing transistors.[5] Although Raytheon captured first place early and retained the position for several years, new companies having nothing to do with tube manufacture soon captured substantial shares of the market. In the early 1950s Germanium Products, which was founded for the purpose of manufacturing transistors, was in second place.[6] Germanium Products was then replaced in second place by Transitron, also founded specifically for this purpose.[7] Texas Instruments, which had been a manufacturer of electronic test equipment but never of electronic components, also entered the market and by 1957 had soared to first place.[8]

Table 3.4, which provides for various years the market shares of the major firms in the semiconductor industry and in some of its submarkets, permits several generalizations about the history of the industry. First, the industry has, throughout its history, been relatively concentrated. Four firm concentration ratios have dipped below 50 percent in only two of the years sampled. Submarkets are often even more concentrated. TTL integrated circuits, which in 1972 were the most important single product line in the semiconductor industry, had a four-firm concentration ratio of 85 percent.

Second, there has been a progressive decline of the role of the major tube manufacturers. Thus, while RCA, G.E., Raytheon, Sylvania, Philco, and Westinghouse together dominated the market in the early 1950s, and each individually has had important moments since, not one of them was among the top five semiconductor manufacturers by the end of the period under study. Third, there has

Table 3.4 Market Shares

Market Shares of Leading Semiconductor Firms
(percentage of total production in terms of value)

1953	*1957*	*1960*
Hughes 18%	Texas Ins. 21%	Texas Ins. 21%
Transitron 17%	Transitron 13%	Transitron 9%
Texas Ins. 10%	Hughes 11%	GE 8%
RCA 10%	GE 9%	RCA 7%
GE 10%	RCA 6%	Philco Ford 6%
Philco 10%	Raytheon 5%	Westinghouse 6%
	Philco Ford 3%	Motorola 5%
		Fairchild 5%

1963	*1966*	*1970*
Texas Ins. 20%	Texas Ins. 19%	Texas Ins. 25%
Motorola 11%	Fairchild 14%	Motorola 19%
Fairchild 9%	Motorola 13%	Fairchild 12%
GE 8%	GE 9%	RCA 5%
RCA 5%	RCA 8%	GE 4%
	Westinghouse 5%	National 4%
		Signetics 3%
		AMI 2%

1972

Texas Ins. 25%
Motorola 19%
Fairchild 10%
National 7%
Signetics 3%
AMI 2%

Market Shares of Leading Producers of Integrated Circuit

1962	*1965*	*1967*
Texas Ins. 70%	Texas Ins. 32%	Fairchild 24%
Fairchild 20%	Fairchild 18%	Texas Ins. 18%
	Signetics 15%	Motorola 15%
	Westinghouse 12%	Signetics 10%
	Motorola 6%	Westinghouse 6%

1968	*1970*	*1972*
Texas Ins. 17%	Texas Ins. 18%	Texas Ins. 31%
Motorola 17%	Motorola 14%	Fairchild 16%

1968	1970	1972
Fairchild 15%	Fairchild 10%	Motorola 14%
Signetics 8%	National 7%	National 10%
	Signetics 6%	Signetics 8%

Market Shares in 1972 of Leading Producers of TTL Integrated Circuits

Texas Ins. 44%
Motorola 15%
Fairchild 13%
Signetics 13%
National 9%

Sources: Tilton, *International Diffusion of Technology: The Case of Semiconductors* (Washington, D.C.: Brookings Institution, 1971), p. 66; *Semiconductor Industry Trends* (New York: Wainwright, 1973); Golding, "The Semiconductor Industry in Britain and the United States: A Case Study in Innovation, Growth, and the Diffusion of Technology," Ph.D. diss., University of Sussex, 1971, p. 152; *Microelectronics: Revolutionary Impact of New Technology* (New York: Samson Science, 1965); *Microelectronics: Shakedown and Shakeout* (New York: Samson Science, 1971); H. Gunther Rudenberg, *The Outlook for Integrated Circuits* (Cambridge, Mass.: Arthur D. Little, 1967); *Trends in Integrated Circuits and Microelectronics* (Cambridge, Mass.: Arthur D. Little, 1965); and various trade and general business journals.

been a continuous infusion of new successful firms into the ranks of the industry leaders: Fairchild in the late 1950s, Signetics in the early 1960s, National and Intel in the early 1970s. Fourth, there is considerable fluidity in firm rankings, although there was some stabilization over the last ten years of the period under study.

This pattern of firm composition has been analyzed by John Tilton and Anthony Golding in explaining the industry facts related above.[9] Both focus on the important role of the new entrant. Tilton demonstrates that large established firms with their extensive research facilities have been responsible for inventing a major portion of the technological advances in the industry, but that the newer entrants have gradually grown to dominate the market. New firms seem more willing to try a new technology. They are able to enter because barriers are relatively low. Once they enter and are successful, learning economies make them the low-cost producers and, according to Tilton and Golding, enable them to maintain themselves in the market served by the new technology even if the big established companies try to compete.[10] Discrete technological advances occurred at such a rate in the 1950s that a complete transformation of method occurred on the average of every two years. Such advances continued to occur in the 1960s and 1970s, although at a somewhat slower pace. With each major technological advance, another company came to the forefront. Examples are Transitron with the gold-bonded diode, Texas Instruments with the silicon transistor, Signetics with integrated circuits, and Intel with semiconductor computer memories.

Horizontal integration played a surprisingly small role in structuring the industry. None of the top five firms in semiconductor market share in the years reported on in table 3.4 had significantly expanded its capacity by horizontal merger or acquisition. Among the other firms in the industry, no consolidations that occurred during the period resulted in a firm with a market share of more than a few percent.

Vertical or conglomerate mergers involving known firms were somewhat more common. In at least one case, the acquisition of Signetics by Corning Glass, a clear reason was to provide substantial additional finance to Signetics (see chapter 4, section 1.32). In other cases the motivation of the acquired firm has not been clear, but the motivation of the acquiring firm has been the desire for vertical integration or diversification.* There has evidently been considerable merger activity on the part of the smaller firms in the industry which have never won fame. It was estimated that only seven of the thirty-six semiconductor firms started in the period 1966–1979 were still independent by the end of that period.[11]

Exit by the discontinuation of semiconductor operations or bankruptcy is not uncommon. Golding estimates the mortality rate for new firms founded to enter the semiconductor industry to be 20 percent after four to five years from the date of entry.[12] During the twenty-five-year period under study, there were several bankruptcies of more minor firms: Western Transistor in 1962, Molectro in 1962, Micro Semiconductor in 1963, and Cogar in 1972. Some of the

---

*Since the end of the period under study, vertical and conglomerate mergers have become much more important in the industry. Schumberger, Ltd., purchased Fairchild in 1979. United Technologies Corp. purchased Mostek in 1980 (and discontinued its operations in 1985). Sprague was taken over by GK Technologies in 1979 which was in turn taken over by Penn Central Corp. in 1981. Financial press reporting on several of these acquisitions suggested that the prime motivation from the point of view of the acquired company was better access to financing. In a transaction that falls somewhere between a conventional financing and vertical integration, Intel sold 6.25 million shares of stock (representing 12% of the total issued and outstanding) to IBM, its largest customer, for $250 million.

major diversified electronics companies which were at one point or another significant factors in the market, including General Electric, Sylvania, Westinghouse, Philco-Ford, and CBS, discontinued their semiconductor operations.

2. *Profitability*

The available evidence suggests that the semiconductor industry was on the whole very profitable during the period under study. For the ten-year period 1964–1973, profits as a percentage of sales averaged 4.3 percent compared with an all-industries average of 4.9 percent.[13] This figure probably represents a return on investment well above the all-industries average. Although a dependable capital/output ratio for the semiconductor industry during the period is not available to compare with an all-industries average, figures are available for the percentage of total value of output represented by labor costs. In 1967 this percentage for semiconductors was 2.1 times the all-industries average, and in 1973 it was 1.6 times that average.[14] Assuming at least a rough inverse relationship between these percentages and the corresponding capital/output ratios, return on capital in the semiconductor industry was 40–80 percent above the all-industries average for the period.

For the period prior to 1964, no industry figures are available, but data on particular firms suggests that at least the most successful firms in the industry were very profitable. In 1960 Transitron was reported to have earned profits of $8.1 million on sales of $47.8 million.[15] In the late 1950s Texas Instruments and Philco were reported to have rates of return on semiconductor investments of 20 percent and 30 percent respectively.[16]

4. Finance and Dynamic Efficiency in the Semiconductor Industry

Critical questions in the study of industrial organization are how technological advances are first implemented and how they then are diffused through an industry. These questions correspond to the fundamental mechanisms that determine an economy's dynamic efficiency. The semiconductor industry's short history has been marked by several distinct generations of products and processes, and the industry is always in the state of shifting from one generation to the next. The decision of a firm to undertake production employing a new technology normally presents itself in the form of a decision whether or not to make an investment embedded with the new technology. The study of these investment decisions is therefore the study of the decisions that determine innovation and diffusion in the industry. This chapter is devoted to an analysis on a case by case basis of how the finance process assesses and selects which investment ideas to implement.

The assessment and selection of potential semiconductor investment ideas by the finance process is the composite result of the decisions of the individual actors and subgroups in the system. As has been suggested in previous chapters, the decisions of individuals are based on motives and expectations. The expectations of each individual actor concerning the results of alternative courses of action are determined by the information he possesses. In tracing the flow of decision from the proponent to the saver, therefore, particular attention is paid to the communications interconnection among the participants in the system.

Chapter 2 suggests that there are three avenues by which a proponent can bring an investment idea forward for funding: offer to sell the idea to an established company, attempt to persuade the top management of the established company for which he works to implement the idea, or try to raise capital and start a new business based on the idea. This chapter breaks down the analysis in terms of three possible "contexts" in which the decision concerning such an investment idea can occur. The first and second contexts are an established firm that is already part of the industry and an established firm that is not. Established firms are the institutions that in the first instance make decisions to fund or not to fund ideas brought forward through offers of sale and through efforts by employees to persuade their top managements. The decisions established firms make are ultimately the result of both forces within the firm and pressures on the firm from the outside finance process. Established firms currently part of the semiconductor industry and established firms that are not are treated as separate contexts because research reveals that the process of decision differs significantly between the two. The third context of decision is the interaction of proponents of new firms and the financial institutions that provide them funds, the other avenue for bringing forward new investment ideas.

This typology of decisions is useful because it permits several kinds of comparison. One is between investment decisions of existing members of the industry versus new entrants (the first context versus the second and third). Another is between the two types of new entrants: existing firms and brand new firms (the second context versus the third). Still another is a comparison between existing firms and brand new firms (the first and second contexts versus the third). Finally, and less obviously, is a comparison between firms whose primary line of business is semiconductors and large, diversified firms. The typology permits this last comparison because, by the time of the interviews, all of the firms, with the exception of IBM, that were major factors in the industry (the first context) had semiconductors as their major line of business, whereas, throughout the history of the industry, almost all established firm new entrants (the second context) were large, diversified firms.

1. *Investment by Established Semiconductor Firms*

The neoclassical model of firm investment recited in chapter 1 suggests that firms decide whether or not to fund an investment project by calculating its expected rate of return and risk and comparing this expected rate, adjusted for the risk, with the market cost of capital. This study reveals that the neoclassical model is not a fully satisfactory simplification for use in the study of the organization of industries displaying rapid technical change. A less parsimonious description of the decision process such as found here, with emphasis on communication and on the multiple motivations of the actors, can yield a number of insights.

In the case of firms already established in the semiconductor industry, the model of the investment decision process that I will use focuses on (a) the source of the investment idea; (b) the calculation of the advantages from the investment to firm management including its effect on the firm's rate of return, growth, and earnings stability; and (c) the calculation of the costs of the investment to firm management including the increased use of organizational resources such as technical staff not fully elastic in supply, the availability and price of capital from the various possible sources, and the characteristics of other investment projects, if any, which might have to be forgone if investment is made in the proposed project.

1.1 Sources of Ideas

For established firms in the semiconductor industry, new product investment proposals are not generally based on a discrete idea from a single source, but rather are the result of an organizational process. The perceived needs of the users of the company's products trigger this process. At Mostek, AMI, and National Semiconductor, marketing men were said to make the initial proposals for new products. At IBM, semiconductor product development decisions were based on the future product plans of the computer division. When the Texas Instruments instrument division was the major portion of its business, the needs of the division explained many of its semiconductor investment decisions. The proponent is a coalition of employees who each identifies an interest in pursuing the project. The research staff tries to develop a workable solution to the customer need, and then the decision is made whether to make a major investment.[1] Only at Fairchild was there any indication that ideas regularly bubbled up independently from the research and development department. Fairchild was generally regarded as having devoted the most effort into research and development.

The interviews and literature have revealed very little about the source of ideas for process improvement investments. This may be because product and process developments normally occur simultaneously and are simply identified by officials as product improvements. A new product may perform the same function but be less costly to make. Process improvement within the life cycle of a particular product is regarded as part of the normal work product of the technical staff of the company, not something involving a discrete investment decision.

The purchase of a major idea through a licensing arrangement usually occurs only well into the product cycle. Because a major idea purchase involves entry into a market which, owing to the learning curve economies achieved by initial producers, already has low prices, such a purchase is only attractive if the purchasing company has slack resources. Such a purchase is not practical in the earlier stages of the product cycle because profitable operation at that time requires an organizational effort constantly to improve the method of production. The result of this effort is not a discrete idea readily summarizable and transferable to another organization.

Earlier in the history of the industry a great deal more licensing took place because Bell Labs was the major source of semiconductor advances but for antitrust reasons could not take full advantage of them.[2] Fairchild, even toward the end of the period under study, still earned a considerable portion of its income from royalties because its research and development group produced more ideas than its production group could digest.[3]

The preponderance of internally generated ideas as the basis for the investments made by established firms in the industry is consistent with the prediction of the general theory proposed in chapter 2. It is also consistent with Edwin Mansfield's findings that in industries with rapid technical change, innovation is much more likely to be based on internally generated ideas than in more sluggish industries where innovative ideas tend to come from outside the firm.[4]

1.2 *Calculation of the Advantages from Investment*

In chapter 2, I suggest that a firm manager seeks to satisfy a variety of personal goals: compensation, perquisites, respect, power, affection of those around him, and a sense of rectitude. The chapter goes on to set out a strategy for managers operating within large management-controlled firms calculated to best further these goals. That description fits some of the firms considered here and not others. But whether any particular investment decision is the result of the firm following that strategy, the reasoning used to develop the strategy suggests that three characteristics would be the most important to a firm's managers in determining the advantages to them of undertaking an investment: rate of return, growth, and stability of earnings. Managers of established semiconductor firms indicated that these are in fact the positive characteristics of an investment that they try to calculate.

1.21. *Rate of Return*

Officials of six of the nine firms interviewed stated that they did make rate of return calculations.[5] There is considerable question as to whether in several of these cases the calculation made fits an economist's definition of the term "rate of return." In the case of Fairchild, for example, the official interviewed immediately went into a discussion of required payback periods for different kinds of investments. There is also considerable question as to the degree of seriousness with which these calculations are taken by the firms that make them. The reasons why are closely related to the reasons why the other three firms did not even bother to make rate of return calculations. To start, there is lack of faith in the accuracy of the calculation because they are so complex. The existence of extensive learning curve economies makes the inevitable uncertainties concerning customer demand and the actions of competitors much more significant than with other kinds of investment. Errors in the calculation of volume in one period will cumulate by affecting cost and hence volume in the next. The effect that the investment will have on the profitability of other investments the firm has already made in other product areas, and hence on its aggregate profitability, is also very hard to assess accurately, particularly for a company whose semiconductor products are predominantly used by its own manufacturing divisions. IBM therefore does not calculate the rate of return expected from its semiconductor investment, but rather makes these investment decisions as part of a grand end product development plan, for which it does make a rate of return estimate. An official of another company suggested that it is easier to justify on a rate of return basis a proposed investment of \$20 million than of \$200,000 because the calculations are so much more open to manipulation when the whole character of the company will be changed.

A second reason why the rate of return calculation may not be taken very seriously is that another constraint on investment—the burden it puts on limited organizational resources—is frequently regarded as more important in ranking competing proposed investment projects. An official at Mostek, for example, said that they did not bother to make rate of return calculations because they choose projects in terms of expected profit per design engineer.

A third reason is that precisely accurate rate of return calculations, even if they could be made, may not be very useful. As will be explored in more detail in the cost section below, the cost of capital is a great deal less clear than neoclassical theory would lead one to assume. Thus, a precisely accurate rate of return calculation cannot act as a razor with which to make a clean cut between worthwhile and unworthwhile investments.

The three companies where rate of return calculations are taken the most seriously are the three most diversified companies in the sample: Texas Instruments, Raytheon, and Sprague. In these companies the initiative to some extent is on division managers to come forward with investment proposals that must then be approved by a central committee which allocates capital. At least in the cases of Texas Instruments and Raytheon, the estimates of the rate of return are made by the proponent of the project. As the micro analysis in chapter 2 predicts, the estimate is often discounted to some extent depending on who has made the estimate.

The procedures of the more diversified companies are interesting because they suggest that such companies, which by their nature have an extra step in the finance process similar to an internal capital market, function in a fashion more closely resembling the neoclassical model of capital allocation than does the outside finance process when it provides funds to undiversified firms seeking external finance for particular projects. With the large diversified firm, the decision process includes at least one point where conscious calculations are made resembling those implied by the neoclassical model. This difference is consistent with the discussion in chapter 2 (sections C 3.312 and C 3.32) of the role of conglomerates in the

finance process. Compared with a company interacting with the outside capital market, there is in a large diversified firm greater symmetry between the level of knowledge of the person dispensing the
capital and the proponent because of the proponent's experience-
based authority (the neoclassical model assumes perfect symmetry).
The capital dispenser knows how to assess the proponent's communications in a manner that reveals to the dispenser a larger portion of the full amount of knowledge possessed by the proponent.

The fact that the less serious rate of return calculations are even
made by some of the undiversified companies reflects the secular
trend in the industry toward increasing business sophistication on
the part of top management.[6] In the 1950s many semiconductor
companies were run by individuals with high scientific ability but
with little business experience. During the first "shakeout" of semiconductor firms in the early 1960s, many of these individuals were
forced out.[7]

1.22. Growth

The officials interviewed uniformly stressed that firm growth was
very important to them, a theme which also comes out repeatedly
in published reports of their views.[8] The term "growth" to them
seems to cover an amalgam of phenomena: growth in sales, firm
assets, organizational size, and, perhaps, profits.

Firm managers said that they recognized there is a trade-off between profits and growth and that they were willing to make the
trade to some extent. A number of interviewees stated that their
companies were growth oriented, not profit oriented. Some of the
industry leaders referred to profit orientation almost derisively. It
was reported that the reason James Riley resigned as president of
Signetics and accepted the same position at Intersil was because
Corning, the controlling stockholder of Signetics, wanted it to be too
profit oriented.[9]

It is not clear exactly what the managers' statements mean because they used both the terms "profits" and "growth" imprecisely.
The trade-off they were referring to may really be between current
profits and future profits. The interviews suggest that the firms that
make expected rate of return calculations of proposed projects do
not look forward for more than a few years. "Growth" may be a
synonym for, or an instrument for reaching, longer-run profits.

There are a number of reasons why a sacrifice of profits now could be associated with greater profits later. To start, when a firm engages in investment, the current profits figure generated by conventional accounting methods is a figure below that which an economist would generate because required accounting methods dictate that some of the expenses associated with the investment cannot be capitalized and must be written off as current expenses. Thus, any investment project, no matter how promising, involves some sacrifice of current accounting profits for future profits.

In addition, a project that contributes to firm growth may also contribute to the overall stability and profitability of the firm. Managers seem universally convinced that a failure to grow will have a disastrous effect on morale. The structure of these firms is inevitably pyramidal, and unless they grow, there will be severe limitations on advancement through time of even their most talented personnel. A firm which is not growing will be unable, therefore, to attract or to keep good people, and its long-run profitability will be impaired.

The most likely way for a project to make a larger contribution to firm growth is by improving the quality of the list of proposed investment projects in future periods. Managers clearly believe that having a significant share of the market for a product in one time period makes it easier to have that share in the next time period. If correct, an investment permitting the capture of a significant share of current sales of a growing product will create future investment opportunities, not otherwise available, to invest in the capacity to satisfy the same share of a much larger market. Such a project will deserve funding even if the expected revenues it produces directly do not justify funding.

The preference for investments in products with growing sales leads, according to most interviewed officials, to a preference for investment in innovative products because it is a general rule in the semiconductor industry that the rate of growth of sales of a product declines throughout its life cycle. For example, the growth orientation of Texas Instruments and Fairchild, not an expectation of a high rate of return on the specific investments made, is said to have impelled these two companies into the rapid development of commercially available integrated circuits.[10]

Growth concerns also result in a preference revealed in the interviews for projects that diversify a company's investments. It is difficult for a firm to increase its market share beyond a certain point in any one market; therefore, if the firm is to grow faster than the industry as a whole, it must enter new markets. Fairchild wished to move from its eighty-twenty to a fifty-fifty ratio of semiconductor sales to other sales. Smaller firms such as Intel were moving into electronic watches, and National Semiconductor, Mostek, and AMI were moving into electronic calculators.

This discussion suggests that the stated willingness of firm managers to trade profits for growth is really in most cases perfectly consistent with seeking to make AACF as large as possible. And since the quality of the proposed investment lists of most of these firms is high, it is consistent as well with share value maximization and efficient allocation of the economy's scarce savings. The combination revealed by the interviews of vague or nonexistent rate of return calculations and a strong growth ideology would appear for most industries to be irrational both from management and shareholder perspectives. But the combination reflects an investment policy which seems well adapted to an industry with a pattern of frequent introduction of new products followed by rapid sales growth and subsequent rapid obsolescence.

1.23. *Stability of Earnings*

A value which management is obviously concerned with is the avoidance of bankruptcy. Stockholders can minimize risk for a given return by diversification. But part of managers' human capital is firm specific, and so the continued viability of their firm serves their personal interests. One official also suggested that they feel a responsibility toward the employees of the firm and the community in which it operates to keep the firm alive. Although one instrument for pursuing this value is the avoidance of a high debt/equity ratio, investment decisions which tend to stabilize aggregate earnings of the company are also important.

One way to increase the stability of aggregate earnings is simply not to invest in projects characterized by high risk, even if they promise a high expected rate of return. No company admitted that they had ever made such a choice, but they did openly discuss their preference for investments which stabilize the total earnings of the firm when choosing among investment projects with similar expected rates of return. Investments which diversify a company's earning base would thus be preferred for stability as well as for growth reasons. Most of the managers interviewed expressed a desire to reduce or avoid "dependence" on a single product area.

The problem with diversification is that companies can run into trouble when they go into areas in which they do not have much expertise. Transitron is a prime example. The company was tremendously successful in the 1950s, having by the end of the decade $50 million in sales and no debt. Its two owners indicated that they wanted the security of size and diversity.[11] After a public offering to raise cash and to establish the value of their stock, the company engaged in a major acquisition program. By 1969 no company in the *Fortune* "Second 500" exceeded Transitron's loss of $18 million, which was on sales of only $81.5 million. The cause of the losses was primarily the nineteen small companies that it had acquired.[12] The diversion of management's attention from the company's semiconductor division also led to poor results within the semiconductor business, including a costly delay in switching to integrated circuits and an inadequate research and development program.[13]

A desire to stabilize earnings may also result in a preference for investments in the older, less hotly contested markets in which most of the price cuts which make accurate prediction so difficult have already taken place. This seemed to be the policy of RCA and General Electric (before it dropped out of the business).[14] The small shares of the market RCA and General Electric maintained can at least partially be attributed to this unadventurous policy which is contrary to the growth concern preference for innovative new products.

1.3 *Calculation of the Cost of Investment*

For managers to choose investment projects that will maximize net benefit to them, they must of course consider the cost of the various proposals as well as the gross benefits. Managers face two basic kinds of costs in making investments: organizational resources and financial resources.

1.31. *Organizational Resources*

Organizational resources are the productive features of the firm which cannot be quickly augmented to any great extent by outside supplement at a reasonable price. Semiconductors is an industry in which key people count very much. Twenty-million-dollar companies have been built on the basis of the skills of a few individuals, and if they leave, the company sometimes crumbles. At the same time, it is also an industry which involves production processes and research projects that are large team efforts. These teams take time to build up and for the individuals within them to learn to work together effectively. When an investment project is proposed, it is unlikely to succeed unless some of these key people lend their time and effort to the project. Although there is considerable mobility among firms by skilled people in the industry, a combination of new skilled people and an expanded, well-functioning organization for them to work in is very difficult to achieve in a short period of time. Good ideas quickly lose value over time (they are either outmoded or they are utilized by a sufficient number of competitors to make entry unrewarding).[15] Therefore, the investment proposals pending at any given time have to be considered with an essentially fixed amount of organizational assets to serve the needs of the projects chosen.

Officials at five of the nine interviewed firms mentioned organizational constraints as soon as the question was raised concerning whether they made rate of return on capital calculations. At the three smaller firms of the five, AMI, Intel, and Mostek, the unprompted reply was that the organizational constraints were more important than capital constraints. At Fairchild, for which financial constraints were particularly pressing because of substantial losses in some of the last years of the period under study, an official still reported that the number of promising ideas coming out of its research and development group greatly exceeded the number which the organization could handle. He cited both a lack of good managers to run that number of projects and the inability of the production group to absorb too many different projects at the same time. The interviews suggested an awareness that the cost of organizational resources of the firm is the opportunity cost in terms of the other projects proposed.

1.32. *Financial Resources*

A firm can finance new investment from three sources: (1) dissipation of its liquid assets accumulated from current and unspent past retained earnings and depreciation and from unspent remains of previous external financings; (2) new debt through the issuance of debt securities or through the negotiation of a loan; and (3) a new equity issue. There are costs that impinge on management values connected with each of these sources that increase with the amount provided, and there are effective limits to the amounts that can be raised by each method.

In a simple neoclassical model of the investment process, a discussion of the cost of financial resources would simply consist of describing a supply curve for capital with the cost of capital on one axis and the amount demanded for the project on the other. The cost of capital would be defined as the value of the income stream diverted from holders of currently outstanding shares of equity. Because of the way that financial markets are assumed to operate, the cost is supposed to be the same whichever way the capital is raised.

The first complexity introduced by the observations of the semiconductor industry is that firm managers, who are the individuals who make the investment decision, do not see an investment in terms of the single cost dimension of income diverted from current holders of equity. The intrusion of their personal values in the decision process leads them to consider costs such as the security of their jobs and their personal notions of what good finance practice is.

The second complexity is that, even in terms of diversion of income from current holders of equity, there is no single cost of capital because the different financial markets are not perceived to mesh perfectly. Different funding sources have different views, and for the reasons discussed in chapter 1 (section C2.211), the best-informed investors may not fully intermediate among them. Furthermore, even where management is trying to choose between two possible funding sources that share the same view of the underlying income stream of the firm, if the sources would make claims on different portions of that income stream, knowing the terms offered by each does not unambiguously reveal which is cheaper. That determination depends on one's own assessment of the probability distribution of the underlying income stream because the expected diversion of the underlying income stream implied by any given set of terms depends on that distribution.

The third complexity is that the cost of, and limits on, the capital provided by the different sources is related to the nature of the project to be invested in because the positive or negative cash flow generated by the investment becomes part of the total income stream of the company.

It is helpful for the purposes of the discussion of the cost of financial resources to approach the problem in two steps. The first step is an analysis of the cost of an investment where 1) the financial sources assume that the project proposed has prospects proportionally identical to those of the current assets (so that these sources' assessment of the distribution of the income stream of the company should the investment be made is simply some constant greater than one times their assessment of the current distribution), and 2) management does not concern itself with the effect of implementing the project on the costs of financing future projects. This first step abstracts out the problem of how financial resources react to the nature of the investment and the effect the making of the investment has on the cost of raising financial resources in the future. The second step drops these assumptions to create a model with greater realism.

a. *The cost of financial resources during the current period if the outside finance process assumes that the proposed investment has prospects proportionately identical to current assets.*

1. *Dissipation of liquid assets.* The first source to which a firm turns is its own liquid assets. The firm needs a certain amount of liquidity to operate so there is a limit on the amount available from this source that is substantially less than the total amount of a firm's liquid assets. Firms in the semiconductor industry do accumulate reserves beyond these liquidity needs to act as a cushion so that in some years without outside financing investments can occur in amounts larger than the sum of retained earnings and depreciation for the particular year. Every firm interviewed but the very new Mostek had in at least one year between 1967 and 1972 reduced its liquid asset position from the previous year while experiencing considerable overall growth.

The firm controls one variable that affects the size of the liquid assets available for investment during the current period: the cash dividend rate. It appears, however, that this variable does not really add much flexibility. At the time of the interviews, the four new companies, Mostek, Intel, AMI, and National Semiconductor, had never paid any dividends. Fairchild, which paid dividends up until 1970, and Sprague, which paid dividends until 1971, had discontinued payment of cash dividends. The discontinuances were not the result of heavy investment programs but the result of financial difficulties. IBM and Texas Instruments were paying dividends, but the officials of these two firms indicated that they were each concerned with maintaining a steady dividend payout ratio.[16] The official at Texas Instruments suggested that this policy was necessary in order to give its stock a "quality image." Texas Instruments did, however, eliminate its dividends from 1954 to 1961 during the period of its rapid expansion into the semiconductor industry.

The cost of using liquid assets to finance any particular project is the return that could be expected from the best alternative which such use forecloses. At a minimum, this cost is the expected rate of return on investments in easily marketable, low-risk securities—the way liquid assets are normally stored. This is easily definable and constitutes the first possible measure of the cost of internal finance, but it is low because of the premium paid for low risk and high liquidity.

A second measure is the rate of return which a company might hope to receive on investment projects in the future, the ideas for which have not yet been put forward. This second measure should be used if 1) the firm anticipates that during the payback period of the proposed project there will be a flow of ideas that have expected rates of return better than that of the proposed project[17] and that require an aggregate amount of funds exceeding the amount of additional retained earnings and depreciation expected in that time period, and 2) either this excess is greater than what can be raised by outside finance, or the expected rates of return on some of these ideas, though better than that on the proposed project, are less than the lowest expected cost source of outside finance. Since the managers interviewed did not make formal cost of capital calculations, they did not address themselves directly to whether they used either the first measure or this second measure. There was a clear implication, however, that something resembling this second measure underlies their investment decisions.

A third possible measure of the cost of capital provided by internal finance would relate to the possibility of returning to stockholders more of the earnings than the current amount returned, if any. The cost to management of not returning money to shareholders is their dissatisfaction should the company invest in projects which have rates of return lower than SROR. Shareholder dissatisfaction manifests itself in lower share price which affects management by reducing the value of stock price based compensation schemes and by increasing the risk of takeover. Despite the resemblance of the third definition to the modern finance theory definition of the cost of capital,[18] no interviewee mentioned anything approaching it. This is perhaps because the firms interviewed all had expectations of good future investment ideas, and so SROR would be unlikely to exceed the second measure, and no proposed project which survives the test of the second measure would be blocked by the third. Also, managers facing what they believe to be only a temporary dearth of good investment ideas are loath to increase the dividend payment ratio because it is difficult to lower it again.[19]

A question which straddles this discussion of internal finance and the discussions below of debt and equity finance is whether or not there exists a management preference for investment by internal finance. The importance of this question relates to which measure of the cost of internally financed capital is more appropriate. The stronger the preference for internal financing, the higher, in the eyes of management, the cost of external financing for future projects and the more likely that management would want to use the second measure. In other words, a management group that has a strong aversion to outside finance but that expects that its future investment ideas will be reasonably good is on the one hand unlikely to resort to external finance and on the other unlikely to want to squander its internal funds by "pricing" them in terms of what they can earn as liquid assets or in the hands of shareholders. The relevant opportunity cost of a proposed project for such management will be, as suggested by the second measure, what they could earn invested in these future ideas.

It does not require econometric analysis of the financial reports of the firms surveyed to determine that there is a strong positive relationship between earnings and investment. The relationship was even stronger during the formative years of the industry when Texas Instruments and Transitron grew into the industry leaders almost entirely on the basis of internal financing.[20] The interviews indicated, however, that the relationship in most cases is primarily due to factors other than an explicit preference for internal financing per se. Rather, there are separate reasons why firms may prefer internal finance to debt and internal finance to equity. Only one of the nine firms, Intel, answered in response to direct questioning that the firm affirmatively desired to grow on the basis of internally generated funds.

There are a number of reasons for the relationship between earnings and investment. One, just alluded to, is that the two methods of external finance each has its own disadvantages in the eyes of management. The more earnings, the more funds are available that have neither set of disadvantages. Another is that there are circumstances, usually related to financial troubles, under which neither debt nor equity outside financing is available on practical terms, so that earnings and depreciation are the only sources of finance. Also, the expectations of managers concerning future prospects of proposed investment projects are closely related to current profitability. As an official at Texas Instruments put it, "Businessmen have a tendency to pull in their horns when profits are down." His rationale for this behavior was essentially an articulation of the mini-max strategy in game theory: the consequences of a large investment, made during a period when profits are already low, can be disastrous if it fails to work out. Heavy investment under such circumstances is worth avoiding even at the cost of some apparent missed opportunities. Furthermore, investment, no matter how it is financed, inevitably involves a drain on current accounting earnings because some items which are really investment are not capitalizable by normal accounting rules. Such a drain is unwelcome when earnings are already down, particularly to high growth companies which must justify their high price/earnings ratio on the basis of continuing growth in accounting earnings.

2. *Debt financing.* The cost of debt financing can be examined by first looking at the limits and costs imposed by the sources of debt financing and then by looking at the additional factors which, from a manager's perspective, may either further restrict the amount considered available or add to its cost.

The cost and the limits on the availability of additional debt for a firm are each a function of the risk of payback as perceived by the sources. There is not a full range of risk-cost options for a firm, and debt finance is simply not available if risk is perceived by the sources to be above a certain moderate level. The two firms in the survey that have experienced considerable financial trouble, Sprague and Fairchild, both reported that during their respective periods of financial difficulties it would not have been possible for them to raise any money by debt except on a short-term basis.

The reason for the restricted range of risk-cost options appears to be closely connected to the information-processing procedures of the debt sources. Several of the officials interviewed suggested that banks were much more concerned with the financial statement of a firm than with an analysis of the prospects of its underlying assets. The items which debt sources look at are the current earnings of the firm, the debt/equity ratio, the liquidity of the assets of the company, and the stock price. If the decision is made that it is safe to extrapolate current earnings into the future and that the company can support at least some additional debt, then the cost gradually rises with the amount desired up to a certain point and then essentially jumps to infinity.

The failure of debt sources to develop a capacity to evaluate loans and debt securities that pose a significant risk of default probably results from their perception that there would not be much of a market for this kind of lending even if they did develop such a capacity. As shown by Jensen and Meckling, when there is a significant risk of default, debt holders can no longer assume that management, by acting in the shareholders' best interests, is acting in the debt holders' best interests as well.[21] Decisions that maximize the shareholders' expected return may well not be the ones that maximize the value of the underlying income stream of the firm but instead may be ones that take risks at the expense of debt holders (who must suffer more of the downside of the risk than they enjoy of the upside). Unless a loan agreement or bond indenture can be drafted to eliminate fully and costlessly all such "moral hazard," which is unlikely, management, to obtain a loan, must pay a rate of interest that reflects the possibility that such decisions will be made and cause a default. That elevation in rate is likely to make debt financing unattractive whether or not internal or external equity financing is possible. In addition to the high expected costs, high fixed debt service payments pose substantial bankruptcy risks, something that management personally wishes to avoid.

AMI is an example of a company in essentially good financial health which had to abandon an investment project because it required more capital than could be raised by debt. In 1971 it purchased a subsidiary called Unicom Systems, Inc., which was a manufacturer of electronic calculators. It became clear that the amount of capital required to build the subsidiary into a major consumer product company would be very large, and the AMI official interviewed stated that amassing so much capital was beyond the capacity of a small company such as AMI. Management did not wish to issue new equity because of control considerations. AMI therefore sold the subsidiary in 1972, for more than a 20 percent after-tax profit, to the much larger North American Rockwell. The inability of AMI to raise the necessary capital to implement a project that was good enough to be seen as very promising by North American Rockwell is probably a demonstration of how debt sources look at the current balance sheet and income statement of the company for security without adjusting for the prospects of the project to which the money is to be applied.

Managers must make investment and financing decisions within the bounds of the interest charged and limits imposed by outside sources, but they consider as well a number of other factors in making the ultimate calculation of the cost to them of debt-financed capital. A high debt/equity ratio is as much a concern to the interviewed firms' managers as to its financing sources. Almost all the firms had target debt/equity ratios. A higher ratio increases the risk of bankruptcy, and this concern was mentioned by several managers. In addition, it was suggested both by an official at Intel and by its original source of venture capital, Arthur Rock, that a complex debt structure, which may develop when debt financing is resorted to frequently, complicates the balance sheet and makes new outside capital, debt or equity, more difficult to raise.

A high debt/equity ratio is seen by some finance authorities to have two advantages, though in each case opinion is divided. The first is that a higher debt/equity ratio permits deduction of a greater portion of capital costs from corporate income taxes (see chapter 6, section B2.12). Interestingly, however, this point was mentioned by only one official despite the fact that everyone interviewed was asked about the advantages and disadvantages of debt financing. The other possible advantage stems from the fact that increased leverage from a higher debt/equity ratio increases earnings if the company is relatively successful.[22] To regard this as an advantage would appear to involve an implicit rejection of the Modigliani and Miller hypothesis. One official interviewed from AMI felt that the public appreciated this result. His rationale was that all the public looked at was increased earnings and was "too unsophisticated" to realize that such increases were the result of leverage. The official may have been making the underlying assumption, perhaps not unrealistic, that because management's knowledge of the prospects of investment proposals is so much greater than the knowledge of those on the outside, they know the chances are good that the leverage is going to work to the stockholders' advantage.[23]

The calculation by managers of the ultimate cost to them of debt-financed capital, like internal finance, involves three possible measures. One measure is to take the rate of interest which must be paid for the amount of borrowing contemplated, plus transaction costs and some kind of differential for the other factors discussed above. The second is to use a "mixed cost of capital" which takes account as well of the hypothetical cost of engaging in additional equity financing to return the firm to its initial debt/equity ratio. This is the classic textbook approach.[24] The third measure is opportunity cost: the rate of return which the company might hope to receive on investment projects in the future, the ideas for which have not yet been put forward. Thus, the third measure of the cost of debt is the same as the second measure of the cost of internal finance.

There are good arguments for using the third measure of the cost of debt in many cases. As long as equity remains unchanged, financing a proposed project by debt increases the debt/equity ratio. That makes future borrowings more expensive and moves the firm closer to the ratio at which no further borrowing is practical. Additional external equity financing may, as subsequent discussion will show, be impractical or limited in availability for considerable periods of time. There are, as we have already seen, limits on the availability of internal funds as a source of finance. Thus, all three sources of funds can be limited. If the flow of ideas in the future is expected to be big enough and good enough, present investment which promises a rate of return greater than the first or second measure of the cost of debt may still be unwise because it would reduce the amount available for future ideas which promise better rates of return.

In the interviews, officials indicated that the third measure of the cost of debt underlay their investment decision process more than the first or second. They tended to worry about a situation in the future in which earnings were down, both reducing the amount of internal financing available and making equity financing impractical. To issue debt during the current period for a project barely justifiable under the first two measures of cost might squander borrowing capacity which might be needed more in the future. An equity issue during the current period, even if current share price is acceptable, may not be practical because the amount of new equity needed to return the debt/equity ratio to its initial position before the debt financing is too small. Public offerings of equity display significant economies of scale. The two firms which calculated expected rates of return for prospective projects and which provided a definite cutoff figure, Texas Instruments and AMI, used cutoff figures of 10 to 12 percent and 12 percent, respectively. These figures were two or three points above the rate at which they could have obtained long-term debt at the time of the interviews, which is consistent with the second and third debt cost measures but not the first.

3. *Equity financing.* The financial cost of equity financing to the holders of the shares currently outstanding at the time the financing occurs is the need to pay dividends to the holders of the newly issued shares at any time in the future that they are paid to the holders of the previously outstanding ones. The firms must first determine what price the market would be willing to pay for newly issued shares. Whether or not equity financing at that price is an economical way of raising investment funds depends on one's assessment of the probability distribution of the firm's earnings for each time period in the future. For any given price, the more pessimistic these estimates, the more desirable equity financing appears for the holders of the currently outstanding shares because the less money will ultimately have to be shared with the holders of the newly issued shares.

The initial question in determining the cost and limits of equity finance is whether it is worth engaging in at all. In the opinion of all those interviewed who spoke about the subject, there are many times when it is not, and the effective limit on equity financing is, therefore, zero. These officials all evinced a faith that stock prices were reasonably rational over the long run but that they greatly overreacted to both good and bad news. (See chapter 1, section C 2.214, for a discussion of theoretical and empirical literature supporting the view of short-run stock market irrationality.) If a firm does choose to engage in equity financing, the cost gradually rises with the amount of stock being offered because, as chapter 1 suggests, a lower price is necessary to induce investors to undertake the de-diversification entailed in making additional purchases.[25]

There are again other factors considered by management besides the financial cost to current stockholders. First, there is the expense of an equity issue. If the issue is a registered public one, the underwriters' fees, printing expenses, and legal fees are substantial (see chapter 2, section C2.412). Registration also requires nonmonetary costs, including executive time and possible disclosures management does not wish to make. A private placement of equity securities does not entail these underwriting and registration expenses, but the purchaser will not pay as much for the securities because he cannot sell them easily without going through similar registration steps himself.

Second, an equity issue dilutes ownership. This is considered a cost if management was put into power by a particular ownership group because it increases the number of votes that might be cast against it in the future. Dilution may be helpful to management's position, if, as in the case of National Semiconductor, large blocks of its stocks are owned by institutional investors with no connection with management.

A third factor, mentioned by officials at Texas Instruments and AMI, is that equity finance can be relatively undesirable because the resulting dilution of earnings runs contrary to the company's goals of maximizing earnings per share. With respect to the choice between debt and equity, this concern does not make sense even on its face, since debt payments also reduce earnings and hence earnings per share. With respect to the choice between external equity finance and internal finance, this concern is reminiscent of the attitudes revealed by Donaldson's study, discussed in chapter 2 (appendix 2.1), of the financial policies of large industrial companies twenty years earlier. Such a concern is consistent with a management desire to maximize AACF—the instrumental goal attributed to management in chapter 2—but it fails to take account of the cost to stockholders of reduced dividends. Notwithstanding what has just been said, there is some evidence that, in pricing certain "growth stocks," the stock market, during the period under study, irrationally overemphasized growth in earnings per share without looking at the dividend pattern, and so a preference for internal finance would have served shareholder interests.

Two officials interviewed also mentioned that equity, unlike debt and internal financing, is inflexible: it cannot be raised in the amount you want and it cannot be paid off when you want. It is difficult to say how important these considerations are to firm managers. Small amounts of equity can be issued through private placements and sales to employees.[26] And capital raised by equity financing can be "paid off," if management so wishes, by the repurchase of shares, though not at a predetermined price.

In terms of using equity finance to raise money for a particular investment project, it would appear that, unlike internal and debt finance, a simple measure of financial cost plus some premium for the other factors considered is the appropriate measure of the cost of equity-financed capital.* If the price of the stock is sufficiently high before new stock sales so that equity financing makes any economic sense at all, then the cost of equity finance increases gradually with the amount demanded without any discrete jump or further limit at some point.

It would appear that with the exception of Intel and Mostek, equity financing is engaged in to raise money for a particular project only after use of the other sources has reached their limits, internally or externally imposed. In each of the other companies,[27] officials stated that the decision to employ equity financing to help raise money for particular investment projects was based on the debt/equity ratio. Most of them explicitly said that they favored debt. Intel and Mostek were very new companies for which equity finance was unusually attractive because of their extraordinary earnings growth and very favorable price/earnings ratios.

To leave at this point the discussion of how management, in mak-

---

*A second measure would be to use the same "mixed cost of capital" that constitutes the second measure of the cost of debt financing referred to above. The theory would be that any time a firm engages in equity financing, it permits the firm to engage as well in some additional debt financing without increasing its debt/equity ratio. Since debt financing is generally less costly than equity financing in terms of the expected diversion from existing shareholders of future earnings, the mixed cost of capital is generally less than the expected "out of pocket" cost of equity financing. None of the managers interviewed, however, indicated that they used a mixed cost of capital measure.

ing its investment decisions, ascertains the cost of equity-raised capital would be misleading, because it appears that much, perhaps most,
equity finance does not occur within the context of raising money
for a specific investment project. Just as equity financing is impossible when a firm's stock is priced too low, equity financing is too
good an opportunity to pass up when the stock is priced higher than
management thinks it is actually worth.[28] Fairchild, Intel, and Mostek officials said that their respective companies engaged in equity
financing when the stock price seemed particularly favorable despite
the fact that they did not have an immediate use for all the funds
raised. The financial statements of several of the other companies
surveyed indicate that this was true of them as well. When this kind
of equity-raised money is eventually used for investment, it would
involve the dissipation of liquid assets, and the cost of its use, as
the discussion concerning use of liquid assets indicated, would
probably be the second measure of the cost of internal finance, i.e.,
the opportunity cost in terms of future investment projects.

It should be noted that there is one way that equity finance may
be available to a firm in financial trouble but able to convince itself
and others who will take enough time to listen in detail that it has
good ideas worth investing in: sell enough of its shares to another
corporation to become a partially or wholly owned subsidiary of that
corporation. The two prominent examples are Signetics, which in
1962 sold a 50 percent interest in itself to Corning Glass, and General Microelectronics, which became a subsidiary of Philco. Signetics, while maintaining relative autonomy, was transformed from a
failing company into a tremendous success. General Microelectronics, the operations of which were eventually almost fully integrated
into those of Philco, was a failure despite some pioneering work in
MOS.

b. *Changes in the assessments of a firm by the outside finance process
because of a new investment and their effect on the cost of financial resources
raised to finance the investment and on the cost of financial resources for
future projects.*

1. *Immediate effect.* As assumed in the discussion immediately above,
financial sources usually act as though a proposed project has prospects proportionally identical to those of current assets so that the
nature of the project does not have much effect on the cost of raising
funds for the project.[29] But certain areas of innovation investment

are in vogue in the investment world at any one time and do have an effect. These are generally areas in which there is expected unusually fast growth in demand, because of expected product improvement, or in the amount demanded, because of expected cost and hence price reductions. A review of security analyst reports and of the annual reports of firms in the semiconductor industry clearly demonstrates that investment in its vogue areas stimulates interest. The analyst reports tend to assume that a company with a good image will have a good chance of making a success out of a new investment if it is in a promising area. Thus, commentary consists of the announcement of new and interesting investment areas and a review of the factors by which the current prospects of the company without the new investment would be judged. If a firm has sufficient authority, it can catapult a proposed investment into the vogue category simply by announcing that the firm finds it especially promising.

Several factors enter into the image of whether a company can succeed with a vogue investment in a promising new area. The most important factor is past success as reflected in reported earnings. The reputation of the individual top managers is important too. An official of one envious competitor suggested that the reason that Intel had twice the price/earnings ratio of his firm, despite very similar earnings growth profiles, was the good reputation that Robert Noyce enjoyed with the financial community. A switch of a top manager who has such a reputation from one firm to another, such as that of Lester Hogan from Motorola to Fairchild and that of James Riley from Signetics to Intersil, can have a real effect on the stock price of the receiving company.[30] Such a manager may be wanted as much for the effect on the image of the company as for the real skills he may bring with him.[31]

The trappings of being established are also important. One such trapping, an official at Intel suggested, was simply having engaged in a public offering. A much more substantial one is being listed on the New York Stock Exchange. In 1953, Texas Instruments, which had forty-seven shareholders, merged with a small company called the Intercontinental Rubber Company. An important motivating factor in the merger was that Intercontinental Rubber was listed on the New York Stock Exchange.[32] Upon the merger, its listing became the listing of Texas Instruments.

The investment itself, if it involves sufficiently high technology, can have an immediate effect on a firm's image and can justify investments that otherwise would not seem worthwhile. More than one commentator has remarked that the transition of firms in the industry into integrated circuits was aided greatly by the favorable, and perhaps overly optimistic, treatment that integrated circuits received in the press.[33] Officials at Sprague and Intel admitted that they decided to develop and produce certain products primarily to enhance or preserve their reputations as technological leaders. This effort is of course directed at customers as well as financial sources. Herbert Kleiman reports the story of an unnamed electronics systems company which refused to drop its perennially losing semiconductor division because the company felt that the financial community would consider such action a sign of weakness. The financial community held the view at that time that the prospects for semiconductors were tremendous.[34] If an investment is so high technology that it appears impractical, it can have an immediately negative effect on a firm's image. AMI officials believed this was the case with its investment in MOS several years in advance of other firms.

2. *Effect in subsequent period.* New investment has both negative and potentially positive effects that are not felt at the time the money must be raised. The negative effect is the short-run drain on accounting earnings because part of what is spent on the investment cannot be capitalized and hence is charged as an operating expense. The potential positive effect, usually longer run, is the effect on profits if the project is successful.

If the reasons are not understood, the drain on accounting earnings from an investment will inevitably, for the period of its duration, worsen the terms on which outside financing can be obtained and hence is part of the cost of capital of the investment. The officials interviewed unanimously believed that the reasons are not fully understood. Anecdotal evidence, at least, indicates that this belief is correct.[35] The effect of a drain on earnings on the stock prices of firms in the semiconductor industry was aggravated because most of these firms had high price/earnings ratios based on the assumption that they would exhibit rapid earnings growth.

The concern with accounting earnings and their effect on stock price does not, of course, create an incentive for no investment at all, since over the long run good investment is the basic source of earnings growth. Furthermore, if accounting earnings each year are the result of a reduction of real earnings (as an economist would define them) by a fixed percentage because of noncapitalized expenses for investment, accounting earnings will grow at the same rate as real earnings. The larger the fixed percentage of reduction, the higher the growth rate of accounting earnings (assuming that there is an adequate supply of good investment ideas to which to apply the increased investment permitted by the greater percentage of reduction). As we saw in chapter 2 (section B 3.221), actions taken to improve current earnings at the expense of future earnings reflect a short time horizon on the part of management. If undertaken regularly in years with disappointing earnings, such actions represent a policy to stabilize the growth path of accounting earnings at the cost of reducing their long-run average growth rate. An emphasis on current accounting earnings carried to its extreme can lead to disastrous long-run results.[36] While none of the nine firm managements that were the focus of this study appeared to have acted in such an extreme fashion, there is evidence that most or all of them made compromises trading off future growth for current earnings by forgoing promising investments. Officials of every firm surveyed (except IBM, at which the subject was not discussed) indicated that their firms did or would reduce investment in order to relieve pressure on accounting earnings in disappointing years. This attitude or response is dramatically displayed by cuts in the aggregate amount of investment in the industry in the low profit years of 1970 and 1971 to half the level of 1969. This cutback was followed by an acute shortage of capacity and rebounding profits in 1972, and by record levels of aggregate investment in 1973.[37]

The interviews revealed a number of specific instances of firms avoiding investment in order to enhance accounting earnings. Raytheon wished to get into MOS but wanted to do so by acquiring a company with already developed competence in the field rather than building up the competence themselves within their own organization. The reason given by the general manager of the semiconductor division was that management was afraid of the reaction of stockholders to a decline in accounting earnings that would result from the noncapitalizable expenses of internal development.[38] During the period of Fairchild's financial problems (1969–1971), all investment projects had to promise a payback period of six months or less in order to be approved. Such a short payback period would mean that, in at least half of the investments, the drain on accounting earnings from investment would be recouped within the same annual accounting period.

The overemphasis of financial sources on current accounting earnings that tempts managers in this fashion appears irrational only from the better-informed perspective of management. Financial sources must make their long-run calculations on the basis of what information they have or can economically obtain. The most easily obtainable and hardest information that they have is recent accounting earnings performance. They cannot be expected fully to grasp the promises of new investment, understanding the subtleties of which requires the expertise for which management was hired. Thus, because of the information differential between management and financial sources, the decisions of these sources, although based on the best long-run calculations these sources can economically make, appear to management to reflect too much concern with the short run.

This overemphasis on current accounting earnings will be moderated if there is an authority relationship between management and the financial sources. Such a relationship permits management to explain convincingly how a short-term reduction in accounting earnings does not forecast a gloomy future. It takes time and stability of personnel to develop such a relationship. Such a relationship may therefore have been rather weak in the case of most members of the semiconductor industry at the time of the interviews. The industry also had a legacy of firms that operated in less than a reputable fashion and collapsed after being glamour stocks.

On the other hand, the effect of analyst focus on current accounting earnings will be accentuated if the stock market pricing has an irrationally speculative component. As we saw in chapter 1 (section C 2.214), some theorists suggest that the fact that the typical investor will hold shares only for the short or medium run causes the price to take on a life of its own independent of expectations concerning long-run dividend flow because the price an investor is willing to pay today is a function of what he thinks other investors will be willing to pay for it at some point in the future. Baumol, for example, suggests that the stock market tends to operate on the basis of cues which coordinate the expectations of buyers, allowing them to anticipate one another's behavior. Earnings reports function as one of these cues.[39]

1.33. *The Nature of the Opportunity Costs*

The discussion so far has entirely been in terms of *current* investment proposals in the area of semiconductors. Three other kinds of investment deserve some attention because, under various circumstances, one or more of them define the opportunity costs of the current investment proposals discussed above. The first is current investment proposals in areas other than semiconductors. The second is meta-investments in research and development and in the expansion of organizational resources. The third, which has been referred to before, is future investment projects, the ideas for which have not yet become sufficiently developed to become current investment proposals.

a. *Current investments outside the area of semiconductors.* The decision process for current investments outside the area of semiconductors is in most respects identical to that discussed above for those within the area. The focus here is on how the fact that the firm is already in semiconductors affects the decision process concerning investments outside of the field.

The advantages (and disadvantages) to diversity have already been considered. Obviously, just as predominance of sales outside semiconductors leads a firm to appreciate the diversity advantages of an investment in semiconductors, predominance of sales in semiconductors leads a firm to appreciate investments outside of the area.

Additional investments of firms with a predominance of sales in semiconductors frequently involve downstream vertical integration. During the period 1950–1970, the progressive development of the semiconductors led to an increase in the percentage of the value of the final electronics end product represented by its components from an average of about 15 percent to an average of 50 percent.[40] Integrated circuits meant that much of the final product's circuitry is within the components instead of between them. Size reduction also meant considerable savings in cabinet costs. Given the large percentage of value added that is already contributed by the component manufacturer, the argument for completing the operation is considerable. An integrated effort permits the company that is manufacturing the end product privacy of design during development, it eliminates marketing costs, it will probably allow better control of component quality and delivery schedule, it puts people in charge of final product decisions who know the full potential of new semiconductor developments,[41] and it increases the component manufacturer's understanding of the needs of the end product manufacturer and of its customers.[42]

The incentive for a firm to engage in a vertically integrative investment is heightened if other companies are already involved in the same kind of integrated operations because of the fear that the market for the firm's components will be foreclosed. Officials at Mostek and National Semiconductor both said that their respective companies entered the calculator business because Texas Instruments had done so.[43]

b. *Meta-investments in R & D and organizational resources.* A firm must make a certain level of investment each year for it to be able to have investment ideas and the organizational capacity to implement them. Although investment ideas can come from outside the organization, for reasons discussed in the idea source discussion above, investments of established semiconductor firms in genuinely innovative areas are generally based on internally developed ideas from the firm's own research and development. A study done by the Business and Defense Services Administration (hereinafter referred to as the BDSA study) compared the research and development expenditures to sales ratios of the twenty-five major firms in the semiconductor industry in the period 1958–59 with the rates of growth of these companies between that period and 1964.[44] The group of companies with the highest ratios experienced the most rapid growth rates, and the group with the lowest ratios had a negative growth rate. This would suggest that there is a substantial long-run return on investment in research and development. Transitron is the classic example of the consequences of avoiding research and development expenditures and concentrating on getting quickly into production ideas developed by others.[45] The company suffered greatly when the industry shifted to integrated circuits. Companies, such as Raytheon and Sprague, which specialized in buying the ideas of others, also met with little success and either exited or started doing more of their own research and development.

A firm can spend too much on research and development, as a

Fairchild official admitted that it had in the past. Such an investment produces more ideas than the firm can handle because of the limits on its organizational and available financial resources. Because the surplus ideas cannot be stored, they tend through the migration of personnel to make their way into the investment proposals considered by competitors.

The interviews were not very revealing on how firms determine how much research and development to conduct because most of the interviewees were intent on demonstrating that they conducted a great deal. One approach would be to match the industry average of the ratio of research and development expenditures to sales and see over time if this seems to produce about the right flow of ideas for the capacities of the organization. As evidence that this approach is used, the discussion in the interviews was usually in terms of comparisons with the spending of competitors. Such an approach is less open to the criticism that there are economies of scale in research than it might appear to be at first glance. Because of static and dynamic economies of scale in production, the difference between firms with larger and smaller semiconductor sales is not primarily due to differences between the two kinds of firms in the amount of sales of any particular product line, but rather to differences in the breadth of product line.

The history of the industry shows a decline, followed by a leveling off, in the ratio of expenditures on research and development to sales. In 1953, RCA had a quarter of its 300-man research staff working on semiconductors, and Bell Labs had one-eighth of its 2,300 researchers working in the area.[46] In 1954 and 1955, annual research and development expenditures were still greater than sales.[47] Various estimates of the amount invested in research and development as a percentage of sales for particular years among the last ten years of the period under study are in the range of 6 to 9 percent.[48]

Investments in organizational resources are not as speculative. The optimal amount is a function of the amount of organizational resources consumption that would be required for the expected number of good investment proposals over the succeeding two- or three-year period for which there will be financial resources available.

c. *Alternative projects in the future.* There does exist an expectation held by firms in the industry that they will have a continuing stream of good investment ideas. They quite properly do not see the future flow of good investment proposals as a random event. They see it as the result of a well-functioning organizational process which develops ideas in its research and development department and searches them out from the outside. Their expectations concerning the future flow of investment proposals are extrapolations of their respective past successes.

2. *Investment by an Established Firm Not Previously in the Semiconductor Industry*

Established firm investment in innovative technology is made not only by firms already operating in the semiconductor industry, but also by new entrants. As indicated earlier, every established firm that entered the industry was large and diversified. Such an entrant, unlike a brand new firm, has an ongoing internal finance process similar to the established semiconductor firms discussed above. However, the nature of the investment proposed is entirely new and is not the highly specified result of an internal idea-generating process within the firm.

The evidence collected concerning firms already established in other industries before entering the semiconductor industry was historical in nature because there had been no recent examples at the time of the interviews. Officers of the firms in the interview group with this history did not provide much helpful information because corporate memories are quite short as a result of personnel turnover.

2.1. *History of the Entry of Established Firms*

The major tube manufacturers, Raytheon, General Electric, Philco, RCA, and Sylvania, were the first to enter the semiconductor industry. Their early success was such as to lead Peter Temin to conclude in 1959 that "the most striking thing is that the big tube manufacturers were among the first to enter the transistor industry, and still generally dominate it."[49] Most other major electronics firms also eventually entered the industry. They did so for a variety of reasons, including a desire to integrate vertically. Texas Instruments entered in 1953 in order to improve its instruments and in order to provide a base for growth which could turn the company from a small firm into a large one. Semiconductors soon grew to constitute more than half its sales. Sprague, the world's largest capacitor manufacturer, entered in 1953 because their research and production skills made semiconductors a natural extension of its current line and because it was in a good marketing position. Fairchild entered the industry by extending finance to a new firm founded by several associates of William Shockley, the inventor of the transistor, in return for an option to purchase the company after eighteen months. Its interest was in finding a new product line in a highly technical area which could be a substitute for its declining aerial photographic and optical equipment business. IBM entered in order to reduce its dependence on sources of supply over which it lacked control and in order to tailor the development of future semiconductor products to fit its future needs as it saw them.

The long-run record of the diversified firms which added semiconductors to their business indicates that unless they lost their diversity and focused on manufacturing semiconductors, they did not succeed. By 1972, of the top seven firms in the industry, only IBM had more than 50 percent of its production outside of semiconductors, and the profitability of its semiconductor operation was unclear. General Electric, Sylvania, Westinghouse, Philco-Ford, and CBS had all dropped out of the market. The semiconductor operations at RCA, Raytheon, and Sprague had clearly not been profitable. At the time of the interviews, their officials claimed that they were becoming profitable, but other industry officials, noting the scale of their operations, expressed doubts. These doubts seem confirmed by the fact that none of them are significant factors in the semiconductor industry today.

2.11. *Idea Sources*

A firm planning to enter semiconductors for the first time does not have a staff already working on current semiconductor problems whose expertise can be used to specify new proposals. In the case of a firm the entry of which is at least partially motivated by the desire to integrate vertically, ideas may come from its end product staff who are familiar with the needs of that industry, but such ideas are of a very different nature than those which would be provided by an ongoing semiconductor staff which, among other things, would be familiar with the complexities of production. This familiarity permits assessments of what is possible and how much it will cost. Thus, even though large diversified electronics companies have had talented scientific personnel, the investment proposals on which they have acted have inevitably been less well specified than those for firms already in the industry. The established new entrant, like an outside investor in securities, must make projections of how profitable will investment in the particular product or process be, based either on the experience of outside consultants or on some kind of a general feeling held by most of those in the company familiar with semiconductor technology, production techniques, and markets. But the established new entrant, unlike the outside investor, must take the initiative: it must assemble the semiconductor organization instead of having a semiconductor organization come to it and try to justify the investment. The basis of projections of profitability and the need to take initiative suggest that an established firm new entrant would be unlikely to make the riskiest semiconductor investments, those at the frontier of the technology.

2.12. *Calculation of the Advantages from Investment*

The calculation of the advantages of an initial investment in semiconductors by an established firm entering the industry should not be significantly different from the calculations of additional investment by a firm already in the industry, except that the level of specificity of the idea is lower. Two particular features of such investments, however, should be explored in more detail: the fact that such investments generally involve downward vertical integration made in anticipation of in-house sales and the fact that by definition such investments are diversifying.

It has already been suggested that in some respects a market relationship between the manufacturer of components and the manufacturer of end products is undesirable, and that these factors have taken on added importance as increasingly complex integrated circuits increase the percentage of value contributed by components.[50] Creating a firm responsive to these factors can be accomplished for many end products by upstream integration of an end product firm as well as by downstream integration of a semiconductor firm.

Systems manufacturers are motivated to integrate vertically by the inverse of the market foreclosure worries of component manufacturers. Supply shortages occur periodically in the boom or bust world of the semiconductor industry. When such shortages occur, the supply is allocated to a great extent among regular customers in a pattern determined by the supplier rather than by price rationing. Vertically integrated manufacturers of components tend to favor their own end product divisions.

Because of these factors, in 1970, 35 percent of all integrated circuits were produced for "captive use," and it was predicted that the proportion would remain at least that high for another five years.[51] Most major diversified systems companies have tried semiconductor production at some point, and concern about internal needs has often been a dominating factor in the decision.[52] The semiconductor divisions of these companies have often shown an open preference for their sibling manufacturing divisions even if they actively competed in the open market as well. RCA's semiconductor division, for example, at one time gave its sibling divisions a 5 percent discount.[53]

The high rate of failure of existing firms making upstream integration investments into semiconductors resulted from both overestimating the benefits and underestimating the costs of the particular projects they chose. One cause of overestimating benefits is that the choice of the technology in which they invest often is distorted by their concern with the immediate needs of their end products divisions.[54] These divisions are the chief internal (and hence most trusted) source of semiconductor investment ideas. Investments based on such ideas would produce products the usefulness of which is well understood. Investments based on current needs result in a conservative bias relative to investments in the industry as a whole. The most innovative semiconductor products, by contrast, tend to be ones that are in demand as much because they create the possibility of new end products as because they satisfy the needs of existing end products. An established diversified firm runs a much larger risk of investing in a technology that will obsolesce before the firm has slid down the learning curve and had an adequate period of payback.

One example of this phenomenon was RCA's overcommitment to germanium transistors when it first engaged in substantial semiconductor production in the mid 1950s. This commitment was shaped by RCA's aim to satisfy the immediate needs of its consumer product division,[55] which did not need transistors able to withstand the wider range of operating conditions that the next generation of transistors made of silicon offered. By not entering the silicon transistor market early, as Texas Instruments did, RCA lost the chance to exploit the military market which at the time turned out to be far larger than the civilian consumer product market.

IBM provides other examples. It first entered semiconductor production by establishing a components group to manufacture germanium transistors which were the kind used in its current generation of computers. When the germanium transistors were made obsolete for this purpose in a year or so, IBM was not prepared to produce the superior silicon ones.[56] Later, in April 1963, IBM designed its 360-series computer with hybrid integrated circuits which it could manufacture itself, because it felt that integrated circuits were not yet sufficiently perfected. IBM subsequently lagged behind its competitors in using monolithic integrated circuits because it was not capable of manufacturing them in volume.[57]

The large systems companies which manufactured tubes faced an additional, somewhat analogous problem in the 1950s because semiconductor investment meant for them quasi-horizontal integration as well as vertical integration. Involvement in the tube business again gave the internal idea sources and assessment functions of the firm investment decision process a conservative bias because such involvement narrowed appreciation of the full range of eventual applications of semiconductors: semiconductors were simply viewed as miniaturized tubes.[58] A Raytheon official, for example, admitted in an interview that the company's initial effort in semiconductors was plagued by the fact that the tube orientation of the people who ran the company led them to try to develop individual transistors which would replace tubes on a one-to-one basis within a traditional circuit design. They failed to realize that full utilization of the potential of semiconductors required whole new circuit design concepts, and that individual transistors should be designed to satisfy the requirements of these new circuits. The conservative bias of the tube manufacturers may have been aggravated by the vested interest that some officials had in maintaining a market for tubes, the product for which they had developed a lifetime of manufacturing skills.

The second problem that established diversified firms tended to overlook when estimating the benefits of an initial semiconductor investment was how difficult it was for such a firm to assemble a good semiconductor staff.[59] As a general matter, such corporate giants never had problems attracting and retaining quality personnel. But it was the universal opinion of the officials interviewed at firms where semiconductors represent at least 50 percent of sales that "good semiconductor people" do not want to work for the more diversified companies. Officials at diversified companies at least admitted it was a problem they needed to deal with. One confirmation is the great success that numerous groups of former employees of diversified firms have had after leaving and founding their own firms. Their motivation for leaving relates to the comparatively inadequate financial incentive structure that is offered by large diversified firms,[60] and, according to several such former employees when interviewed, irritation at the level of central management interference in their work.

2.13. *Calculation of Costs*

The process by which an established firm contemplating its first investment in semiconductors calculates its costs should be the same as the way firms already in the semiconductor industry calculate the costs of semiconductor project proposals. There are, however, again special features of established firm new entrants that affect this process to some extent and that lead them to overestimate the costs of highly innovative investment and underestimate the costs of large investments.

It was suggested in several of the interviews that large diversified firms are more accounting rate of return oriented and less growth oriented than firms relatively more specialized in semiconductors. This orientation would make diversified companies less tolerant of the more innovative semiconductor investments. Although such investments clearly have more growth potential, they involve more development time with noncapitalizable expenses and hence more drain on current accounting income. A firm oriented toward short-run accounting rate of return will therefore tend to avoid the most innovative investment proposals. This tendency is aggravated by the fact that an initial investment in the semiconductor industry will inherently involve a greater delay before the appearance of positive accounting profits than an additional investment.

A large diversified firm has much larger absolute limits on the total amount of finance it can raise by debt, equity, and dissipation of liquid assets. On average it will have proportionally more current and future alternative investment proposals to consume the finance that can be raised. However, if the firm should choose to invest in semiconductors, the cost of the financing will not increase as fast with the size of investment as is the case with a smaller firm. If the appropriate measure is outside cost, each additional dollar of investment in semiconductors raised by debt alters the debt/equity ratio, the main determinant of the price of debt, less in the case of a large company than of a small one. Each additional dollar of investment in semiconductors raised by equity requires less of a decline in the price of stock to induce additional people to hold it because the company is better known. If the appropriate measure is instead opportunity cost, the company will have more potential investment projects at each level of expected rate of return so that increased investment in semiconductors will foreclose investment in more projects with one level of expected rate of return before beginning to foreclose projects at a higher level of expected rate of return.

This analysis suggests that large diversified firms do not face the same limits on the size of their investments as do their smaller, specialized brethren. The record shows that large diversified firms have made a number of unusually large investments in semiconductors. Sprague in the early 1970s spent $57 million to develop a wide range of integrated circuits in an effort to reenter the semiconductor market with a full line. Motorola had invested a total of $33 million in 1963 and 1964 to establish its integrated circuit operations before making its first profit from them in 1965.[61] Philco-Ford put a million dollars a month into its General Microelectronics subsidiary between 1966, when Philco-Ford purchased the company in order to reenter the semiconductor industry, and 1968, when it closed the operation.[62] This investment was on top of $19 million Philco-Ford spent prior to 1966 in developing a microcircuit capacity.[63] These figures are tenfold and more greater than what most of the successful semispecialized semiconductor firms spent on their entry before they became profitable operations capable of self-sustained growth (see section 3.22 for specific figures). Thus, the availability of a "deep pocket" to which to go for financing is either no help, or it is not sufficient help to compensate for whatever disadvantages are connected with a semiconductor operation within such a firm.

The foregoing survey of the process by which established diversified firms decided to make investments that enter them into the semiconductor industry suggests several causes for their record of failure. In many cases, the cause was that the firm backed a project that was overly conservative in terms of the technology it implemented. In many others, however, the choice of technology was appropriate,[64] but the large diversified firm failed to provide an incentive structure capable of attracting and retaining high-quality personnel the way smaller firms can by providing significant equity interests to such individuals. Another cause of failure was the result of two seemingly contradictory tendencies frequently displayed by large diversified companies. On the one hand, they were willing to make very large initial investments, while on the other hand they did not tolerate a period of sustained accounting losses. Investment was larger than the new unit was organizationally capable of handling and was accompanied by impatience for positive accounting earnings. The impatience distorted the ongoing flow of decisions related to running the investment project. After a period of time it caused undue central management interference in the work of the semiconductor specialists heading the project, and eventually resulted in termination of the project.

3. *Investment by New Entries Founded To Be Semiconductor Firms*

The serious economic literature that exists on the semiconductor industry stresses the importance for innovation and diffusion of new firms founded for the purpose of entering the industry. Anthony Golding concludes that "the real contribution of the spin-off phenomenon [the forming of new firms by personnel working for old firms] lies in the stimulus given to established producers. Entrenched firms have often been galvanized into action by fast-reacting, early innovative spin-offs intent upon the aggressive exploitation of advanced technology."[65] John Tilton emphasizes the importance of new entries within the first few paragraphs of his book: "The central hypothesis examined is the following: The diffusion of new technology is accelerated by a market structure that allows new firms to enter an industry and supplant the established leaders whenever the latter fail to employ new techniques as quickly as economic conditions warrant."[66] Although Tilton's hypothesis covers all new entries, not just ones by firms founded for that purpose, he later goes on to recount some of the difficulties that established large diversified firms have had in entering the field of semiconductors. The thrust of his hypothesis is therefore also centered on firms founded to produce semiconductors. The list of firms founded to produce semiconductors that now are, or at some time in the past were, among the leaders in the industry testifies to the importance of this investment context: Fairchild,[67] Signetics, Intel, Mostek, AMI, National Semiconductor, Transitron, General Transistor, and Germanium Products.

3.1. *Idea Sources*

In the case of a firm founded for the purpose of manufacturing semiconductors, the source of the idea for the investment and the group of persons who make the decision to organize the firm are one and the same. The pattern has never been one in which a proponent without scientific skills decides that the field is ripe for investment and gathers a scientific staff around him.

In the early years of the industry, firms were founded by individuals who simply had good training in solid state physics. Transitron, for example, was founded by two brothers, one of whom was a physicist still in his twenties. However, because the technology quickly became a highly specialized combination of skills including metallurgy, mechanical engineering, and electronics as well as solid state physics, soon no firm could enter the business that was not manned by individuals who had previous experience in the industry. Since the later part of the 1950s, all the new firms to enter the industry have been spin-offs from established firms: the individuals who founded each of them had been working for some other semiconductor firm and left as a group to form a new one. Thus, most firms in the market today can trace their origins back through successive generations to AT&T. The published family trees of the industry show that aside from its grandparent, AT&T, Fairchild spawned by far the most descendants.[68] This appears to be related to Fairchild's unusually large research and development effort.

3.11. *Calculation of Benefit*

Individuals who start a new firm are motivated by the same constellation of human values that motivates the managers of large established firms: compensation, perquisites, respect, power, affection of those around them, and a sense of rectitude. However, because control is coupled with ownership of a substantial portion of the company, the course of action that satisfies these motives is much simpler than in the managerial case and is much closer to the neoclassical model. The decision to start a spin-off is based on the calculation that the benefits from receiving an income directly related to the performance of a new company are greater than those which can be negotiated in the organizational division of the spoils of an established company. A proponent may also feel that he can pursue other values more effectively in the context of a new firm which may involve trade-offs with economic values that the established firm is unwilling or unable to make or which are only available in a small organization.

The calculation of economic benefit to an individual from the decision to found a new semiconductor company is simply the calculation of the risk-return characteristics of the investment. How they go about making this calculation is not completely clear. The individuals who found new firms are the same kind as those who form the intelligence backbone of established firms and who are responsible for most of the expert input into an established organization's calculation of the expected return from investment. Indications from the interviews are that the calculations made by those founding new firms are not quantified in rate of return form and instead represent a feeling about the potential of a new company built on a new technology. The disinclination to make quantified rate of return calculations is undoubtedly reinforced by the fact that the founding of a new corporation involves start-up costs incurred in building an extended organization, achieving brand recognition, and establishing marketing channels. Instead of precise calculations, founders of new firms appear to act on the combination of the feeling that the project has good enough prospects to be practical and an awareness of the tremendous financial rewards reaped by the luckier founders of other firms. The eight founders of what is now the Fairchild semiconductor operations shared $3 million when their company was purchased by Fairchild Camera and Instrument a year and a half after they began;[69] the two brothers who founded Transitron received $30 million for the sale of 13 percent of its stock seven years after its founding;[70] the founders of General Microelectronics received $300,000 each when the company was sold to Philco-Ford three years after its founding.[71]

3.2 *Calculation of Costs*

3.21. *Opportunity Cost of the Founder's Time*

Those founding a firm face two kinds of costs: the opportunity cost of their own time and the cost of financial resources. The opportunity cost for the time of each of the usually several founders of a semiconductor firm is high: people of the quality that have founded successful firms in the early 1970s could command annual salaries of $50,000 to $150,000 plus valuable stock options.[72] This is really an advantage which encourages the formation of firms. It means that the founders, who are the individuals who believe in the project the most because of their intimate knowledge of its prospects, can supply a significant portion of the initial capital through "sweat equity." In addition, because this income-earning ability is derived from a generally marketable scientific skill rather than the occupation of a vital position within a particular organization, founders leaving an established firm face a relatively secure future even if the new firm fails.

3.22. *Cost of Financial Resources*

The cost of financial resources is a function of how the company is assessed by the sources of finance and how much finance is required beyond the sweat equity and cash contributions of the founders themselves.

a. *Assessment by financial sources.* There are a number of sources that new companies can look to for their initial capital. The most direct, in terms of the finance process, is the direct investment of wealthy individuals, which normally comes in the form of equity. Leo Bakalar, who had made his money in entirely different areas of industry, lent and invested a million dollars to start Transitron, which was the brainchild of his younger physicist brother.[73] The fraternal relationship between the financier and the idea source, however, shows the level of personal trust that is required for this source to produce significant amounts of money.

Another conventional way in which new firms in other industries are founded is through the support of an investment banking house. Signetics, which was backed by Lehman Brothers, is the only major example of the use of this source in the semiconductor industry.[74] Hayden, Stone, primarily at the instigation of its then employee Arthur Rock, did play a brokerage role by helping to arrange the deal between Fairchild Camera and Instrument and the founders of the Shockley Labs spin-off, whereby the firm was financed and later taken over by Fairchild.[75] This general lack of involvement by investment banks may be caused by the effectiveness of their competitors, the venture capital firms, which are perhaps more knowledgeable because they specialize because of a growth orientation in extending founding capital in areas of advanced technology.[76]

Officials of two such firms were interviewed in connection with this study: New Business Resources–Venture Capital Partnership, Ltd. (NBR), and Arthur Rock & Co., which furnished founding capital for Mostek and Intel, respectively. The first of these two firms raised most of its money from private individuals and their trusts; the second raised money as well from endowments, bank trust departments, and established corporations.[77] The money was raised by convincing these sources that the managers of the venture firms have the sagacity to pick a few winners among the investments they make. In the case of Arthur Rock, his success in launching two previous winners, Scientific Data Systems and Teledyne, and his instrumental role in getting Fairchild interested in the founders of what was later to become Fairchild's semiconductor division, were strong selling points. The managers of NBR, according to the interview, treated the raising of money as a sales job and tried to capitalize on their personal experience and technical competence in the semiconductor field.

These venture capital groups can augment their importance by acting as a broker to find other investors to contribute founding capital. NBR, for example, succeeded in persuading Sprague to add $2½ million of its own money to the $½ million that NBR itself was investing in Mostek.

Corporations with extra resources are an important source of founding capital with or without the partnership of a venture capital firm. Sometimes, as in the case of Fairchild, the ultimate desire is to integrate the new firm into its own operations. In other cases, as in the case of Sprague investing in Mostek, the intention is merely to make a good securities investment. Other companies which have tried this kind of investment less successfully are Beckman Instruments (Shockley Labs, which was eventually sold to ITT after losing much of its talent spawning Fairchild), Union Carbide (control of its semiconductor subsidiary was sold to Solitron in 1969), Rheem (control of its semiconductor subsidiary was sold to Raytheon), and Stewart Warner.[78] The technical orientation of most of these companies indicates that they were able to act as expert investors who would have more confidence in their judgment of the prospects of investment in the innovation proposed than most kinds of investors.

Although the different sources of founding capital have somewhat different information-processing systems, they all look for roughly the same characteristics in deciding whether to make an investment in a brand new semiconductor firm and the terms.

The characteristic that was stressed over all others in the interviews and in published reports was the quality of the people founding the firm and their apparent level of desire to make money.[79] The fact that a "good person" is willing to devote his time to the implementation of an idea is a certification of the quality of the idea. Despite the problems with an approach that relies so much on personal contacts, better analysis of the ideas is very difficult for an investment group, usually consisting of a few men at most.[80] Even in the case of the scientific-based corporate investor Sprague, the interest in the Mostek project was generated by personal contacts: officials of NBR were acting as consultants to Sprague on some technical matters and suggested the idea to them.

A related characteristic is the length of time the source expects the founding individuals to stay with the new firm. Because they are primarily investing in people, rather than ideas or equipment that is of value separate from the founders, the investors will be left with an empty shell if the founders leave the firm.[81] There are two aspects of the initial financial structure of a new firm that both constitute incentives for the founders to stay and act as indicators to investors of the intention of the founders to do so: significant personal investment in the company by the founders; and a financial plan which emphasizes the substitution of founders' shares for salary.

Although the characteristics of the technology are in general not carefully studied, attention is paid to how advanced the level is.

Investors are not interested in new companies in the semiconductor industry planning to replicate current technology. Investors recognize (a) the large amount of capital necessary to make up for the learning economies achieved by established competitors in current technology products, (b) the static economies of scale in the production of standardized products by use of automated machinery that large companies with substantial capital resources may be able to accomplish,[82] (c) the advantage of an innovative product in establishing brand recognition,[83] and (d) the growth potential of new products. For a period of time before the first "shakeout" in 1962, the interviewees and the published sources both suggested, the level-of-technology factor may have been the dominant consideration in investment source decisions.[84]

b. *Size of investment necessary for entry.* The semiconductor industry on the whole became more expensive to enter over the twenty-five-year period of the study, but the minimum investment necessary in 1974 was still relatively small given the size that successful entrants could attain in a period of a few years. Table 4.1 lists some representative experiences of new entrants. While the figures are not entirely comparable, all relate in one way or another to the underlying concept of the cost of entry: the amount of money which must be put into a firm before its cash flow becomes positive.

Considering the fifteen-fold increase in the dollar sales of semiconductors between 1956 and 1973 (see Chapter 3, section B) and the relatively steady level of concentration in the industry (see chapter 3, section C1), the increase in entry cost seems very modest. This is particularly so in light of the fact that these figures are for entries with relatively broad-based intentions. The BDSA study indicates that entry with the intention of specializing in a very narrow field was much less costly still: such specialized operations could be successful with only a few employees.[85]

The reason for this modest level of entry cost in an industry with sales dominated by a small number of firms, each with sales in the hundreds of millions of dollars, is that there is a difference between the size necessary to start successfully and the size necessary to stay in business over the long run as a broad-based company. The scale of operations necessary for success immediately after entry is small for a number of reasons. Such firms entered by investments in the newest technology which lessened the applications of automation

Table 4.1

Company	Year of Entry	Cost
General Transistor	1954	$100,000[a]
Transitron	1952	$1 million[b]
Texas Instruments	1954	Entry into semiconductors, $4.25 million ($3.0 million in assets and $1.25 million in uncapitalizable losses)[c]
Fairchild	1957	$700,000 in "unusual expenses" (presumably uncapitalizable losses)[d]
Siliconix	1962	$2 million[e]
Intel	1968	$4 million[f]
Mostek	1969	$3 million[g]

[a] William Harris, "The Battle of Components," *Fortune*, May 1957, p. 138.

[b] "Semiconductors," *Business Week*, March 26, 1960, p. 110.

[c] A. Golding, "The Semiconductor Industry in Britain and the United States: A Case Study in Innovation, Growth, and the Diffusion of Technology," Ph.D. diss., University of Sussex, 1971, p. 117.

[d] "Semiconductors," p. 113.

[e] H. Kleiman, "The Integrated Circuit: A Case Study of Innovation in the Electronics Industry," D.B.A. diss., George Washington University, 1966, p. 122.

[f] N. Lindbergen, "Building a Two-Headed Monster," *Innovation* (1971), no. 20, p. 46.

[g] Interview with Richard Hanschen of NBR, which backed Mostek.

and its associated static economies of scale. Marketing costs in the industry were not high: in the late 1960s there were only about 4,000 potential customers, of which a few hundred accounted for 95 percent of sales.[86] Marketing costs were about 8 percent of sales in 1965.[87] Sales were made on the basis of reputation spread by word of mouth and published characteristics in trade magazines; not by brand name identity built up by expensive mass advertising. Initial research and development costs were low because the spin-off group normally took the technology with it from its last employer.

After a firm becomes successful, however, it is necessary that it continue to grow in order to survive. If it stays merely in the narrow line of products in which it initially began, it faces high risks because of lack of diversity and eventual diminution of market through obsolescence. Becoming a broad-based company and entering new product lines at the beginning of their product cycle in order to compensate for the gradual obsolescence of current lines both require an extensive research and development program. Because the ideas generated by research and development are not readily salable, expenses related to such an effort tend to be lump sum overhead which allow economies of scale. Lester Hogan estimated in 1968 that a company must spend annually $10 million to $15 million just to stay abreast of the latest technology.[88] A firm cannot spend a great deal more than the industry average per unit on any input (in the case of R & D expenditure in semiconductors, 6 to 9 percent of sales; see section 1.33b) and stay in business in a reasonably competitive industry. Thus, a broad-based company would at that time have required sales in the neighborhood of $200 million to be viable. A company may not need to be fully broad based to remain viable, but the narrower the base, the greater the risk of extinction by a sudden change in technology or the market. In addition, there are probably not proportionate savings in necessary research and development expenditures, as the range of products offered is narrowed because certain general research is necessary no matter what the width of product line is. This appears to be empirically confirmed, at least historically, by the BDSA study finding that the percentage of sales spent on research and development by firms covered in their 1964 survey with less than $15 million of sales was twice as high as the percentage spent by such firms with sales of more than $15 million.[89]

The cost of entry into the semiconductor industry would have been greater if it had been necessary to be vertically integrated into the end product industry in order to have access to a sufficient market for the semiconductors produced. Despite the trend toward such integration discussed earlier, there is no evidence that it was necessary for survival, and certainly no firm that entered had founders that felt that a simultaneous vertical integration investment was necessary.

3.3 *Why Spin-offs Occur*

The spin-off phenomenon represents a failure of the finance process of established semiconductor corporations. The reason that a proponent employed by such a corporation took his idea elsewhere was, in the case of at least three highly successful spin-offs, that the parent firm simply did not perceive the idea to be worth substantial investment: the Signetics group breaking from Fairchild in 1961 over integrated circuits, the Intel group breaking from Fairchild in 1968 over semiconductor computer memories, and the Mostek group breaking from Texas Instruments over MOS. The reason in several other cases is that the established corporation, while interested, was not interested enough to offer the proponent sufficiently attractive terms to persuade the proponent to stay and implement the project within the established corporation. The fact that the success rate of semiconductor spin-off firms has been high and that they have been the initiators of so many innovations suggests that in many instances established firms missed good opportunities.[90]

The first question raised by the phenomenon is why did the established firms fail to realize the potential of the proposed projects? The proponent who proposes an investment idea has, because of his expertise, the capacity to predict more accurately than anyone else the outcome of the project. He must, however, convince the sources of finance that his announced assessment of the project's prospects is not inflated by his self-interest. As we saw in chapter 2, a proponent who is an employee of an established firm proposing a project to his top management is confined to relying primarily on his experience-based authority relationship with his funding source. The problem for established firms is that those proponents with the most experience-based authority are unlikely to be the ones proposing the most innovative ideas. And proponents with innovative ideas but little experience-based authority cannot substitute with structure-of-incentive authority. For example, officials at one established firm, Raytheon, admitted that the most important cause of Raytheon's semiconductor problems in the 1950s and 1960s (after its initial flush of success) was an overly rigid salary structure.

It might be suggested that the way around these problems is for a parent corporation to establish a subsidiary for each investment proposal they undertake, granting to the proponent a substantial equity interest in return for a commitment of money and time. Signetics actually did this in the case of semiconductor computer memories in order to forestall a spin-off. Generally, however, this has not been viewed as a practical technique. It would extend the conglomerate concept to a company in a single line of business and deny the firm what undoubtedly are the numerous advantages of more integrated operations for the production and marketing of similar products.

An established corporation may also fail to finance an idea which becomes the basis of a successful spin-off because certain officials within it may have developed a vested interest in the current semi-conductor technology, which would be displaced by the technology embedded in the proposed new investment.[91] This parallels the tepid reaction of many managers of diversified electronics companies to their semiconductor operations because the managers had vested interests in tubes.

The reasons why the established firms missed these opportunities do not of themselves explain, however, how the proponents were more successful in persuading funding sources in the outside capital market to provide funds for the project.

The proponent of a good idea is likely to have even less experience-based authority with which to persuade outside funding sources of the sincerity of his predictions (see chapter 2, sections B 2.122 and B 2.124). Fortunately, however, a new semiconductor firm proponent has the potential for establishing significant authority in the eyes of outside funding sources both on the basis of reputation and through the structure of incentives that the proponent operates within. The availability of these alternative sources of authority, given the relatively low experience-based authority of those proponents within established firms proposing the most innovative ideas, goes a long way in explaining the dominance of new firms as the vehicles for introducing new technology into the industry.

The semiconductor industry is one characterized by "rising stars" who are known throughout the industry because of their technical achievements and because of their tendency to move among firms. It is also an industry in which prior academic achievements are more reliable indicators of business promise than most. These factors give potential funding sources a better idea of the kind of person they are dealing with in the case of a new semiconductor firm proponent than in the case of a new firm proponent in a more traditional industry.

As discussed in chapter 2, a proponent of founding a new firm on an investment idea has more potential to develop structure of incentive based authority than does a proponent of an investment idea within an established organization. Whether that potential can be realized depends on how practical it is for the proponent to make a significant investment in his new firm. Statistics suggest that during the period under study it was practical for the typical proponent of a good innovative idea to make such an investment.

The founders of new firms received considerable portions of the original shares issued by the companies they began. The founders of AMI, for example, received, according to one official who was interviewed, 70 percent of the stock for an investment of $250,000 plus their time. Outside financiers received 30 percent of the stock for $1 million. As late as 1957, the top management of Texas Instruments owned over 25 percent of the stock of the company.[92] It is difficult, of course, to separate out in these figures the component that represents the provision for entrepreneurial surplus, the profit due to the proponent for a good idea capable of earning more than the market rate of return, from shares given for actual investment of money and time.[93] But if the initial capital necessary in 1974 to start such a firm was, as has been suggested, in the neighborhood of $5 million to cover capital equipment and losses for perhaps two years, four founders whose time was worth $50,000 to $100,000 a year could, by working at low salary for two years plus investment of personal savings of the size that persons in this income bracket could then have accumulated, have contributed perhaps 20 percent of the initial capital. This would seem to meet the two criteria for convincing others of the soundness of the investment: substantial personal sacrifice and a significant enough portion of ownership so that the sacrifice does not seem worth it simply on the basis of a small chance of making an enormous fortune (the entrepreneurial surplus of a very large project). The high portion of originally issued shares which has gone to founders combined with the ability that founders have for providing a significant share of initial capital at least suggest that the demonstration of sincerity arising from investments by founders accounts in part for the success of new firms.

4. *Summary*

This chapter examines the role of investment decisions in innovation and diffusion of new technology in the semiconductor industry. Innovative project proposals were likely to be considered in one of three contexts: a proposal by an employee to the top management of a firm already a member of the industry, a proposal by an employee to the top management of an established, diversified firm not a member of the industry, and a proposal to found a new firm made to participants in the outside finance process.

When the management of a firm already in the industry evaluated the benefits of a new project proposal, it put heavy emphasis on the extent to which the proposed project would contribute to firm growth. This emphasis was not necessarily inconsistent with a policy of long-run profit maximization, however, because the managers interviewed believed organizational growth was needed in order to attract and retain the kind of personnel necessary for the firm to be profitable. The evaluation of benefits also stressed the contribution the proposed project could make to the stability of firm income. This stress put a premium on proposed projects that would diversify the firm's portfolio of real investments. A number of diversification ventures implemented by established semiconductor firms proved to be failures.

When the management of a firm already in the industry evaluated the costs of a proposed project, it was typically as concerned with the project's consumption of organizational resources, such as design engineers and experienced production teams, as with the cost of funding the project. This suggests that investment decisions in such firms proceeded at two levels: meta-investments in organizational resources (including R & D) and project investments. The statements of managers suggest that the process by which they evaluated the funding costs of a project proposal focused primarily on opportunity costs: the return that could otherwise be earned using the funds to implement alternative projects that might be proposed in the future. Managers were very explicit about their concern with the negative effect of new real investments on short-run accounting earnings. They stated that because of this concern they reduced their level of investment when accounting earnings were already low for other reasons.

The end product division was the idea source of most project proposals considered by established, diversified firms that were not at the time of the proposal members of the semiconductor industry. This factor gave a conservative cast to many of the proposals. The conservatism of proposals was complemented by a conservatism in evaluation because of a management emphasis, greater than in firms dominated by semiconductors, on quick returns in order to minimize the drain of the investment on short-run accounting earnings.

Firms of this type were willing to invest large amounts in the projects they did choose to implement, but, in the cases where the choice of technology was wrong, this simply magnified the size of the failure.

Proposals to form new firms based on an innovative investment idea invariably came from employees of firms already in the industry who wished to "spin off." A spin-off represents a failure on the part of the internal finance process of the spawning firm. One reason for the failure was often a rigidity in the spawning firm's interest rules, which were shaped by experiences of earlier successes. Another reason the old employers did not fully recognize the value of the ideas of spin-off proponents may be that the proponents lacked experience-based authority in the eyes of their top managers. Spin-off proponents succeeded at obtaining funds from outside sources because they could easily establish structure of incentive based authority in the eyes of these sources. The cost of entry into the industry was low relative to the income-earning potential of the proponents. This permitted proponents to provide a significant amount of sweat and cash equity.

5. Finance and Competition in the Semiconductor Industry

The degree of competition in the economy with respect to any particular product line without close substitutes is closely related to a structural characteristic of its market organization: the number of firms among which the aggregate capacity of the industry to produce the product is divided. Finance is relevant to the development of this structural characteristic because a share of the market is only available to those entrepreneurs who have access to finance for investment.

This chapter attempts to answer why the semiconductor industry and the product lines within it have been as concentrated as the figures in chapter 3 describe. This question is particularly vexing because it was concluded in chapter 4 that the initial costs of entry are surprisingly low and should not constitute an entry barrier of the type discussed in traditional industrial organization literature in industries where massive amounts of capital are necessary.[1] Finance, it will be argued, still has much to do with the answer.

There is almost total agreement among officials in, and commentators on, the semiconductor industry that firms that implement innovations quickly grow, while those that do not wither.[2] The relationship between early implementation and growth is so strong that when an idea for a new product or process develops to the point of practical implementation, often only the handful of firms that become aware of the idea and act on it quickly succeed with it. As a result, these few firms tend to dominate the relevant product line for the life of the innovation. If one can explain the reason for the success of early entrants, one can therefore explain the high level of concentration in most semiconductor product lines.

The conventional wisdom is that success is limited to the early implementers of semiconductor innovations because of the existence of the learning curve. Later implementers face a huge cost disadvantage relative to the earlier ones. What follows challenges to some extent that conventional wisdom. A model is developed showing that, given plausible parameters, a learning curve will result in only a very modest decline from one period to the next in the marginal costs of the quantities produced (where marginal cost for a given quantity in a given period is defined as the full cost consequences— both in the period in question and, discounted to present value, in all subsequent periods—of the decision to produce the last unit, i.e., the figure to which a share value maximizing firm would set marginal revenue equal when choosing what quantity to produce in the given period). Assuming, along the lines of the Chamberlain model of oligopoly, that an initial entrant and a later one face identical demand curves, the price in any given period that maximizes the profits of one should not be very different from the price that maximizes the profits of the other because the marginal cost curves of the two are not very different. Thus, the learning curve will not present a substantial barrier to the later entrant because the initial entrant and the later entrant will not experience largely different long-run profits charging the same price. This suggests that the learning curve is not a major explanation of product line concentration in the semiconductor industry unless one accepts a nonneoclassical theory of the finance process that recognizes a firm bias toward projects that enhance short-run accounting profits. It also suggests that even if one does accept such a theory—as the preceding discussion suggests one should—the learning curve can only be a partial explanation unless the bias is much larger than it appears from the case study.

The failure of the learning curve theory to explain much of the product line concentration in semiconductors leaves us searching for other explanations. One explanation is that a late entrant can never enjoy the profit margin enjoyed by the early entrant from a "skimming" pricing policy in the first few periods of a product's availability. This factor, however, should not be a major contributor to concentration because most profits are earned later in the product cycle on large volume sales even though the profit margin is less. A more powerful explanation, we will see, is that, given the retained earnings bias of the finance process, the initial entrants, which enjoy greater profitability from the innovation, can expand easily, while potential later entrants, which will suffer a decline in profitability because of the increased competition from the initial entrants, will have trouble financing entry.

A. Concentration Effects of Technical Change Involving Substantial Learning Economies

Tilton and Golding both find learning economies to be the primary reason for the link between early implementation of innovation and success. Late implementation of an innovation forces the company involved to operate at high costs when firms that implemented the innovation earlier have moved down the learning curve.[3] Firms tend to withdraw from, or not to enter, markets in which they are not initial implementers. Semiconductor product lines tend to be concentrated in the hands of the initial implementers because the spreading of a new idea to all those potentially ready to use it takes time, and only those few who get the idea early and are willing and able to act on it quickly find it profitable to do so.[4] This is an appealing explanation for the high level of concentration in the semiconductor industry, but it requires more rigorous analysis.

1. *Marginal Cost with Dynamic Economies of Scale*

There is no doubt that in the semiconductor industry the extra input cost incurred in a given period to produce during that period an additional unit of a new product (its "unit cost") and its price both drop significantly over time, even absent any further technological innovation.[5] It is not obvious, however, that dropping unit cost and price demonstrate that marginal cost, defined in a way that will guide the firm to make price and quantity decisions which will yield a maximum discounted net revenue stream, necessarily drops proportionally. Intuitively, it seems that a firm making these decisions should take into account the unit cost during the periods when dynamic economies of scale are finally fully realized (the "eventual unit cost"). The decision to produce an additional unit in an earlier period will require the expenditure during that period of an amount equal to its unit cost. But in calculating the ultimate cost to the firm of this decision, the firm should subtract from this expenditure an amount reflecting the savings, given dynamic economies of scale, in subsequent period input costs. The model presented below sets forth, given the assumptions employed, the true "marginal cost" of producing an additional unit in a given period. Marginal cost is determined in part by the eventual unit cost but, because of the existence of a positive interest rate, is also in part determined by the unit cost for the period for which the production decision is being made. As will be seen, given plausible parameters, 1) marginal cost, even in an early period of production, is much closer to eventual unit cost than to current unit cost, and 2) marginal costs decline from one period to the next much less sharply than do unit costs.

1.1 A Model of Marginal Cost Over the Life Cycle

When a firm facing dynamic economies of scale decides on an increase in production in one period, it will, by definition, experience a decrease in costs, for any given level of production, in subsequent periods. Thus, the decision a firm makes on the quantity to produce in one particular period must take into account not only the cost functions pertaining to that period but also the effect that the chosen quantity of production will have on costs in subsequent periods. The model presented here employs the assumption (without loss of generality) that unit input cost (UC) in any one time period is constant except for the effect of learning economies, which are a function of cumulative production including production in time periods preceding the one involved. This assumption allows us to focus on the intertemporal aspects of the marginal cost definition.

Definitions and Characteristics of the Model

(a) q_k = quantity produced in period k

(b) $Q_k = \sum_{i=1}^{k} q_k$

(c) n = the number of periods in the life of the innovation investment

(d) FC = initial fixed cost before production is undertaken

(e) $PC_k(q_1, q_2 \ldots, q_k) =$ expenditure in period k to permit production of q_k. Because of economies of scale, PC_k is a function of $q_1, \ldots, q_{k-1}$ as well as of q_k.

(f) $PR_k(q_k) =$ the revenue in period k from sale of q_k

(g) $TVC_k(q_1, \ldots, q_k) = \sum_{i=1}^{k} PC_i =$ aggregate of expenditures in each period up to and including period k in order to permit production of $q_1 \ldots q_k$

(h) $TVC_k(q_1, \ldots, q_k) = PC_1 \left(\sum_{i=1}^{k} q_i \right)$,

i.e., aggregate undiscounted cost of producing any given number of units does not depend on allocation of production among time periods. Marginal cost in each time period would be constant if it were not for dynamic economies of scale.

Therefore,

$$PC_k = TVC_k(q_1, \ldots, q_k) - TVC_{k-1}(q_1, \ldots, q_{k-1})$$

$$= PC_1 \left(\sum_{i=1}^{k} q_i \right) - PC_1 \left(\sum_{i=1}^{k-1} q_i \right)$$

(i) $d^2 PC_1/dq^2 < 0$ for $q < q_o$
$\qquad\qquad\quad = 0$ for $q \geq q_o$
where q_o is the aggregate level of production at which learning economies disappear.

(j) Revenue in one period is independent of quantity sold in another period, and the revenue function is the same for each period.

(k) $P_k =$ price in period k

(l) $\pi =$ total profit from the investment discounted to its present value in period 1

Pattern of Marginal Cost Over Time

(5.1) $\pi = \sum_{i=1}^{n} \frac{1}{(1+r)^{i-1}} PR_i(q_i) - \sum_{i=1}^{n} \frac{1}{(1+r)^{i-1}} PC_i(q_1, \ldots, q_i) - FC$

(5.2) $\quad = \sum_{i=1}^{n} \frac{1}{(1+r)^{i-1}} PR_i(q_i) - \sum_{i=1}^{n} \frac{1}{(1+r)^{i-1}} \left[PC_1 \left(\sum_{j=1}^{i} q_j \right) - PC_1 \left(\sum_{j=1}^{i-1} q_j \right) \right] - FC$

Taking the derivative of π with respect to q_k

$$(5.3) \quad d\pi/dq_k = \frac{1}{(1+r)^{k-1}} \frac{dPR_k(q_k)}{dq_k} - \sum_{i=1}^{n} \frac{1}{(1+r)^{i-1}} \left[\frac{dPC_1\left(\sum_{j=1}^{i} q_j\right)}{dq_k} - \frac{dPC_1\left(\sum_{j=1}^{i-1} q_j\right)}{dq_k} \right]$$

$$(5.4) \quad = \frac{1}{(1+r)^{k-1}} \frac{dPR_k(q_k)}{dq_k} - \sum_{i=1}^{k-1} \frac{1}{(1+r)^{i-1}} \left[\frac{dPC_1\left(\sum_{j=1}^{i} q_j\right)}{dq_k} - \frac{dPC_1\left(\sum_{j=1}^{i-1} q_j\right)}{dq_k} \right]$$

$$- \frac{1}{(1+r)^{k-1}} \left[\frac{dPC_1\left(\sum_{j=1}^{k} q_j\right)}{dq_k} - \frac{dPC_1\left(\sum_{j=1}^{k-1} q_j\right)}{dq_k} \right]$$

$$- \sum_{i=k+1}^{n} \frac{1}{(1+r)^{i-1}} \left[\frac{dPC_1\left(\sum_{j=1}^{i} q_j\right)}{dq_k} - \frac{dPC_1\left(\sum_{j=1}^{i-1} q_j\right)}{dq_k} \right]$$

$$(5.5) \quad = \frac{1}{(1+r)^{k-1}} \left[\frac{dPR_k(q_k)}{dq^k} - \frac{dPC_1\left(\sum_{j=1}^{k} q_j\right)}{dq_k} \right]$$

$$- \sum_{i=k+1}^{n} \frac{1}{(1+r)^{i-1}} \left[\frac{dPC_1\left(\sum_{j=1}^{i} q_j\right)}{dq_k} - \frac{dPC_1\left(\sum_{j=1}^{i-1} q_j\right)}{dq_k} \right]*$$

For convenience, the terms of this equation will be reexpressed in a form using the symbols MR and UC:

(A) Marginal revenue in each particular period is the function of the number of units produced in that period and is the same function for each period, so if $q_k = q_j$, then

$$\frac{dPR_k(q_k)}{dq_k} = \frac{dPR_j(q_j)}{dq_j} = MR(q_k) = MR(q_j).$$

(B) Unit cost (UC) in each particular period is the function of the number of the units produced not only in that period but also in all previous periods.

---

*The second expression in equation (5.4) drops out because both of the terms within the brackets equal 0 for all $i = 1, \ldots, k-1$. The second term within the brackets of the third expression in equation (5.4) similarly drops out.

$$UC(q_k) = \frac{dPC_1\left(\sum\limits_{j=1}^{k} q_j\right)}{dq_k} = UC(Q_k)$$

Equation (5.5) can therefore be rewritten as follows:

(5.6) $d\pi/dq_k = \dfrac{1}{(1+r)^{k-1}}[MR(q_k) - UC(Q_k)]$

$$- \sum_{i=k+1}^{n} \frac{1}{(1+r)^{i-1}}[UC(Q_i) - UC(Q_{i-1})]$$

The model is now sufficiently developed to answer the question of whether or not a profit-maximizing firm will have declining marginal costs in succeeding periods as it experiences dynamic economies of scale. A profit-maximizing firm will, of course, set $\dfrac{d\pi}{dq_k} = 0$ for all k's $= 1, 2 \ldots, n$. By doing so, we can for each period derive from equation (5.6) an expression (in terms of unit cost for that and each succeeding period) to which marginal revenue must be equal; i.e., an optimizing firm should choose a quantity of production for the period such that the value of marginal revenue equals the value of this expression. By the definition of marginal cost we have adopted, this expression gives the marginal cost for any given level of production during such period.

(5.7) $MC(q_k) = UC(Q_k) + \sum\limits_{i=k+1}^{n} \dfrac{1}{(1+r)^{i-k}}[UC(Q_i) - UC(Q_{i-1})]$

(5.8) $= (1+r)^{n-k} \dfrac{UC(Q_k)}{(1+r)^{n-k}} + \sum\limits_{i=k+1}^{n} \dfrac{(1+r)^{n-i}[UC(Q_i) - UC(Q_{i-1})]}{(1+r)^{n-k}}$

(5.9) $= \sum\limits_{i=k}^{n-1} \dfrac{[(1+r)^{n-i} - (1+r)^{(n-i)-1}]UC(Q_i)}{(1+r)^{n-k}} + \dfrac{1}{(1+r)^{n-k}}UC(Q_n)$

(5.10) $= \sum\limits_{i=k}^{n-1} \dfrac{r(1+r)^{(n-i)-1}}{(1+r)^{n-k}}UC(Q_i) + \dfrac{1}{(1+r)^{n-k}}UC(Q_n)$

because $(1+r)^{n-i} - (1+r)^{(n-i)-1} = r(1+r)^{(n-i)-1}$.

Equation (5.10) demonstrates that if $r=0$, then, for any k, $MC(q_k) = UC(Q_n)$. That is because even if $UC(Q_k)$ exceeds $UC(Q_n)$, the ultimate cost consequence of producing an additional unit in period k is that among all the units produced in succeeding periods, one less will be produced at a unit cost equal to $UC(Q_k)$ and one more will be produced at a unit cost equal to $UC(Q_n)$. All that prevents marginal cost from being equal in each period to the unit cost in the last period is the existence of a positive interest rate. However, as the example in the next section demonstrates, given real world interest rates and the relatively short period between the initial period of production and the final period of production (usually just a few years), the final period unit cost is still predominantly important.

Assume, as in the real world, $r > 0$. What, if any, are the conditions under which a firm faces declining marginal costs in succeeding periods? To analyze this question, utilize equation (5.10) to obtain expressions for $MC(q_{k-1})$ and for $MC(q_{k-1}) - MC(q_k)$.

$$(5.11) \quad MC(q_{k-1}) = \sum_{i=k-1}^{n-1} \frac{r(1+r)^{(n-1)-1}}{(1+r)^{n-(k-1)}} UC(Q_i) + \frac{1}{(1+r)^{n-(k-1)}} UC(Q_n)$$

$$(5.12) \quad MC(q_{k-1}) - MC(q_k) = \sum_{i=k-1}^{n-1} \frac{r(1+r)^{(n-i)-1}}{(1+r)^{n-(k-1)}} UC(Q_i) + \frac{1}{(1+r)^{n-(k-1)}} UC(Q_n)$$

$$- \sum_{i=k}^{n-1} \frac{r(1+r)^{n-i}}{(1+r)^{n-(k-1)}} UC(Q_i) - \frac{(1+r)}{(1+r)^{n-(k-1)}} UC(Q_n)$$

$$(5.13) \quad = \frac{r(1+r)^{n-k}}{(1+r)^{n-(k-1)}} UC(Q_{k-1}) + \sum_{i=k}^{n-1} \frac{r[(1+r)^{(n-i)-1} - (1+r)^{n-i}]}{(1+r)^{n-(k-1)}} UC(Q_i)$$

$$- \frac{r\, UC(Q_n)}{(1+r)^{n-(k-1)}}$$

$$(5.14) \quad = \sum_{i=k}^{n} \frac{r(1+r)^{n-i}}{(1+r)^{n-(k-1)}} [UC(Q_{i-1}) - UC(Q_i)]$$

$$= \sum_{i=k}^{n} r(1+r)^{k-i-1} [UC(Q_{i-1}) - UC(Q_i)]$$

If $Q_{i-1} \geq q_o$, i.e., the aggregate level of production has reached the point where the potential for learning economies has been exhausted, $UC(Q_{i-1}) = UC(Q_i)$. From 5.14, $MC(q_{k-1}) = MC(q_k)$. If $Q_{i-1} < q_o$, $UC(Q_{i-1}) > UC(Q_i) \geq UC(Q_{i+1}) \ldots \geq UC(Q_n)$. From 5.14, $MC(q_{k-1}) > MC(q_k) \geq MC(q_n)$. Thus, as long as the learning curve is still affecting unit costs, marginal cost will decline from one period to the next.

1.2 *An Example of the Relationship Between Unit Cost Reduction and Marginal Cost Reduction*

Working through an example with an arbitrary but plausible set of parameters demonstrates how small are marginal cost changes given substantial dynamic economies-of-scale unit cost reductions. Imagine a semiconductor product with, as is not unusual, a three-year life cycle. We can choose to analyze the behavior of costs and revenues during the cycle by breaking it into 36 time periods of one month each (i.e., $n = 36$).[6] After a year on the market, the product will display relatively steady unit cost changes because of dynamic economies of scale. The industry experience has been a unit cost drop of 20 to 30 percent for each doubling of production.[7] We will assume 30 percent in this example. If the product has a unit growth rate of 100 percent a year (clearly not too low given an industry unit growth rate of 27 percent; see chapter 3, section B), the unit cost of the product might be expected to decline 30 percent per year (3 percent per period). If we assume an interest rate that compounded monthly equals 12 percent annually, i.e., .95 percent monthly, we can calculate, using equations (5.7) and (5.14), the expected percentage decline in marginal cost between periods 12 and 13 (i.e., $k = 12$). This figure can be compared with the 3 percent unit cost decline.

(a) From (5.7), $MC(q_{12}) = UC(Q_{12}) + \sum_{i=13}^{36} (1+r)^{12-i}[UC(Q_i) - UC(Q_{i-1})]$.

(b) Using a series of calculations, for $i = 13, 14 \ldots, 36$, of $(1+r)^{12-i}$ and of $[UC(Q_i) - UC(Q_{i-1})]$ (on the assumption that $UC(Q_i) = .97UC(Q_{i-1})$), we find that $MC(q_{12}) = UC(Q_{12}) - .469UC(Q_{12}) = .531UC(Q_{12})$.

(c) Again assuming $UC(Q_i) = .97\ UC(Q_{i-1})$, $MC(q_{36}) = UC(Q_{36}) = .481\ UC(Q_{12})$.

Thus, $MC(q_{12})$ is much closer to final unit cost than to unit cost in period 12.

(d) From (5.14), $MC(q_{11}) - MC(q_{12}) =$

$$\sum_{i=12}^{n} r(1+r)^{k-i-1}[UC(Q_{i-1}) - UC(Q_i)].$$

(e) Using a set of calculations similar to those above, $MC(q_{11}) - MC(q_{12}) = (.0048)\ UC(Q_{12})$ and

$$\frac{MC(q_{11}) - MC(q_{12})}{MC(q_{12})} = \frac{.0048\ UC(Q_{12})}{.531\ UC(Q_{12})} = .0090.$$

Therefore, a decline in UC of 3 percent leads to a decline in MC of less than 1 percent.

2. The Effect of Delayed Implementation of an Innovation on the Attractiveness of Entry Given Dynamic Economies of Scale

Not every firm which at some point might be inclined to enter a market involving a new innovation will enter the market at the same time as do the initial implementers of the innovation, because there are differences in the speed with which firms can easily raise capital and there is an unevenness with which new ideas are spread. If learning economies of the initial implementers make implementation of the innovation in a subsequent period by an additional firm less profitable than it would have been if the additional firm had joined the initial implementers in the initial period of implementation, this potential entrant may decide not to enter and concentration would be greater than would otherwise be the case.*

To determine the effect on late entry of dynamic economies of scale unit cost reductions, we need to compare the profitability of firm "n+1" if it were an initial implementer joining n other firms implementing the innovation in period 1 with the profitability of firm n+1 if it were not an initial implementer and joined the original n

---

*Stated more precisely, in the case of a product innovation having a low cross-elasticity of demand between it and other semiconductor products so that it creates a new product line (hereinafter referred to as a "market-creating innovation"), entry into the new market may be discouraged. In the cases of a process innovation or a product innovation involving a close substitute for preexisting products (hereinafter both referred to as "market-affecting innovations"), not only will potential entrants be discouraged from entering, but firms currently producing in the market (using the old process or producing the preexisting product) may be encouraged to exit. The following analysis will be presented in terms of a market-creating innovation, but it is equally applicable in the case of a market-affecting innovation.

implementers at some subsequent period after the original n implementers had already been producing the innovation product for one or more periods. In order to isolate the salient factors, we can use a simple Chamberlain oligopoly model and assume that whatever number of firms are in the market at any one time, they will divide the market equally, charging a uniform price. It will also be assumed that all firms entering at the same time will have identical cost curves. If all $n+1$ firms enter in period 1, the Chamberlain model suggests that each firm faces a marginal revenue curve derived from a demand curve which equals the industry demand curve divided by $n+1$. The resulting price (P_1) is one that, given the division of the market, maximizes profits for each of the firms, i.e., where $MC_1 = MR_1$ for each firm. If firm $n+1$ does not enter in this initial period when the other n firms enter and instead enters the market in a subsequent period, its marginal cost for any given level of production will, as we have just seen, be higher than the marginal cost of the n other firms. Firm $n+1$ and the other n firms would now each face the same MR curve as if firm $n+1$ had entered in the first period. Firm $n+1$ would maximize its profits at P_1, just as it would have if it had entered in period 1, because it faces the same costs as if it had entered then and, as we have assumed in the preceding section, the demand in each period for the product is the same. If the price were P_1, the firm would make the same amount of profits its first period of production as it would have had it entered at the same time as the initial implementers. The other n firms would, because their marginal cost curves for that period have been lowered as a result of learning economies, maximize profits at a price P_2 lower than P_1. The industry price resulting from tacit or overt bargaining among the $n+1$ firms will almost certainly be below P_1 and in all likelihood much closer to P_2. The situation will be repeated in each subsequent time period until the marginal costs of firm $n+1$ equal those of the other n firms. Thus, entry is not as profitable for firm $n+1$ as it would have been had it implemented the innovation in the initial period of production. The question is, how much less profitable?

P_2 and P_1 correspond to the points on the marginal revenue curve where it is crossed respectively by the marginal cost curve shared by each of the initial implementers and the marginal cost curve of firm $n+1$. The parameters used in the preceding example of the relationship between learning curve induced declines in unit cost and declines in marginal cost are representative of the factors they represent in the real world. The example suggests that the marginal cost curves are not nearly as far apart as differences in unit costs would suggest. Since $P = MR/(1 - 1/e)$, where e is the elasticity of demand which can be assumed to be constant over this small range, P_2 and P_1 will differ by about the same percentage as the marginal revenues and marginal costs do. The compromise price will differ from P_1 by even less. *Thus, learning economies enjoyed by initial entrants do not reduce dramatically the potential profits of other firms considering subsequent entry.*

3. *Bias for Short-Run Accounting Earnings*

The preceding model and example assume that the firm involved is a rational maximizer of its long-run profit stream discounted to present value at a rate reflecting SROR. The model suggests such a firm would price in a fashion that reduces current revenues in order to increase current sales and enjoy the resulting lower input costs in subsequent periods. The reduction in current revenues is in essence an investment. Although the case study did reveal examples of this kind of behavior,[8] it also revealed that many managers are as a general matter very concerned with short-term accounting profits (see chapter 4, section 1.32b). An investment of the kind being discussed here is not capitalizable and therefore counts against current accounting earnings. Managers having such a concern might trade off future for current accounting income at an implicit interest rate considerably higher than the 12 percent depicted as representative in the example. That would make current unit costs a more important determinant in management's calculation of marginal cost. Thus, if one accepts a nonneoclassical view of the workings the finance process, the existence of learning economies is more of an explanation of the concentration in semiconductor product lines than if one does not. But it is still not a powerful explanation. Consider the following change in the preceding example: management discounts capitalizable investments at 12 percent but discounts investments that count against current accounting earnings at 18 percent, i.e., a 50 percent premium. Calculations show that the $MC(q_{12})$ would be $.576$ $UC(Q_{12})$ instead of $.531$ $UC(Q_{12})$. Thus, while marginal cost is not as far from unit cost as in the original example, it is still much closer to the final unit and marginal cost, i.e., $.481$ $UC(Q_{12})$, than to $UC(Q_{12})$. Similarly, the 3 percent decline in unit cost from the eleventh to the twelfth month is still two and a half times the 1.2 percent decline in marginal cost.

4. Explanations for Observed Extent of Price Declines and Their Relationship to the Profitability of Late Entry

Observed price declines over the life cycle of the typical semiconductor product have been much greater than the declines in marginal cost as analyzed above. Despite appearances, however, these price declines do not necessarily suggest that the learning curve imposes on late entrants a bigger loss in profits than the foregoing analysis suggests. There are two factors which account for the greater decline in prices than in marginal cost. One is an erosion of monopoly profits. In terms of the Chamberlain model, it is the division of the industry demand curve by n + 1 instead of by n (and the increasing problems for oligopolistic cooperation as the number of firms grows). This will occur whenever firm n + 1 enters the market, whether with the initial implementers or later. Erosion of monopoly profits is the result of entry, not a deterrent to entry. Much of the rest of the amount by which the reduction in price exceeds that of marginal cost, at least in the case of product innovations, may be explained by a dynamic kind of price discrimination in which the small number of producers tacitly agree to "skim" the market in the initial periods of production, charging high prices to those customers with an inelastic demand for the new product (e.g., the military) and later "penetrate" the full market with lower prices (contrary to the assumption of identical marginal revenue for each period).[9] Price reductions that are the result of this dynamic price discrimination may make later implementation somewhat less attractive than initial implementation, but it is the mass market that represents most of the dollar volume over the life cycle of a semiconductor product and, despite a lower margin, is where most of the profits are to be made.[10]

B. Alternative Explanations of Concentration: The Effects of Technical Change in an Industry with a Substantial Retained Earnings Bias

If the effect of learning economies on the prices charged by the few initial implementers are at best only a partial explanation of why most semiconductor product lines are concentrated in their hands, we need to look for other explanations.

One explanation might be that the market is simply too small relative to the optimal scale of production to support more than a few firms. The combination of significant static and dynamic economies of scale give this explanation plausibility. What keeps it from being more than just a second partial explanation is the fact that there are not great differences in the degree of concentration of relatively low-volume product lines and of product lines ten or twenty times as great.

A second explanation might be that the high rate of technical change makes late entry less attractive because the investments involved would have a shorter useful life before the product or process became obsolete. This would be a particularly serious problem for the late entrant if the point of obsolescence arrived before the late entrant had a chance to exhaust the potential learning economies associated with the new product or process. This explanation also has some plausibility. However, one would expect that most participants in an industry with this kind of history would devote resources to be in the position to enter any market involving a new product or process without so much delay that impending obsolescence makes the investment not worthwhile. Not everyone can win the race to be among the first few, but everyone who wants to stay a factor in the industry needs to be fast enough to meet the test being discussed here.

Both the general theory and the case study set out in the preceding chapters suggest a potentially more powerful explanation for product line concentration than any suggested so far: the retained earnings funding bias of the finance process.

Because firms regard retained earnings as a source of cheap finance, the likelihood that a firm will invest in a new innovation is related to its profit position. The initial implementers of an innovation will have their profits enhanced relative to the potential implementers. This advantage accruing to the handful of initial implementers is important because first period investment constitutes only a fraction of the economy's eventual aggregate investment in production capacity utilizing the new innovation.

Both market-creating and market-affecting innovations cause disequilibrium (see the textual note in section A2 for a discussion of these terms). In the case of market-creating innovation, disequilibrium is caused by the establishment of a new production function for a product for which there has been a latent demand. In the case of market-affecting process innovation, disequilibrium is caused by a shifting of the production function for a product already in existence. Market-affecting product innovation can be analyzed like a process innovation. The result in each case is the creation of an economic vacuum the filling of which is called diffusion. Capacity cannot be purchased instantaneously so that in the first period there exists exactly the amount of innovation-utilizing capacity that would be predicted by a model employing the assumption of competitive supply and demand with fully informed profit-maximizing firms. The number of firms that participate over time in the creating of this innovation-utilizing capacity will affect the level of concentration within the product line involved. If the initial implementers have an advantage in obtaining capital, concentration is encouraged.

1. *Market-Creating Innovations*

The case of the effect of a market-creating innovation on concentration in an industry such as semiconductors is relatively easy to analyze. The firms in the newly created market, which will number a few at most, are earning monopoly or oligopoly profits. The rate of return on capital invested is even higher than a normal monopoly situation because short-run marginal cost is well above long-run marginal cost, owing to the inability of the firms in the market to create in a very short period of time all the innovation-utilizing capacity called for by long-run marginal cost calculations. Thus, companies that have had the good fortune to enter the market at the beginning have a substantial source of investment funds which, given their retained earnings finance bias, are regarded as cheaper than outside funds.

An increase in retained earnings increases capital investment if the expected marginal efficiency of investment at a level of investment equal to the amount of retained earnings is greater than the perceived cost of using the retained earnings. This perceived cost is artificially low for a firm with a retained earnings bias. The increase in investment that results from an increase in retained earnings can be seen by using the Meyer and Kuh type figure 5.1 (utilizing the conventional textbook presentation of the Meyer and Kuh theory).

Figure 5.1 illustrates the effects of an increase in the level of retained earnings under three different assumptions concerning the level of the marginal efficiency of investment curve. MEI_1 depicts the situation in which, despite the artificially low opportunity cost (r_i) that the firm puts on use of its retained earnings, investment opportunities are not sufficiently promising to exhaust the supply of retained earnings even at the initial level of profits. MEI_2 depicts a firm fully utilizing its internal funds but which does not have sufficiently good investment opportunities to spur it to seek outside finance, the case depicted by MEI_3. The increase in the level of retained earnings is depicted by a movement outward in the financial supply curve from fsc_1 to fsc_2. Given MEI_1, the level of investments, I_1, is unaffected by the increase in profits resulting in the shift from fsc_1 to fsc_2. Given MEI_2, the level of investment increases from I_2 to I_3. Given MEI_3, the level of investment increases from I_4 to I_5.

The opportunity to invest in a major innovation should normally raise the marginal efficiency of investment curves of firms in a fast-growing industry such as semiconductors at least to such a point (if they were not there already) that the expected return on investment

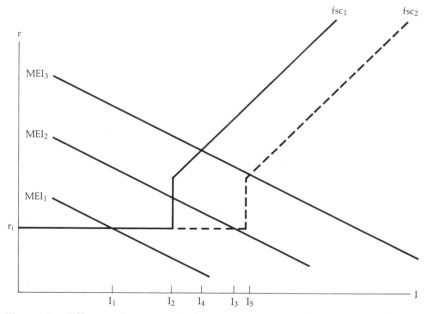

Figure 5.1 Effect on Investment of Increase in Earnings of a Firm with Retained Earnings Bias

at a level equal to initially available retained earnings is higher than the perceived cost of using retained earnings. If this is the case, the increase in earnings derived from being one of the initial firms manufacturing the innovation will normally result in such firms making larger further investments in innovation-utilizing capacity than firms in the same position but without innovation-induced increases in earnings. This analysis applies as well to the semiconductor divisions of large diversified companies because, as related above, such divisions find it easier to invest earnings attributable to their operations than to obtain from central management other investment funds.

Texas Instruments and Intel are two examples in the semiconductor industry of firms which grew very rapidly using large amounts of retained earnings that accrued from being an initial manufacturer of an innovation, in the first case the silicon transistor and in the second the semiconductor computer memory. In each case the firm grew to occupy a dominant position in the new market involved, but, unlike the market-affecting innovations to be discussed below, the growth was not predominantly at the expense of other firms. Growth in the new market was simply easier for them than for later entrants because of ample supplies of cash to finance new investment.

2. Market-Affecting Innovations

The analysis of a market-affecting innovation's effect on concentration in an industry such as semiconductors is more complex.

Profits of an initial implementer will increase: that is the reason the innovation is undertaken. In the case of a process innovation, the input costs of producing an identical product to that of a competitor is lowered when the process is utilized. In the case of a product innovation, the demand for the innovation product is greater than for the noninnovation product, raising the implementer's MR curve.

Profits of competing firms decline. In the case of process innovation, the lowered MC of the initially innovating firms means that the intersection of their MC and MR curves will be at larger quantities of output, thus moving out the industry supply curve and lowering the prices at which noninnovating higher-cost competitors can sell. In the case of product innovation, the MR curves of the noninnovating firms will be lowered because of the increased attractiveness of their innovating competitors' product.[11]

The unveiling of an innovation by the initial implementer raises the MEI curve of each nonimplementing firm as well as that of each implementing firm. The effect of a rise in the MEI curve on the level of investment performed by firms experiencing a gain in retained earnings (from increased profits) and those firms experiencing a fall in retained earnings (from decreased profits) in a system characterized by a bias for retained earnings financing is analyzed in figures 5.2–5.5.

Figures 5.2 and 5.3 illustrate the situation where the rise in the MEI curve is not as great as the perceived difference between the cost of internal and external finance in the cases, respectively, of a firm (an initial implementer) experiencing a substantial gain in retained earnings (enough to illustrate the maximum effect on investment of such a rise in the MEI curve) and a firm (not an initial implementer) experiencing a substantial decrease in retained earnings. The financial supply curves after the change in earnings are depicted

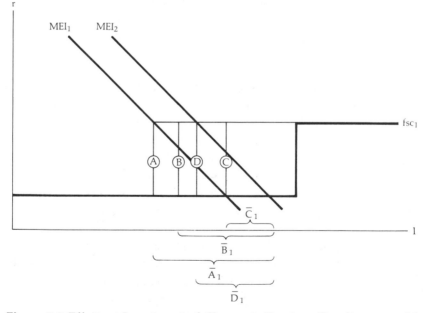

Figure 5.2 Effect on Investment of Change in Earnings Simultaneous with an Increase in the Marginal Efficiency of Investment

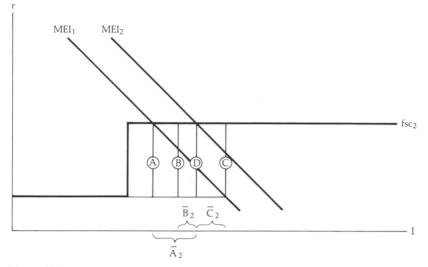

Figure 5.3

by the dark curves marked, respectively, fsc_1 and fsc_2. In each case, the amount and direction of change in investment depends on the position of the dogleg in the fsc curve prior to the change in earnings, relative to MEI_1 and MEI_2, the marginal efficiency of investment curves before and after the initiation of the innovation with its resulting change in the level of retained earnings. The four prior positions of the dogleg in figures 5.2 and 5.3, the lighter vertical lines marked A, B, C, and D, set out the range in which the position of the dogleg affects the change in investment. The increases in investment in figure 5.2 corresponding to these four positions are $\overline{A}_1$, $\overline{B}_1$, $\overline{C}_1$, and $\overline{D}_1$. If the dogleg is to the left of A, investment will still increase by $\overline{A}_1$; if the dogleg is to the right of C, investment will still increase by $\overline{C}_1$. $\overline{B}_1$ and $\overline{D}_1$ illustrate how the amount of increase in investment varies depending on the location of the dogleg between A and C. Likewise, in figure 5.3, if the dogleg is to the left of A, the increase in investment will still be $\overline{A}_2$, and if it is to the right of C, the decrease in investment will still be $\overline{C}_2$. $\overline{B}_2$ illustrates how the amount of increase varies depending on the location of the dogleg between A and D. Similarly, the decrease will vary depending on the location of the dogleg between C and D.

Figures 5.4 and 5.5 illustrate the situation where the rise in the

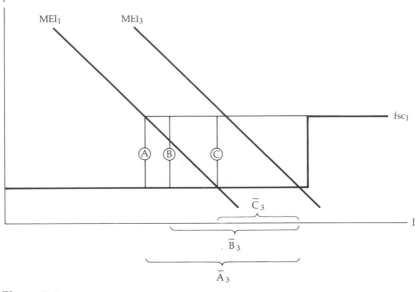

Figure 5.4

MEI curve is greater than the perceived difference between the cost of internal and external financing, again in the cases of a firm experiencing a substantial gain and a firm experiencing a substantial loss in retained earnings. The increases in investment corresponding to dogleg positions A, B, and C are $\bar{A}_3$, $\bar{B}_3$, and $\bar{C}_3$, and $\bar{A}_4$, $\bar{B}_4$, and $\bar{C}_4$, respectively. If the dogleg is to the left of A, the increases will still be $\bar{A}_3$ and $\bar{A}_4$. If the dogleg is to the right of C, the increases will still be $\bar{C}_3$ and $\bar{C}_4$.

The important conclusions are the following: 1) a firm which experiences an increase in retained earnings always invests more than a firm which experiences a loss; 2) if, as in figure 5.3, the shift up in the MEI curve is not as great as the perceived difference between the cost of internal and external financing, and if the position of the dogleg is such that it would result in external financing at the original level of retained earnings after the shift up of the MEI curve, the level of desired investment for firms experiencing a decline in retained earnings will actually be below that desired if the innovation had never been introduced into the industry.

These figures theoretically demonstrate that if firms in an industry have retained earnings finance bias, initial implementers of market-

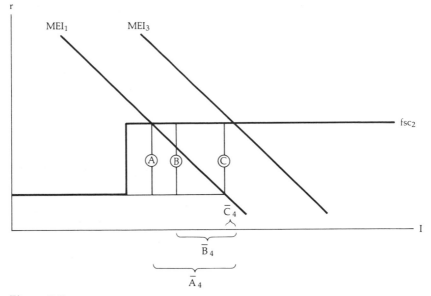

Figure 5.5

affecting innovation can, because of the innovation-induced supply of investment funds, grow relative to, and in some cases absolutely at the expense of, their actual competitors in the market and have distinct advantages over any potential competitors. Because the number of initial implementers is usually small, the contribution of this factor to concentration is obvious. No direct evidence on the application of this theoretical conclusion to the semiconductor industry is available. But we do know that semiconductor firms (and the semiconductor divisions of diversified firms) do have a retained earnings finance bias and that market-affecting innovations can produce large profits quickly.

Part III

A Study in Policy

6. Applications to Policy

The preceding chapters address the question of how the workings of the finance process affect the level of industrial performance in our economy. One function of their findings is as input for scholars of industrial organization. These findings relate to a number of concerns of such scholars, such as the extent of X-inefficiencies in the economy, the degree to which project choice in the economy corresponds to consumer preferences, the rates of innovation and of its diffusion in the economy, and the relationship between innovation and market structure.

A second function of these findings, one which requires more elaboration, is to serve as the basis of policy recommendations. The impact of the finance process on industrial performance depends on how the finance process is regulated. Several bodies of law contribute to the structure in which it operates: corporations, securities, investment companies, tax, banking, insurance, and trusts. If one reflects upon the preceding chapters, one sees that a number of the issues to which these laws speak are related to industrial performance. Of particular importance, and the major focus of this chapter, is the impact of this legal structure on whether large corporations use their cash flow to finance real investment internally or to pay dividends. This is a key question in the functioning of our economy. The behavior of large corporations in this regard determines who participates in what ways in the decision of the finance process as to which proposed real investment projects are implemented and which are not.

This chapter begins with a recapitulation of the findings of the previous chapters that lead to the conclusion that the industrial performance of our economy could be significantly improved by larger corporate dividend payments with the consequent increase in the role of outside finance process participants in making project choice decisions. This conclusion leads us to ask what aspects of the legal structure are responsible for the existing pattern of dividend decisions and whether there are practical reforms that should be made in the legal structure to change this existing pattern.

The analysis of the legal structure that follows is divided into two parts. The first part concerns laws that have as their primary purpose something other than the regulation of the corporate dividend decision but that operate in a fashion that influences management in making that decision. Two bodies of law are of special importance here: laws relating to the issuance of new securities and tax law. Both these bodies of law have the unfortunate effect of making retention of earnings for internal finance of investment projects more attractive to management than is the payment of larger dividends. Reforms are suggested that would reduce or eliminate the incentives they create. The recommendations for reform are necessarily tentative because each of these two complex bodies of law impinges upon a variety of important values, the full weighing of which is outside the scope of this work. But the fact that they are tentative should not subtract from their force. The point of the recommended reforms is that one important value, achieving a high level of industrial performance, calls for their change.

The second part of the analysis of legal structure concerns corporation law, the body of law that purports directly to regulate the dividend decision. The analysis finds that existing corporate law places no effective restraints on the discretion of the management of large, management-controlled corporations in deciding the level of dividend. Changing this situation would involve a much more radical assault on the current pattern of dividend decision than the removal of the unintended incentives for earnings retention contemplated by the proposed reforms of securities and tax law. Nevertheless, the potential improvement in industrial performance that could result from a change in the current pattern is large, and that fact makes corporate law reforms well worth considering. Several possible avenues are explored. The conclusion is that the reform that would be both most practical and offer the greatest prospect of benefit would be a rule requiring large public corporations to finance externally a certain minimum percentage, perhaps all, of their capital investments. Such a reform would lead to a general increase in dividend payments because a failure by management of a firm to increase dividends would lead to an accumulation of liquid assets. Management would not want such an accumulation because liquid assets beyond a firm's working capital needs would be of no utility to management and, assuming adoption of the recommended tax reforms, would be detrimental to the interests of shareholders.

A. A Recapitulation

The starting point for an investigation of whether any changes in the legal structure are desirable is a recapitulation of the findings of the preceding chapters concerning the pattern of participation in the decision as to which real investment projects are selected for implementation and the consequences of that pattern.

Consider first what we have found out about the pattern of participation.

1. The largest 100 U.S. industrial corporations control over 40 percent of the sector's assets; the largest 200, between 50 and 60 percent; and the largest 500, almost 75 percent (chapter 2, section B 3.1).
2. The data available suggest that these groups are responsible for roughly comparable percentages of the sector's new real investment (chapter 2, section B 3.1).
3. The proponents of these investment projects are almost always employees of these firms (chapter 2, section C 2.422).
4. Internal cash flow after payment of dividends has in recent years been sufficient to fund an average of close to 90 percent of the real investment of these corporations. This average is the result of a significant portion of these firms having sufficient internal cash flow after dividends to fund fully their real investment and others having a level of internal cash flow after dividends well below what would be necessary to fund fully their real investment (chapter 2, section B 3.1).
5. For most large corporations, no one individual, family, or institution holds as much as 10 percent of its shares. Management of such a corporation has a certain amount of discretion in the real investment decisions it makes without fearing loss of control by hostile takeover (chapter 2, section B 3.221).
6. Management of such a corporation has incentives not to release

as much information about the firm as investors might want even if this has some negative effect on the corporation's share price. These incentives arise from fears that releasing more information both is useful to competitors and increases the chance of take-over. Pressures to release information are much less on corporations that do not engage in outside financing, particularly equity financing (chapter 2, section B 3.222).

7. Members of the outside sector of the finance process—financial intermediaries and individual savers—do participate more directly in a portion of the economy's real investment decisions. They are the primary sources of funds for projects being sponsored by new firms, and they also supply funds for the projects of large corporations whose cash flow after payment of dividends is less than their level of real investment. But the role of the outside sector is much smaller than it would otherwise be because of the decision by most large corporations to restrict payment of dividends in order to finance all or a large portion of their real investment internally (chapter 2, section C 2.422).

What are the consequences of this pattern? Chapter 2 suggests four criteria for evaluating the finance process.

1. How closely does the list of projects chosen by the system for implementation resemble the list of most promising projects that one would create if one had access to the best prediction being made concerning the prospects of each and every proposed project in the economy?
2. How accurate is the best prediction being made concerning each proposal? In essence, is information going to the persons best able to assess the proposal, and is it the right information?
3. What secondary effects does the finance process have on industrial performance, specifically on the level of industrial competition?
4. How much does the system cost to operate?

There are, as we have seen in trying to apply these criteria, good theoretical and empirical reasons to believe that some firms are investing in projects inferior in predicted return to some projects that go unfunded, and that if these firms paid out more in dividends, they would forgo these inferior investments and the projects with greater predicted promise would receive the freed-up savings. The cost of moving funds appears to be low enough that, if we could identify specifically which firms are investing in inferior projects and by how much, the gains from their increasing their dividends would substantially exceed the costs. We have also seen that there are good reasons to believe that a greater dividend payout by all large public corporations would improve the sensitivity of the system to innovative investment proposals and would increase competition in innovative industries.

B. Laws with Unintended Influence on the Dividend Decision

Two bodies of law, the law relating to the issuance of new securities and tax law, have significant unintended influence on the decision of management whether to use any given portion of the firm's cash flow to pay dividends* or to finance internally new real investment. This part of the chapter considers what aspects of each of these bodies of law leads to this unintended influence and considers reforms that would reduce or eliminate this influence.

1. *The Public Issuance of New Securities: Registration Under the Securities Act of 1933*

When the management of a firm is making the decision how to use some portion of its cash flow—whether to finance a real investment internally or to pay dividends—one consideration is the comparative cost to the issuer of financing the project externally, since payment of the dividend will require either seeking such financing or abandoning the project. The largest source of long-term external finance is the public issuance of new securities.[1] The Securities Act of 1933 (the "Securities Act") in essence requires any issuer making a public offering of its securities to go through a disclosure-oriented registration procedure. This procedure, and the provisions of the Securities Act relating to false or misleading statements made in connection with the procedure, impose three interrelated kinds of costs of importance to management that will not be incurred if a public offering

---

*Throughout this chapter, unless the context suggests otherwise, references to payment of dividends also includes all methods by which a corporation transfers money from its treasury to shareholders: other corporate distributions to shareholders not legally considered "dividends" and repurchases by the corporation of its own securities.

is avoided: additional disclosure, additional potential liability for both the issuer and its directors and top management, and the need to pay more in underwriter's fees to recompense the underwriter for the potential liability the Securities Act imposes on it. A public offering also may involve large legal, accounting, and printing expenses.[2] These costs of registration are significant in terms of their impact on the personal values of management and are likely to create a substantial incentive to retain earnings in order to avoid a public offering.

1.1 *The Questions Asked*

As a formal matter, for a large, publicly held corporation, most of the disclosure required by the Securities Act in connection with registering a public offering is not really additional because it has already been required of the corporation in another context. Whether or not the corporation engages in any public offerings, the Securities Exchange Commission, pursuant to Section 13 of the Securities Exchange Act of 1934 (the "Exchange Act"), requires the corporation to file annually with the Commission a disclosure document on Form 10-K. Information updating the answers to some of the questions on Form 10-K are required quarterly on Form 10-Q, and certain events relating to 10-K questions trigger an obligation to disclose their occurrence by making a filing on Form 8-K within fifteen days. The only new disclosures concerning the affairs of a corporation required as a result of the registration of a public offering under the Securities Act are (a) material changes that have occurred in the affairs of the corporation since the filing of the last 10-K that have not been reported in a subsequent 10-Q or 8-K, and (b) the principal purposes for which the corporation intends to use the net proceeds of the issue.[3]

The requirement that material changes be disclosed at the time of the public offering is sometimes sufficiently unattractive to management that it chooses to fund a project internally instead.[4] But disclosure of the changes in any case can only be delayed until the due date of the next Exchange Act filing requiring the information. Often the timing of the public offering is not crucial, and it can be postponed until disclosure is less unattractive or is required anyway by an Exchange Act filing.

The use of proceeds requirement is more likely to elicit new information. Since funds are fungible, the requirement that the use of proceeds be disclosed inevitably requires the corporation to say something about its near term capital spending plans. No question required by form 10-K is likely to elicit as much information on a regular basis with respect to such plans. A random survey of recent registration statements for public offerings conducted by me shows that the use of proceeds question is often answered in a rather general fashion.[5] When specific projects are mentioned, they have often been the subject of prior voluntary public announcements of the corporation. Nevertheless, my personal experience is that this question is often one of the most difficult ones for an issuer to answer, an impression reinforced by discussions with other practicing securities lawyers. On the one hand, management is very reluctant to disclose future plans of this sort. On the other hand, there is a very real fear of potential liability if the corporation subsequently undertakes an investment that is not discussed in the answer and that turns out badly. Once one statement is made about a project, something more often needs to be said in order to make the statement made not misleading.[6] Since one conclusion of chapter 2 is that real investment is the most likely place for there to be a divergence between management behavior and shareholder interest, any additional disclosure in this area is potentially valuable to investors and costly to management.

1.2 *Liability of the Issuer and Its Principals for False or Misleading Statements*

A false or misleading statement or omission contained in a Securities Act registration statement creates a greater risk of liability to the issuer and its directors and top officers than does the same statement contained in an Exchange Act filing. The formal comparison of the questions asked in connection with an Exchange Act filing with those asked in connection with a Securities Act registration statement thus understates the amount of additional disclosure that results from a decision to raise funds externally through the public issuance of new securities. This greater risk of liability often results in a different answer being given to the same question. The need to disclose more in a registration statement than the formal comparison of questions suggests thus adds to the unattractiveness of a public offering and to the attractiveness of retained earnings financing.

1.21 *Exchange Act Filings*

Consider first the risk to the issuer of paying damages for a false or misleading statement with respect to a material fact made in an Exchange Act filing, a risk which must be incurred whether or not the issuer engages in a public offering. Such a statement may give rise to a cause of action under Section 18(a) of the Exchange Act and possibly under Section 10(b) thereof as well.

Section 18(a) provides that an issuer who makes such a statement shall be liable to any person who "in reliance upon the statement, shall have purchased or sold a security at a price affected by the statement, for damages caused by such reliance, unless the [issuer] can prove that [it] acted in good faith and had no knowledge that the statement was false or misleading." If the burden placed on the issuer of proving the "acted in good faith and had no knowledge" exception is interpreted as restricting the availability of the exception to matters where the issuer has no actual knowledge after conducting a "reasonable investigation",[7] Section 18(a) would appear to make false or misleading statements in an Exchange Act filing very dangerous to an issuer. But this appearance is deceptive because the courts have generally interpreted the "in reliance" requirement to mean "eyeball reliance": the plaintiff must have seen the statement in the actual filed document, as opposed to, for example, a newspaper or brokerage house report based on the statement.[8] This requirement not only severely limits the number of potential plaintiffs, but it also may make impractical class actions, which are the only effective way of vindicating the rights of the average investor, given the relatively small amount of damages suffered by any one individual.[9]

There may, however, exist a second basis of liability for a false or misleading statement in an Exchange Act filing. There is authority for the proposition that Section 10(b) of the Exchange Act and Rule 10b-5 promulgated thereunder give rise to an implied private right of action for damages for, among other things, a false or misleading statement made publicly by an issuer of publicly traded securities.[10] While the existence of Section 18(a) with its explicit provisions relating to damages permits an argument that this right does not extend to statements made in Exchange Act filings, there is substantial authority to the effect that it does.[11] Assuming it does, the test for reliance for a plaintiff proceeding under a Rule 10b-5 theory appears to be much easier than under Section 18(a). Using either a theory that the reliance requirement under Rule 10b-5 is really just a causation requirement or a theory that an investor relies on the fact that the market price of a security reflects the information contained in the filed statements of the issuer, several courts have found that in the case of publicly traded securities the plaintiff establishes a prima facie case of reliance if he can show that the false or misleading statement was publicly disseminated and was material.[12] But the easier reliance requirement is counterbalanced by a stricter standard concerning the knowledge of the issuer: the false or misleading statement must be made with "scienter," i.e., the issuer must have an intent of some sort to deceive; mere negligence as to the truth of the statement is not enough.[13] Furthermore, it is the plaintiff who must prove scienter to succeed in his action, not the issuer who must show the absence of it to defeat the action.

This discussion suggests that any false or misleading material statement that appears in an Exchange Act filing of a large, reputable issuer is unlikely to give rise to liability. Such an issuer, whatever the state of the law, will not in the ordinary course intentionally make false or misleading statements, at least not ones that deviate so far from the truth that a plaintiff could meet its burden of proof on the question of scienter.* That means that Rule 10b-5, even if

---

*The question of how false or misleading a statement is relates to its materiality, which analytically is separate from the question of scienter. A definition of materiality in line with current authority could be formulated as follows: a false or misleading statement of a material fact is one where there is a substantial likelihood that a reasonable investor would have attached importance to the difference between the statement made and the true state of affairs in determining whether to buy, hold, or sell the securities in question.[14] In reality, however, a fact finder in a legal proceeding will be looking at much of the same evidence to answer the questions of materiality and scienter, so they tend to blur. It is much easier to argue that minor deviations from the truth were accidental than that major ones were. A large, reputable issuer is not likely to make a statement that is in direct contradiction to important facts known to the persons drafting the statement. Such persons may, however, "shade" the truth or be less than totally forthcoming concerning what they know. The twin requirements that the statement must be materially false or misleading and that it be made with scienter tends to protect this level of deviation from the truth. The main danger to an issuer under rule 10b-5 is where the finder of fact cannot withstand the temptation to judge the materiality of a statement with the benefit of hindsight.

applicable, is not a large threat. And the strict reliance requirement of Section 18(a) renders it a largely ineffective remedy.[15]

1.22 *Securities Act Filings*

Now consider the potential consequences to an issuer that decides to engage in a public offering of its securities and files a registration statement containing a false or misleading statement of a material fact. Section 11 of the Securities Act provides that any person acquiring a security registered under a registration statement containing such a statement may sue the issuer for damages.* Liability is absolute: the plaintiff need not demonstrate scienter, and the issuer is not even allowed the defense of reasonable care or good faith lack of knowledge. And for a period of approximately one year after the registration statement becomes effective, the plaintiff need not show reliance on the false or misleading statement, so a class action can easily be brought.† The plaintiff need not be the initial purchaser of the security. The measure of damages is the difference between the price the plaintiff paid for the security (not exceeding the public offering price) and the value thereof at the time the suit is brought (or, if the plaintiff sold the security prior to bringing the suit, the price at which he sold it). Under Section 11(e), if the issuer can prove that some portion of the depreciation in the value of the security is due to factors other than the market becoming aware of the false or misleading nature of the statement, it can reduce its damages accordingly. But this defense is of limited usefulness except for issues of debt with the highest credit ratings, where the risk of default is perceived to be so low that the securities are traded on the basis of yield. For other securities, the process by which a securities market prices a security is complex, so it is difficult for the issuer to prove that any particular event has been a cause in a change in price or

---

*Section 11 also applies to an omission of a material fact required to be stated in the registration statement. Section 18(a) of the Exchange Act and rule 10b-5(2) do not cover an omission unless it can be characterized as an omission of fact necessary to make the statements that were made not misleading.

†Specifically, Section 11(a) requires a plaintiff to establish reliance, though not "eyeball reliance," if he acquires the security after the time that the issuer makes "generally available to its security holders an earning statement covering a period of at least 12 months beginning after the effective date of registration statement."

how much of the change is due to that event.[16] Thus, an issuer deciding to engage in a public offering faces the prospect that if the registration statement for any reason turns out to contain a false or misleading material statement and the security depreciates in value over the succeeding year, it will have to pay out damages equal to all or a substantial portion of the amount of depreciation times the number of securities sold in the offering.[17]

1.23 *The Disincentive for Public Offerings*

This comparison of the potential consequences of a false or misleading statement in an Exchange Act filing and in a registration statement for a public offering suggests that an issuer significantly adds to its risk of paying damages if in the registration statement it simply repeats, or where permitted incorporates by reference from a prior Exchange Act filing, a material statement that turns out to be false or misleading.[18] To reduce this risk, an issuer engaging in a public offering, when it answers in the registration statement the same questions required by its Exchange Act filings, must be more straightforward and more forthcoming and must gather its facts more carefully. The prospect of making the additional disclosure involved is a cost of engaging in a public offering.*

The comparison also suggests a second cost of engaging in a public offering that Exchange Act filings do not involve: the possibility of issuer liability for an innocently made false or misleading statement, something that can happen no matter how straightforward, forthcoming, and careful an issuer is.

These two costs of a public offering are reinforced by the added risk of liability for the directors and top officers of the corporation.

---

*Under the integrated disclosure system, firms may answer most of the questions asked of them through incorporation by reference to their most recent Exchange Act filings. There are specific eligibility requirements for firms using these Forms, which relate to how widely followed the issuer is. For a firm that qualifies to use an S-2 or S-3, the cost of putting itself in the position to engage in a public offering is the additional disclosure that results from being more straightforward, forthcoming, and careful in its Exchange Act filings. Any statement incorporated by reference from an Exchange Act filing gives rise to the same potential liability under Section 11(a) of the Securities Act as if it were actually made in the registration statement. See, however, the discussion in section B 1.41 concerning the effect of the integrated disclosure system on the level and quality of disclosure.

If an Exchange Act filing contains a false or misleading material statement, an individual director or officer will be liable for damages under Section 18(a) or Rule 10b-5 only if the plaintiff can both prove all the facts necessary for a successful action against the corporation and also the facts necessary to show that the individual, in the case of an 18(a) claim, "caused" the statement to be made,[19] or, in the case of a 10b-5 claim, "aided or abetted" the issuer in making the false statement.[20] If any part of a Securities Act registration contains the same statement, each of the directors and top officers* is jointly and severally liable with the issuer under Section 11(a) of the Act, unless the director or officer can sustain the burden of proof that after reasonable investigation he had reasonable grounds to believe the statement was true.†

1.3 *Liability of the Underwriter*

The liability scheme imposed by the Securities Act discourages the management of large corporations from engaging in public offerings in another way. Most corporations, when they engage in a public offering, do not offer the securities directly to the public but sell them to one or more investment banks that then distribute the securities to their ultimate purchasers.[21] An investment bank performing this function is defined as an "underwriter" under Section 2(11) of the Securities Act. Section 11(a) of the Act provides that any person acquiring a security registered by a registration statement containing "an untrue statement of a material fact or omit[ting] to state a material fact required to be stated therein or necessary to make the statements therein not misleading" may sue every underwriter of such security for damages unless such underwriter can "sustain the burden of proof . . . that . . . he had, after reasonable investigation, reasonable ground to believe and did believe" that the registration statement did not contain such untrue statement or omission.[22] The investigation and review of the registration statement motivated

---

*Specifically, the principal executive officer or officers, the principal financial officer and the principal accounting officer.

†This so-called "due diligence defense" is the same one available to underwriters and is discussed in more detail in the immediately succeeding section. A defense less burdensome on the director or officer, not requiring investigation, is imposed with respect to any part of the registration statement prepared by an expert or purporting to be the statement of a public official or an extract from a public official document.

by these sections are referred to as "due diligence," and the defense under Section 11(b) as the "due diligence defense."[23]

The legislative history of Section 11 and its subsequent interpretation by the courts make clear that its function is more to assure, through an *in terrorem* effect, that the true condition of the issuer is disclosed than to compensate those who suffer losses if the true condition is not.[24] While Section 11 imposes liability on a variety of participants in a public offering including, as we have just seen, the issuer, its directors, and certain of its top officers, underwriter liability is a crucial part of the legislative plan.[25] There are good reasons to believe that such imposition of liability, in accord with the expectations of those courts that have interpreted the statute, results in the underwriter playing a somewhat adverse or "devil's advocate role" in the drafting of the registration statement.[26] The persons staffing the underwriter are organizationally independent of the persons staffing the issuer,[27] enabling them to view facts with greater objectivity. For the same reasons, a person associated with the underwriter is generally able to ask a person associated with the issuer more pointed questions than one person associated with the issuer can ask of another such person. A person associated with the underwriter is also in a better position to seek verification of the answers because a given level of distrust by an outsider is more socially acceptable than it is by an insider concerning another insider.[28] Because an underwriter participates in numerous public offerings each year and the management of an issuer does so just occasionally, the underwriter is much more likely to develop the resources and skill necessary to perform a thorough investigation than is the management of the issuer.[29] Furthermore, the issuer might find that the gains to be reaped in a successful offering outweigh the risks of liability for damages from being less than forthcoming or shading the truth, but the underwriter has little to gain from taking these risks.[30]

Underwriter liability thus gives rise to two more reasons for the management of a large corporation to consider a registered public offering costly. First, the involvement of an underwriter results in added disclosure. Second, the issuer must compensate the underwriter for the unavoidable residual risks of liability for damages.*

---

*Even if an underwriter acts in a fashion that to an omniscient observer meets the standard required for the underwriter to be entitled to the due diligence defense, the underwriter, who has the burden of proof on the question, may not be able to persuade a finder of fact in a legal proceeding that such is the case.

1.4 *Changes in Securities Laws to Alter Incentives*

The foregoing discussion suggests that the additional costs that the Securities Act imposes on the management of a firm engaging in a public offering creates an incentive for management to avoid such offerings and their attendant costs by using the firm's cash flow to finance projects internally instead of to pay dividends. This incentive can be reduced by either of two possible approaches. The first approach is to reduce the costs that the Securities Act imposes on management when it decides to engage in a registered public offering. The second approach is to take costs traditionally imposed by the securities laws only on firms engaging in public offerings and impose them on all firms all of the time, whether or not they are engaging in public offerings.

The SEC's integrated disclosure program is a reform utilizing the first approach. The program is a series of changes in rules and procedures instituted in the late 1970s and early 1980s that are aimed at making the process of registering public offerings less burdensome on the issuer. The concept behind the program is that Securities Act disclosure can "piggyback" on the requirements of periodic disclosure imposed by the Exchange Act. The analysis below suggests that, despite a number of positive features, the program has serious shortcomings. Much of the reduction in cost accomplished by the program comes from changes that have the effect of reducing pressures for disclosure to the public. Much of the incentive to retain earnings remains because significant pressures for disclosure and risks of liability remain that can be avoided by avoiding a public offering.

The proposal presented here is to complete the integration of the disclosure requirements of the Securities Act and the Exchange Act. To some extent the proposal utilizes the first approach to reducing the incentive to retain earnings created by the Securities Act because the starting point would be the current program's near elimination of the huge rush printing and handling expenses that had been associated with a traditional registration. But the proposal also utilizes the second approach to reducing the incentive because it would impose on issuers the same pressures for disclosure and risks of liability traditionally associated with a public offering—pressures and risks that the integrated disclosure program has let slip somewhat—on firms that choose not to engage in public offerings as it would on firms that do choose to engage in them.

1.41 *The Integrated Disclosure Program*

The starting point for understanding the integrated disclosure program is a brief review of how the registration process in the typical underwritten public offering operated traditionally.[31] After this, the important components of the program will be summarized, followed by an analysis of their effect on underwriter due diligence and disclosure.

1.411 *The Traditional Underwritten Public Offering*

The two registration statement forms generally used before the advent of the integrated disclosure's short form registration, the S-1 and the S-7, called for the firm to answer a wide range of questions concerning the operations of the firm and its management as well as about the characteristics of the particular security being offered and the proposed method of their distribution. There was a great deal of overlap between the information sought by Forms S-1 and S-7 concerning operations and management and the information required to be provided by a publicly traded firm in its Exchange Act filings. But the format was somewhat different,[32] and in any case, the information needed to be all written out again. Most of this information was required to be included in the "prospectus," the part of the registration statement that would be printed up in thousands of copies and distributed to each potential purchaser of the securities being registered. The drafting of the registration statement was a group exercise involving the issuer, the underwriter, and their respective counsel. While the first draft, which was usually prepared by the issuer, might in many places track the language of the issuer's annual Exchange Act filing, the 10-K, there was a general understanding that none of the language was sacred, and the underwriters and their counsel participated in redrafting the registration statement on a line by line basis.[33] There was a concern in the sequence of presentation both with providing appropriate emphasis for particularly material facts and avoiding a presentation of facts out of context.[34]

For a firm that had not engaged in a recent public offering, preparation of the registration statement often took a month or more before the statement was initially filed.[35] The SEC then reviewed and commented upon the initial filing. One or more amended filings, in response to these comments, would be made.[36] Altogether two to three months or more might elapse before the registration statement in its final form became effective and the public offering could commence. During this time, particularly prior to the initial filing, the underwriter would make an examination of the whole company, including interviews of top management and operating personnel in key areas, a review of what had been written about the firm and its industry, a review of the firm's projections and plans, a review of the minutes of its board meetings and of its material contracts, and, in some cases, visits to the firm's facilities.[37]

The line by line participation of the underwriter in the drafting of the registration statement, the concern with presentation, and the extensive examination of the company permitted by the time schedule interacted with each other to make a process that often by the final draft revealed a great deal about the issuer not revealed in its Exchange Act filings.[38] The exercise of choosing particular words by persons becoming increasingly familiar with the issuer led to further, more sharply defined questions. The universal view of those who have commented on this process is that time and again it resulted in significant additional disclosure.[39]

1.412 *Nature of the Integrated Disclosure Program*

The traditional registration process had the one clear disadvantage of involving a number of costs to issuers: large amounts of time of highly paid executives, lawyers, investment bankers, and accountants, substantial fees to printers for reproducing on short notice thousands of copies of long complex documents with pages of financials, and an inability to take quick advantage of possibly temporary favorable market conditions. The integrated disclosure program is an effort on the part of the SEC to reduce these costs significantly.[40] The program has a number of cost-saving components, but the following are the three most important in terms of their effects on due diligence.

1. *New Securities Act registration statement forms.* In March 1982 the SEC adopted three forms, S-1, S-2, and S-3, for the registration of a public offering of a new issue of securities for cash.[41] The nature of the issuer determines which of the three forms is to be used. Any large established public company, unless it has recently been in se-

rious financial trouble, would qualify to use the short form S-3.[42] Instead of requiring the issuer to answer the questions asked of it in Form 10-K, the issuer incorporates by reference into the registration statement its latest 10-K and any subsequently filled 10-Qs and 8-Ks. The only information relating to the affairs of the issuer that must actually be set out in the registration statement is, in most cases, the use of proceeds and a description of any material changes since the last 10-K not described in a 10-Q or 8-K. The theory behind the S-3 is the efficient market hypothesis. Individual investors do not need to receive information concerning a heavily traded security; they can count on the fact that the information provided in the Exchange Act filings is already reflected in the price of the security. The fact that the registration statement and prospectus are so much shorter greatly reduces the amount of executive, lawyer, and accountant time needed to prepare it, slashes the printing fees, and permits the filing of a registration statement in a matter of a few days from the time the offering was first conceived.

2. *Selective SEC review and accelerated effectiveness.* Starting in November 1980 the SEC as a general matter abandoned the practice of giving even "cursory" or "summary" review to the registration statements of issuers of the type qualifying to use a form S-3.[43] With the elimination of review and the reliance on prior Exchange Act filings to inform the market concerning the issuer, the SEC apparently saw no reason why there should be a significant waiting period after the filing of the registration statement before it becomes effective. The staff has begun permitting most S-3 registration statements, upon "acceleration" requests by the issuers, to become effective in forty-eight hours.[44]

3. *Shelf registration.* An issuer qualifying to use Form S-3 is permitted under Rule 415 to register debt or equity securities that are to be offered on a delayed or continuous basis during a two-year period following the effective date of the registration statement. The issuer need not amend the registration statement during the two-year period unless there has been a fundamental change in the reported information that has not been disclosed in a subsequent 10-K, 10-Q, or 8-K. A number of managing underwriters can be named in the registration statement and then just one of them be used when any particular portion of the registered securities is actually offered. The effect of Rule 415 is to permit the issuer wishing at any point

during the two-year period to sell some or all of the registered securities to contact the several managing underwriters named in the
registration statement, determine which underwriter will give it the
best terms, and offer the security to the market through that underwriter in a matter of hours.[45]

1.413 *Probable Changes in level of Disclosure*

1. *Changes in the environment in which due diligence occurs.* It will be
recalled that underwriter due diligence is a crucial part of the legislative plan to make Section 11 liability an engine for disclosure. The
integrated disclosure program is bound to have a dramatic effect on
the environment in which an underwriter conducts due diligence in
connection with a short form S-3 offering, whether or not it is shelf
registered. Since most of the registration statement consists of language from prior Exchange Act filings incorporated by reference—
language that in a long form registration statement was set out in
full—the underwriter no longer plays a part in the drafting of this
material at the time of registration. In theory, any language incorporated by reference that does not please the underwriter can be
explicitly corrected either by an 8-K filing or in the registration statement itself, but an issuer is likely to resist strenuously undertaking
such an action because it would imply that one of its prior filings
was somehow defective.[46] Incorporation by reference also makes obsolete concerns with sequence of presentation and emphasis. The
reforms alter radically the potential speed with which securities may
be offered to the public. Mechanically it takes very little time to prepare an S-3 registration statement, and once it is filed, it can become
effective in as little as forty-eight hours. A process that once inevitably took a few weeks to a few months now can be undertaken in
a few days, a period far shorter than underwriters traditionally devoted to due diligence.

Shelf registration accentuates the·effects of these changes in environment. There is unlikely to be even the minimal underwriter involvement in the preparation of the registration statement that occurs with a non-shelf-registered S-3. Several potential managing
underwriters can be named in a registration statement by the issuer
(without their permission) and then one selected to underwrite any

particular block of shares at the time the issuer decides to offer the block. For an issuer that has an inventory of shelf-registered securities, the time that it takes to bring an offering to the public once a decision is made to do so is further reduced to a few hours as compared with the few days needed for a non-shelf-registered S-3 offering.

In response to criticisms that these changes in environment would impede due diligence, the SEC has suggested the following possible scenario.[47] The integrated disclosure program would shift the locus of interaction between the issuer and the underwriters from the point where the registration statement is drafted to the points where the 10-K, 10-Qs, and 8-Ks are drafted. The disciplining effects on due diligence traditionally associated with the drafting of the registration statement would become associated instead with the drafting of the issuer's Exchange Act filings. The speed with which public offerings could be consummated need not hinder due diligence because the underwriter would be examining the issuer on an ongoing basis.

There are, however, a number of reasons to believe that underwriters will not often participate in the drafting of Exchange Act filings and that, in those cases where they do, the nature of their participation will differ from what it was in the drafting of the traditional registration statement. In most cases, neither the issuer nor any particular investment bank can be confident at the time the Exchange Act filing is drafted that the issuer will engage in a public offering or that the investment bank in question will be the managing underwriter of the offering if it does occur.[48] Under these circumstances the issuer is not likely to permit one or perhaps several potential underwriters to intrude in the process of drafting what the issuer considers to be its document. Nor is the issuer going to be willing to provide the same amount of "soft" information to such potential underwriters as it would in the context of a traditional registration, because the more distant relationship between the two reduces the likelihood that the information would stay confidential. The investment bank, in turn, is not going to invest the same amount of resources in drafting and in examining the firm as it would with a traditional registration because it is far from certain that it will receive any return for its efforts. Nor is the investment bank likely to ask as pointed, potentially antagonizing, questions because the issuer has much less stake in ultimately consummating an offering using that bank and can easily give the business to another, more deferential one.

There is some empirical evidence confirming the limited extent of underwriter participation in the preparation of Exchange Act filings. A survey of issuers conducted by the Securities Industries Association in 1982 revealed that only 13 percent involved underwriters and only 24 percent involved underwriter's counsel in the preparation of their 10-Ks.[49] The respective percentages were much lower for 10-Qs and 8-Ks.[50] Of those issuers that did not at the time of the survey involve underwriters in the preparation of their Exchange Act filings, only 22 percent expressed a willingness to do so in the future.[51] These rather dramatic findings may, however, need to be discounted to some extent because the association actively opposed Rule 415 and conducted this survey in preparation for its testimony concerning the rule.

2. *Effect on the information available to the market assuming no change in the standard of underwriter liability.* The changed environment in which due diligence will occur and the probable lack of underwriter participation in issuers' Exchange Act filings do not by themselves prove that the quality of issuer disclosure will suffer as a result of the integrated disclosure program. As the SEC argues, "Nothing compels an underwriter to proceed prematurely with an offering"[52] before the underwriter feels it has completed as thorough an investigation of the issuer as it did traditionally and obtained whatever additional disclosure that investigation suggests is necessary. One might argue that underwriters are unlikely to bring offerings to market unless they have engaged in just as much due diligence as traditionally because to do otherwise would be irrational. Assuming for the moment that the standard of underwriter liability under Section 11 remains unchanged, the consequences of an inadequate investigation remain the same.

This argument, however, has a number of problems. To begin, there are two reasons why a reduction in due diligence is likely to be a perfectly rational response to the new reforms. First, the language now incorporated by reference in an S-3 would in a traditional registration have appeared in the prospectus, a document distributed to thousands of investors and market professionals that had on its cover the name of the managing underwriter in letters almost as bold as those used in the name of the issuer. Thus, the underwriter's reputation was more closely associated with this language than it is now. Second, the time necessary to undertake the traditional amount of due diligence would, given the integrated disclosure reforms, inevitably result in a significant delay of the offering, whereas undertaking such due diligence caused no delay previously. Such a delay might be viewed by an issuer as too costly because of the increased volatility of securities markets and the perceived existence of short-lived "windows" of financing opportunity.[53] Given the cost of the delay in the eyes of the issuer, it may be rational for the underwriter to proceed to market having engaged in less due diligence rather than lose the deal.

At least as important, the argument's assumption that underwriters will react rationally to the change in environment is questionable. Assuming participation by an underwriter in the drafting of Exchange Act filings is limited or nonexistent, the level of disclosure resulting from these filings will be less than was the case with a traditional registration statement. An issuer, as we have seen, will be reluctant to grant an underwriter involved in an S-3 registration the time for conducting a thorough investigation or to agree to make additional disclosure through language in the registration statement (or through the filing of an 8-K) superseding what otherwise would be incorporated by reference. To the extent that the underwriter insists on obtaining this additional time and disclosure, it will be only out of fear of liability. Christopher Stone in his work on enterprise liability argues persuasively that large organizations tend not to act rationally when calculating the trade-off between short-run gain (in this case, getting the issuer's business) and an increased risk of future liability for damages (in this case, resulting from having to accept the issuer's terms concerning due diligence in order to get the business).[54] The problem is accentuated because, at least for a few years, the possibility of liability is going to seem more remote than it really is. In the past there have been relatively few cases where an underwriter has had to pay out a large amount of damages as a result of an adverse judgment or settlement in connection with a Section 11 claim.[55] But this historical record is the product of a time period in which underwriters played their traditional due diligence role.

There is some empirical evidence, again from the Securities Industry Association, that the integrated disclosure program has in fact reduced the amount of underwriter due diligence. The association conducted a survey of underwriters in July 1982 that found that only 9 percent of underwriters believed they were performing as much due diligence as two years before.[56]

3. *Effect on the standards of underwriter liability.* The assumption that the integrated disclosure program will have no effect on the standards of underwriter liability is, in any case, probably incorrect. Section 11(c) of the Securities Act provides that the standard by which the reasonableness of an underwriter's investigation and belief in the truth of the registration statement is judged for purposes of establishing a due diligence defense is that of a "prudent man in the management of his own property." The legislative history of this language suggests that the conduct necessary for an underwriter to be entitled to the due diligence defense depends on the surrounding circumstances.[57] One circumstance that may be relevant is whether an underwriter is the one managing the issue or a minor participant in the syndicate selling the issue. There is some judicial authority that can be used in support of the argument that the managing underwriter must engage in a more thorough investigation because of its close contact with the issuer.[58] Similarly, the SEC has in official releases taken the position for several years that the fact that language in a registration statement is incorporated by reference is a circumstance a court would take into account in determining the reasonableness of an underwriter's investigation and belief concerning such language.[59] In March 1982 the SEC went one step further by promulgating Rule 176, which provides in part that in determining whether or not the conduct of a person meets the standard set out in Section 11(c), relevant circumstances include "whether, with respect to a fact or document incorporated by reference, the particular person had any responsibility for the fact or document at the time of the filing from which it was incorporated."[60] Obviously, an underwriter, unlike an officer, generally would not have any such responsibility.

The likelihood that the integrated disclosure program will lower standards of liability is reinforced by the fact that in most areas of the law where courts are charged with determining whether particular behavior is reasonable or not, they are influenced by prevailing behavior.[61] If initially there were no change in the standard of liability but, for any of the reasons discussed above, integrated disclosure in fact results in less due diligence activity, over time the courts will not require underwriters to have performed as much due diligence as they had before in order to be entitled to the defense.

1.414 *The Effect of Integrated Disclosure on the Incentive to Retain Earnings*

The integrated disclosure program reduces the cost to management of a public offering in a number of ways. In doing so, it has undoubtedly reduced somewhat the incentive that the Securities Act has traditionally created to retain earnings in order to avoid public offerings. It is appropriate to ask, however, how socially desirable these various methods of cost reduction are.

The near elimination of the huge mechanical costs of preparing, printing, and distributing thousands of copies of complex documents is almost certainly an improvement. The flexibility in the timing of an offering probably helps capital markets function more smoothly.

Other aspects of the cost reduction require more scrutiny, however. Management undoubtedly appreciates the reduction in the amount of additional information that must be disclosed as a result of a decision to engage in a public offering. The elimination of the many hours of valuable professional and executive time required to achieve the level of disclosure associated with the traditional registration process also means significant savings to the firm. But these cost reductions come at the price to the economy as a whole in the form of a reduced flow of information concerning corporate operations. It is the function of management to know more about its firm's operations than do outside investors. Because the market could not make good use of all of this information possessed by management, it would not be cost effective to require that the firm provide it. But, notwithstanding the arguments of adherents of agency theory and signaling theory,[62] we have seen in the preceding chapters reasons for believing that management often will not voluntarily provide as much information as can be justified when social benefit is weighed against social cost. Emitting accurate predictions and little else can be in management's interest because it provides maximum protection from takeover for any given deviation of the decisions of management from those that would be in the best interests of shareholders (see chapter 2, section B 3.222). Withholding information that could be helpful to actual or potential competitors, suppliers, or customers may be in the interests of both management and the shareholders of the firm. But release of such information may still be socially justified. The harm to the shareholders of the firm will be canceled out by a gain to the shareholders of another firm.* And the release of the information will improve the functioning of the finance process in its project choice and control reassignment functions.[63]

The review of the integrated disclosure program also makes clear that it by no means completely eliminates the incentive to retain earnings in order to avoid a public offering, because a management that avoids a public offering avoids significant pressures for disclosure, risks of liability, and expenses that continue to be imposed when a firm does engage in an offering.

1.42 *An Alternative: Total Integration of Securities Act Disclosure*

Under the current integrated disclosure program, Exchange Act filings have become the central documents for disclosure, whether a firm engages in a public offering or not. Unfortunately, the changes in procedures and rules mean that even when it is contemplated that the firm will engage in a public offering, these Exchange Act documents do not display a quality of disclosure of the level traditionally associated with the registration of public offerings. The problems associated with the existing program of integrated disclosure suggest that we should consider a full merger of the disclosure requirements of the two acts by imposing on all firms when they prepare their periodic reports the same pressures for disclosure and risks of liability whether or not they subsequently engage in public offerings. They also suggest that the standard of disclosure that we should aim for should be the one associated with the traditional registered public offerings. Doing so would accomplish the twin objec-

---

*If all firms live under a regime requiring forced disclosure of information that might be useful to competitors, suppliers, or customers, any particular firm would sometimes be a gainer and sometimes a loser. Unless there is a reason to believe that the firm systematically would be one more than the other, in the long run the effects should balance out.

tives of increasing the amount of meaningful disclosure from public companies and of decreasing the amount of internal finance.

There is an apparent logic to the current legal regime, which, despite the somewhat equalizing effect of integrated disclosure, still places much less pressure to provide honest, forthcoming disclosure on firms that do not engage in public offerings than on firms that do. But as we shall see, closer examination shows that the apparent logic is not entirely compelling because it stems from regarding the firm as a single entity rather than as an amalgam of management on the one hand and an ever-changing group of investors on the other. To illustrate, consider two firms, A and B, each of which is a management-controlled corporation in which management has little or no equity stake. On February 1 each has one million shares outstanding which are trading at $50. In each case management, through a false or misleading statement in a current Exchange Act filing, is withholding information concerning the prospects of existing assets that, if it were known to the public, would, given an SROR of 10 percent, cause the shares to be trading at $40. In the case of firm A, its existing productive assets have, in the eyes of a fully informed observer, a perpetual expected return to $4 million per year. The false or misleading statement leads the public to expect instead $5 million per year. Firm A has no other assets because it just paid out all its cash in the form of a dividend. In the case of firm B, its existing productive assets have, in the eyes of a fully informed observer, a perpetual expected return of $3.5 million per year. The false or misleading statement leads the public to expect $4.5 million per year. Firm B also has $5 million in cash.

On February 1 each firm expends $5 million on an investment project that, in the eyes of both the best-informed observer and the market, has a perpetual expected return of $500,000, i.e., a rate of return just equal to SROR. The money for firm A's project comes from a simultaneous public offering of 100,000 shares made pursuant to a registration statement that repeats (or incorporates by reference) the false or misleading statement. The shares will sell at $50. The money for firm B's project comes from internally generated funds. Announcement of the project by firm B will have no effect on the $50 price of its shares, since shareholders will be indifferent between receiving a dividend of $5 million and having that amount invested in a project with an expected rate of return equaling SROR. For the sake of clarity of the example, assume that no one trades in the secondary market in A's shares during the month of February. Firm B does not engage in a public offering, but 100,000 shares are traded during the month on the secondary market, all at $50. On March 1 each firm announces the true state of affairs. No other factors have influenced the market's evaluation of either firm between February 1 and March 1.

Who gains and who loses and by how much? In the case of firm A, the price will drop to $40.90. Each of the persons who bought the 100,000 newly issued shares loses $9.10 a share. The firm has gained $910,000 from not stating the true state of affairs at the time of the public offering. This gain results because 10/11 of what the new shareholders were buying was a pro-rata interest in the existing assets of the firm. That interest was overpriced by $910,000 because of the false or misleading statement. Restitution, i.e., reversing the transaction by the firm giving each of the buyers $50 in return for each share he bought, or its damages equivalent, i.e., the payment by the firm to each of the buyers of $10 per share,* makes the innocent buyers whole and forces a wrongdoer, the firm, to disgorge the gains obtained as a result of its wrongdoing. Such a result, forcing someone who lies to transfer the gains of his lie to the person injured by it, is consistent with a broadly held basic norm of our legal system.

In the case of firm B, the announcement will cause the price to drop to $40. The buyers of the 100,000 shares traded during February lose $10 per share; they paid $50 for something worth $40. The sellers of the 100,000 shares, assuming none of them knew the information, are innocent windfall gainers in the amount of $10 per share. Restitution is barred as a legal matter because of the innocence of the sellers and as a practical matter as well in many cases because of the impersonal nature of stock exchange transactions.[64] The legal system could require the firm to pay the buyers damages of $10 per share under the theory that the firm's wrongdoing caused the losses. But the correctness of such a result is not nearly as clear as in the case of firm A because firm B may have gained little or nothing from its wrongdoing.

---

*A payment of $10, rather than $9.10, is necessary because the buyers, as shareholders, will derivatively be paying part of their own damages, since their shares will lose value from the payment.

The apparent logic of the current legal regime putting less pressure on firms like B than on ones like A breaks down, however, if we disassemble the legal fiction known as a corporation and look at two of its component parts, the shareholders and management. Looking at the shareholders, the two cases now become very similar. Existing holders of firm A shares on January 1 are innocent windfall gainers to the extent of $.90 per share, and the buyers in the public offering are innocent losers to the extent of $9.10 per share. From the point of view of shareholders, there is no more compelling reason to provide for restitution or restitutionary damages in the case of firm A than there is, where the seller can be found, in the case of firm B. *Thus, we need to look to management motivation to find a justification for the difference in treatment.* One might speculate that false or misleading statements need to be treated more severely in connection with the sale of new shares by a firm because they are a way to increase share value, something management is motivated to do because it pleases shareholders. Firm A's shares increased $.90 as a result of the public offering. But at least in the case of a sale of equity (where a misstatement is likely to have the most significant effect on the price of a security of a financially sound firm), the pleasure it brings existing shareholders is exactly counterbalanced in dollar amount by the displeasure it brings the new shareholders. So it is not a very promising tactic unless management itself has a significant direct stake in share value.

The preceding discussion is not intended to suggest that the law should be amended so that firms are no longer liable when they engage in a public offering of securities pursuant to a registration statement containing a false or misleading statement of a material fact. There is nothing unjust about imposing liability on such a firm— even for the innocent gainers, liability would simply reverse their windfalls—and there are many situations where management would identify with the interest of existing shareholders (for example, where the offering is of debt securities or where management owns a significant number of shares), so that the gains to existing shareholders if issuer liability were eliminated would be an incentive for management to make false or misleading statements. But the discussion does suggest that in the case of the financially sound large, management-controlled corporations—the type that dominate real investment decision making in our economy—the best single rationale for laws pressuring management to make honest forthcoming disclosure should be, as has been argued in this book, to discipline management in its production and project choice decisions, a purpose which is of equal concern whether or not the corporation is engaging in public offerings.*

What practical steps could be undertaken to impose on managements that do not engage in public offerings the same pressures for disclosure as are imposed on those that do? Again, consider our two hypothetical firms. Applying what was discussed in the preceding section, what are the pressures on the management of firm A to disclose the true state of affairs on February 1 instead of March 1? The first pressure is that the firm itself would face liability if it does not disclose. As we have just seen, imposition of liability on the firm affects the welfare of existing shareholders, which is at least some-

---

*Another argument for treating false and misleading statements with greater severity when made in connection with a public offering is that only then can the statements affect the firm's cost of capital and result in misallocation. The management of firm A has to dilute its total equity outstanding by only 100,000 shares to raise $5 million compared with the 120,000 shares required if the true state of affairs were known. This, the argument goes, will make investment in inferior projects attractive when it would not be if greater dilution were necessary. Less dilution means the project needs to generate less return in order to maintain any given level of dividends per share outstanding.

Adherents of the pure neoclassical theory of corporate finance would find this reasoning unpersuasive, however. If management wants to maximize the share value of current holders, its cost of capital for a project, whatever the source of funds, is the opportunity cost to shareholders of not receiving in dividends the amount of money that is instead expended on the project. The decisions of the firm as to whether to raise money and whether to spend it are separate. A newly issued security in large part represents a pro-rata interest in the earnings of a firm's existing assets. If a firm wishing to maximize share value can sell the security at a price reflecting an evaluation of this interest greater than it is really worth, the firm should engage in the offering regardless of the quality of its investment opportunities. If none of its opportunities promise as great a rate of return as its shareholders could earn by reinvestment, management should just distribute the proceeds of the offering or use them to reduce the firm's debt.[65]

The theory set out in chapter 2 (section B3.221), in contrast to the pure neoclassical theory, assumes that management under some circumstances will make investments with an expected return less than SROR, i.e., ones that do not maximize share value. But the chapter 2 theory also assumes that a firm which would act in this fashion would avoid outside finance because the additional disclosure involved might make obvious its strategy. Thus, the chapter 2 theory leads to the same conclusion as the pure neoclassical theory, that additional disclosure should lead to the same level of improvement in project choice in the case of a firm that does not engage in outside financing as in the case of a firm that does.

times of concern to management. It can also cause a financially weak firm to become insolvent, something of great concern to management. The liability of the firm would equal ($5 million/$50) × ($50 − $40) (the "Total Liability")* less the total contribution, if any, that would be legally required from the officers and directors and the underwriters. (Each of the directors, officers, and underwriters would, pursuant to Section 11(f) of the Securities Act, be jointly and severally liable with the issuer for the Total Liability if it could not maintain its due diligence defense.)[66] Ironically, however, this pressure just counterbalances the gain from the sale of each newly issued share at a price approximately $10 in excess of its value. Rather than really being a disincentive to misrepresent, the imposition of Section 11 liability *on the firm* is just an antidote for what otherwise is an extra incentive to misrepresent that is present when a firm issues new securities.† The second pressure on management is the risk that it would be legally required itself to contribute to payment to the purchasers of the public offering. This risk can only be avoided by a careful investigation to ascertain the true state of affairs and disclosure of what is discovered. The third pressure on management comes from the fact that the underwriter faces the risk of being legally required to contribute to payment of the Total Liability. The underwriter will try to avoid this risk by conducting its own investigation of the true state of affairs and insisting, by threat of withdrawal if necessary, on disclosure of what it finds.

How would equivalent pressures be put on the management of firm B to disclose the true state of affairs on February 1 instead of March 1? The first pressure—liability on the firm—is unnecessary to replicate because there is no need for an antidote for the extra incen-

---

*If a court did not take account of the fact that the purchasers of the public offering would be paying for part of the damages they were receiving, the Total Liability would be slightly less: ($5 million/$50) × ($50 − $40.90).

†When (unlike the hypothetical) the whole decline in the price of the security is not due to the firm's failure to disclose the true state of affairs at the time of the offering, the burden is on the defendant to show what portion of the decline is due to other factors. Because this is a difficult burden, Total Liability might well exceed the gain in a real world case. On the other hand, the measure of damages set out in Section 11(e) of the Securities Act does not provide for any recovery in a situation where, notwithstanding the initial failure to disclose, random positive developments counteract the effect of the true state of affairs being revealed, resulting in a security price equal to or above the offering price. In this situation, the firm experiences a gain from its nondisclosure for which it never pays damages.

tive to misrepresent that is present when a firm issues new securities. The second pressure could be replicated by making each of the top officers and directors who could not meet a Securities Act type due diligence defense be liable for an amount equal to his likely contribution to the Total Liability if firm B, failing to disclose the same information, had instead financed its investment by a public offering. Similarly, the third pressure could be replicated by requiring firm B to have an investment bank which, akin to an accountant, acts as a disclosure guarantor even though the corporation is not engaging in a public offering. The bank, if it could not meet a due diligence defense, would be liable in an amount equal to its likely contribution to the Total Liability if firm B, failing to disclose the same information, had financed its investment by a public offering and the bank had been its underwriter.

To whom should the officers, directors, and underwriters be liable (the aggregate amount of such liability being referred to as "Total Contributions")? One's first reaction might be to suggest that the Total Contributions be paid to those who purchased the 100,000 B shares during the month of February at $50 before the true state of affairs was revealed. But there are a number of arguments against giving the money to the purchasers. To start, they are chance losers from not knowing the true state of affairs, there being an equal number of chance gainers in the form of the sellers. Thus, investors who maintain reasonably diversified portfolios will over time experience in approximately equal amounts chance losses and chance gains from not knowing the true state of affairs concerning the securities they buy and sell. Furthermore, the amount which the purchasers would receive per share would be entirely arbitrary. Total Contributions is some ascertainable fraction of Total Liability which in turn is a function of the amount of real investment that occurs during the period when the true state of affairs is not known, something which has no necessary connection with the number of shares that exchange hands in the secondary market during that period.* In the real world the number of secondary trades may be so great that dividing Total Contributions among all the purchasers would result in an amount of the recovery per share that would not even equal the

---

*In the hypothetical example, the 100,000 shares traded in the secondary market just coincidentally equaled the number of shares that would have to have been issued in a public offering on February 1 to raise $5 million, the amount of the investment.

considerable transaction costs that would be involved in locating all of the members of the class and delivering them the money.

The rationale suggested here for disclosure—that it results in management making better production and project choice decisions— suggests that the better recipient of the money is the corporation itself. Since deviation from shareholder best interests is more likely to involve implementation of projects using the internally generated funds that management decides not to distribute to shareholders, Total Liability, and hence Total Contributions, would have some rough proportionality to the harm to shareholders from a misuse of this money permitted by a failure to disclose. The transaction costs involved in giving the money to the corporation would also be far less.

The change in legal regime suggested by this hypothetical example could be implemented in accordance with the following scheme. The 10-K filed during the first quarter of an issuer's fiscal year (covering the preceding fiscal year) and the subsequent three 10-Qs filed in the three remaining quarters could each be treated as the equivalent to a registration statement to which is applied liability of the kind imposed by Section 11 on public offerings. The filing would be treated as if it were a phantom public offering of the number of common shares that, given P_0 (the share price immediately after the filing), would need to be issued to fund I (the total of the real investment and the net increase in other nonliquid assets during the quarter). Thus, Total Liability for an untrue statement or an omission of a material fact would be determined by the formula $(I/P_0) (P_0 - P_1)$, where P_1 is the price of the shares at the time the suit is brought, or such other amount as is suggested by Section 11(e) of the Securities Act.* Each filing would be required to be signed by an investment bank (with sufficient assets to cover its potential liability

---

*Under current law, the accuracy of a registration statement for Section 11 purposes is judged as of the date of its effectiveness. The equivalent in this scheme would be the filing date of the 10-K or 10-Q. Absent the issuance of a "stop order" by the SEC pursuant to Section 8(b) or 8(d) of the Securities Act, no amendment to the registration statement is, as a formal matter, required because of subsequent events. Subsequent events are instead handled under the prospectus requirements of the Securities Act. A prospectus which fails to reflect material changes occurring after the effective date of the registration statement does not meet the requirements of Section 10(a) of the Securities Act, and as a consequence, sale by the issuer of the related security violates Section 5(b)(2) and may give rise to issuer liability pursuant to Section 12(1) even if the issuer is unaware of the problem. If the issuer is or should be aware, it would be liable under Section 12(2).[67] A prospectus can be revised to satisfy Section 10(a) simply by filing copies of the revised document pursuant to Rule 424(c) or by

from this and any other filings it signed), by the officers currently required to sign a registration statement, and by a majority of the directors. The investment bank, each officer signing the registration statement, and each director would be liable to the issuer in the amount of the portion of the Total Liability that it would be required to contribute if the action were under Section 11 of the Securities Act. The statute of limitations could be one year.* The action could be brought derivatively on behalf of the corporation by any shareholder in the same fashion as is possible under Section 16(b) of the Exchange Act, the incentive to bring the action, as in Section 16(b), being the prospect of a legal fee if the action is successful.[68] Actions by shareholders on their own behalf brought pursuant to Section 18(a) or Rule 10b-5 under the Exchange Act would be barred. Indemnification of officers, directors, and underwriters by the issuer and insurance purchased by the issuer would need to be prohibited or severely restricted in order to preserve the *in terrorem* effect that justifies imposition of the liability in the first place.† In order to assure

the filing of a posteffective amendment containing the revised prospectus. There is no analogy to the prospectus in the scheme being set out here, so changed circumstances would need to be handled another way. A possible solution would be to treat an 8-K as an equivalent to a posteffective amendment. Failure to file an 8-K when subsequent events require its filing would result in the original 10-K or 10-Q being judged as to its accuracy for purposes of liability as of the date the 8-K should have been filed instead of as of the date the original document was filed.

*A prohibition on bringing a suit more than a year after the failure to disclose would be the rough equivalent of the requirement under Section 11(a) of the Securities Act, that the plaintiff must establish reliance if he brings his action after the issuer makes generally available an earnings statement covering a period of at least twelve months beginning after the effective date of the registration statement. The imposition of this reliance requirement effectively bars any further Section 11 suits in most cases.

†Indemnification and insurance are controversial and confused issues under the Securities Act that are themselves in need of clarification.[69] Here, since liability is to the issuer, indemnification and issuer-paid insurance seem particularly inappropriate. Whatever legal regime is established on paper, there is going to be a natural reluctance on the part of those administering the law to put individual officers and directors in a position where they are forced to pay out of their own pockets huge amounts of money in situations where they did not personally profit from the violation. This reluctance arises both out of a concern for the human consequences of imposing such massive liability and from a fear of deterring qualified persons from becoming officers and directors. The reluctance may be reflected in a refusal to find the existence of a violation notwithstanding facts warranting such a finding, in a refusal to find a civil action for damages available, or in a tolerance of indemnification or insurance arrangements that seem contrary to the statutory scheme. Perhaps the best way to deal with the problem is to limit the damages owing by such officers or directors to an amount in the range of one or two year's compensation from the issuer.[70]

that investment bank liability to the issuer did not create an incentive for officers and directors to be less than forthcoming, officer and director liability should be a necessary condition for bank liability. The integrated disclosure program's short form registration statements, selective review, and shelf registration for public offerings would be continued, but it would now rest on a process producing disclosure comparable in quality to what was produced by the traditional registration process.

There are, of course, a wide variety of technical problems that would need to be solved if a change in legal regime of the type contemplated were actually to be implemented. But this brief description does suggest the basic practicality of a regime that would bring to bear on all public corporations on an ongoing basis the unique forces for disclosure contained in the Securities Act and that would eliminate a significant incentive for internal funding of investment.

2. *Federal Taxation of Corporate and Personal Income*

2.1 *Current Regime*

Federal tax law is the second body of law that has a significant unintended influence on the decision of management whether to use any given portion of the corporation's cash flow to pay dividends or to finance internally new real investment. Under existing tax law, a corporation is regarded as a legal person distinct from its shareholders, and its earnings, net of interest payments on its debt, are taxed as corporate income. Dividends and interest payments received by individual holders of equity and debt are taxed the year of receipt as ordinary individual income. Any increase in the value of a share is not taxed unless and until such time as the holder sells the share and then at the prevailing capital gains rate, which historically has been lower than the rate on ordinary income. If the share is held until the holder's death, the increase in value during his period of holding is not taxed at all. This structure of taxation influences the financial decisions of management in two ways: the choice between internal and external financing and the choice between debt and equity when external financing is sought.

2.11. *Choice Between Internal and External Financing*

A large portion of a firm's shareholders enjoy tax benefits if the firm retains and reinvests its earnings because the gains they derive from these earnings come in the form of increases in the value of their shares instead of in the form of dividends. Other things being equal, it is to management's advantage to make decisions that confer tax benefits on most of the firm's shareholders. Thus, compared with a world without taxes, the current tax regime is likely to reduce the level of dividend payout by most corporations, thereby limiting the sensitivity of the finance process to innovative proposals. The tax benefits of retention and reinvestment are sufficiently great that under many circumstances retention and reinvestment are in the shareholders' best interests even where the investment opportunities available to the firm are inferior to those that could be found by the shareholders. Thus, the existing tax regime also facilitates the funding of projects with a lower expected return than some that go unfunded.

It has been argued that the dividend decision of any individual corporation should not be influenced by these tax considerations. The investment community consists of a group of different "clienteles," each with its own tax-induced preferences in terms of the dividend payout policies of the firms in which it invests. Some investors, such as nonprofit organizations and pension funds, pay no taxes on dividends, and others are individuals in low tax brackets who hold stock for current income.[71] If any clientele does not find a sufficient number of firms in which to invest with payout policies suiting its preferences, it would be willing to pay a premium for the shares of the ones that have such policies. Thus, an equilibrium will develop in which the distribution of payout policies among firms will just match the distribution of preferences among clienteles. Any individual firm is too insignificant for a change in its dividend policy to upset the equilibrium. If it did undertake such a change, holdings of its shares would simply shift without premium or penalty to the clientele with preferences matching its new policy.

Even if this argument is correct, however, it in no way undermines the point that the current tax regime reduces the aggregate dividend payout ratio of corporations as a group and thus the sensitivity of the finance process to innovative investment. The bulk of all equity investments are held by investors who pay taxes on dividends[72] and at high rates (see note 92). This clientele, the one that has a strong tax-induced preference for a low payout ratio, is the one that most corporations will tailor their policies to satisfy.[73]

2.12. *Choice Between External Debt and External Equity*

The second influence of the current tax structure is that to the extent that corporations do engage in outside finance, debt is preferable to equity because payments to debt holders reduce the corporation's taxable income and payments to equity holders do not. This is also unfortunate. The range of factual issues relevant to an outside financing source deciding whether or not to provide a firm with equity financing is broader than that of one deciding whether or not to provide debt financing. Consequently, both the quality and extent of outside finance process involvement in project choice and the resulting amount of public disclosure concerning the firm is likely to be much greater in the case where a firm seeks outside equity financing.

A full exposition of the effect of the current regime on the amount of debt issued requires us to take account of the fact that for most investors holding equity has tax advantages over holding debt. This fact to an extent counteracts the corporate tax based attraction of using debt financing. Miller has constructed a model that shows (a) that the aggregate debt/equity ratio of corporations as a group is a function of the corporate tax rate (t_c), the personal tax rate on income from bonds (t_b) for the marginal clientele buying bonds, and the personal tax rate on income received from holding shares (t_s), but (b) that in equilibrium any individual corporation should be uninfluenced by tax considerations in determining its debt/equity ratio.[74]

Miller starts by deriving a formula to show the gain, G, in the value of the cash flows to investors from leverage, i.e., from having perpetually outstanding debt with a market value of B:

$$(6.1) \quad G = \left[1 - \frac{(1 - t_c)(1 - t_s)}{(1 - t_b)} \right] B$$

Miller then examines how this formula would work in a world where $t_s = 0$ (which he argues is not implausible), firms issue risk-free bonds, and the rate of return on tax-free, risk-free municipal bonds (and, presumably, on a risk-adjusted expected basis, equity) is r_o. No one but tax-exempt investors will hold corporate bonds unless they pay a rate of return in excess of r_o, since investors are interested only in after-tax income flows. As the premium over r_o increases, investors in higher and higher tax brackets (additional clienteles) will find it desirable to hold corporate bonds. Corporations as a group will find it worthwhile to issue bonds up to the point at which the premium that must be paid, $\dfrac{1}{(1 - t_b)}\, r_o$, just cancels out the corporate tax benefits. At this point, t_b for the marginal clientele equals t_c, and Miller's formula shows that there would be no gain for any individual firm to issue more bonds, i.e., its degree of leverage is irrelevant to its value. The model can easily be generalized to cover the situation where t_s is greater than 0: corporations as a group issue bonds up to the point where the t_b for the marginal clientele is such that $(1 - t_b)$ just equals $(1 - t_c)(1 - t_s)$.

For our purposes, the point of Miller's model is that despite the personal tax induced attractions of equity financing, i.e., $t_s < t_b$, the existence of a corporate income tax that permits deduction for interest payments but not dividend payments (i.e., $t_c > 0$) means that the tax regime as a whole creates incentives for more corporate leverage in the aggregate than would be the case in a world without taxes (i.e., where $t_c = t_b = t_s = 0$). The tax regime creates an incentive for outside funding to be predominantly debt, since the personal tax advantages of already outstanding equity depend on corporate income being used to accumulate equity internally, whereas debt, the issuance of which is also tax induced, can only be externally funded.

The empirical evidence relating to the validity of Miller's model is mixed,[75] but the alternative possibility—that an individual corporation can increase its value by the judicious use of leverage—is at least as consistent as Miller's model with the proposition that the current tax regime creates incentives to issue debt rather than equity.

2.2 *Proposed Tax Reforms: "Total Integration" and "Partial Integration"*

The "total integration" of corporate and personal income taxes along the lines of the taxation of a partnership is a reform that would eliminate the tendency of the current tax regime both to encourage internal over external financing and to encourage the use of debt when external finance is sought. With total integration, the corporate tax is eliminated and each shareholder is taxed each year on the full amount of the earnings during that year attributable to his shares, whether or not they are paid out in dividends. The basis of each share for the calculation of capital gains tax is increased by the amount of the retained earnings attributable to such a share during the period it was held. If shareholders are taxed for the full amount of earnings whether they are paid out or not, obviously there is no personal tax-induced incentive for corporate managers to retain. Miller's formula, equation (6.1), can be used to show that a fully integrated tax regime would create no incentives for a higher debt/equity ratio and outside debt financing than would exist in a world without taxes. With total integration, $t_c = 0$, and, assuming that under an integrated regime taxable capital gains and losses would on average cancel each other out, $t_s = t_b$ for all clienteles. According to Miller's formula, $G = 0$; so there is no tax-induced gain for corporations as a group to issue any debt. Thus, the aggregate corporate debt/equity ratio should be the same in a world without taxes, where $t_c = t_s = t_b = 0$, and lower than under the current regime.

Total integration has been advocated by persons possessing a variety of goals not well served by the existing tax regime.[76] One such goal is horizontal equity in the total effect of taxation on individuals: individuals experiencing equal gains in a year should have their wealth position affected by the tax regime equally. The current regime violates this principle in a number of ways. An individual whose money is invested in a project held by a corporation is subject to double taxation of the income from that project to the extent it is paid out in dividends. An individual who invests in a project held personally or by a partnership is taxed only once on that income, as is an individual whose income is derived from the sale of his labor and skills. On the other hand, to the extent that the income of the corporation is not paid out in dividends, the individual whose money is invested in the corporation enjoys the tax deferral and rate reduction effects of the current regime's treatment of his gains as capital gains that are considered unrealized until his interest is sold. Obviously, tax costs and benefits of corporate investment often do not balance each other in individual cases.

Vertical equity in the total effect of taxation on individuals is another goal possessed by some persons advocating integration. Proponents of vertical equity want individuals with higher incomes to have their gains taxed at a higher rate than persons with lower incomes. The current regime violates this principle because the corporate tax has the same impact on low-income shareholders as on high-income shareholders.

A third goal of some persons advocating integration is efficient allocation of resources. The current regime distorts choices by individuals between corporate and noncorporate forms of investment. Some types of real investment, such as real estate development, lend themselves more readily to partnership or individual holding than do other activities, such as automobile manufacture. It also distorts choices between consumption and saving. But the advantages of integration in correcting the allocational concern expressed here—the distortion by the current regime of the allocation of investment funds among corporations—while having received some attention, deserves, the analysis in this book would suggest, a great deal more.[77]

A more modest proposed reform, "partial integration," involves maintaining the corporate income tax but providing some kind of relief from the double taxation of dividends, as is done in a number of European countries. This could be accomplished by calculating the corporate income for tax purposes net of dividend payments as well as of interest payments. Or the corporate income tax could continue to be calculated in the same way it is now, but the portion of the tax corresponding to the percentage of earnings paid out in dividends could be credited to shareholders (just as a withholding tax is). Part of the attraction of partial integration stems from the fact that full integration of corporate and personal taxes raises a host of problems, including how to treat existing corporate tax preferences, the status of tax-exempt shareholders, and the treatment of international capital flows.[78] Partial integration does not eliminate these problems but it makes them easier to deal with administratively. For example, in the credit version of the reform, the relief can be denied foreign and tax-exempt holders by simply denying them the credit. And the only corporate tax preferences that would be passed on would be ones with respect to which there had been an affirmative decision to do so by increasing the credit to reflect the tax that would have been payable but for the preference.

Partial integration has its own problem, however. It has been criticized because it will make the total tax structure less progressive in its impact. Shareholding is concentrated among high-income individuals who, with the more modest proposal, will receive relief from double taxation but still have available the tax shelter and rate reduction benefits of reinvested earnings.[79] For that reason, partial integration does not further the goals set out in this book to the same extent that total integration does because there is still some incentive for management to retain earnings. But partial integration would still be very helpful.[80] Management's choice between paying a dividend and reinvestment would be, in terms of its tax effect on the shareholder, between a gain taxed once now at the ordinary income rate and a gain taxed now at the corporate rate and later (assuming sale before death) at the capital gains rate. The 1982 changes in the federal tax law set the marginal corporate tax rate at 46 percent, the maximum marginal rate on ordinary personal income at 50 percent, and the maximum marginal rate on capital gains at 20 percent. At these rates, if a partial integration scheme were implemented that passed through most corporate tax preferences, few shareholders of any public corporation would derive tax benefits from corporate earnings retention. Even if the preferences were not passed through, few shareholders of corporations not enjoying such preferences would derive tax benefits from retention.*

---

*The existence of a wide variety of corporate tax preferences reduced the effective tax rate paid for 1982 by the average large corporation on its U.S. operations to 16% of these operations' pretax earnings.[81]

If none of these preferences were passed through to shareholders, the average large corporation would under partial integration still have a considerable incentive to retain earnings if it wished to please most of its shareholders in terms of their tax situation. To see this, consider, given the credit version of partial integration, a 50% bracket shareholder of such a corporation whose pro-rata share of pretax earnings is $100, and compare his situation if the corporation pays out all of its posttax earnings in dividends with his situation if it retains all of its posttax earnings. In the full payout case, the shareholder will receive $84 in dividends and be entitled to a $16 tax credit. Since the tax credit is treated like a withholding tax, his taxable income will increase by $100 as a result of receipt of the dividend. In total, $50 will be paid in current taxes—$16 by the corporation and $34 by the shareholder—and there will be no gain to be taxed in a later period. In the full retention case, a total of $16 will be paid in current taxes, all by the corporation, and the tax on the $84 gain that is retained will be deferred until such time, if ever, as the holder sells his shares and then will only be at the 20% capital gains rate.

However, if all the preferences are passed through to the shareholder under a re-

Partial integration would also significantly reduce the other influence of the existing regime concerning us here, the preference for debt over equity when the corporation does seek outside financing. To start, the aggregate corporate debt/equity ratio can be expected to decrease because the reform eliminates the tax disadvantage of equity compared with debt as a security for providing current income, while leaving untouched equity's tax advantages to the extent that earnings are reinvested. This effect can be demonstrated analytically in the case of the dividend deductibility version of the reform by a simple modification of equation (6.1), Miller's formula. Assume that 1) the ratio of payout to earnings for each corporation in the economy equals X^*, 2) the capital gains portion of the returns on equity are effectively taxed at a 0 rate, and 3) the dividend portion is taxed at t_b, the same rate as interest on bonds are taxed. Thus, an investor in any given clientele will have an effective overall rate of taxation on his equity returns of Xt_b. Modifying (6.1) to reflect these assumptions,

$$(6.2) \quad G = \left[1 - \frac{(1-(1-X)t_c)(1-Xt_b)}{(1-t_b)}\right]B$$

The effects of partial integration in the extreme cases, $X=1$ and $X=0$, are straightforward. Where $X=1$, full payout, the tax gains from leverage are completely eliminated by the reform: firms will act

gime of partial integration, tax considerations will create little or no incentive for retention. To see this, consider the same shareholder. If the corporation pays out in dividends all of its posttax income, the shareholder receives $84 in dividends and a total tax credit of $46, $16 for the taxes paid and $30 for the tax preferences being passed through. His taxable income would again increase $100 as a result of receipt of the dividend. In total, $20 will be paid now in taxes—$16 by the corporation and $4 by the shareholder—and none will need to be paid later. The full retention case remains the same as the case where no preferences are passed through. Thus, the relative attractiveness of dividends versus retention is that dividends eliminate the later 20% capital gains taxation that will be imposed on the retained $84 if the shareholder sells before death, while retention reduces by $4 total current taxes paid on the $100 in earnings.

Tax reform legislation moving through Congress in 1986 will, if adopted, affect the magnitudes involved in this discussion, but it will not affect the basic validity of my comparison between the current tax regime and one involving total or partial integration.

*Obviously, corporations in fact vary in terms of their payout ratio. An assumption that they all are equal to the average payout ratio separates out clientele effects on dividends from clientele effects on the debt/equity ratio.

no differently from in a world without taxes. Where $X=0$, full retention, the gains from leverage are identical to those under the current tax regime (assuming, as Miller does, that $t_s=0$), and corporations as a group will issue bonds up to the point that t_b for the marginal clientele equals t_c.

Where $O<X<1$, firms will issue bonds up to the point where the gains from leverage in (6.2) become 0, i.e., where the t_b for the marginal clientele has value such that:

$$(6.3) \quad (1-t_b)=(1-(1-X)t_c)(1-Xt_b)$$
$$=(1-t_c)+X[(1-X)t_bt_c+t_c-t_b]$$
$$t_b=t_c-X[(1-X)t_bt_c+t_c-t_b]$$
$$(1-X)t_b=(1-X)t_c-X(1-X)t_bt_c$$
$$t_b=t_c-Xt_bt_c$$

$$(6.4) \quad t_b=\frac{t_c}{(1+Xt_c)}$$

Since X and t_c are both positive, the t_b of the marginal clientele will be less than t_c, and therefore firms will issue less debt than under the current tax regime. The greater the payout ratio, the greater the decrease in the issuance of debt and in the aggregate corporate debt/equity ratio. Partial integration's increase in the equity portion of firm capitalization combined with its decrease in retained earnings will create significantly more need for external equity issues.

C. Direct Regulation of the Dividend Decision

Having considered the two bodies of law that have significant unintended effects on corporate dividend decisions, it is now time to consider the body of law that purports directly to regulate the decision: corporate law. The current state of the law is easy to describe: it imposes no effective limits on the discretion of the management of a large corporation in choosing whether to use its cash flow to pay dividends or to finance internally new investment.[82] Research does not reveal a single case in the last 100 years where the directors of a management-controlled corporation were ordered by a court to increase the dividend on its common stock. This final section of the chapter will explore what changes in the existing law of dividends, if any, would be desirable in light of the goals set out at the beginning of this chapter.

Specifically, three questions will be addressed. First, is it practical to ask courts to identify specific firms which have a practice of investing in inferior projects and force them to increase their dividends? Second, is it practical to identify one or more classes of firms whose members on average have displayed such a practice and require of all members of the class a larger dividend payout? Third, should all large, publicly traded corporations be forced, directly or indirectly, to pay out as dividends some minimum portion, perhaps all, of their earnings and depreciation?

1. *Requiring Individual Firms Investing in Inferior Projects to Increase Their Dividend Payouts.*

There already exists a legal mechanism, the shareholder suit to compel payment of dividends, that in theory should force corporations investing in inferior projects to increase their dividend payouts. While the general rule is that directors have unfettered discretion in setting dividends, an exception exists where a larger dividend can be distributed without harm to the business and the refusal to do so constitutes bad faith toward the shareholders.[83] A corporation whose management is using internally generated cash for investment in projects which the directors know, or should know, have expected rates of return below SROR—the rate shareholders could earn if instead they received the cash as dividends and reinvested it—would appear to fit within this exception.

The burden of showing that management is behaving in such a fashion, however, is placed on the shareholder. The apparent failure of plaintiffs ever to succeed in suits to increase the dividends of large, management-controlled corporations shows how heavy this burden is.[84] There is so much uncertainty associated with what investment policies are in fact in the shareholders' best interests that the directors of such a corporation would have to deviate radically from what is required of them before a case would be sufficiently clear that a shareholder could meet the burden. Other pressures on such directors make it highly unlikely that their policies would deviate to this extent. The only way to make shareholder suits for dividends a practical way to increase the dividend payout is to lighten the burden of proof and to grant relief where it is only probable, not certain, that management is engaging in a practice of investing in projects which it knows, or should know, have inferior prospects to the opportunities available to shareholders.

The existing heavy burden of proof reflects the policy behind the "business judgment rule" in corporate law: judges are not business experts and should not with hindsight second-guess the business decisions of directors made in good faith.[85] As a practical matter, this means that judges will not overrule such decisions unless they are clearly contrary to the best interests of shareholders. Stated as a general principle, the business judgment rule reflects sound policy. Since we have chosen in large part a decentralized system of private decision making in our economy, it does not make sense for us to entrust to judges decisions we are unwilling to entrust to the kind of real experts we could have making them in an economic planning ministry. The desirability of applying the business judgment rule becomes questionable, however, where the decision of the board of directors in question involves an actual or potential conflict of interest between the directors and the shareholders. In certain types of conflict situations, discussed below, state corporation law has recognized a need to condition the application of the rule or eliminate altogether the protection it provides. Although not recognized yet by any state court, an argument can be made for conditioning or eliminating the protection of the business judgment rule as a matter of course in the case of the dividend decision also because, as the theory set out in chapter 2 argues, the dividend decision in a management-controlled corporation involves a potential conflict of interest between management and shareholders.[86] Conditioning or eliminating this protection could turn the suit for payment of dividends into a practical remedy against corporations that fund inferior projects with internally generated funds. Unfortunately, however, a comparison of the dividend decision with the types of decisions that currently result in a conditioning or outright elimination of the business judgment rule reveals that doing so in the case of the dividend decision would create far more problems than in the cases of the other types of decisions.

The most common type of decision involving a conflict is where the directors authorize the firm to enter into a transaction in which the party on the other side is a director or an entity in which a director has an interest or to which he owes a duty. Board decisions of this type are still accorded the judicial deference embodied in the business judgment rule, but only if the transaction is approved by the shareholders or a majority of the directors who are independent of the transaction.[87] If neither of these conditions is met, the law swings to the opposite extreme and places on the party wishing to uphold the transaction the difficult burden of proving that the transaction is clearly fair to the corporation.[88] Either way, the court avoids making the complex business determination of choosing which argument is better when plausible arguments can be made both in favor and against the wisdom of the board's decision to approve the transaction.

A derivative suit is a second situation that often creates a conflict for board members. A derivative suit is one brought by a shareholder on behalf of a corporation to pursue a cause of action belonging to the corporation. If the board determines that the suit is not in the best interests of the corporation and no member of management is a defendant in the suit or is otherwise personally interested in the suit's dismissal, a court typically will, by application of the business judgment rule, respect the board's determination and dismiss the suit.[89] However, if one or more members of management are defendants in the derivative suit or are otherwise personally interested in its dismissal, courts in some states, before applying the business judgment rule to the board determination, insist on more than just that it be the determination of the members of the board who are formally not interested. These courts also want the board to show that the formally disinterested directors making the determination are genuinely independent of the members of management that are interested in the dismissal of the derivative suit and that the procedures the disinterested directors follow in investigating the claim raised by the suit demonstrate their good faith. Deciding whether these additional conditions are met, while not simple, still involves issues of a kind that are familiar to courts.[90]

Hostile takeover bids often create yet another conflict situation. The decision of the board to undertake a defensive measure in the face of such a bid often gives rise to a challenge under state corporation law. Undertaking such a defensive measure is not necessarily contrary to the best interests of the corporation and its shareholders, but the decision to do so is one in which all the directors are clearly interested because they will be likely to lose their positions if the bid succeeds. Recognizing this conflict, some authorities suggest the business judgment rule be abandoned altogether in suits challenging a board decision to invoke such a defensive measure. Abandoning the business judgment rule places on the directors the burden of justifying their decision as being in the shareholders' best interests.[91] Again, as with the conditioning of the business judgment rule in cases of interested transactions and derivative suits, its abandonment here does not put the court in the position of making a complex business decision. The court need not decide whether incumbent management is better or worse for the corporation than the challengers. It can focus instead on the nature of the measure. Some of these measures, for example, simply involve limited delay—making court affirmation, according to one view, potentially beneficial to shareholders and at worst relatively harmless—and others make the corporation permanently more difficult to take over with no apparent benefit to the corporation—according to this view, making the case for overturning the board's judgment easy.*

Would the approaches used in any of these three types of decisions work well as a substitute for the current policy of automatically applying the business judgment rule in the case of dividend decisions? Conditioning application of the rule on disinterested director or shareholder approval, the approach used in interested transaction cases, is unlikely to produce significantly different results from the current policy of applying the rule automatically. Requiring approval of the dividend decision by directors who are formally disinterested in it, i.e., the nonofficer directors, would be ineffective because, in a management-controlled corporation, these outsiders, if they oth-

---

*According to this view, in some percentage of cases a delay in a takeover is in the shareholders' best interests because it provides time either for the market to realize the true value of the target under its current management, which value is higher than the tender offer price, or for another offeror to come along and offer a higher price. In the rest of the cases, neither of these developments occurs, so delay does not benefit shareholders. But it may not be very harmful, since a company that is a desirable target today, as evidenced by the takeover attempt, will still be a desirable target a few months later either to the original offeror or another one. A judge holding this view who evaluates a board decision to take an antitakeover measure that results in limited delay, not knowing whether or not one of these developments favorable to shareholders will result, can thus feel reasonably comfortable affirming the board's decision, since the cost, if one of these developments does not result, is low. On the other hand, any antitakeover action that permanently makes the corporation more difficult to take over is never, at least by reason of that effect, in the best interests of shareholders according to this view.[92]

erwise support management, are unlikely to vote differently from
the insiders with respect to a decision that is tied to something as
fundamental as management's general investment practices.[93] Conditioning application of the rule to dividend decisions that receive
shareholder ratification would be ineffective because shareholders
are generally uninformed concerning these practices.

A second approach is a further investigation by the court into the
outside directors' independence from the officer directors along the
lines of the investigations employed by some courts in derivative
suit cases. This approach is also unlikely to be helpful. The proposition that outside directors who otherwise support management are
unlikely to vote against them in a matter concerning the quality of
management's general investment practices applies both to directors
who are independent only as a formal matter and those who are
truly independent. Thus, conditioning application of the business
judgment rule on whether the approving outside directors are truly
independent or not would divide corporations along irrelevant lines.
In the case of corporations found to have truly independent outside
directors, the courts would apply the business judgment rule and,
as they do today, would approve essentially all their dividend decisions. In the case of corporations whose outside directors are not
found to be truly independent of management, the courts would
have to review dividend decisions without the benefit of the rule.
This, as we will see in a moment, is very difficult for them to do
unless they swing to the opposite extreme and find to be insufficient
almost all declarations of dividends in an amount less than earnings.

A third approach, akin to the one some authorities urge in the
review of challenges to takeover defenses, is to abandon the business judgment rule altogether in the review of dividend decisions.
The problem with this approach is that, unlike takeover defenses,
dividend decisions do not fall into certain identifiable types that are
either generally good or generally bad for corporations and their
shareholders. The ultimate issue that must be determined in a dividend decision case is whether management is retaining too much
earnings in order to facilitate funding of investment projects with
expected returns below SROR. Making this determination involves
a very complex business question. The court would not be able to
avoid that problem by placing on the directors the burden of proving that the corporation was clearly not engaging in such a practice

because such an approach is tantamount to invalidating almost all decisions to declare dividends in amounts that are less than earnings.

Dividend decisions are thus different from each of the other types of decisions reviewed involving conflicts of interest because there is no way meaningfully to alter the current policy of automatically applying the business judgment rule without putting the court in the position of making complex business determinations. Such an alteration would put the court in exactly the position that the rule is meant to avoid. This difference suggests that it is unwise to change the current policy. Given this conclusion, we need to look elsewhere than the shareholder suit to find a remedy for corporations that fund inferior projects with internally generated funds.

2. Requiring a Larger Dividend Payout of Certain Classes of Firms

Another approach to regulating the dividend decision would be to identify one or more classes of firms whose members on average have displayed a practice of investing in inferior projects and require of all members of the class a larger dividend payout. Is such an approach practical? The empirical studies reviewed in chapter 2 (appendix 2.1) reveal three classes of firms whose members on average invest in inferior projects:

1. Firms that engage in no significant amount of outside equity finance.
2. Firms where a majority of the directors are managers of the corporation.
3. Firms that meet Grabowski and Mueller's definition of "mature."

With respect to each of these classes of firms, if these studies are correct, the performance of the finance process would be improved by forcing all its members to increase their dividend payout. The discussion in chapter 2 (section C2.412) shows that the benefits resulting from the increased payout—the better matching of funding decisions with the projects having the highest predicted return— would well exceed the costs associated with the additional movement of funds. The question is whether it is practical legally to require members of one or more of these classes to increase their dividend payout.

The problem with the first two classes is that if a rule requiring a greater payout from their members were implemented, a firm within either class could easily take actions to remove itself: just engage in a little outside equity finance or put some friendly outsiders on the board of directors. A court or other administrative body could attempt to frustrate these efforts at evasion by trying to determine in each case whether the amount of equity finance is "enough" or whether the outsiders were sufficiently independent. But this would present the legal decision maker with difficult line-drawing problems.

The third class, "mature firms," presents line-drawing problems even before evasion techniques are considered. Grabowski and Mueller, it will be recalled, define mature firms as those which were in existence before World War II and which predominantly produce products in existence before World War II. This rough categorization is satisfactory for purposes of running an empirical study, but it may not be satisfactory as a definition to which significant legal consequences attach. Issues would arise as to whether a firm existing today is the same as one existing forty years earlier despite reincorporations, mergers, acquisitions, sales of divisions, etc. The question of whether a product in existence forty years ago that has been significantly modified since is still the same product for purposes of the payout rule raises the same kind of questions. Multidivisional firms raise more questions.

The problem of line drawing with each of these three classes of firms is aggravated by the fact that in the relevant studies there is no evidence of a dependable causal relationship between the factors used in the definition and observed inferior investment, just evidence of different average investment behavior between firms defined to be within the class and those defined to be outside. This means there are not clear policy criteria to guide a court or other administrative body deciding a particular case as to which side of the line a firm should be placed on. Thus, a rule requiring an increased dividend payout by members of one of these classes is in application certain to involve much arbitrariness if the legal decision maker does not engage in detailed fact finding and might well involve almost as much arbitrariness even if the decision maker does engage in such fact finding.

This conclusion does not mean that such a rule necessarily could not accomplish its purpose for the economy as a whole of a better matching of funding decisions with the projects having the highest return. A certain amount of randomness in the application of the rule and a certain level of administrative cost, while reducing the net gains that could be expected from the rule, would not eliminate them. On the other hand, the conclusion probably does mean that such a rule is not a practical means of regulating dividend behavior of firms within a legal system such as ours that takes seriously the claims of individual firms. Given the significant consequences to a firm of being placed within the class, there would be enormous pressures for the procedures used by the legal decision maker charged with applying the rule to undertake costly, in-depth fact finding. Even if it does not create due process problems, the likely large remaining degree of arbitrariness would undermine the authority of the legal system. In addition, the difficulty of knowing in advance whether for any given period a particular firm will be legally determined to be within or outside the class will create a kind of uncertainty in the minds of many finance process participants that may negatively affect the functioning of the system in terms of the goals we have set out. The cost of administration of such a rule, the demoralizing effect of the residual arbitrariness, and the possible damage to the functioning of the finance process from the added uncertainty all suggest that we need to look yet further for a remedy for corporations that fund inferior projects with internally generated funds.

3. *Increasing the Dividend Payout of Large Public Corporations Generally*

We have seen that a change in the legal system aimed at identifying specific firms that have inferior investment practices and requiring from them a greater dividend payment appears not to be practical. The same conclusion is reached with respect to a change aimed at identifying the members of groups of firms that on average have inferior investment practices. That leaves us with the question of whether we should adopt a universal payout rule, a rule that would assure that large, publicly traded corporations would generally pay out to shareholders some minimum portion, perhaps all, of their earnings and depreciation flows.[94] I will first address whether a rule with this effect would be economically desirable. Then I will address how to formulate a universal payout rule that would be administratively practical.

3.1 *The Economic Desirability of a Universal Payout Rule*

A universal payout rule would cause far more funds to flow into the outside sector than the other proposals considered above. That result has both advantages and disadvantages. The first advantage is that such a rule, by its very breadth, is bound to increase the payout by the firms that in fact are engaging in inferior investment practices. This increased payout will lead to a better matching of the system's funding decisions with the projects having the highest predicted returns. The second advantage is, as chapter 2 suggests, that the large role of the outside sector of the finance process makes the system more sensitive to innovative real investment proposals. The third advantage is a reduction in the tendency of the finance process to encourage concentration in the presence of innovation. Thus, the rule would result in changes in the finance process that would be clear improvements in terms of the first three criteria set out at the beginning of this chapter.

The disadvantage is in terms of cost, the fourth criterion. Chapter 2 suggests that the cost of the movement of funds contemplated by rules aimed at specific firms that have inferior investment practices or at groups of firms that have on average inferior investment practices would be more than justified simply by the improvement in the matching of funding decisions with projects having the highest predicted return. The problem with such rules, as we have just seen, is administratability. But a universal payout rule would involve moving funds out of many firms where there is no indication that they are overinvesting. A lot of funds would make a round-trip out of firms and back into the same firms and be invested in the same projects that retained earnings would otherwise have funded. Such a round-trip involves costs but yields no benefits. To determine whether or not a universal payout rule would be economically desirable, we need to assess the probable magnitude of its cost and then compare it with the probable magnitude of the combination of benefits, just outlined, that the rule promises.

3.11 *The Costs of a Universal Payout Rule*

What would the cost be of cycling through the outside finance process the increase in funds resulting from imposition of a universal payout rule? That question breaks down into parts: what would be the amount of that increase and what would be the average cost per dollar of the cycling?

The amount of the increase depends on the rule adopted. The most extreme version of the rule would result in each large publicly traded corporation distributing to its shareholders 100 percent of its profit and depreciation flows. The extreme version of the rule would mean that dividend payments would be about three times their current levels, since the average corporation currently pays out somewhat more than half of its earnings in dividends,[95] and retained earnings represent only about a third of its total domestic internally generated funds for investment.[96] The capital expenditures of the 500 largest firms represent about 75 percent of all business expenditures (excluding public utilities) for new plant and equipment ("BENE"; see chapter 2, section B 3.1). Currently internally generated funds are sufficient to finance about 90 percent of their capital expenditures (chapter 2, section 3.1). Therefore, the most extreme version of the rule would involve an increase in the amount of funds cycled through the outside sector of the finance process in an amount equal to 67 percent of BENE. Less extreme versions of the rule would result in proportionally smaller increases. For example, a rule that would require a payout of 100 percent of profits but no depreciation would increase the amount of funds cycled through the outside sector by an amount equal to 24 percent of BENE.

It is also possible to qualify a universal payout rule in a fashion which would cut out a large portion of funds that would otherwise under such a rule make a round-trip out of a firm through the outside sector and back to the same firm, thus reducing the aggregate amount of real costs associated with the reform. The qualification would be to allow a firm to give each shareholder the option, if he takes the initiative, of using some or all of his dividends to purchase, at the current market price and without charge, newly issued shares of the corporation.

The starting point for an examination of the average per dollar cost of cycling additional funds through the outside finance process is the estimate made in chapter 2 of the costs associated with the payment of a dividend of $1,000 and its reinvestment in the shares of another firm. These costs were composed of "saver's costs"—the cost to a saver of finding a new place to invest money received as a dividend—and "recipient's costs"—the transaction's costs to a firm of obtaining new funds. The total cost was conservatively estimated to be 4–7 percent of the dividend amount, which for a fifteen-year project receiving the funds translates into a annual cost (taking account of the time value of money) of .50–.90 percent per year (see chapter 2, section C2.412). For a number of reasons considered below, the 4–7 percent range is higher, by a factor of perhaps two or more, than what the average cost would be of moving funds through the outside sector of the finance process if a universal payout rule were adopted. If that is correct, the range under a universal payout rule would be 2.0–3.5 percent (or .25–.45 percent annually for a fifteen-year project).

First, the range is estimated on the basis of transfers involving the highest possible saver's costs, which is well above what during the period studied was the average cost to savers per dollar of dividend paid. The assumption used to calculate saver's costs is that the saver was an individual receiving $1,000 in dividends during a year and reinvesting this at one time in a single stock.* In fact, shareholding by individuals in our economy is sufficiently concentrated that the bulk of dividends go to persons who receive significantly more than $1,000 in dividends, and saver's costs display very significant economies of scale. Over half of all dividends were received by persons in the top 1 percent of income in the country in 1971. If this is still true, the average amount of dividends received by a member of this group in 1983 was over $4,000.[97]

Second, the data used to make the calculation of recipient's costs were prior to the advent of the integrated disclosure system (so as to be comparable to the data with which it was being compared). Prior discussion suggests integrated disclosure has reduced the re-

---

*Financial intermediaries are considered in this analysis as competitive substitutes for the individual holding of shares. An individual who holds a share in the intermediary holds an indirect interest in the shares held by the intermediary and in this sense can benefit from these economies of scale. Counterbalanced against this benefit are the fees he must pay the managers of the funds for the services they perform.

cipient's costs associated with public offerings of securities (see section B1.41). If the securities law reforms proposed in this chapter were undertaken, the recipient's costs associated with a public offering would be even lower because the offering would require no additional due diligence.

Third, the average cost of moving funds through the outside sector today is higher than it would be with the much larger amount of funds moving through under a universal payout rule. In the most extreme version of the rule, the 90 percent of capital spending that is presently internally financed would need to be raised externally. Thus, the net amount of funds raised externally (i.e., above and beyond refinancings) would increase nine-fold. Each saver would, from his larger dividends, be reinvesting much more than today, and as just noted, there are significant economies of scale with saver's costs. Each recipient will be seeking much more financing from the outside sector, and a larger public financing typically involves lower recipient's costs per dollar raised.

Wholly aside from these calculations, which suggest a reduction in the cost of cycling funds to the range of 2–3½ percent, if the universal payout rule is qualified by allowing a dividend reinvestment option, much of the funds would not have to cycle through the outside sector in any ordinary fashion. For funds that a firm has freed up because of shareholder exercise of the option, there are, if one of the tax reforms discussed earlier is adopted, no saver's costs at all: the shareholder who decides as a general policy to exercise without further consideration every reinvestment option he receives is in no different a position than he would have been if the universal payout rule had not been adopted and firms continued to retain earnings as they do now.* If the saver decides to take the dividends in cash and reinvest them, the saver's costs associated with that decision are voluntarily undertaken, presumably because the saver thinks

---

*The position of the shareholder under a qualified universal payout rule who decides to exercise the option of reinvesting the dividends under the reform is in one respect in a different position from the holder under the current regime of shares of a firm that retains earnings. The shareholder under the reform who reinvests is reinvesting in a firm in which he has no guarantee that other shareholders are also reinvesting. The current regime, while it gives the shareholder no choice over whether or not his pro-rata share of the firm's earnings will be retained, assures him that if they are retained, the pro-rata shares of all the other shareholders will also be retained.

he can do better notwithstanding these costs. The only costs associated with funds freed up by exercise of the reinvestment option would be the recipient's costs that the corporation incurs persuading shareholders. The cost of persuading current shareholders would almost certainly be less than normal recipient's costs of raising funds from the external sector.

A qualification of the universal payout rule to permit dividend reinvestment, while lowering costs, would also make the rule less effective in sensitizing the finance process to the potentialities of innovative investment proposals, because a qualified rule would not increase the involvement of the outside sector in the workings of the finance process as much as it would without qualification. But the need to persuade existing shareholders, especially if combined with the disclosure reforms discussed earlier, would guarantee some of the advantages of this kind of involvement for the portion of the funds raised by dividend reinvestment.

3.12 *The Direct Benefits of a Universal Payout Rule*

a. *Better matching of funding decisions with proposals having the highest expected returns.* The studies discussed in chapter 2 concerning groups of firms that on average have a record of inferior investment performance suggest that there are gains to be had from moving funds from firms in these groups to firms outside them. The studies do not permit us to assess with any precision the extent of the difference in expected return of the marginal projects of firms within these groups and those outside them. Appendix 2.1 sets out an array of differences in rates of return. These data suggest that the difference in average rates of return between firms within these groups and those outside might be as much as an astounding 20 percent, but this figure depends on choosing the most unfavorable definition of earnings and lags, and there are questions as to its statistical significance. Furthermore, we know neither what the 20 percent difference implies about differences in marginal rates (though one approach to that question suggests that the difference in marginal rate exceeded 12.6 percent) nor how much funds would have to be transferred from firms within the groups to those outside them before the rates on the marginal projects were equal. Nevertheless, the range of results produced by these several different studies does suggest that a difference in annual rates of return of the marginal projects of the two groups does exist and that a conservative estimate is that it is at least several percent. The portion of all major firms that fall into one or more of these groups is significant. According to the prior discussion, moving funds through the outside sector costs in annualized terms perhaps .25–.45 percent of the amount moved.

This comparison of benefits and costs suggests that, simply in terms of a better matching of funding decisions with the project proposals having the highest return, a universal payout rule can conservatively be cost justified if only one dollar in ten is moved by the rule out of a firm investing in inferior projects and the other nine dollars simply make round-trips out of and back to the firms where they originated to be used in the same projects that otherwise would have been funded internally. If one believes that the cost of moving funds under the rule would be at the low end of the probable range and that the differences in the expected returns among firms on their marginal projects is at the high end of the probable range, a universal payout rule would be cost justified if only one dollar in one hundred is moved from an inferior project firm to a superior project firm and the other ninety-nine dollars simply make a round-trip.

Equally interesting, if our concern is only the better matching of funding decisions with the most promising proposed projects, much or all of what could be accomplished with an unqualified universal payout rule could be accomplished at considerably lower cost with a qualified version of the rule that would permit a corporation's shareholders the option at their initiative of reinvesting cost-free the dividends they receive in newly issued shares of the corporation.

b. *Increasing the sensitivity of the finance process to innovative proposals.* The potential for a universal payout rule to be cost justified in terms of its effect on the sensitivity of the finance process can be explored by considering a hypothetical example and then examining the plausibility of that example. Consider a version of the rule that would result in large, publicly traded corporations generally paying out 100 percent of their profits but none of their depreciation in dividends and that would not be qualified by a reinvestment option. Although this falls well short of the most extreme possible version of the rule, it is still revolutionary and would nearly double the average dividend payout of these corporations. Suppose that the resulting increase in the economy's innovativeness increased the annual growth rate of GNP by one-quarter of 1 percent. This would represent an annual gain to the economy equal in amount of about 2.5 percent of BENE, since BENE averages approximately 10 percent of GNP. The total cost would be the cost of moving through the outside finance process an additional amount of funds equal to 24 percent of BENE. That would be something in the range of .45 to .80 percent of BENE if the probable per-dollar cost range given above is correct. Thus, in this hypothetical example, the benefits from imposing the universal payout rule are three to six times the costs without even considering the benefits from the better matching of funding decisions and project proposals discussed above.

We of course do not know that the imposition of this version of a universal payout rule will generate an increase in the GNP growth rate of one-quarter of 1 percent. But an increase of this much or more is very possible. Since technical change is thought to be responsible for between one-third and one-half of an annual growth rate that has averaged 3–4 percent in the last few decades,[98] only a moderate increase in the rate of technical change is necessary to result in a one-quarter percent increase in the GNP growth rate. As noted in the Introduction, transnational comparisons of product competitiveness and intertemporal comparisons with the rates of GNP and productivity growth in the 1950s and 1960s suggest that the current rate of innovation in our economy is not as great as it could be. Certainly our base of scientific knowledge has been growing very rapidly during the last ten or fifteen years. Many of the calls for a "national industrial policy" are at their heart condemnations of the insensitivity of the finance process to innovative investment proposals. A universal payout rule is a way of utilizing private institutions to meet this problem.

One important conclusion from the macro theory developed in chapter 2 is that there is a trade-off between the cost of operating the finance process and its sensitivity to innovation. Thus, when we ask the question whether the costs of a universal payout rule are in part justified by the increased sensitivity to innovation, we are asking about what the terms of this trade-off are. While it is not possible to answer that question with any certainty because we have no range of experience to examine, it is very important to note a second conclusion from the macro theory: the existing level of innovativeness of the finance process, whatever that level is, can be expected to be self-reinforcing. There are no inexorable forces pushing the system toward the optimal point in the trade-off between cost and innovativeness. The current point may in fact be suboptimal. Our economic disappointments of recent years are evidence that it is. The feeling that it is suboptimal is substantially reinforced by the semiconductor study, which showed how much less sensitive the internal finance processes of established diversified firms in that industry were compared with the outside finance process.

One of the features of the universal payout rule is that when introduced, it can require a percentage of payout well below the version in the hypothetical example, and it can be qualified to permit shareholders a reinvestment option. The results of the rule in such an introductory form can be monitored so that we can begin to develop an understanding of the terms of the trade-off between the costs of operating the finance process and innovativeness. This understanding can then be used to determine how much, if any, the percentage of payout should be increased and whether the qualification should be abandoned.

This cost-benefit analysis, despite its "back of the envelope" quality, makes a powerful case for trying a universal payout in some form on the basis of its effect on innovation alone. To start, the hypothetical gains postulated in the example are perfectly plausible. The example also shows that imposition of the rule would still be worthwhile even if the resulting increase in GNP growth were much less than the example assumes. And the flexibility of the rule permits it to be introduced in a more modest and less costly version that would educate us about the potential of taking the reform further.

3.13 *Indirect Benefits of a Universal Payout Rule: Facilitation of New Offerings by Its Effect on the Secondary Trading Market*

There is good reason to believe that, other things being equal, a universal payout rule would improve the accuracy of pricing in the market for secondary trades of already issued securities. The argument rests on a view of the existing secondary market, discussed in chapter 1 (section C2.214), as having an irrational component in its pricing mechanism. Briefly reviewing, a potential purchaser of a share of stock determines the return he expects to earn on the stock on the basis of two factors: how much the share will sell for at the point in the future he expects to sell it and how much in dividends he will receive in the interim. The second factor requires making a best guess about real events. But the first factor requires guessing today at what the market will "think" the stock will be worth at the point he expects to sell. If the market is rational, what the market at that future point will "think" the stock is worth is equal to the best prediction of subsequent distributions to shareholders discounted to then present value. That suggests the potential purchaser should focus on his estimate today of what that future flow of distributions will be. But the potential purchaser may not believe that the market is rational and may instead focus on the "psychology" of the market. If enough potential purchasers share this belief over time, it is self-confirming. The market becomes inward looking. A potential purchaser who focuses solely on fundamentals—real events—will not do as well as one who also considers the psychology of the market. The "fundamentalist" will not have as accurate a guess as the "market psychologist" concerning the first factor determining the rate of return from purchasing the stock, i.e., the value the market will assign to the stock at the point he expects to sell. None of the evidence supporting the efficient market hypothesis is inconsistent with this view of the market as having an irrational component.

In any potential purchaser's determination of his expected return, a universal payout rule increases the importance of the second factor, dividends, and decreases the importance of the first factor. If the first factor is less important, the psychology of the market is less important and participants will focus more of their attention on predicting real events.

This effect of a universal payout rule on the secondary market would in turn have a salutary effect on the role of the outside sector of the finance process in determining project choice. Primary offerings of established public companies are in essence sold into the secondary market. More accurate pricing in the secondary market is thus likely to increase the accuracy of the price of primary issues when sold into that market, thereby improving the matching of funding decisions with the projects having the highest predicted expected return. More accurate pricing in the secondary market would also improve the functioning of the market for corporate control in its disciplining effect on corporate management and the effectiveness of stock price based compensation schemes as incentives for good managerial performance.[99]

Some of this increased accuracy in the pricing of primary issues may be traded off for a reduction in the real resources—saver's costs and recipient's costs—devoted to moving funds through the outside sector. As we saw in chapter 2, most of these expenditures are devoted to the processing of information to achieve a given level of matching funding decisions with the projects having the highest predicted return. The more accurate the prices are in the secondary market, the less resources need to be devoted to such information processing in order to achieve the existing level of matching. In any event, whether the change in the stock market's focus leads to more accurate pricing of primary issues and a better functioning market for corporate control or to lower costs in the operation of the finance process, the economy gains.

3.14 *Impact of a Universal Payout Rule on Corporate Debt/Equity Ratios*

Because a universal payout rule would cause firms to substitute external finance, which would be either debt or equity, for internal finance, which is inevitably equity, it is possible that the rule would lead to a general increase in corporate debt/equity ratios. Whether a significant increase in corporate debt/equity ratios would be harmful to the economy is a matter of debate,* but in any event the possibil-

---

*An increase in corporate debt/equity ratios is likely to lead to an increase in bankruptcies and, for our purposes, their equivalent—reorganizations in anticipation of bankruptcy. One argument that debt/equity ratio increases are therefore harmful starts with the proposition that a firm in bankruptcy or reorganization may discontinue an operating business even if, absent this financial event, the operating business would, shorn of fixed payments on debt, have had a positive expected cash flow. A profit-maximizing, all-equity firm would choose to continue to operate such a business, but the firm facing bankruptcy may not. This is because the complexity of the additional financial rearrangements necessary to permit continuation of the operating business by the bankrupt firm may involve administrative costs that are higher than the parties are willing to bear, because the operating business misses essential opportunities while it is tied up in the proceedings, or because of a breakdown in consumer or supplier confidence in the continued viability of the business. While some of the expected costs associated with business discontinuation of this sort may be considered by the actors whose actions determine the debt/equity ratio and weighed against whatever expected benefits that the chosen ratio offers, other costs, in particular worker displacement and community decay, may not be.

Another possible problem arises from the fact that under the current tax regime,

ity that the rule would lead to such a major financial restructuring deserves investigation. The question is examined here by first considering the likely effect of a universal payout rule in a world without taxes and then considering its effect given the existing tax regime and given the proposed reforms discussed above—full and partial integration of corporate and personal income taxes. The conclusion is that a universal payout rule without a change in the existing tax regime would increase corporate debt/equity ratios but that if either of the reforms were adopted, the combined effect of the payout rule and the reform would be to reduce corporate debt/equity ratios from their current levels.

3.141. *World Without Taxes*

There are good theoretical reasons for believing that in a world without taxes there exists an equilibrium debt/equity ratio for each individual firm and one for all corporations in the aggregate, each

some of the benefits of leverage are pecuniary rather than real. The actors whose actions are determining the ratio are weighing expected real costs—the "agency" costs of monitoring a levered firm and the adminstrative and other costs of bankruptcy and reorganization—against these pecuniary benefits. Thus, the real costs of the ratio chosen may exceed the real portion of the benefits. If a universal payout rule would exacerbate this problem by adding to the tax incentives for leverage, that would be a cause for concern.

Finally, a significant increase in corporate debt/equity ratios may be harmful from a macroeconomic point of view. Because the performance of corporations are positively correlated, an economy of highly levered corporations might be susceptible to a massive wave of bankruptcies occurring during a general economic downturn much less severe than the Depression of the 1930s. Such a wave might be disastrous because of its effect on the confidence of investors, who by living previously in a less levered world are used to thinking of bankruptcy as a very occasional thing, and because of the organizational strains it would impose on financial institutions.

Balanced against these arguments are a series of claims relating to their assumptions: the administrative and other costs of bankruptcy may be exaggerated,[100] the expected costs of bankruptcy on workers and communities may be reflected in firm contracts with these constituencies and thus considered in the determination of the debt/equity ratio,[101] and investors may rationally interpret the bankruptcy of a highly levered corporation as a less significant indicator of bad economic times than the bankruptcy of a less levered one. Furthermore, to the extent, as discussed in the text below, that there are real benefits from leverage as a way of economically satisfying different investor tastes and beliefs, management-controlled corporations may currently be underlevered because the managers who choose the ratio are risk averse and, unlike investors, cannot diversify. If a universal payout rule increases corporate debt/equity ratios, it will act as an antidote to this problem.

of which would be unaffected by a universal payout rule. At the firm level, this proposition stems from the agency theory of the firm. Jensen and Meckling suggest that outside shareholders and debt holders each need to monitor management to control for conflicts, in the first case, between the interests of outside shareholders and management and, in the second case, between the interests of debt holders and shareholders. In the case of each group, the costs of its monitoring increase more than proportionally as the share of its contribution to the capital of the firm increases. There is a crossover point representing the debt/equity ratio with the lowest total monitoring costs. Market forces should push the firm toward this least cost solution.[102] Particularly important is the concept that the monitoring costs associated with a level of debt less than the scrap value of the firm's assets are much lower than these costs when the debt increases to a level greater than the scrap value.[103] There is some empirical evidence supporting this theory. Corporations carried long-term debt on their balance sheets before the introduction of the corporate income tax, and, as is the case today, firms in physical capital intensive industries such as steel and utilities had high debt/equity ratios and firms in service industries had low debt/equity ratios.[104]

As discussed in chapter 1 (section C1.2), heterogeneous expectations on the part of investors concerning the probability distribution of the future earnings of the firm can also lead to an optimal debt/equity ratio with the group that views the distribution as having a lower mean preferring bonds and the group with the opposite view preferring equity.

The proposition that there is an equilibrium aggregate corporate debt/equity ratio for corporations as a group arises from the fact that investors vary in their taste for risk. While unsystematic risk can be eliminated by diversification, systematic risk cannot. The existence of a premium for systematic risk suggests that some investors are, for a price, willing to take on risks that other investors are willing to pay the same price to be rid of. One way that this allocation of risk could be handled would be for corporations to issue only equity securities and for investors to make risk-reallocating transactions among themselves. Thus, if A is less risk averse than B and their portfolios are otherwise the same, A might purchase 100 shares of the all-equity X corporation by borrowing half the purchase price from B. The loan would be secured by a pledge of the shares and be on a nonrecourse basis. The financial position of A is the same as if he held 50 shares of X and X had a debt/equity ratio of 1/1; it is riskier than if he had purchased 50 shares of the actual all-equity X with all cash. The financial position of B is the same as if he held a bond of X and X had a debt/equity ratio of 1/1; it is less risky than if he had purchased 50 shares of the actual all-equity X with all cash.

If there are thousands of investors like A and thousands like B, it may be preferable for this reallocation of risk to be accomplished by the corporation itself through maintenance of a 1/1 debt/equity ratio. There will be economies of scale from the corporation doing the borrowing because of reduced transaction costs (though these in part could be replicated by the As' and Bs' investing in a financial intermediary which would act in a fashion parallel to the way the As and Bs would otherwise act independently). More important, management representing shareholders who all hold shares on margin will presumably be just as inclined to follow the same policies intended to enrich the shareholders at the expense of the lenders as would the management of a firm with no margin shareholders but a 1/1 debt/equity ratio. But lenders to individual shareholders cannot establish constraints on corporate behavior and monitor adherence to these constraints as easily as lenders to corporations, so they are likely to insist on a higher rate of interest.*

In equilibrium, no one corporation needs to satisfy the preferences of the As and Bs because its securities will satisfy the tastes of some group of investors. If the range of securities offered by all corporations does not match the range of investor taste in risk characteristics and quantity, some corporations can take advantage of their economies in reallocating risks among investors and, by altering their debt/equity ratios, obtain funds at a bargain rate. Eventually an equilibrium will be reached at which point any single corporation need not concern itself with its debt/equity ratio in terms of any possible gain by reallocating risk among investors.

If these theories as to equilibrium debt/equity ratio for firms individually and for corporations in the aggregate are correct and the system is in equilibrium, a universal payout rule would have no effect on debt/equity ratios in a world without taxes. An individual

---

*Lenders to individual shareholders could insist on a proxy to vote the shares pledged to them, but this arrangement switches the relevant governance group to the opposite extreme.

firm that in response to the rule substituted external debt for internal equity would incur higher agency costs of capital than would one that substituted external equity for internal equity. Market forces would encourage the first firm to return to its initial debt/equity ratio. If imposition of the rule initially leads to an increase in the aggregate corporate debt/equity ratio, some firms would take advantage of their low-cost ability to reallocate investor risk and reduce their cost of capital by lowering their debt/equity ratios until the equilibrium was reestablished.

3.142 *A World with Taxes*

We saw earlier in this chapter (section B2.12) that the aggregate corporate debt/equity ratio is higher under the current tax regime than in a world without taxes. If the current tax regime were unaltered, the imposition of a universal payout rule would be likely to aggravate the problem. Under the current regime without a payout rule, the attractiveness of debt arising from the corporate income tax deductibility of interest is counteracted to some extent by the fact that the individual tax on the portion of the return on equity constituting capital gains is tax deferred and has historically been at a lower rate (zero if held to death) than the rate applying to the return on bonds and to the dividend portion of the return on equity. The overall effective tax rate on the return on equity, t_s in equation (6.1), is a weighted average of the rate on the capital gains portion and the rate on the dividend portion. Imposition of a universal payout ratio would increase t_s by increasing the portion of equity return paid in dividends and thereby reduce or eliminate the attraction of equity that counteracts the interest deductibility of debt.

Miller's model, described in the earlier discussion, can be easily used to show this effect. It can be seen from equation (6.1) that the gains from leverage disappear when the value of t_b (the personal income tax rate of the marginal bond-buying clientele) reaches the point such that $(1 - t_b) = (1 - t_c)(1 - t_s)$. That value of t_b increases when t_s increases. Thus, to reach equilibrium, corporations will issue more debt because, with equity less attractive, a smaller premium over the risk-adjusted rate of return on equity needs to be paid persons in higher tax brackets for corporate bonds to be attractive to them.

A universal payout rule is not likely to be adopted, however, without the accompaniment of some kind of changes in tax law because it would otherwise result in a large increase in the amount of taxes derived from investment income. Full integration and partial integration of corporate and personal income taxes are two types of proposed reforms that, by eliminating the double taxation on dividends, would respond to this problem, and, as discussed earlier, have broad support because they serve a number of other goals as well.

We have seen that if full integration were adopted, there is no tax-induced gain for corporations to issue any debt (see section B2.2). Applying (6.1), $t_c = 0$ and $t_s = t_b$ for all clienteles. Debt/equity ratios are determined by the actions of the relevant actors as in a world without taxes where $t_c = t_s = t_b = 0$. Therefore, total integration would reduce the existing aggregate debt/equity ratio to the level it would be at if there were no taxes, and if the analysis above concerning a world without taxes is correct, imposition of a universal payout rule would leave the aggregate ratio at this reduced level. Similarly, imposition should have no effect on the reduced individual firm ratios.

If only partial integration were adopted, the analysis of the effect of the imposition of a universal payout rule depends on the proportion of earnings required to be paid out. A rule requiring payout of all earnings would, as with full integration, result in there being no tax-induced gain for corporations to issue debt. This can be seen by referring back to equation (6.2) and setting $X = 1$ to represent full payout. The relevant actors should act as if they were in a world of no taxes, and the equilibrium values of individual firm and aggregate corporate debt/equity ratios should remain unchanged. If less than all earnings are required to be paid out, there will continue to exist a tax inducement to issue some debt. But, as shown in the discussion earlier concerning the effect of partial integration on the aggregate corporate debt/equity ratio (section B2.2), the combined effect of partial integration and a universal less than total payout rule (i.e., $0 < X < 1$) will be to reduce the aggregate debt/equity ratio from the one existing under the current tax regime. And, by referring back to equation (6.4), one can see that the higher the payout ratio (i.e., the value of X), the lower t_b and the less debt is issued by corporations.

3.2 *Formulating an Administratively Practical Universal Payout Rule*

The discussion of the universal payout rule has so far been in terms of its effect: a rule that would assure that large, publicly traded corporations would generally pay out to shareholders some minimum portion, perhaps all, of their earnings and depreciation. That leaves the question of what the actual content of the rule should be to make it administratively practical.

Fortunately we have some historical experience to help guide us in our effort at formulation. New Jersey, North Carolina, and New Mexico each enacted statutes in the late nineteenth or early twentieth century requiring all, or a set percentage of all, profits to be paid out as dividends.[105] Each of the states had a somewhat different formula and each amended its statute once or more in significant ways. In some cases there was a proviso allowing an amount to be set aside as an addition to working capital, and in some cases there was a proviso that permitted a majority of shareholders on an annual basis to ratify a greater retention of earnings for any purpose. None of the statutes is still in effect, and the general consensus of scholars who have studied the cases decided under them is that they did not work well.[106] This suggests that we should survey these cases in order to identify the types of problems that arose under these older universal payout rules. Such a survey will permit us to determine which of these problems are still relevant and how to formulate a modern universal payout rule that would avoid them.

The first type of problem revealed by the cases was the interpretation of key statutory terms, such as "accumulated profits."[107] The terms were not defined in the statutes and they had no clear meaning on their face. Modern accounting conventions combined with more careful statutory drafting would make this kind of problem much less severe today. These problems of interpretation were aggravated by the fact that the statutes appear to have been viewed unsympathetically by most judges who applied them. The statutes were in derogation of common law in an era when most judges believed that statutes in derogation of common law should be construed in a fashion that would result in the minimum deviation from what the result would have been under the common law.[108] The opinions also suggest that many judges clearly believed that corporations would be hobbled if they were not able to expand their real investment base using internally generated funds.[109] Furthermore, the statutes appear to be the result of populist antibusiness sentiments, which were better represented in state legislatures than on the judiciary. The development of a vast outside capital market and the changes in judicial attitude toward statutory interpretation and business in general suggest that a universal payout statute would not today encounter the same kind of judicial resistance.

A second type of problem was shareholders who waited a number of years while the corporations in question violated the statute and then brought actions demanding payment of all back dividends owed.[110] By that point most of the accumulated profits were in the form of fixed assets or inventory. Judges were understandably reluctant to hand down orders that would force large-scale liquidation of these assets. This problem too would be less significant with the development of outside capital markets. It could be largely eliminated by providing that an action for dividends based on violation of the universal payout rule would have a relatively short statute of limitations.

The final problem that the cases reveal is that any rule that directly requires a large percentage of profits to be paid out in dividends will, if enforced without exceptions, work an extreme hardship on some corporations.[111] Unlike the other problems, modern developments are not likely to have reduced its importance. A growing firm, for example, may require increases in working capital at a time when it may not be easy to borrow for such purposes. A firm may feel a need to retain profits in the form of liquid assets to cover possible financial reverses in the future. A firm also may need to retain earnings in order to comply with restrictions on dividends that were necessary to agree to in order to obtain debt financing. Provisos in some of the statutes tried to deal with these problems to some extent, but in rather awkward ways.[112] Because the amount of retention genuinely needed for these kinds of reasons is difficult for anyone but management to ascertain, any effort to draft exceptions into a rule directly requiring a percentage of profits or cash flow to be paid out in dividends is likely to have one of three results: the exception ends up being too narrow and the rule still imposes hardship on certain firms; the exception, by being broad enough to cover all these cases, ends up being a gaping loophole; or the exception gives a great deal of discretion to the court, which is likely to apply it in an unpredictable hit-or-miss fashion because it must second-guess management without having management's knowledge of the specific facts or general expertise. Thus, any formulation of a universal payout rule directly requiring payment of dividends that does not impose severe hardships but is still effective enough to accomplish its underlying purposes is likely to come at the cost of imposing on corporate management significant uncertainty concerning its applicability in particular cases and of significantly increasing the amount of corporate litigation.

A different, more indirect approach to increasing corporate payouts from that taken in the old statutes offers a way out of this quandary. Rather than focusing on the level of dividends per se, the rule could focus on the real concerns of this chapter: the relationship between how much a corporation invests and how much outside financing it seeks. This rule would require each large, publicly traded corporation to seek outside financing each year in the form of long-term debt or equity in an amount (the "base amount") equal to a given percentage of all additions to property, plant, and equipment as revealed by its accounting statements. Liberal carryforward and carryback provisions would give management the flexibility to raise outside finance at the times it considers most advantageous rather than require perfect annual synchronization of the amount of capital spending and the amount of outside capital raised. Were it thought desirable in order to reduce costs, the rule could be qualified along the lines discussed above to count funds freed up by the exercise of a dividend reinvestment option as outside financing.

Management under the proposed formulation would have the same freedom to determine its level of dividends as it does now. Therefore it could determine without restriction how much of its earnings to retain to increase working capital, to cover future contingencies, to meet restrictions imposed by debt financings, etc. Management would not be motivated to retain earnings in any given year in excess of the amount needed for these purposes and for any portion of expenditures on property, plant, and equipment allowed to be internally financed (either because the percentage of the base amount that must be externally financed is less than 100 percent or because the current expenditure is being made in anticipation of a future external financing that will be credited to the current period through a carryback). The only use for the excess would be long-term investment in liquid assets, a type of investment that does not produce any special benefits for management. Thus, the typical corporation in an average year would distribute to shareholders a percentage of its total earnings and depreciation approximately equal to the percentage of the base amount that must be financed externally.

Consideration should be given to adding two items to the base amount for each year. The first is any principal repayments made on long-term debt outstanding at the beginning of the year. If such payments are not included, even a growing firm (i.e., one that during the year undertakes more real investment than the loss in value of its existing investments because of obsolescence or wear) could, through recapitalization of existing debt, satisfy the rule and maintain its debt/equity ratio without engaging in any outside equity finance. This may be undesirable, since external equity finance involves more outside finance process involvement and greater disclosure than does debt finance. The second item is acquisitions of shares of other firms in amounts large enough to be illiquid. If such acquisitions are not added to the base amount, imposition of the rule in the form proposed might result in some corporations building up "war chests" for takeovers of other corporations instead of increasing their dividends.

D. Conclusion

This chapter demonstrates how the findings of this book concerning the relationship between finance and industrial performance can illuminate issues of public policy. The chapter focuses on the impact of the legal structure on one component of the finance process: the dividend behavior of large corporations. The law has a blind spot concerning dividends. Almost no attention is paid to the consequences for industrial performance of the significant, unintended impact of securities law and tax law on the dividend behavior of large corporations. And the part of the law that purports to regulate this behavior directly regulates by not regulating: there are essentially no limits on the discretion of the managers of large corporations to determine the level of dividends.

One reason for this blind spot is that the neoclassical theory of finance leads one to underestimate the importance of dividend behavior for industrial performance. If one believes that the finance process operates as if all participants were equally well informed, money and good ideas should not have trouble finding each other. There is no need for the law to interfere purposefully in the dividend decision of corporate managers for this happy union to happen, and if the law interferes accidentally, forces within the process are likely to find a way around the problem. But if one abandons the equal information assumption, dividends become very important because they determine who participates in what ways in the decision of the finance process concerning which proposed real investment projects are implemented and which are not.

A second reason for the blind spot is that even among persons who suspect that the dividend decision is important, they do not know what to do with that suspicion.[113] The preceding chapters provide criteria by which to judge what pattern of dividends we want and empirical information useful in applying these criteria. The conclusion is that a greater flow of dividends would be desirable, particularly from certain firms but generally as well.

This conclusion suggests certain changes in law. First, the SEC's integrated disclosure program should be completed so that firms face the same pressures for disclosure and risks of liability whether they choose to engage in public offerings or not. This change would eliminate the current incentive to retain earnings in order to avoid a public offering. At the same time it would improve the quality of periodic disclosure by firms not regularly engaging in public offerings. Second, the partial or total integration of corporate and personal taxes should be implemented. This would largely eliminate the pressure on management to retain earnings in order to improve the tax positions of most shareholders. The final, most radical suggestion is that large, public corporations should be required to finance externally a certain minimum percentage, perhaps all, of their real investments. Such a proposal would accomplish the twin goals of moving funds out of firms that fund inferior projects with retained earnings and of increasing the participation of the outside finance process in project choice generally with the attendant effect of increasing the economy's dynamic efficiency.

The increased understanding of the relationship between finance and industrial performance yielded by the approach of this book has policy relevance that goes beyond the issue of dividends. Several other issues associated with the regulation of the finance process could be fruitfully explored. Consider these examples.

1. How great are existing incentives for a participant in the outside finance process to seek out and analyze bits of information in order to make a better assessment of its prospects and thus enhance the accuracy of the firm's share price? This question is related to the regulation of insider trading, since these incentives will depend on how much of the nonrandom profits in the trading of the firm's shares go to those with inside information.
2. What kinds of information should a corporation be able to keep secret from outside investors? This question is related to the kinds of questions asked of public corporations in securities law filings and the policy of the SEC in granting confidentiality in certain cases to the answers.
3. How easy is it for an employee of a corporation who has an investment idea to form a "spin-off" to implement the idea if his employer will not implement the idea or will not implement it on terms sufficiently rewarding to the employee to attract him to stay? In essence, should the legal system in this situation favor rewards for talent or for capital? This question relates to the rules in agency and corporate law of employee loyalty and corporate opportunity.

A better understanding of these issues, as in the case of dividends, could make a real contribution to the improvement of the industrial performance of our economy in the coming decades.

Notes

Part I

1. The Question of Approach

1. M. Friedman, *Essays in Positive Economics* (Chicago: University of Chicago Press, 1953).

2. There is the possibility that the proponent can sell the idea to another firm, but this is an infrequent route to implementation. See chapter 2, section B 2.11.

3. The contexts in which a proponent may propose its idea are elaborated in chapter 2; see section B 2.12. The reasons why it is unlikely that a proponent can have an idea considered in more than one context are discussed in chapter 2, section C 2.422.

4. At least at a theoretical level, there is always a conflict of interest between debt holders and shareholders in terms of the desirable level of riskiness of the firm's investments. Shareholders can be viewed as having sold the firm to debt holders subject to the grant to shareholders of a call option that is exercised by timely payment of debt service. For any given expected return on investment, a call option holder prefers as much risk as possible and the grantor of the option as little as possible. Black and Scholes, "The Pricing of Options and Corporate Liabilities," *J. Pol. Econ.* (1973), 81:637–654. However, as will be elaborated in chapter 2, the management of a large corporation, even though elected by shareholders, is likely under most circumstances to share the conservative bias of the debt holders. Jensen and Meckling make the same point: "Theory of the Firm: Managerial Behavior, Agency Cost, and Ownership Structure," *J. Fin. Econ.* (1976), 3:305–360, p. 353.

5. This is not always made explicit in the models, but it is implied. J. March and H. Simon point out that it is difficult to give meaning to the term "rationality" if the actors cannot assign a probability distribution to the various states of nature. *Organizations* (New York: Wiley, 1958), p. 138. For the behavior of the actors to be objectively rational, their internal perception of the real probability distribution must be an accurate one.

6. Modigliani and Miller, "The Cost of Capital, Corporation Finance, and the Theory of Investment," *Am. Econ. Rev.* (1958), 48:261–297. Modigliani and Miller do not deal explicitly with the question of differing beliefs; they assume the market will assign a firm to an appropriate "risk class." J. Stiglitz demonstrates that uniform expectations, when combined with the existence of a fixed-rate safe asset infinitely elastic in supply and with investors evaluating income streams in terms of mean and variance only, constitute a sufficient condition for the Modigliani and Miller proposition. "A Re-examination of the Modigliani-Miller Theorem," *Am. Econ. Rev.* (1969), 59:784–

793. He also shows that any one of three other conditions is sufficient, but as Stiglitz has observed elsewhere, none of the other conditions bears much resemblance to institutional reality. See "Some Aspects of the Pure Theory of Corporate Finance: Bankruptcies and Takeovers," *Bell J. Econ.* (1972), 3:458–482.

7. A. Berle and G. Means, *The Modern Corporation and Private Property*, rev. ed. (New York: Harcourt, Brace and World, 1968).

8. W. Baumol, *Business Behavior, Value, and Growth*, 2d ed. (New York: Harcourt, Brace and World, 1967), pp. 45–53; R. Marris, "A Model of 'Managerial' Enterprise," *Q. J. Econ.* (1963), 77:185–209; O. Williamson, "Managerial Discretion and Business Behavior," *Am. Econ. Rev.* (1963), 53:1032–1057; O. Williamson, *Corporate Control and Business Behavior* (Englewood Cliffs, N.J.: Prentice-Hall, 1970). Other studies generally considered to constitute part of the "managerial school" include: R. Marris, *The Economic Theory of Managerial Capitalism* (London: Macmillan, 1974); R. A. Gordon, *Business Leadership in the Large Corporation* (Washington: Brookings Institution, 1945); A. G. Papandreos, "Some Basic Problems in the Theory of the Firm," in B. Haley, ed., *A Survey of Contemporary Economics*, (Homewood, Ill: Irwin, 1952), pp. 183–219; R. Mosan, J. Chiu, and R. Cooley, "The Effect of Separation of Ownership from Control on the Performance of the Large Firm," *Q. J. Econ.* (1968), 82:435–451. The managerial theory is discussed further in chapter 2, section B 3.221.

9. H. Simon, "Theories of Decision-Making in Economics and Behavioral Science," *Am. Econ. Rev.* (1959), 49:253–283; J. March and H. Simon, *Organizations;* R. Cyert and J. March, *A Behavioral Theory of the Firm* (Englewood Cliffs, N.J.: Prentice-Hall, 1963).

10. H. Simon, "Theories of Decision-Making," p. 263.

11. March and Simon, *Organizations*, p. 139.

12. Oliver Williamson, in an important and pioneering work, does try to apply the learnings of the managerial and behavioral literature on the theory of the firm to a number of antitrust policy issues. *Markets and Hierarchies: Analysis and Antitrust Implications* (New York: Free Press, 1975). However, the specific industrial organization policy issues which he addresses do not require him to develop a managerial or behavioral theory of industrial organization. See chapter 2, section C 3, for an extended discussion of Williamson's work as it relates to the finance process and industrial performance.

13. See J. Stiglitz, "Some Aspects of the Pure Theory of Corporate Finance," on which this discussion is based. See also J. Stiglitz, "On the Irrelevance of Corporate Financial Policy," *Am. Econ. Rev.* (1974), 64:851–866; A. Robicheck and S. Myers, "Problems in the Theory of Optimal Capital Structure," *J. of Financial and Quantitative Analysis* (June 1966), 1:1–35; J. H. Scott, Jr., "A Theory of Optimal Capital Structure," *Bell J. Econ.* (1976), 7:33–54. Stiglitz's second article ostensibly supports the Modigliani and Miller conclusion but only on the basis of a set of assumptions which Stiglitz admits are seriously flawed. He analogizes the Modigliani and Miller proposition to a theorem in physics which does not take account of friction.

The discussion here abstracts away three considerations that lead most applied finance theorists to conclude that there is an optimal financial structure: taxes, "agency costs," and administrative and transaction costs associated with bankruptcy. A small amount of debt deprives the firm of the tax deductions arising from interest payments. A large amount of debt creates a significant conflict of interest between debt holders and shareholders that requires expensive supervision by debt holders to prevent management from making decisions contrary to debt holder interests. It also increases the chances of bankruptcy, which involves significant real costs. See, for example, Brigham, *Financial Management: Theory and Practice*, 3d ed. (Chicago: Dryden Press, 1982), pp. 641–666. The fact that there is an optimal debt/equity ratio means that if the firm is not at that ratio, the cost of capital from using one source of funds is different from using the other.

14. See appendix 1.1 for a more complete description of this way of looking at the respective subjective probability distributions of a future event of two persons with different levels of information.

15. J. Meyer and E. Kuh, *The Investment Decision* (Cambridge: Harvard University Press, 1957). These findings are confirmed and extended in J. Meyer and R. Glauber, *Investment Decisions, Economic Forecasting, and Public Policy* (Boston: Graduate School of Business Administration, Harvard University, 1964). Other adherents of the "cash flow" theory of investment for use in macroeconomic forecasting include J. Duesenberry, *Business Cycles and Economic Growth* (New York: McGraw-Hill, 1958); W. L. Anderson, *Corporate Finance and Fixed Investment* (Boston: Graduate School of Business Administration, Harvard University, 1964).

16. Meyer and Kuh, *The Investment Decision*, p. 138. Internal funds are still the dominant source of corporate finance. See chapter 2, section B 3.

17. G. Donaldson, *Corporate Debt Capacity* (Boston: Graduate School of Business Administration Harvard University, 1961), pp. 51–67. See a more extensive discussion of this study in appendix 2.1.

18. Meyer and Kuh, *The Investment Decision,* pp. 142–153.

19. A. Alchian, "Uncertainty, Evolution, and Economic Theory," *J. Pol. Econ.* (1950), 58:211–221; M. Friedman, *Essays in Positive Economics*, pp. 19–23.

20. S. Winter, "Economic Natural Selection and the Theory of the Firm," *Yale Econ. Essays* (1964), 4:225–272.

21. Williamson, *Markets and Hierarchies*, pp. 216, 229.

22. Winter, "Economic Natural Selection and the Theory of the Firm."

23. S. Grossman and O. Hart, using a somewhat different analysis, come to the conclusion that the management of firms which have financed large fixed costs with equity are less constrained in their discretion by product competition than other firms. "Takeover Bids, the Free Rider Problem, and the Theory of the Corporation," *Bell J. Econ.* (1980), 11:42–64.

24. H. Manne, "Mergers and the Market for Corporate Control," *J. Pol. Econ.* (1965), 73:110–120; See also, H. Manne and H. Wallich, *The Modern Corporation and Social Responsibility* (Washington, D.C.: American Enterprise Institute, 1972).

25. Manne, "Mergers and the Market for Corporate Control," p. 112. Manne states, "A fundamental premise underlying the market for corporate control is the existence of a high positive correlation between corporation managerial efficiency and the market price of shares of that company," and then goes on to propose his arbitrage theory. It appears that Manne includes among his best-informed investors corporate management, but, given restrictions on trading by management, particularly on short selling, it seems unlikely that they, as opposed to the best-informed nonmanagement investors, could perform this function.

26. There are other defenders of the modern corporation who believe that control reassignment via hostile takeover is an extremely sensitive mechanism. See, for example, S. Peterson, "Corporate Control and Capitalism," *Q. J. Econ.* (1965), 79:1–24. Few persons would argue, however, that a takeover via a pure proxy battle, with the alternative management group owning only a few shares, is likely to succeed in any but the most egregious case of mismanagement. See O. Williamson, *Corporate Control and Business Behavior*, p. 98. A proxy context may succeed in giving the dissidents

some minority representation on the board. See Dodd and Warner, "On Corporate Governance: A Study of Proxy Contests," *J. Fin. Econ.* (1983), 11:401. But for control reassignment, the focus must be on the hostile tender offer.

27. The seminal article reviewing the work to its date that formed the basis for the hypothesis is E. Fama, "Efficient Capital Markets: A Review of Theory and Empirical Work," *J. Finance* (1970), 25:383–417. For a recent overview of literature associated with the hypothesis, see K. Garbade, *Securities Markets* (New York: McGraw-Hill, 1982), pp. 241–259.

28. W. Beaver, "Market Efficiency," *Accounting Rev.* (1981), 56:23–37.

29. It is highly unusual in economics for a hypothesis to evolve without an explicit causative theory. The lack of such a theory has continued to cause some commentators concern since the inception of the hypothesis. See A. Boness and F. Jen, "A Model of Information Diffusion, Stock Market Behavior, and Equilibrium Price," *J. of Financial and Quantitative Analysis* (1970), 5:279–296; S. Figlewski, "Market Efficiency in a Market with Heterogeneous Information," *J. Pol. Econ.* (1978), 86:581–597; R. Verrecchia, "On the Theory of Market Information Efficiency," *J. Accounting and Econ.* (1979), 1:77–90; Beaver, "Market Efficiency," p. 24.

30. Paul Cootner, one of the pioneers in developing the hypothesis, states, for example: "If any substantial group of buyers thought prices were too low, their buying would force up the prices. The same would be true for sellers. Except for appreciation due to earnings retention, the conditional expectation of tomorrow's price, given today's price, is today's price." "Stock Prices: Random vs. Systematic Changes," in P. Cootner, ed., *The Random Character of Stock Market Prices* (Cambridge: MIT Press, 1964), p. 232. Commentators in recent reviews of the efficient market literature suggest that the behavioral paradigm in the minds of most of the adherents of the hypothesis continues to be the simple arbitrage model. T. Copeland and J. Weston, *Financial Theory and Corporate Policy*, 2d ed. (Reading, Mass.: Addison-Wesley, 1983), p. 307; R. Gilson and R. Kraakman, "The Mechanisms of Market Efficiency," *Virginia Law Rev.* (1984), 70:549–644, p. 629 (specifically relating to trading on inside information). Although Paul Samuelson seems at one point to imply the existence of an arbitrage mechanism in his seminal piece establishing that random walk securities prices are consistent with market efficiency, he makes clear at the end of the article that his purpose is not to explain how a market resolves the existence of heterogeneous expectations among its participants. "Proof That Properly Anticipated Prices Fluctuate Randomly," *Industrial Management Rev.* (1965), 6:41–49, pp. 43–44, and 48–49.

The empirical studies have given rise to some recent theoretical studies, discussed in section 2.213, that posit considerably more complex, less intuitive models than the arbitrage model.

31. The simple arbitrage model referred to here should not be confused with the arbitrage pricing theory originated by S. Ross, which predicts that security prices will be a linear function of k factors. "The Arbitrage Theory of Capital Asset Pricing," *J. Econ. Theory* (1976), 13:341–360.

32. Gilson and Kraakman, "The Mechanisms of Market Efficiency," p. 570, n.67.

33. For a general proof, see M. Fox, "The Role of Finance in Industrial Organization" (Ph.D. diss., Yale University, 1980), pp. 445–447.

34. J. Lintner, "The Aggregation of Investors' Diverse Judgments and Preferences in a Purely Competitive Securities Market," *J. of Financial and Quantitative Analysis* (1969), 4:347–400.

35. See, for example, S. Alexander, "Price Movements in Speculative Markets: Trends or Random Walks," and other essays collected in P. Cootner, ed., *The Random Char-*

acter of Stock Market Prices. For reviews of studies in this group, see Fama, "Efficient Capital Markets," pp. 391–396; Garbade, *Securities Markets,* pp. 241–249.

36. Samuelson is credited with first identifying the consistency between random walk pricing and the efficient market hypothesis: "Proof That Properly Anticipated Prices Fluctuate Randomly." He does not, however, claim that such pricing is inconsistent with situations where the price does not reflect every bit of information held by one or more investors. In a subsequent article that elaborates upon his seminal piece, Samuelson finds no incompatibility between the existence of a group of better-informed persons that do better than average investors without affecting prices appreciably and stock prices behaving like a random walk. *Bell J. Econ. and Management* (1973), 4:369–373.

37. See, for example, E. Fama, L. Fisher, M. Jensen, and R. Roll, "The Adjustment of Stock Prices to New Information," *International Econ. Rev.* (1969), 10:1–21; W. Beaver, "The Information Content of Annual Earnings Announcements," *Empirical Research in Accounting: Selected Studies, 1968* (Chicago: Institute of Professional Accounting, University of Chicago, 1969); R. Pettit, "Dividend Announcements, Security Performance, and Capital Market Efficiency," *J. Finance* (1972), 27:993–1007. For reviews of studies in this group, see Fama, "Efficient Capital Markets," pp. 404–409; Garbade, *Securities Markets,* pp. 249–259.

38. M. Jensen, "The Performance of Mutual Funds in the Period 1945–1964," *J. Finance* (1968), 23:389–416.

39. *Ibid.,* p. 410.

40. *Ibid.,* pp. 410, 415.

41. See, for example, W. Sharpe, "Mutual Fund Performance," *J. Business* (1966), 39:119–138; P. Williamson, "Measuring Mutual Fund Performance," *Financial Analysts J.* (November-December 1972), 28:78–84; J. McDonald, "Objectives and Performance of Mutual Funds, 1960–1969," *J. of Financial and Quantitative Analysis* (1974), 9:311–333.

42. *Institutional Investor Study Report of the Securities and Exchange Commission* (Washington, D.C.: GPO, 1971), House Doc. 92–64, 2:327.

43. N. Mains, "Risk, the Pricing of Capital Assets, and the Evaluation of Investment Portfolios: Comment," *J. Business* (1977), 50:371–384.

44. Friend, Blume, and Crockett, *Mutual Funds and Other Institutional Investors: A New Perspective* (New York: McGraw-Hill, 1970), pp. 57–58 (using a market average weighted by market values of the stocks involved); R. Carlson, "Aggregate Performance of Mutual Funds, 1948–1967," *J. of Financial and Quantitative Analysis* (1970), 5:1–32. Carlson maintains that results of this type of study are highly dependent on the index used as a surrogate for a market portfolio. He concludes that "generalizations based on all types of mutual funds with a single market index for one selected period are of limited value," p. 11. K. Cohen and J. Pogue, "An Empirical Evaluation of Alternative Portfolio-Selection Methods," *J. Business* (1967), 40:166–193 (comparison of funds with efficient portfolios calculated from *ex ante* efficiency frontiers). Roll points out a paradox connected with the CAPM that both explains why the choice of index can affect the conclusions about mutual fund performance and casts serious doubt on the validity of tests of fund performance that use market-derived cross-sectional measures of systematic risk to adjust the observed returns of each fund. If the index represents a portfolio which happens to be *ex post* efficient, i.e., on a mean/variance efficiency frontier constructed using the performance on individual securities during the period under study, no adjusted deviation from the index of the performance of a fund's portfolio will show up as anything but chance. If instead the

index represents a portfolio that is *ex post* inefficient, the comparison between the performance of the fund and the index is entirely arbitrary and depends on which index is chosen. R. Roll, "A Critique of the Asset Pricing Theory's Tests," *J. Fin. Econ.* (1977), 4:129–176.

45. F. Arditti, "Another Look at Mutual Fund Performance," *J. of Financial and Quantitative Analysis* (1971), 6:909–912. Arditti maintains that the distribution of returns are in fact not normal but have fat tails, which means that it may be rational to take an additional variability in exchange for a better chance at a big gain.

46. This percentage is as of 1977. M. Blume and I. Friend, *The Changing Role of the Individual Investor* (New York: Wiley, 1978), p. 4. Homer Kripke makes the same argument: *The SEC and Corporate Disclosure: Regulation in Search of a Purpose* (New York: Harcourt Brace Jovanovich, 1979), pp. 84–85. The assumption underlying the argument is that on average other institutional traders have information of similar quality and quantity to that possessed by the mutual fund managers.

47. J. Murphy, "Efficient Markets, Index Funds, Illusion and Reality," *J. Portfolio Management* (1977), 4:5–20.

48. See T. Copeland and J. Weston, *Financial Theory and Corporate Policy*, 2d ed. (Reading, Mass.: Addison-Wesley, 1983), pp. 204–211, 305–307.

49. *Ibid.* See also discussion of Roll, "A Critique of the Asset Pricing Theory's Tests," in note 44.

50. Watts, "Systematic Abnormal Returns After Quarterly Earnings Announcements," *J. Fin. Econ.* (1978), 6:127; Charest, "Split Information, Stock Returns, and Market Efficiency–I," *J. Fin. Econ.* (1978), 6:265.

51. J. Gordon and L. Korhnauser, "Efficient Markets, Costly Information, and Securities Research," *N.Y.U. Law Rev.* (1985), 60:761–849.

52. For a model that divides investors into two such classes, see Grossman and Stiglitz, "The Impossibility of Informationally Efficient Markets," *Am. Econ. Rev.* (1980), 70:393–408.

53. See, for example, R. Verrecchia, "On the Theory of Market Information Efficiency," *J. Accounting and Econ.* (1979), 1:77–90.

54. M. Fox, "The Role of Finance in Industrial Organization," pp. 418–427. I set out a model of the relationships between an investor's level of knowledge and his influence on prices from which it is clear that the accuracy of the market price as a forecast of future returns is a positive function of the accuracy of each investor's forecast.

55. See, for example, Grossman, "On the Efficiency of Competitive Stock Markets Where Traders Have Diverse Information," *J. Finance* (1976), 31:573–585; Grossman, "Further Results on the Informational Efficiency of Competitive Stock Markets," *J. Econ. Theory* (1978) 18:81–101.

56. Grossman and Stiglitz, "The Impossibility of Informationally Efficient Markets."

57. Keynes, *The General Theory of Employment, Interest, and Money* (New York: Harcourt, Brace, 1936), p. 156.

58. W. Baumol, *The Stock Market and Economic Efficiency* (New York: Fordham University Press, 1965).

59. See, for example, J. Tobin and W. Brainard, "Asset Market and the Cost of Market," in B. Belassa and R. Nelson, eds., *Economic Progress, Private Values, and Public Policy: Essays in Honor of William Fellner* (Amsterdam: North-Holland, 1977), pp. 235–262.

60. Modigliani and Cohn, "Inflation, Rational Valuation, and the Market," *Financial Analysts J.* (March-April 1979), 35:24–44.

61. See, for example, J. Tobin, "On the Efficiency of the Financial System," mimeo, Hirsh Memorial Lecture, May, 15, 1984, pp. 6–10.

62. R. Shiller, "Do Stock Prices Move Too Much To Be Justified by Subsequent Changes in Dividends?" *Am. Econ. Rev.* (1981), 71:421–436.

63. See, for example, Sheffrin, *Rational Expectations* (Cambridge: Cambridge University Press, 1983), pp. 145–150 (reviewing possible explanations of the data consistent with stock market rationality).

64. K. Arrow, "Control in Large Corporations," *Management Science* (1964), 10:404. See also Stigler, "The Economics of Information," *J. Pol. Econ.* (1961), 69:213.

65. Adherents of the "agency theory" of the firm, for example, view the firm as a set of "contracts" among factors of production, in particular between suppliers of capital and of managerial services. It is in the interest of both parties to establish structures for monitoring and controlling managerial behavior because such devices increase the value of the firm, which increase can be shared by the two parties. See chapter 2, section B 3.3, for a further discussion of this theory.

"Signaling theory" is another approach to the question of management motivation to supply useful information to the market. Firms with good news will want to disclose it, and firms that say nothing will be assumed by the market not to be in possession of good news. See S. Ross, "The Economics of Information and Disclosure Regulation," in F. Edwards, ed., *Issues in Financial Regulation* (New York: McGraw-Hill, 1979). This assumes that managers' motivation in deciding what information to disclose is motivated by the desire to maximize share price.

66. Kripke, *The SEC and Corporate Disclosure*, pp. 121–122.

67. Williamson makes both these points: "On the Governance of the Modern Corporation," *Hofstra Law Rev.* (1979), 8:63–78, p. 76.

68. J. Lorie and V. Niederhoffer, "Predictive and Statistical Properties of Insider Trading," *J. Law and Econ.* (1968), 11:35–53. See also J. Jaffe, "Special Information and Insider Trading," *J. Business* (1974), 47:410–428; and J. Finnerty, "Insiders and Market Efficiency," *J. Finance* (1976), 31:1141–1148.

69. M. Scholes, "The Market for Securities: Substitution Versus Price Pressure and the Effects of Information on Share Prices," *J. Business* (1972), pp. 179–211.

70. O. Williamson, *Markets and Hierarchies*, p. 142.

71. Monsen and Downs, "A Theory of Large Managerial Firms," *J. Pol. Econ.* (1965), 73:225.

72. The 13% figure comes from R. Smiley, "Tender Offers, Transaction Costs, and the Theory of the Firm," *Rev. of Econ. and Statistics* (1976), 58:22–32, p. 32. Smiley also concludes that in his sample the value of the equity of the average firm that was the target of a successful tender offer was half what it would have been if the firm had been run in an optimal fashion during the ten years preceding the offer. S. Hayes and R. Tausig, in a survey of tender offer premiums in the 1960s (friendly, hostile, and in-between), found a range from 0 to 44% of the market price prevailing two days before the offer is announced with the figure tending toward the high side in hostile situations. "Tactics of Cash Takeover Bids," *Harvard Business Rev.* (1967), 45(2):135–148, p. 140. These figures would be significantly larger if, like Smiley, the authors added in fees paid investment bankers, share solicitors, and lawyers. Bradley found the average premium in a successful tender offer to be 49%. "Interfirm Tender Offers and the Market for Corporate Control," *J. Business* (1980), 53:345–376, p. 345. Jarrel and Bradley found that the state takeover statute movement in the 1970s raised the average takeover premium to 70%. "The Economic Effects of Federal and State Regulation of Cash Tender Offers," *J. Law and Econ.* (1980), 23:371–407. Subsequent

legal developments have probably reduced their role as an impediment to takeovers, however. See *Edgar v. Mite Corp.*, 457 U.S. 624 (1982), which declared the Illinois statute unconstitutional.

73. Brian Hindley uses a different approach to estimate how much incumbent management has to underperform before it need fear a takeover and comes up with a figure within the range suggested by the other studies. He compares the ratio of book value to market value for corporations which are taken over to the ratio for those in the same industries which are not taken over. From this, he estimates that the ones taken over have on average the potential of increasing earnings by 30% with better management. "Separation of Ownership from Control in the Modern Corporation" *J. Law and Econ.* (1970), 13:185–221, pp. 199–200.

74. O. Williamson, *Corporate Control and Business Behavior*, p. 99.

75. D. Kuehn, "Stock Market Valuation and Acquisitions," *J. of Industrial Econ.* (1969), 17:132–144 (relationship of firm size to risk of takeover).

76. E. Herman, *Corporate Control, Corporate Power* (Cambridge: Cambridge University Press, 1981), p. 50.

77. See, for example, J. Coffee, "Shareholders versus Management: The Strain in the Corporate Web,"mimeo, presented at the Conference on Takeovers and Contests for Corporate Control, Columbia University Center for Law and Economic Studies, November 14, 1985.

78. Martin Shubik, for example, has suggested that there are two different markets, one for individual shares and one for the control of corporations. "Corporate Control, Efficient Markets, the Public Good, the Law and Economic Theory and Advice," mimeo, presented at the Conference on Takeovers and Contests for Corporate Control, Columbia University Center for Law and Economic Studies, November 14, 1985.

79. M. Jensen, "The Takeover Controversy: Analysis and Evidence," mimeo, presented at the Conference on Takeovers and Contests for Corporate Control, Columbia University Center for Law and Economic Studies, November 15, 1985.

80. Schumpeter, *The Theory of Economic Development*, Redvers Opie, tr. (Cambridge: Harvard University Press, 1934).

81. The literature in this area is now enormous. The following are some of the seminal works: E. Mansfield, *The Economics of Technical Change* (New York: Norton, 1968); R. Nelson, M. Peck, and E. Kalachek, *Technology, Economic Growth, and Public Policy* (Washington, D.C.: Brookings Institution, 1967); J. Jewkes, D. Sawers, and R. Stillerman, *The Sources of Invention*, 2d ed. (New York: Norton, 1969).

82. Formal modeling of this essentially Schumpeterian approach to industrial organization dates back to A. Alchian, "Uncertainty, Evolution, and Economic Theory." For increasingly sophisticated efforts at describing the entry and exit conditions, growth paths, and technology search processes, see S. Winter, "Economic Natural Selection and the Theory of the Firm"; S. Winter, "Satisficing, Selection, and the Innovating Remnant," *Q. J. Econ.* (1971), 85:237–261; R. Nelson and S. Winter, "Neo-classical vs. Evolutionary Theories of Economic Growth: Critique and Prospectus," *Econ. J.* (1974), 84:886–905; R. Nelson and S. Winter, "Simulation of Schumpeterian Competition," *Am. Econ. Rev.* (1977), 67:271–276; R. Nelson and S. Winter, "Forces Generating and Limiting Concentration Under Schumpeterian Competition," *Bell J. Econ.* (1978), 9:524–548; R. Nelson and S. Winter, "The Schumpeterian Tradeoff Revisited," *Am. Econ. Rev.* (1982), 72:114–132; R. Nelson and S. Winter, *An Evolutionary Theory of Economic Change* (Cambridge: Harvard University Press, 1982). Nelson and Winter attribute their interest in the Schumpeterian approach to their difficulty in reconciling much of the modern literature concerning innovation with neoclassical theory. Their fundamental

objection to the neoclassical approach is the lack of reality in the assumption that production functions are well defined. Without this assumption, they point out, the concept of profit maximization is meaningless.

83. Nelson and Winter, "Neo-classical vs. Evolutionary Theories of Economic Growth," p. 895.

84. For a more formal exposition of the points of this appendix, see Samuelson, "Proof That Properly Anticipated Prices Fluctuate Randomly."

85. See, for example, S. Ekern and R. Wilson, "On the Theory of the Firm in an Economy with Incomplete Markets," *Bell J. Econ.* (1974), 5:171–180.

2. A General Theory

1. R. Coase, "The Nature of the Firm," *Economica* (1937), N.S. 4:386–405. See also J. Commons, *Industrial Economics* (New York: Macmillan, 1934). Problems with the price mechanism include: the costs of discovering what the relevant prices are; and the dilemma between the cost of negotiating and concluding a separate contract for each exchange transaction and the inflexibility of a long-term contract to avoid these transaction costs.

2. Coase, "The Nature of the Firm," p. 391.

3. Kenneth Arrow discusses these second and third reasons why an employment relationship may be the superior forum for information transfer in "Economic Welfare and the Allocation of Resources for Invention," in R. R. Nelson, ed., *The Rate and Direction of Inventive Activity* (Princeton: National Bureau of Economic Research, 1962), pp. 616–618. For discussions by Arrow that more explicitly consider the aspects of information that help define the borderline between decisions made by formal organizations and those made by the market, see K. Arrow, *The Limits of Organization* (New York: Norton, 1974), pp. 33–43; K. Arrow, "Vertical Integration and Communication," *Bell J. Econ.* (1975), 6:173–183.

4. O. Williamson, *Markets and Hierarchies* (New York: Free Press, 1975), p. 36.

5. *Ibid.*, pp. 197–199.

6. Arrow, "Comment," in R. R. Nelson, ed., *The Rate and Direction of Inventive Activity*, p. 355.

7. Williamson, *Markets and Hierarchies*, p. 205.

8. T. Kuhn, in his analysis of revolutions in scientific thinking, identifies an ability to separate oneself from existing paradigms as a precondition for revolutionary new discovery. *The Structure of Scientific Revolutions*, 2d ed. (Chicago: University of Chicago Press, 1970), pp. 77–109. It is reasonable to believe the same concept applies in the case of innovation with respect to much narrower and more specific paradigms. See also Schumpeter, *The Theory of Economic Development* (Cambridge: Harvard University Press, 1934).

9. Z. Block, "Can Corporate Venturing Succeed?" *J. Business Strategy* (Fall 1982), 3:21–33; N. Fast, "A Visit to the New Venture Graveyard," *Research Management* (March 1979), 22:18–22.

10. J. Jewkes, D. Sawers, and R. Stillerman, *The Sources of Invention*, 2d ed. (New York: Norton, 1969). There are a number of other studies that give a feeling of the different ways an inventor or proponent can put forward an idea for implementation in a particular industry or a particular period in history. See W. Strassmann, *Risk and Technological Innovation: American Manufacturing Methods During the Nineteenth Century* (Ithaca: Cornell University Press, 1959); F. Scherer, "Invention and Innovation in the

Watt-Boulton Steam Engine Venture," *Technology and Culture* (1965), 6:165–187; M. Peck, "Inventions in the Postwar American Aluminum Industry," in R. Nelson, ed., *The Rate and Direction of Inventive Activity: Economic and Social Factors*, pp. 279–298; J. Enos, "Invention and Innovation in the Petroleum Industry," in R. Nelson, ed., *The Rate and Direction of Inventive Activity*, pp. 299–322; W. Mueller, "The Origins of the Basic Inventions Underlying DuPont's Major Product and Process Innovations, 1920–1950," in R. Nelson, ed., *The Rate and Direction of Inventive Activity*, pp. 323–346; A. Bright, *The Electric Lamp Industry* (New York: Macmillan, 1949); J. Enos, *Petroleum Progress and Profits* (Cambridge: MIT Press, 1962); R. Miller and D. Sawers, *The Technical Development of Modern Aviation* (London: Rutledge and Kegan Paul, 1968). Some sense of the problems of implementing an innovation by establishing a new company can be obtained from W. Miller, *Men in Business* (Cambridge: Harvard University Press, 1952); J. W. Gough, *The Rise of the Entrepreneur* (London: Batsford, 1969); E. Roberts, "Entrepreneurship and Technology," *Research Management*, 1 (1958).

11. J. Schumpeter, *Capitalism, Socialism, and Democracy*, 3d ed. (New York: Harper, 1950), p. 106; J. K. Galbraith, *American Capitalism*, rev. ed. (Boston: Houghton Mifflin, 1956).

12. Jewkes, Sawers, and Stillerman, *Sources of Invention*, pp. 152–162.

13. F. M. Scherer, *Industrial Market Structure and Economic Performance*, 2d ed. (Boston: Houghton Mifflin, 1980), pp. 417–418.

14. See, for example, R. Monsen and A. Downs, "A Theory of Large Managerial Firms," *J. Pol. Econ.* (1965), 73:221–236; A. Downs, *Inside Bureaucracy* (Boston: Little, Brown, 1967).

15. Williamson, *Markets and Hierarchies*, pp. 135–148, 158–162. For further discussion of Williamson's M-form hypothesis, see section C 3.

16. E. Herman, *Corporate Control, Corporate Power* (Cambridge: Cambridge University Press, 1981), pp. 61–62.

17. *Ibid.*, pp. 62–63.

18. As an indication, of the largest 200 nonfinancial corporations (a more inclusive group than the industrials), an individual or family held more than 10% of the shares of only 21. *Ibid.*, pp. 59–60. These figures are almost exactly the same as those of John Palmer, "The Separation of Ownership from Control in Large U.S. Industrial Corporations," *Q. Rev. Econ. and Business* (1972), 12:55–62. For evidence that shareownership becomes more concentrated as one goes further down the list of industrial firms ranked by size, see H. Demsetz, "The Structure of Ownership and the Theory of the Firm," *J. Law and Econ.* (1983), 26:378–390.

19. These estimates were assembled from several different sources of data. The first was the *Fortune* 500 list of the largest industrial corporations (manufacturing and mining) for 1977. "The Fortune Directory of the 500 Largest Industrial Corporations," *Fortune*, May 8, 1978, pp. 240–259. This list ranks corporations by sales but it lists the assets of each. Assuming that the largest 500 by sales includes the largest 200 by assets, the *Fortune* 500 list can be used to generate lists of the largest 100 and the largest 200 industrial corporations ranked by assets. The total assets for the largest 100 and 200 ranked by assets can each be divided by the figure for the total assets of manufacturing and mining sectors of the U.S. economy developed by the Internal Revenue Service on the basis of 1977 tax returns. U.S. Bureau of the Census, *Statistical Abstract of the United States: 1981*, 102d ed., Washington, D.C., chart 921, p. 543 (hereinafter *1981 Statistical Abstract*). This showed that 42% of the sector's assets were controlled by the top 100 and 53% by the top 200.

Another approach is to look at the percentage of manufacturing sector assets that are controlled by the largest manufacturing firms. Manufacturing dominates the industrial sector, with 499 of the largest 514 in the industrial sector being manufacturing firms. U.S. Federal Trade Commission data show that in 1980 the largest 244 manufacturing firms ranked by asset size, those with over $1 billion in assets, controlled 64% of the manufacturing sector's assets and the largest 613, those with over $250 million in assets, controlled 77% of the sector's assets. *1981 Statistical Abstract*, chart 921.

A third approach, using the Internal Revenue Service 1977 tax return figures again, shows that the largest 514 industrial corporations, those with over $250 million in assets, controlled 74% of the sector's assets.

Consistent with these other figures, Michael Pertschuk, then chairman of the FTC, estimated in congressional testimony that in 1977, the largest 200 manufacturing corporations controlled 60% of all manufacturing assets and that in 1976, 451 firms controlled 70% of all manufacturing assets. U.S. Congress, Senate Judiciary Committee, Subcommittee on Antitrust and Monopoly, *Mergers and Industrial Concentration*, 95th Cong., 2d sess. (Washington, D.C.: GPO, 1978), p. 155.

20. U.S. census figures show that in 1977 the 100 largest manufacturing firms, ranked by value added, were responsible for 40% of the sector's new investment, and the largest 200 were responsible for 49% of the sector's new investment. U.S. Bureau of the Census, *1977 Census of Manufacturers*, vol. 1: *Subject Statistics* (Washington, D.C.: 1977), table 4, p. 9–9.

21. Federal Reserve data show that for the period 1976–1980 for all nonfarm, nonfinancial corporations, internal sources of funds (domestic undistributed profits, depreciation, and foreign earnings) as a percentage of capital expenditures averaged 87%. *1981 Statistical Abstract*, chart 938. A private survey cited by Herman of U.S. corporations in mid-1979 revealed that they planned to finance 90% of their 1979 capital expenditures by internal funds. *Corporate Control, Corporate Power*, p. 357.

22. See G. Donaldson, *Corporate Debt Capacity* (Boston: Harvard University School of Business Administration, 1961), pp. 39–44. This study is discussed in appendix 2.1, together with an updating study performed by me.

23. There is a limited body of serious scholarship concerning the use of new ideas by established firms. See, for example, T. Burns and G. Stalker, *The Management of Innovation* (London: Tavistock Publications, 1961); J. Bright, *Research, Development, and Technological Innovation* (Homewood, Ill.: Irwin, 1969); A. Rubenstein, "Organization and Research and Development Decision-Making Within the Decentralized Firm," in R. Nelson, ed., *The Rate and Direction of Inventive Activity*, pp. 385–394; E. Roberts, "Entrepreneurship and Technology"; Burton Klein, *Dynamic Economics* (Cambridge: Harvard University Press, 1977). There are a number of studies which employ the interview methods of empirical social science to explore how businesses evaluate investment opportunities and choose which to invest in. See, for example, R. Eisner, *Determinants of Capital Expenditures* (Urbana: University of Illinois Press, 1956); J. Bower, *Managing the Resource Allocation Process* (Boston: Harvard Business School, 1970); C. Istivan, *Capital Expenditure Decisions* (Bloomington: Indiana University Press, 1961); M. Solomon, *Investment Decisions in Small Firms* (Lexington: University of Kentucky, 1965). See also R. Wright, *Investment Decision in Industry* (London: Chapman Hall, 1964); A. Chandler, *Strategy and Structure* (Cambridge: MIT Press, 1962); W. Strassmann, "The Risks of Innovation in Twentieth Century Manufacturing Methods," *Technology and Culture* (1964), 5:215–223.

24. Williamson, *Markets and Hierarchies*, pp. 122–127; Monsen and Downs, "A Theory of Large Managerial Firms," *J. Pol. Econ.* (1975), 73:221–236, pp. 227–231.

25. Klein, *Dynamic Economics*, pp. 78, 82. The assumption behind this explanation is that each firm has a somewhat different range of tolerance. The combined range of four to eight firms would presumably be broad enough to give a good new idea a chance to be picked up by at least one firm. To the extent that intensity of research and development effort is a surrogate measure for technological advance, Klein's conclusion is supported by Scherer's study of industries in "low or intermediate technological fields." Scherer found the maximum research and development intensity was in industries with four-firm concentration ratios of 50–55%. "Market Structure and the Employment of Scientists and Engineers" *Am. Econ. Rev.* (1967), 57:524–531, esp. pp. 529–530.

26. A. Downs, *Inside Bureaucracy* (Boston: Little, Brown, 1967), pp. 18–20.

27. R. Mack, *Planning on Uncertainty* (New York: Wiley-Interscience, 1971), pp. 55–58.

28. J. Meyer and E. Kuh, *The Investment Decision* (Cambridge: Harvard University Press, 1957), p. 94.

29. C. F. Carter and B. R. Williams, *Investment in Innovation* (London: Oxford University Press, 1958). The unstated assumptions behind the causal link they see are that the supply of capital is not perfectly elastic and that investors demand no risk premium for risks uncorrelated with other risks in the economy.

30. See discussion in appendix 2.2 of H. Grabowski and D. Mueller, "Life-Cycle Effects on Corporate Returns and Retentions," *Rev. of Econ. and Statistics* (1975), 57:400–416.

31. R. Marris, "The Corporation and Economic Theory," in R. Marris and A. Wood, eds., *The Corporate Economy* (London: MacMillan, 1971), pp. 270–317.

32. See H. Wilensky, *Organizational Intelligence* (New York: Basic Books, 1968), pp. 94–109.

33. See, for example, J. Van Horne, *Financial Management and Policy*, 6th ed. (Englewood Cliffs, N.J.: Prentice-Hall, 1983), pp. 182–206. The capital asset pricing model is discussed in chapter 1, section C 2.2123.

34. The idea that managers gain utility simply from the size of the firm they run has a long history. See, for example, F. Knight, *Risk, Uncertainty, and Profit* (Boston: Houghton Mifflin, 1921); J. A. Schumpeter, *The Theory of Economic Development*; R. Gordon, *Business Leadership in the Large Corporation* (Washington, D.C.: The Brookings Institution, 1945).

35. This point was repeatedly made in the interviews conducted in connection with the semiconductor industry study; see chapter 4, section 1.22. Williamson also points out that expansion is a way of settling disputes among managers. *Markets and Hierarchies*, p. 120.

36. See, for example, R. Hayes and W. Abernathy, "Managing Our Way to Economic Decline," *Harvard Business Rev.* (July-August 1980), 58(4):67–77; S. Loescher, "Managerial Perogatives of Corporate Secrecy: Monopolizing 'Private' Information and Deterrence of (Nonconsented) Wrongs," unpublished paper presented at session on Asymmetric Information at the annual meeting of the American Economic Association, December 28, 1982.

37. W. Fellner, *Competition Among the Few* (New York: Knopf, 1949), pp. 172–173.

38. R. Gordon, *Business Leadership in the Large Corporation*, p. 324; R. Monsen and A. Downs, "A Theory of Large Managerial Firms," pp. 225–226.

39. K. Boudreaux, " 'Managerialism' and Risk-Return Performance," *Southern Econ. J.* (1973), 39:366–372.

40. See J. Palmer, "The Profit Variability Effects of the Managerial Enterprise," *Western*

Econ. J. (1973), 11:228–231; R. Larner, *Management Control and the Large Corporation* (New York: Dunellen, 1970), p. 31.

41. W. McEachern, *Managerial Control and Performance* (Lexington, Mass: Lexington Books, 1975), pp. 104–107.

42. The increasing diversity of large U.S. firms since the turn of the century, and particularly since World War II, is impressive. For a survey, see F. Scherer, *Industrial Market Structure and Economic Performance*, pp. 74–78.

43. W. Baumol, *Business Behavior, Value, and Growth* (New York: Macmillan, 1959).

44. W. Baumol, *Business Behavior, Value, and Growth*, rev. ed. (New York: Harcourt, Brace and World, 1967).

45. R. Marris, *The Economic Theory of "Managerial" Capitalism* (London: Macmillan, 1967).

46. O. Williamson, *Corporate Control and Business Behavior* (Englewood Cliffs, N.J.: Prentice-Hall, 1964).

47. See *Prudent Real Estate Trust v. Johncamp Realty, Inc.*, 599 F.2d 1140, 1147 (2d Cir. 1979) (Judge Friendly discusses the importance of the offeror's financial position to the shareholder's decision); Exchange Act Release 5844, July 28, 1977, 42 FR 38341–51, which explains the filing and disclosure requirements under Schedule 14D-1 of the Williams Act; and Borden and Weiner, "An Investment Decision Analysis of Cash Tender Offer Disclosure," *N.Y.L.S.L. Rev.* (1978), 23:553–646

48. J. Lintner, "Distribution of Incomes of Corporations Among Dividends, Retained Earnings, and Taxes," *Am. Econ. Rev.* (May 1956, Papers and Proceedings), 46:97–118.

49. See, for example, J. Freund, *Anatomy of a Merger*, 2d ed. (New York: Law Journal Press, 1976).

50. F. Scherer, "Mergers, Sell-Offs, and Managerial Behavior," mimeo draft, 1985, pp. 7–9.

51. See Financial Accounting Standards Board, "Financial Reporting for Segments of a Business Enterprise" (Statement of Financial Accounting Standards No. 14); SEC Form 10-K, Item 1; SEC Regulation S-K, Item 101(b); and Securities Act Release 5910 (March 3, 1968).

52. See J. Lorie and M. Hamilton, *The Stock Market: Theories and Evidence* (Homewood, Ill.: Irwin, 1973), pp. 142–156, for a discussion of how the wide variety of available accounting options can lead to like firms having very different reported incomes. See also, "What Are Earnings? The Growing Credibility Gap," *Forbes*, May 15, 1967, pp. 28–34.

53. J. Kamin and J. Ronen, "The Effects of Corporate Control on Apparent Profit Performance," *Southern Econ. J.* (1978), 45:181–191.

54. Meyer and Kuh report that businessmen in an interview survey suggested that concern with maintaining market share is second only to the liquidity restraint in determining the level of their investment. *The Investment Decision*, p. 22.

55. F. Easterbrook, "Two Agency-Cost Explanations of Dividends", *Am. Econ. Rev.* (1984), 74:650–661, p. 654.

56. It should be noted that while agency cost explanations of management behavior often have suggestive value, their power of explanation has, as discussed in Section B 3.3, often been exaggerated. See also V. Brudney, "Corporate Governance, Agency Costs, and the Rhetoric of Contract," *Columbia Law Rev.* (1985), 85:1403–1444.

57. This may be a partial explanation for what Williamson describes as a tendency for organizations to display "persistence," a phenomenon also noted by Downs and March and Simon. *Markets and Hierarchies*, p. 121.

58. See, in general, M. Zausner, *Corporate Policy and the Investment Community* (New York: Ronald Press, 1968); J. Derriman, *Company Investor Relations* (London: University of London Press, 1965); T. A. Wise, *The Insiders: A Stockholder Guide to Wall Street* (Garden City, N.Y.: Doubleday, 1962), pp. 117–169.

59. Interviews taken in the semiconductor study confirmed the importance that managers put on good press relations. See chapter 4, section 1.32.

60. See, for example, Alchian and Demsetz, "Production, Information Costs, and Economic Organization," *Am. Econ. Rev.* (1972), 62:777–795; Jensen and Meckling, "Theory of the Firm: Managerial Behavior, Agency Costs, and Ownership Structure," *J. Fin. Econ.* (1976), 11:305–360; Fama, "Agency Problems and the Theory of the Firm," *J. Pol. Econ.* (1980), 88:288–307; Fama and Jensen, "Separation of Ownership and Control," *J. Law and Econ.* (1983), 26:301–325.

61. Jensen and Meckling, "Theory of the Firm," p. 310.

62. *Ibid.*, p. 313.

63. Fama, "Agency Problems," p. 295.

64. Jensen and Meckling, "Theory of the Firm," pp. 327–328.

65. *Ibid.*, pp. 313–319.

66. See, for example, D. Carlton and D. Fischel, "The Regulation of Insider Trading," *Stanford Law Rev.* (1983), 35:857–895, p. 869.

67. Jensen and Meckling, "Theory of the Firm," p. 356.

68. Fama, "Agency Problems," p. 295.

69. *Ibid.*

70. *Ibid.*, pp. 295–302.

71. *Ibid.*, p. 301.

72. The desirability of such an arrangement results from three factors: such investments have increasing returns to the firm in relation to the length of employment; the marginal cost of exercising the skill is less than the cost of acquiring it; and long-term labor contracts have inherent problems. For a discussion of the effects of these factors and of both causes of deviation between the internal and external wage, see M. Aoki, *The Cooperative Game Theory of the Firm* (Oxford: Clarendon Press, 1984), pp. 24–27.

73. J. Veiga, "Mobility Influences During Managerial Career Stages," *Academy of Management J.* (1983), 26:64–85, p. 81; G. Cohn, "An Executive's Quest for a New Job," *The Wall Street Journal*, November 19, 1985, p. 35.

74. Fama, "Agency Problems," pp. 292–293.

75. *Ibid.*

76. Fama and Jensen, "Separation of Ownership and Control," p. 308.

77. *Ibid.*, p. 309.

78. *Ibid.*

79. *Ibid.*, pp. 314–315.

80. *Ibid.*, p. 315.

81. *Ibid.*

82. Fama, "Agency Problems," p. 294.

83. Schmidt, "Does Board Composition Really Make a Difference?" *Conference Board Record* (1975), 12:38–50; L. Solomon, "Restructuring the Corporate Board of Directors: Fond Hope—Faint Promise?" *Michigan Law Rev.* (1978), 76:581–610; V. Brudney, "The Independent Director—Heavenly City or Potemkin Village?" *Harvard Law Rev.* (1982), 95:597–659, p. 616; L. Soderquist, "Toward a More Effective Corporate Board: Reexamining Roles of Outside Directors," *New York University Law Rev.* (1977), 52:1341–1363, pp. 1350–1357.

84. Fama and Jensen, "Separation of Ownership and Control," p. 301.

85. Fama, "Agency Problems," p. 289.

86. Securities and Exchange Commission, *Monthly Statistical Review* (August 1981), 40:8.

87. R. Soldofsky, *Institutional Holdings of Common Stock, 1900–2000* (Ann Arbor: University of Michigan, 1971), p. 209.

88. Edward Herman carefully surveyed the role that financial intermediaries play in the governance of nonfinancial corporations. He finds: "The picture conveyed by the given data suggests that holdings among institutional majors are large enough to have an inherent control significance are sparse." *Corporate Control, Corporate Power*, p. 146. With respect to the smaller holdings financial intermediaries do have, he also concludes that they still generally adhere to the "Wall Street Rule," i.e., they sell the stock of firms the management of which they find inept rather than using their share votes to seek a change in management. This corresponds with the conclusion of the SEC's *Institutional Investor Study Report* ten years earlier, that institutional votes against managements and abstentions from voting in general "seem to be a relatively infrequent phenomenon having little discernible impact on portfolio companies." 92d Cong., 1st sess., House Doc. No. 92–64 (Washington, D. C.: GPO, 1971), 5:2755.

89. The mechanisms by which funding sources outside the firm influence the composition of management are discussed in chapter 1, section A 2. Herman surveys a number of these mechanisms, including the conditioning of future underwriting services, lending, and waiver of restrictive covenants in loan agreements on management changes. He also examines voting and purchase and sale behavior by financial intermediaries at the time of an all-out proxy fight or hostile tender offer. *Corporate Control, Corporate Power*, pp. 114–161. Herman's general conclusion is that while such mechanisms can be very influential in specific cases, generally "financial power in the 1970's appears to constitute a strongly conservative force, accommodating and serving the dominant nonfinancial elements in the community. It does not dominate the large corporation, but what influence it has tends to press for actions that will enhance credit worthiness and profit growth" (p. 161). Baum and Stiles come to a similar conclusion, *The Silent Partners: Institutional Investors and Corporate Control* (Syracuse: Syracuse University Press, 1965), p. 176. This discussion suggests that the main role of financial intermediaries in limiting management discretion is indirect: their influence on security prices as highly knowledgeable investors improves the functioning of the takeover threat.

90. Since principals work within an organization, the fact that they are motivated to obtain as accurate evaluations as possible does not guarantee success. See chapter 2, section B 4.2.

91. Henry Manne discusses in detail networks by which confidential information is exchanged. *Insider Trading and the Stock Market* (New York: Free Press, 1966), pp. 61–75. While his focus is on bits of information which individually are sufficiently important to be considered "material" under the securities law, such networks are also important for bits which individually do not assume that degree of importance but which, when received in a flow over time, improve the recipient's ability to evaluate the firm.

92. U.S. Dept. of Commerce Advisory Committee on Technology and Innovation, *Technological Innovation: Its Environment and Management* (Washington, D.C.: GPO, 1967) p. 43.

93. The relationship between intermediaries and technically based new companies is explored in A. Shapero et al., *The Role of the Financial Community in the Formation,*

Growth, and Effectiveness of Technical Companies: The Attitude of Commercial Loan Officers (Austin, Texas: Multidisiplinary Research, 1969) A. Rubenstein, *Problems of Financing New Research Based Enterprises in New England* (Boston: Federal Reserve Bank of Boston, 1958).

94. S. Ross,"The Determination of Financial Structure: An Incentive Signaling Approach," *Bell J. Econ.* (1977), 8:23–40.

95. Judge Medina's opinion in *United States v. Morgan* contains an excellent, though somewhat dated, survey of the investment banking industry, which stresses the limited number of such relationships possessed by each existing firm. 118 F. Supp. 621, 817 (S.D.N.Y. 1953). Herman suggests that because of the difficulties that commercial banks have assessing the risks of lending to firms, particularly short-term, the typical firm only has one or a few banks to which to turn. *Corporate Control, Corporate Power*, p. 122. The combination of the need for a firm to have authority in the eyes of the funding source with the high degree of concentration of U.S. capital markets in the late nineteenth century may explain much of the increase in industrial concentration at that time, a period when technological change suddenly forced firms to seek large amounts of capital. L. Davis, "The Capital Markets and Industrial Competition: The U.S. and the U.K., a Comparative Study," *Econ. History Rev.* (1966), 19:255–272, pp. 263–268.

96. H. Kripke, *The SEC and Corporate Disclosure: Regulation in Search of a Purpose* (New York: Harcourt Brace Jovanovich, 1979), pp. 121–122.

97. Under the Internal Revenue Code, a fund need pay no income tax if it distributes to its shareholders 90% of its gross income from dividends and interest. Most funds make a practice of distributing all of their net income. J. Springer, *The Mutual Fund Trap* (Chicago: Henry Regnery, 1973), p. 174.

98. The determination of management fees is not entirely an unregulated market phenomenon. Section 36(b) of the Investment Company Act provides that the management company shall have a fiduciary duty to the fund with respect to the compensation it receives. There has been very little litigation involving this section, but the language implies that there must be a reasonable relationship between the management fee and the value of the services rendered. Jennings and Marsh, *Securities Regulation*, 5th ed. (Mineola, N.Y.: Foundation Press, 1982), pp. 1398–1402.

99. Banks in the United States had a sufficiently difficult time in the nineteenth century developing authority in the eyes of savers and in the eyes of each other that Lance Davis concludes that a national capital market cannot really be said to have existed until about 1914. There was a wide divergence of interest rates offered by the major city banks in different regions of the country before that date. This suggests that savers simply did not trust banks they did not know well, and intermediaries did not trust each other sufficiently to arbitrage away the difference. "The Investment Market, 1870–1914; The Evolution of a National Market," *J. Econ. History* (1965), 25:355–393.

100. Underwriters performed this function long before the passage of the Securities Act. See Herman, *Corporate Control, Corporate Power*, pp. 114–121; Douglas and Bates, "The Federal Securities Act of 1933," *Yale Law J.* (1933), 43:171. The function has continued to be important since passage. C. Israeals and G. Duff, *When Corporations Go Public* (New York: Practicing Law Institute, 1962), p. 43. Gilson and Kraakman suggest that the concern of underwriters with their reputation explains the evidence that suggests they underprice new securities. "The Mechanisms of Market Efficiency," *Virginia Law Rev.* (1984), 70:549–644, pp. 613–622.

101. There is evidence, however, that investors who follow the advice of the Value

Line Investor Survey, a subscription service, can make risk-adjusted rates of return substantially above the return of the market as a whole. A survey of several articles concerning this issue is found in Copeland and Weston, *Financial Theory and Corporate Policy*, 2d ed. (Reading, Mass.: Addison-Wesley, 1983), pp. 340–342.

102. Cyert and March conducted a case study of an investment trust officer that was used as empirical support of their behavioral theory of the firm. *A Behavioral Theory of the Firm* (Englewood Cliffs, N.J.: Prentice-Hall, 1963), pp. 253–268. Other organizational studies of financial intermediaries include C. Argyris, *Organization of a Bank* (New Haven: Labor and Management Center, Yale University, 1954); and D. Hayes, *Bank Lending Policies*, 2d ed. (Ann Arbor: Michigan Business Studies, 1977).

103. G. Richardson, *Information and Investment: A Study of the Working of Competitive Economy* (London: Oxford University Press, 1960), p. 59. Compare F. Hayek, "The Use of Knowledge in Society," *Am. Econ. Rev.* (1945), 35:519–530, who states that the central problem in society is whether a centralized or decentralized economy better takes advantage of the information spread among actors in the system and argues strenuously in favor of a market-based decentralized economy.

104. Cybernetics has been used as a heuristic device in the analysis of certain macro-economic stabilization problems. See, for example, R. Allen, *Mathematical Economics* (New York: St. Martin's Press, 1960), pp. 281–313; A. Tunstin, *The Mechanism of Economic Systems* (Cambridge: Harvard University Press, 1953). These studies treat the interrelations among variables as automatic and not as a function of communication flows per se. An interesting study on the cybernetics of the firm is R. McCain, "Competition, Information, Redundancy: X-Efficiency and the Cybernetics of the Firm," *Kyklos* (1975), 28:286–308. McCain argues that competition allows more precise control of firm functions and hence reduces x-inefficiencies (a) because of the information in the form of competitor prices as to the attainable levels of efficiency and in the other forms as to techniques, and (b) because it heightens the importance of a common goal, firm survival, held by all groups within the firm. Oscar Lange observed that the neoclassical model, with its pareto optimal results at equilibrium, is a cybernetic model. *Introduction to Economic Cybernetics* (Warsaw: Polish Scientific Publishers, 1970).

105. K. Deutsch, *The Nerves of Government* (London: Free Press of Glencoe, 1963).

106. *Ibid.*, pp. 185–192. See also chapter 1, section D.

107. See generally, K. Deutsch, *Nerves of Government*; R. Mack, *Planning on Uncertainty*; A. Downs, *Inside Bureaucracy*.

108. J. March and H. Simon, *Organizations* (New York: Wiley, 1958), p. 164.

109. R. Mack, *Planning on Uncertainty*, pp. 123–124.

110. Deutsch, *Nerves of Government*, p. 170.

111. Klein, *Dynamic Economics*, pp. 160–162.

112. Deutsch, *Nerves of Government*, pp. 150–151.

113. Meyer and Kuh, *The Investment Decision*, p. 202.

114. C. Carter and B. Williams, *Investment in Innovation*, p. 72.

115. E. Mansfield, "Entry, Gibrat's Law, Innovation, and the Growth of Firms," *Am. Econ. Rev.* (1962), 52:1023–1051, p. 1036. See also R. Marris, "A Model of 'Managerial' Enterprise," *Q. J. Econ.* (1963), 77:185–209.

116. There has historically been a link between the rate of asset growth and the need for external finance. N. Jacoby and R. Saulnier, *Business Finance and Banking* (New York: National Bureau of Economic Research, 1947), p. 93.

117. Items 501 and 511 of Securities and Exchange Commission Regulations S-X, which is incorporated by reference into the standard forms used to register primary public offerings for cash.

118. See the discussion in Deutsch, *Nerves of Government*, pp. 108–109, 163–165, 172–176.

119. *Ibid.*, p. 174; Mack, *Planning on Uncertainty*, pp. 150–163; Klein, *Dynamic Economics*, pp. 143–144.

120. Klein, *Dynamic Economics*, pp. 160–162.

121. Wilensky, *Organizational Intelligence*, pp. 94–109. Wilensky gives as an example of such a group the Council of Economic Advisers as it functioned in the 1950s and 1960s.

122. *Ibid.*, pp. 76–78.

123. Not all commentators have been as pleased as Wilensky with the creativity in the approach to the Cuban missile crisis. Dean Acheson, a member of the executive committee handling the crisis, later concluded that President Kennedy had been "phenomenally lucky." The President took a "gamble to the point of recklessness" when he decided to answer not the official Soviet note, which conditioned the withdrawal of Cuban missiles on the withdrawal of the (obsolete and soon-to-be-removed) U.S. missiles in Turkey, but rather Khrushchev's "confused" earlier note, which suggested that the Soviets would remove the missiles if the United States would promise not to attack Cuba and end the naval blockade. Although Acheson acknowledged the informality of the "leaderless, uninhibited group" which came to this fortuitous decision, he did not think that this was the proper way to conduct foreign affairs at a moment when the consequence of error would be the end of civilization. See generally, Robert A. Divine, eds., *The Cuban Missile Crisis* (Chicago: Quadrangle Books, 1971), which contains Dean Acheson, "Homage to Plain Dumb Luck," pp. 197, 204–207. See also, Garry Wills, *The Kennedy Imprisonment: A Meditation on Power* (Boston: Little, Brown, 1982).

124. Wilensky, *Organizational Intelligence*, pp. 77, 83, 88–93.

125. Klein, *Dynamic Economics*, pp. 41–42.

126. *Ibid.*, pp. 179–180.

127. *Ibid.*, p. 40. See also a review of several case studies making the same point in Scherer, *Industrial Market Structure and Economic Performance*, p. 431.

128. Klein, *Dynamic Economics*, pp. 82, 95.

129. Deutsch, *Nerves of Government*, p. 254; Mack, *Planning on Uncertainty*, p. 196.

130. Mack, *Planning on Uncertainty*, p. 126.

131. *Ibid.*

132. Deutsch, *Nerves of Government*, pp. 189–190.

133. For a review, see F. Scherer, *Industrial Market Structure and Economic Performance*, pp. 437–438.

134. Comanor, "Market Structure, Product Differentiation, and Industrial Research," *Q. J. Econ.* (1967), 81:639–657. Industries with moderate entry barriers also were found to have a higher R & D intensity than industries with low entry barriers. That finding is consistent with the often-noted observation that industries which resemble textbook perfect competition tend not to be very innovative, apparently because the prospect of rapid imitation means that investment in innovation will not yield high returns. See Scherer, *Industrial Market Structure*, pp. 430–431.

135. *Technological Innovation: Its Environment and Management*, p. 13.

136. R. Greenthal and J. Larson, "Venturing Into Venture Capital," *The McKinsey Quarterly* (Spring 1983), pp. 70–90, p. 74.

137. N. Fast, "Pitfalls of Corporate Venturing," *Research Management* (1981), 24:21–24, p. 22.

138. B. Hunstman and J. Hoban, Jr., "Investment in New Enterprise: Some Empirical Observations on Risk, Return, and Market Structure," *Financial Management* (Summer, 1980), 9:41–51.

139. Ibbotson and Sinquefield, "Stocks, Bonds, Bills, and Inflation: Year by Year Historical Returns (1926–1974)," *J. Business* (1976), 49:11–43, p. 22.

140. For a comprehensive review of the theoretical and empirical literature concerning this relationship, see M. Kamien and N. Schwartz, *Market Structure and Innovation* (Cambridge: Cambridge University Press, 1982).

141. Schumpeter, *Capitalism, Socialism, and Democracy* (New York: Harper, 1942).

142. See, for example, A. Phillips, *Technology and Market Structure: A Study of the Aircraft Industry* (Lexington, Mass.: Heath Lexington, 1971); and D. Webbink, *The Semiconductor Industry*, Federal Trade Commission Staff Report (Washington, D.C.: GPO, 1977). Burton Klein in *Dynamic Economics* uses these two studies along with a study of his own of the U.S. automobile industry (comparing the period before 1930 and the period since 1930) to make his point concerning the virtues of competition in promoting innovation. The study of the semiconductor industry contained in this book also supports this proposition.

Evidence in support of the first theory also comes from several studies that suggest that cartels lower the rate of innovation of an industry. See *Dynamic Economics*, p. 40; Scherer, *Industrial Market Structure*, p. 431.

143. Scherer, *Industrial Market Structure*, pp. 426–430, 435–437.

144. A number of studies have examined the relationship between innovation and the distribution of market shares in an industry. See, for example, E. Mansfield, "Entry, Gibrat's Law, Innovation, and the Growth of Firms," pp. 1023–1051; O. Williamson, "Dominant Firms and the Monopoly Problem: Market Failure Considerations," *Harvard Law Rev.* (1972), 85:1512–1531; R. Nelson and S. Winter, "Forces Generating and Limiting Concentration Under Schumpeterian Competition," *Bell J. Econ.* (1978), 9:524–548. None, however, has focused in any detail on the interaction between innovation and finance as a contributor to concentration.

145. Kamien and Schwartz summarize the debate concerning the "Schumpeterian hypothesis" in *Market Structure and Innovation*. See also F. Scherer, *Industrial Market Structure*, pp. 423–438. Of course, if the "Schumpeterian hypothesis" is correct that the prospect of monopoly profits is a vital inducement for innovation, the tendency of the finance process to encourage concentration when innovation occurs just adds to the inducement.

146. These figures are calculated on the basis of the figures set out in chapter 6, section C 3.11.

147. See section B 3.1 and Grabowski and Mueller, "Life-Cycle Effects on Corporate Returns on Retentions," *Rev. of Econ. and Statistics* (1978), 60:400–409 (discussed in appendix 2.2).

148. In terms of the long "incubation period" of investment in new ventures, see Greenthal and Larson, "Venturing Into Venture Capital," pp. 74–75; N. Fast, "Pitfalls of Corporate Venturing," p. 22; Huntsman and Hoban, "Investment in New Enterprises," pp. 45–47. The problem of starting a new venture capital firm is aggravated by the fact that the minimum scale in terms of the amount of funds that must be attracted is large. The average investment in an innovative new firm, to justify the high search costs, must be large (in the Huntsman and Hoban study, $227,000 in the early 1960s, p. 47). There is a need to make numerous such investments in order to achieve most of the advantages of diversification (in the same study, a series of port-

folios composed of ten venture investments showed a wide variation in returns, showing that significantly more than ten are needed to achieve most of the advantages of diversification, pp. 47–49).

149. Williamson has developed his concept of the M-form firm in numerous pieces over the last ten years. For the most comprehensive treatments, see *Markets and Hierarchies*, pp. 132–175, and "The Modern Corporation: Origins, Evolution, Attributes," *J. Econ. Lit.* (1981), 19:1537–1568.

150. Williamson, "The Modern Corporation," p. 1559.

151. Williamson refers to the M-form conglomerate as a form of organization "whereby the corporation deliberately took on a diversified nature" and that "substitut[es] an administrative interface between an operating division and the stockholders where a market interface had existed previously." "The Modern Corporation," pp. 1557–1558.

152. Williamson, *Markets and Hierarchies*, p. 136; "The Modern Corporation," pp. 1559–1560.

153. Williamson, *Markets and Hierarchies*, pp. 147–148; "The Modern Corporation," p. 1559.

154. Williamson, *Markets and Hierarchies*, pp. 135, 141–143.

155. A. Chandler, *Strategy and Structure* (New York: Doubleday, 1966); A. Chandler, *The Visible Hand: The Managerial Revolution in American Business* (Cambridge: Belknap Press of Harvard University Press, 1977).

156. Williamson, *Markets and Hierarchies*, pp. 133–135, 137; "The Modern Corporation," pp. 1548–1556.

157. Williamson, *The Modern Corporation*, pp. 1558–1560; "Corporate Governance," *Yale Law J.* (1984), 93:1197–1229, p. 1225.

158. Williamson, *Markets and Hierarchies*, pp. 1558–1559; *Markets and Hierarchies*, pp. 145–148.

159. Williamson, *Markets and Hierarchies*, pp. 155–162; "The Modern Corporation," p. 1558. As a basic premise of his "transaction cost economics," Williamson assumes that "transactions will be organized by markets unless market exchange gives rise to serious transaction costs." "The Modern Corporation," p. 1547. Where an organization is substituted for a market relationship, such as the substitution of the M-form conglomerate for independent firm operating units linked only by the external capital market, there is a rebuttable presumption that the organizational substitute economizes on transaction costs (p. 1540).

160. Williamson, "Organization Form, Residual Claimants, and Corporate Control," *J. Law and Econ.* (1983), 26:351–374, p. 357.

161. Williamson, "The Modern Corporation," p. 1559.

162. Williamson implicitly recognizes this point when he discusses the issue of whether line-of-business disclosure (as opposed to only composite disclosure) should be required of diversified corporations. "On the Governance of the Modern Corporation," *Hofstra Law Rev.* (1979), 8:63–78, pp. 75–77.

163. Williamson, *Markets and Hierarchies*, pp. 159–160; "Corporate Governance," pp. 1224–1225.

164. Scherer, "Mergers, Sell-offs, and Managerial Behavior," mimeo draft (1985), p. 1.

165. *Ibid.*, p. 25.

166. *Ibid.*, pp. 7–18.

167. Williamson, *Markets and Hierarchies*, p. 147.

168. *Ibid.*, p. 148.

169. Williamson, "The Modern Corporation," pp. 1558–1559.

170. N. Fast, "A Visit to the New Venture Graveyard," *Research Management* (March 1979), 22:18–22; G. Hardymon, M. DeNino, and M. Salter, "When Corporate Venture Capital Doesn't Work," *Harvard Business Rev.* (May–June 1983), 61(3):114–121; Z. Block, "Can Corporate Venturing Succeed?" *J. Business Strategy* (Fall 1982), 3:21–33; D. Dunn, "The Rise and Fall of Ten Venture Groups," *Business Horizons* (October 1977), 20:32–41.

171. G. Donaldson, *Corporate Debt Capacity* (Boston: Harvard University School of Business Administration, 1961).

172. *Ibid.*, pp. 39–44.

173. *Ibid.*, pp. 57–59.

174. Baumol et al., "Earnings Retention, New Capital, and the Growth of the Firm," *Rev. of Econ. and Statistics* (1970), 52:345–355. See also earlier studies of British firms coming to similar conclusions: I. M. D. Little, "Higgledy, Piggledy Growth," *Bul. of the Oxford Institute of Statistics* (1962), 24:387–412 I. M. D. Little and A. C. Rayner, *Higgledy, Piggledy Growth Again* (Oxford: Blackwell, 1966).

175. G. Whittington, "The Profitability of Retained Earnings," *Rev. of Econ. and Statistics* (1972), 54:152–160; I. Friend and F. Husic, "Efficiency of Corporate Investment," *Rev. of Econ. and Statistics* (1973), 55:122–127; R. Brealey, S. Hodges, and D. Capron, "The Return on Alternative Sources of Finance," *Rev. of Econ. and Statistics* (1976), 58:469–477.

176. Baumol et al., "Efficiency of Corporate Investment: Reply," *Rev. of Econ. and Statistics* (1973), 55:128–131.

177. J. Lorie and M. Hamilton, *The Stock Market: Theories and Evidence* (Homewood, Ill.: Irwin, 1973).

178. Meyer and Kuh, *The Investment Decision*, p. 153. See also, F. Easterbrook, "Two Agency-Cost Explanations of Dividends," discussed in section B 3.222 The semiconductor study found evidence in interviews that management considers dividends desirable if it plans any equity offerings because dividends give shares a "quality image." See chapter 4, section 1.32.

179. H. Grabowski and D. Mueller, "Life-Cycle Effects on Corporate Returns on Retentions."

180. See the survey of nine such studies in W. McEachern, *Managerial Control and Performance* (Lexington, Mass: Lexington Books, 1975), pp. 39–51. McEachern's own study, in which he divided the sample into management-controlled, owner-manager, and externally controlled firms, shows that management-controlled firms have a rate of return only half of that of the owner-manager firms and somewhat less than that of externally controlled firms.

181. Williamson, "Managerial Discretion and Business Behavior," *Am. Econ. Rev.* (1963), 53:1032–1057, pp. 1047–1051.

182. McGuire, Chiu, and Elbing, "Executive Incomes, Sales, and Profits," *Am. Econ. Rev.* (1962), 52:753–761.

183. Lewellen and the Huntsman, "Managerial Pay and Corporate Performance," *Am. Econ. Rev.* (1970), 60:710–720.

184. F. Scherer, *Industrial Market Structure*, p. 36.

185. Masson, "Executive Motivations, Earnings, and Consequent Equity Performance," *J. Pol. Econ.* (1971), 79:1278–1292.

186. Grabowski and Mueller, "Life-Cycle Effects on Corporate Returns on Retentions," p. 407.

Part II

Introduction to Part II

1. The companies interviewed were Texas Instruments Incorporated, Raytheon Company, Fairchild Camera & Instrument Corporation, National Semiconductor Corp., Intel Corp., Sprague Electric Co., American Micro-Systems, Inc., Mostek Corporation, and International Business Machines Corporation. The venture capital groups interviewed were New Business Resources–Venture Capital Partnership, Ltd., and Arthur Rock & Co.

2. The percentage of sales represented by these firms is somewhat less than the percentage of manufacture because the sales figures do not include the sales from IBM's components division to its products divisions. While IBM was estimated to be the fourth largest manufacturer of semiconductors, it did not engage in any outside sales.

3. There are three serious books on the economics of the industry as a whole: John Tilton, *International Diffusion of Technology: The Case of Semiconductors* (Washington, D.C.: Brookings Institution, 1971); Douglas Webbink, *The Semiconductor Industry*, Federal Trade Commission Staff Report (Washington, D.C.: GPO, 1977); and R. Wilson, P. Ashton, and T. Egan, *Innovation, Competition, and Government Policy in the Semiconductor Industry* (Lexington, Mass.: Lexington Books, 1980). Also valuable is A. Golding, "The Semiconductor Industry in Britain and the United States: A Case Study in Innovation, Growth, and the Diffusion of Technology," Ph.D. diss. University of Sussex, 1971. E. Sciberras, *Multinational Electronic Companies and National Economic Policies* (Greenwich, Conn.: Jai Press, 1977), focuses primarily on the United Kingdom. To the extent that it deals with U.S. firms, it is primarily concerned with their overseas investment and export decisions.

3. The Semiconductor Industry: A General Description

1. For a more complete description of the physics involved, see J. Brophy, *Semiconductor Devices* (London: Allen and Urwin, 1966); and W. Hittinger, "Metal-Oxide-Semiconductor Technology," *Scientific American*, August 1973, pp. 48–57. For discussions of the specific technological advances since 1948 and the trends involved, see *Patterns and Problems of Technical Innovation in American Industry* (Cambridge, Mass.: Arthur D. Little, 1963), pp. 138–164; Golding, "The Semiconductor Industry in Britain and the United States: A Case Study in Innovation, Growth, and the Diffusion of Technology," Ph.D. diss., University of Sussex, 1971, pp. 34–84; Tilton, *International Diffusion of Technology: The Case of Semiconductors* (Washington, D.C.: Brookings Institution, 1971), pp. 15–18; *Trends in Integrated Circuits and Microelectronics* (Cambridge, Mass.: Arthur D. Little, 1965), pp. 31–40; and Hittinger, "Metal-Oxide-Semiconductor Technology," pp. 48–57.

2. *Patterns and Problems of Technical Innovation in American Industry*, p. 171.

3. The description is by Dr. Solomon Miller quoted in "Where Time Moves at a Dizzying Pace," *Business Week*, April 20, 1968, pp. 77–78.

4. L. Lessing, "The Electronics Era," *Fortune*, July 1951, p. 79.

5. F. Bello, "The Year of the Transistor," *Fortune*, March 1953, p. 128.

6. *Ibid.*, p. 129.

7. Tilton, *International Diffusion of Technology*, p. 66.

8. W. Harris, "The Battle of the Components," *Fortune*, May 1957.

9. Tilton, *International Diffusion of Technology*, pp. 51–97; Golding, "The Semiconductor Industry in Britain and the United States," pp. 85–125, 150–177, 237–274.

10. The importance of this effect may be exaggerated. See chapter 5, section A.

11. "Can Semiconductors Survive Big Business?" *Business Week*, December 3, 1979.

12. Golding, "The Semiconductor Industry in Britain and the United States," p. 238. Tilton is essentially in accord: *International Diffusion of Technology*, p. 55.

13. R. Wilson, P. Ashton, and T. Egan, *Innovation, Competition, and Government Policy in the Semiconductor Industry* (Lexington, Mass.: Lexington Books, 1980), p. 108.

14. *Ibid.*, pp. 3–34.

15. H. Kleiman, "The Integrated Circuit: A Case Study of Innovation in the Electronics Industry" (D.B.A. diss., George Washington University, 1960), p. 148.

16. Golding, "The Semiconductor Industry in Britain and the United States," pp. 159, 167.

4. Finance and Dynamic Efficiency in the Semiconductor Industry

1. Sometimes this relationship between customer needs and research and development is formalized. Westinghouse, which did most of the pioneering work on integrated circuits, was under a defense contract. Texas Instruments had an agreement in the late 1950s with IBM to do research on computer components in return for an agreement by IBM to buy from Texas Instruments a certain percentage of its needs of the products developed.

2. J. Tilton, *International Diffusion of Technology: The Case of Semiconductors* (Washington, D.C.: Brookings Institution, 1971), pp. 73–75.

3. According to its 1972 annual report, Fairchild received $6.3 million in "royalties and other income" out of a net operating income of $7.7 million.

4. E. Mansfield, *The Economics of Technical Change* (New York: Norton, 1968).

5. Sprague, AMI, Raytheon, Intel, Mostek, and Texas Instruments.

6. There was no indication, however, that at the time of the interviews any of the firms used the types of investment decision-making techniques (e.g., Bayesian estimates) that are part of a modern business school curriculum. See, for example, E. Pessemier, *New Product Design* (New York: McGraw-Hill, 1966).

7. A. Golding, "The Semiconductor Industry in Britain and the United States: A Case Study in Innovation, Growth, and the Diffusion of Technology," Ph.D. diss., University of Sussex, 1971, p. 100; B. Miller, "Competition Tightens in Semiconductors, *Aviation Week and Space Technology*, September 23, 1963, p. 60; "Glamour Industry Takes Its Lumps," *Business Week*, November 11, 1961, p. 109.

8. A strong concern with growth was made explicit in the plans of several companies. Texas Instruments had goals of being a $200 million company by 1960, $1 billion company by 1970, and $3 billion by 1976. Intel had the goal to be a $100 million company within its first ten years. Nilo Lindbergen, "Building a Two-Headed Monster," *Innovation* (1971), no. 20, p. 41.

9. "A Fast Switch in Semiconductors," *Business Week*, September 5, 1970, p. 16.

10. H. Kleiman, "The Integrated Circuit: A Case Study of Innovation in the Electronics Industry" (D.B.A. diss. George Washington University, 1960).

11. W. Harris, "The Company That Started with a Gold Whisker," *Fortune*, August 1959, p. 98.

12. "Transitron Fights Back," *Fortune*, June 1970, p. 180.

13. "Dream Deferred," *Forbes*, January 15, 1971, pp. 16–17.

14. "The Semiconductor Industry: Madness or Method," *Forbes*, February 15, 1971, pp. 20–26.

15. An AMI official estimated that one cannot stockpile research and development work for more than six to twelve months because, with job mobility, the idea will by that time be in the hands of competitors. Fairchild officials claimed that when it reduced its research and development budget because it could not use all the ideas being generated, the research and development budgets of its competitors immediately increased.

16. IBM in fact raised its ratio from about ⅓ to about ½ in the last years of the period under study.

17. The payback period, according to the interviews and published reports, can be as short as six months and is frequently only two or three years because of rapid obsolescence.

18. See, for example, Farrar and Meyer, *Managerial Economics* (Englewood Cliffs, N.J.: Prentice-Hall, 1970), pp. 63–67.

19. In the case of IBM's raising its payout ratio from ⅓ to ½, the interviewed officials did not expect it to be lowered again.

20. J. McDonald, "Where Texas Instruments Goes from Here," *Fortune*, December 1961, p. 228; "Semiconductors," *Business Week*, March 26, 1960, p. 106; W. Harris, "The Company That Started with a Gold Whisker," p. 99.

21. Jensen and Meckling, "Theory of the Firm: Managerial Behavior, Agency Costs, and Ownership Structure," *J. Fin. Econ.* (1976), 3:305–360. See generally, chapter 2, section B 3.23, and chapter 6, section C 3.141.

22. For an exposition of this point of view, see Graham, Dodd, and Cottle, *Security Analysis*, 4th ed. (New York: McGraw Hill, 1962), pp. 539–549.

23. The more persuasive argument is that the superior knowledge of management would lead it to favor internal finance over debt or a new equity issue. See chapter 1, section C 1.2.

24. See, for example, E. Brigham, *Financial Management: Theory and Practice*, 3d ed. (Chicago: Dryden Press, 1982), pp. 552–570.

25. See chapter 1, section C 2.211. The proposition that an increase in the supply of a security pressures its price downward is not free from controversy. Gilson and Kraakman, for example, argue that it is inconsistent with the capital asset pricing model. "The Mechanisms of Market Efficiency," *Virginia Law Rev.* (1984), 70:549–644, p. 570, n.67. Scholes also argues against the proposition based on his empirical study of secondary offerings which found no relationship between the size of the offering and the reduction in share price following the offering. "The Market for Securities: Substitution Versus Price Pressure and the Effects of Information on Share Prices," *J. Business* (1972), pp. 179–211. For a brief review of alternative explanations for Scholes' findings, see S. Levmore, "Efficient Markets and Puzzling Intermediaries," *Virginia Law Rev.* (1984), 70:645–669, pp. 653–654.

26. IBM has received about $200 million a year, or about ⅙ of their total capital spending, from equity sales to employees.

27. Except Raytheon, with which the subject was not discussed.

28. Press reports suggest that, out of fear of the legal and investor relations consequences of a later price fall, managers in the industry have avoided taking advantage of gross overpricing. Transitron, for its first public offering, chose a price at which ten times as many shares were demanded than offered. "Transitron Sets Investors Agog," *Business Week*, December 5, 1959, p. 123. Similarly, Intel chose to make its initial equity financing through a private placement with highly sophisticated

investors who offered a considerably lower price than the company, with Robert Noyce's name, could have received in a public offering. N. Lindberg, "Building a Two-Headed Monster," p. 45.

29. This would not be true if the size of the new investment was very large in comparison with the current assets of the firm, in which case the whole financing process would be more like that of a brand-new firm entering the market.

30. "Transitron Sets Investors Agog," p. 123; A. Golding, "The Semiconductor Industry in Britain and the United States," p. 168.

31. It has been suggested that this was the case with James Riley: he had excellent contacts in investment banking circles. See "A Fast Switch in Semiconductors," *Business Week*, September 5, 1970, p. 16.

32. McDonald, "The Men at Texas Instruments," *Fortune*, December 1961, p. 116.

33. H. Kleiman, "The Integrated Circuit," pp. 162–63.

34. *Ibid.*, p. 109, 131–132; John Hack, "Glamour of Industry Stock Credited to Analysts," *Electronic News*, May 15, 1967, p. 46.

35. One apparent example is Texas Instruments, which appeared to be undergoing an earnings slump in the mid-1960s which was reflected in its stock price. During that period of time, the company was developing then very advanced integrated circuits which when introduced allowed the company to dominate its competition. "Texas Instruments: Full Steam Ahead," *Magazine of Wall Street*, September 13, 1969, p. 16.

36. Litton Industries, a conglomerate with an electronics base, is a prime example. Because the company was very acquisition oriented, the price of its stock was particularly important. Its past record of earnings growth and reputation for research and development had blessed it with a very high price/earnings ratio. There was tremendous pressure after its acquisition program began for each year's earnings to show dramatic gains over the year before. One means for attaining this goal was a return on gross assets incentive system for division managers under which their salaries were determined by the ratio of accounting earnings to the assets under their control. This led the managers to eschew investments heavy in research and development because most research and development costs cannot be capitalized. By 1968, real earnings had been sufficiently damaged by the paucity of research and development investment that even this high-pressure system could not produce continued growth of accounting earnings, and the value of the stock collapsed. "Litton's Shattered Image," *Forbes*, December 1, 1969, pp. 26–37.

37. J. Haenichen, "Expansion Won't End Semicon Lag," *Electronic News*, October 22, 1973, p. 54.

38. Management was particularly afraid of the reaction of shareowners who received substantial blocks of stock when their companies were acquired by Raytheon and who, in recognition of their concentrated ownership, were represented on the board of directors.

39. William Baumol, *The Stock Market and Economic Efficiency* (New York: Fordham University Press, 1965), p. 53.

40. A. Golding, "The Semiconductor Industry in Britain and the United States," p. 120; "TI Tilts at IBM's Market," *Business Week*, June 27, 1970, p. 80.

41. Lack of imagination on the part of end product manufacturers has not been an uncommon problem. In the middle 1950s, Texas Instruments developed a transistor radio in order to show manufacturers its practicality. In the early 1960s, it developed a small computer employing integrated circuits to demonstrate their potential to computer manufacturers.

42. The official interviewed at Intel, for example, said that their investment in the

electronic watch business had led them to develop better C/MOS circuits, a particularly advanced kind of integrated circuit with very low power usage. IBM justifies its manufacture of components on the grounds that it knows its needs better than outside suppliers.

43. John Tilton and a report published by Arthur D. Little each suggest that component and end product divisions within the same company tend to treat each other like outsiders, but my interviews suggested the opposite. J. Tilton, *International Diffusion of Technology*, p. 83; *Patterns and Problems of Technical Innovation in American Industry* (Cambridge, Mass.: Arthur D. Little, 1963). It may be that Tilton's and Little's focus was on the large systems companies, most of which have subsequently dropped their semiconductor operations.

44. Unpublished report prepared by the Business and Defense Services Administration (hereafter referred to as the "BDSA Study") and given to the OECD in its preparation of a 1965 book entitled *Electronic Components: Gaps in Technology*.

45. C. Silberman, "The Coming Shakeout in Electronics," *Fortune*, August 1960, p. 186; "Transitron Sets Investors Agog," p. 123.

46. F. Bello, "The Year of the Transistor," *Fortune*, March 1953, p. 168.

47. W. Harris, "The Battle of the Components," *Fortune*, May 1957, p. 138.

48. The BDSA study estimates the ratio in 1965 to be 6.1%. Anthony Golding estimates the ratio for the same year to be about 8%. A. Golding, "The Semiconductor Industry in Britain and the United States," p. 134. Samson Reports estimated the ratio at 9% for 1971. *Microelectronics: Shakedown and Shakeout* (New York: Samson Science, 1971), p. 15. *Electronic News* estimated the ratio to be 7% for 1972 and 6.6% for the first half of 1973. "Semicon Firms Cash In on Skyrocket," *Electronic News*, August 6, 1973, p. 45.

49. "The Early Years of the Transistor Industry," unpublished paper prepared for U.S. Air Force Project RAND, 1959, p. 19.

50. See section 1.33. The response of companies already vertically integrated to the increased share of value contributed by components has been put to their components and products divisions under more central control in order to increase communication between them. "The New Shape of Electronics," *Business Week*, April 14, 1975, p. 177.

51. *Microelectronics: Shakedown and Shakeout*.

52. "Surge in Semiconductors," *Electronics*, January 9, 1967, p. 132; "The New Shape of Electronics," *Business Week*, April 14, 1975, pp. 176–179; *Trends in Integrated Circuits and Microelectronics* (Cambridge, Mass: Arthur D. Little, 1965), p. 16; P. Seikman, "In Electronics, the Big Stakes Ride on Tiny Chips," *Fortune*, June 1966, p. 125.

53. *Electronics*, April 18, 1966, p. 25.

54. A. Golding, "The Semiconductor Industry in Britain and the United States," pp. 172–175.

55. *Ibid.*, p. 174.

56. *Microelectronics: Revolutionary Impact of New Technology*, (New York: Samson Science, 1971), p. 12.

57. P. Seikman, "In Electronics, the Big Stakes Ride on Tiny Chips," p. 122.

58. W. Harris, "The Battle of Components," *Fortune*, May 1957, pp. 286–288; A. Golding, "The Semiconductor Industry in Britain and the United States," pp. 172–175.

59. *Microelectronics: Revolutionary Impact of New Technology*, pp. 11–12.

60. J. Tilton, *International Diffusion of Technology*, pp. 72, 80.

61. H. Kleiman, "The Integrated Circuit," pp. 127–128.

62. "Silicon Valley," *Electronic News*, January 11, 1971, p. 4.

63. "Philco Expands Solid State Setup," *Electronic News*, April 4, 1966, p. 1.

64. Westinghouse with the initial integrated circuit, Sylvania with the TTL integrated circuit, and Philco-Ford with MOS.

65. A. Golding, "The Semiconductor Industry in Britain and the United States," p. 261.

66. J. Tilton, *International Diffusion of Technology*, p. 2.

67. The group that founded Fairchild's semiconductor organization was financially backed by Fairchild and granted the company an option to buy them out, which Fairchild exercised. By 1974 semiconductors dominated the larger firm, constituting 80% of its sales.

68. Don C. Hoefler, "Semiconductor Family Tree," *Electronic News*, July 8, 1968, p. 1; chart from this article reprinted in J. Tilton, *International Diffusion of Technology*, p. 79; Don C. Hoefler, "Silicon Valley, U.S.A.," *Electronic News*, January 11, 1971, p. 1.

69. B. Miller, "Competition Tightens," *Aviation Week and Space Technology*, September 23, 1963, p. 61.

70. "Transitron Sets Investors Agog," p. 123.

71. Don C. Hoefler, "Silicon Valley, U.S.A.," p. 14.

72. For the example of Lester Hogan, see J. Tilton, *International Diffusion of Technology*, p. 80.

73. "Semiconductors," *Business Week*, March 26, 1960, p. 110.

74. Even Signetics, when it discovered that it would require considerably more outside capital before it could develop into a profitable broadline semiconductor firm, chose to raise the money by issuing a sufficient quantity of stock to Corning to give Corning a majority interest. Signetics reportedly felt that Lehman would not be willing to give it continued backing through the period of losses still ahead. B. Miller, "Competition to Tighten in Semiconductors," *Aviation Week and Space Technology*, September 23, 1963, p. 56.

75. *Ibid.*, p. 113.

76. BDSA study, p. 8.

77. G. Bylinsky, "Little Chips Invade the Memory Market," *Fortune*, April 1973, p. 102.

78. D. Hoefler, "Silicon Valley, U.S.A.," p. 1; D. Hoefler, "Semiconductor Family Tree," p. 1.

79. "Managers Seen as Secret Ingredient," *Electronic News*, January 27, 1969, p. 6; "Venture Capital with a Solid Reputation," *Business Week*, May 30, 1970, p. 102.

80. Some venture capital groups do retain scientists and engineers who are active in their professions, as consultants, or include them on their boards of directors.

81. "Managers Seen as Secret Ingredient," p. 6.

82. *Electronic News*, September 19, 1966, pp. 1ff., p. 6.

83. *Ibid.*

84. *Electronic News*, March 7, 1966, p. 1.

85. BDSA study, p. 8.

86. "Where Time Moves at a Dizzying Pace," *Business Week*, April 20, 1968, p. 174.

87. BDSA study, p. 4.

88. J. Tilton, *International Diffusion of Technology*, p. 82.

89. BDSA study, p. 4.

90. A. Golding, "The Semiconductor Industry in Britain and the United States," p. 241.

91. *Ibid.*, p. 259.

92. J. McDonald, "The Men Who Made TI," *Fortune*, December 1961, p. 218. Substantial investment by a founder is not a guarantee of success to other investors, however. George Cogar, perhaps the biggest single individual investor in the history of the semiconductor industry, put in $12 million of his own money out of the Cogar Corporation's original capitalization of $20 million in return for 67% of the common stock. "Cogar's Letdown," *Duns Rev.*, March 1972, p. 66; "How the High Fliers Take Off," *Business Week*, November 22, 1969, p. 112. In early 1973, the company went through a financial reorganization to avoid bandruptcy in which trade creditors accepted 20¢ on the dollar. "Cogar Proposes Plan," *Wall Street Journal*, February 5, 1973, p. 24, col. 3. Letters I sent to Cogar in the fall of 1973 were returned with the marking "Moved, left no forwarding address."

93. Cases where there appears not to have been any cash investment by the founders vary considerably in the percentage of founding shares. Each of the eight founders of the Fairchild semiconductor division received 10% of the shares of the company for no cash investment but had to grant an option to the funding source, Fairchild Camera. "Semiconductors," *Business Week*, March 26, 1960, p. 113. The founders of Signetics received together 20% of the original shares issued.

5. Finance and Competition in the Semiconductor Industry

1. Bain, *Barriers to New Competition* (Cambridge, Mass.: Harvard University Press, 1956), pp. 146–148, 156–162.

2. The discussion in chapter 4 concerning the relationship between research and development spending and success supports this conclusion because research and development spending is a precondition for fast implementation of innovation on the part of established firms. See chapter 4, section 1.33. The semiconductor sales of firms that employed a second sourcing strategy such as Raytheon and Sprague experienced severe losses and reoriented their efforts toward innovation in order to rectify the situation. Transitron, which tried to save research and development costs by being a quick imitator rather than an initiator of innovations, faded rapidly from prominence.

3. J. Tilton, *International Diffusion of Technology: The Case of Semiconductors* (Washington, D.C.: Brookings Institution, 1971), pp. 86–87; A. Golding, "The Semiconductor Industry in Britain and the United States: A Case Study in Innovation, Growth, and the Diffusion of Technology," Ph.D. diss., University of Sussex, 1971, p. 119. This explanation was widely accepted among industry officials as well.

4. Neither Tilton nor Golding directly attributes concentration to dynamic economies of scale. Golding, however, says, "Dynamic scale economies have often allowed early innovators to achieve a virtually impregnable position over established rivals . . . within the space of a few short years." Golding, "The Semiconductor Industry in Britain and the United States," p. 251. Tilton finds that the semiconductor business is dominated by new firms despite the fact that in the first fifteen years of its existence most research and development breakthroughs were achieved by established diversified electronics companies. He attributes the success of the new companies to the fact that they implemented the innovations more quickly. Tilton, *International Diffusion of Technology*, p. 71.

5. A. Golding, "The Semiconductor Industry in Britain and the United States," pp. 103–106.

6. The results of this example would not be materially different if the time periods chosen were quarters ($n = 12$) or years ($n = 3$).

7. A. Golding, "The Semiconductor Industry in Britain and the United States," p. 105; J. Tilton, *International Diffusion of Technology*, p. 85.

8. The literature contains at least two examples, one involving Motorola and the other RCA, where the firm involved openly admitted that it priced products below current cost in anticipation of future declines in cost resulting from learning economies. See J. Tilton, *International Diffusion of Technology*, p. 86; A. Golding, "The Semiconductor Industry in Britain and the United States," p. 108.

9. W. E. Gustafson, "Research and Development: New Products and Productivity Change," *Am. Econ. Rev.* (May 1962), 52:77–85.

10. Initial implementers sometimes eschew this strategy and move directly into penetration pricing, as would be predicted by the model. See note 8.

11. This analysis ignores the possibility of any oligopolistic coordination. If such cooperation exists to one extent or another, the direction of the effect would be the same. The optimal price and quantity for each implementing firm will shift. In the case of explicit agreement, this leads the implementing firms to demand renegotiation. In the case of coordination by awareness of mutual interdependency, this will force other firms to act according to the new realities if they want cooperation to continue.

Part III

6. Applications to Policy

1. In the five-year period 1977–1981, term bank loans supplied only 28% of the long-term funds raised by U.S. nonfinancial business corporations. The rest of the funds came from new debt security issues (52%), new equity security issues (6%), mortgage debt (4%), and industrial revenue bonds (10%). D. Wooley and B. Lowen, *Credit and Capital Markets, 1983* (New York: Bankers Trust, 1983), p. T 26. For the same period, 69% of the all new debt securities (presumably including mortgage bonds) and 93% of all equity securities issued for cash were publicly offered. U.S. Bureau of the Census, *Statistical Abstract of the United States: 1982–1983* (Washington, D.C.: GPO, 1982), p. 518.

2. A survey by me of "long form" registration statements filed prior to the integrated disclosure reforms of the early 1980s (discussed in section B 1.41) suggests that these expenses represented between .25 and .50% of the proceeds of the issue of a major established issuer and a much higher percentage of newly established smaller issuer's issues.

3. Forms S-1, S-2, and S-3 also require a registrant to discuss any factors that make the offering speculative or high risk, matters not covered by form 10-K, but an offering by a large public corporation rarely involves such factors.

4. If a mineral company makes a test drilling that suggests a commercially minable body of ore and decides to purchase land adjacent to the drilling site, disclosure would raise the purchase price of the land. This company would not wish to engage in a public offering until after the land was acquired.

5. For the purpose of sampling the disclosures concerning the use of the proceeds derived from the securities being registered, I selected at random twenty-six registration statements from among all those filed by *Fortune* 500 companies between May 1982 and November 1983. Sixteen registration statements simply stated that the proceeds would be used for general corporate purposes. Five provided specific information as to the location and type of facility to which the funds would be applied. The remaining five were between these two extremes. See also, A. Levenson, "Preparation of the Registration Statement," in *Going Public: Filing Problems* (New York: Practicing Law Institute, 1970), pp. 103–104.

6. Any mention of a specific project would normally, for example, require mentioning the project's total predicted cost. An inaccurately low prediction or the use of the proceeds for a different project can create problems. See *Blakely v. Lisac,* 357 F. Supp. 255 (D. Ore. 1972); *MFT Investment Co. v. Diversified Data Services and Sciences, Inc.,* CCH Federal Securities Law Reporter (hereinafter Fed. Sec. L. Rep.) ¶93,691 (1972–1973 Transfer Binder).

7. Placing the burden of proof on the issuer concerning good faith action and no knowledge clearly negates any need for the plaintiff to prove the issuer's intent to deceive ("scienter"). It is unclear whether the defendant, to be entitled to the defense, needs to show no actual knowledge after a reasonable investigation or whether something less will do. See Bromberg and Lowenfels, *Securities Fraud and Commodities Fraud* (New York: McGraw-Hill, 1984), vol. 3, section 8.4(460); and "Civil Liability for Misstatements in Documents Filed Under Securities Act and Securities Exchange Act," *Yale Law J.* (1935), 44:456–477, p. 474.

8. See *Wachovia Bank and Trust v. National Student Marketing Corp.,* CCH Fed. Sec. L. Rep. ¶96,603 at 94,573 (D.D.C. 1978); *Gross v. Diversified Mortgage Investors,* 438 F. Supp. 190, 195 (S.D.N.Y. 1977); *Barotz v. Monarch General,* CCH Fed. Sec. L. Rep. ¶94,933 (1974–1975 Transfer Binder) (S.D.N.Y. 1975).

9. Louis Loss has stated, "The ultimate effectiveness of the federal remedies, when the defendants are not prone to settle, may depend in large measure on the applicability of the class action device." *Fundamentals of Securities Regulation* (Boston: Little, Brown, 1983), p. 1007. Although there is little case law on point, two district courts have dismissed class actions under Section 18(a) because the plaintiffs failed to offer evidence of "specific individual class member reliance." *Adams v. Standard Knitting Mills, Inc.,* CCH Fed. Sec. L. Rep. ¶95,683 (E.D. Tenn. 1979) (1978–1979 Transfer Binder), *rev'd* on other grounds, 623 F.2d 422 (6th Cir. 1980) *cert. denied* 449 U.S. 1067 (1980); and *Elster v. Alexander,* 76 F.R.D. 440, 442–443 (N.D. Ga. 1977).

10. An issuer publicly making a materially false or misleading statement can violate Rule 10b-5. *SEC v. Texas Gulf Sulphur Co.,* 401 F.2d 833, 862 (2d Cir. 1968) cert. denied 394 U.S. 976 (1969) (hereinafter cited as *TGS*). See also Bromberg and Lowenfels, *Securities Fraud and Commodities Fraud,* vol. 3, section 7.6(26). Whether such a violation gives rise to an implied private right of action for damages (as opposed to simply an SEC enforcement action) is not absolutely settled. The cases on point, ones relating to false statements, hold that it does. *Mitchell v. Texas Gulf Sulphur,* 446 F.2d 90 (10th Cir. 1971). But see *Fridrich v. Bradford,* 542 F.2d 307 (6th Cir. 1976), *cert denied,* 429 U.S. 1053 (1977).

11. The trend has been to allow these particular cumulative remedies. See *Ross v. A.H. Robins Co.,* 607 F.2d 545, 556 (2d Cir. 1979), *cert. denied,* 446 U.S. 911 (1980); Bromberg and Lowenfels, *Securities Fraud and Commodities Fraud,* vol. 1, section 2.4 (440)(5).

12. See *Blackie v. Barrack,* 524 F.2d 891, 906 (9th Cir. 1975), *cert. denied,* 429 U.S. 816 (1976); *Panzirer v. Wolf,* 663 F.2d 365 (2d Cir. 1982), *vacated sub nom. Price Waterhouse v. Panzirer,* 459 U.S. 1027 (1982) ("in light of the respondent's suggestion of mootness and the petitioner's response"), Bromberg and Lowenfels, *Securities Fraud and Commodities Fraud,* vol. 3: section 8.6.

13. *Ernst & Ernst v. Hochfelder,* 425 U.S. 185 (1976). The Court left open the question of "whether, in some circumstances, reckless behavior is sufficient for civil liability." *Id.* at fn. 12, 194. Most of the courts that have considered the issue after *Hochfelder* have concluded that Rule 10b-5 does cover recklessness. See, e.g., *Mansbach v. Prescott, Ball, & Turben,* 598 F.2d 1017, 1023–1025 (6th Cir. 1979); Bromberg and Lowenfels, *Securities Fraud and Commodities Fraud,* vol 2, section 5.7(240)–(242).

14. In *TSC Industries v. Northway, Inc.*, the Supreme Court set out the concept that materiality relates to a situation where there is a "substantial likelihood that a reasonable shareholder would consider it important in deciding" how to act with respect to a security. 426 U.S. 438, 449 (1976). Although that case involved Section 14(a) of the Exchange Act, the same concept has been applied in a 10b-5 case involving the purchase of securities. *Huddleston v. Herman & McClean*, 640 F.2d 534, 543–544 (5th Cir. 1981), cert. granted 456 U.S. 914 (1982), affirmed in part and reversed in part, 459 U.S. 375 (1983). See also Jennings and Marsh, *Securities Regulation*, 5th ed. (Mineola, N.Y.: Foundation Press, 1982), pp. 1023–1025.

15. Bloomenthal, *Securities and Federal Corporate Law* (New York: Clark Boardman, 1984) vol. 3A, section 3.19(6). Research reveals no reported cases sustaining issuer liability under Section 18. *See* CCH Fed. Sec. L. Rep. ¶26,226; 70 West's Federal Practice Digest, section 122 (2d ed. 1978 and Supp. 1982); Bromberg and Lowenfels, *Securities Fraud and Commodities Fraud*, vol. 1, section 2.4(440)(1); and Greene, "Determining the Responsibility of Underwriters Distributing Securities Within an Integrated Disclosure System," *Notre Dame Lawyer* (1981), 56:755–812, p. 758.

16. Bloomenthal, *Securities and Federal Corporate Law*, vol. 3A, section 8.26(3). For example, in *Escott v. BarChris Construction Corp.*, the defendant tried to argue that all of the plaintiffs' damages were due to the "decline in the bowling industry which came about because of the fact that the industry was overbuilt and because popular enthusiasm for bowling diminished." 283 F. Supp. 643, 703 (S.D.N.Y. 1968). The court rejected this general defense at least as to the entire class of plaintiffs. *Id.* at 704. However in *Feit v. Leasco Data Processing Equipment Corp.* the defendant was able to reduce damages under Section 11(e) because of "the very drastic decline in the stock market in 1969." 332 F. Supp. 544, 586 (E.D.N.Y. 1971).

17. This statement requires one significant qualification in the case of equity securities. Plaintiff must prove that the securities purchased were part of the securities subject to the registration statement. Unlike with debt, corporations often register and sell additional shares of a class which is already outstanding and being publicly traded. For investors with shares held in "street name," who owns which specific shares is not specified so the investor will not be able to show that his shares were not previously issued ones. Even where a shareholder does obtain the possession of his certificates, he may not be able to show that they stand for shares issued pursuant to the offering in question. While in theory this could be ascertained by tracing the ownership of his shares on the transfer books of the corporation, at least one court has refused to put the burden of such tracing on the issuer. *Lober v. Beebe*, CCH Fed. Sec. L. Rep. ¶95,363 (1975–1976 Tranfer Binder) (S.D.N.Y. 1975).

18. The SEC has acknowledged this added risk of liability. Securities Act Release 6176 (January 15, 1980). There is also evidence that the difference in risk that arises from the two statutory schemes was deliberate on the part of Congress. Comment, *Yale Law J.* (1934), 44:456–477, pp. 476–477.

19. It is not clear when, if ever, an officer or director who does not participate in the preparation of an Exchange Act filing containing a false or misleading statement will nonetheless be considered under Section 18 as a person who "caused" the statement to be made. The SEC maintains that under appropriate circumstances all directors are liable regardless of whether or not they participated in its preparation. Securities Act Release 6176 (January 15, 1980). At least one commentator is not very impressed by the SEC argument or the cases cited. See Bloomenthal, *Securities Law Handbook* (New York: Clark Boardman, 1982), p. 179. In 1980, the SEC amended its instructions relating to the filing of Form 10-K to require that the 10-K be signed by a majority of the board of directors and certain principal officers. Exchange Act Release

17114 (September 2, 1980). The position of a plaintiff arguing that a director or officer "caused" a statement should be enhanced if the director or officer is one of the persons who signed the document.

20. See *SEC v. Coffey*, 493 F.2d 1304 (6th Cir. 1974), *cert. denied*, 420 U.S. 908 (1975). To be an aider and abettor, one must "knowingly and substantially assist the violation." *Id.* at 1316. If "inaction" is the only form of "assistance," then it must be "shown that the silence . . . was consciously intended to aid the securities law violation." *Id.* at 1317 (footnote and citations omitted).

In regard to outside directors, the court in *Lanza v. Drexel & Co.* held that under Section 10(b) and Rule 10b-5, such a director had "no duty to insure that all material, adverse information is conveyed to prospective purchasers of stock," even if the director negligently failed to discover that officers were making misrepresentations to other parties to the transaction. 479 F.2d 1277, 1289 (2d Cir. 1973).

21. See statistics in *SEC Monthly Statistical Rev.* (February 1981), 40:28.

22. Section 11(b)(3)(A), relating to portions not purporting to be made on the authority of an expert. Section 11(c) of the Securities Act provides that the standard by which the reasonableness of a section 11(b)(3)(A) investigation is to be determined is that "of a prudent man in the management of his own property."

23. H. Bloomenthal, *Securities and Federal Corporate Law*, vol. 3A, sections 8.14–8.15.

24. The legislative history emphasizes that the primary aim of the legislation was to assure the "full disclosure of every essentially important element attending the issue of a new security." H.R. Rep. No. 85, 73d Cong., 1st sess., p. 3(1933). An early commentator, Harry Shulman, quickly picked up on this *"in terrorem* function of the Act" as a means to attain accurate "disclosure of significant matters." "Civil Liability and the Securities Act," *Yale Law J.* (1933), 43:227–253, p. 227; see also Douglas and Bates, "The Federal Securities Act of 1933," *Yale Law J.* (1933), 43:171–226, p. 173. The courts have upheld this view. *Escott v. BarChris Construction Corp.*, 283 F. Supp. 643, 697 (S.D.N.Y. 1968); *Feit v. Leasco Data Processing Equipment Corp.*, 332 F. Supp. 544, 577 (E.D.N.Y. 1971).

25. Greene, "Determining the Responsibility of Underwriters," pp. 767–770.

26. *Escott v. BarChris*, p. 696; *Feit v. Leasco*, p. 581.

27. This degree of organizational separateness is reflected in the fact that only 14.5% of all publicly held companies in the United States had one or more investment bankers on their boards. Exchange Act Release 17,518, 21 *SEC Docket* 1551, tables 5 and 6 (February 5, 1981).

28. Robert Haft, in an article about the emergence of corporate directors that are independent of management, discusses at length the positive role that outsiders can play in increasing the accuracy of the corporation's view of itself and its operations. "Business Decisions by the New Board: Behavioral Science and Corporate Law," *Michigan Law Rev.* (1981), 80:1–67. See also Folk, "Civil Liabilities Under the Federal Securities Acts: The BarChris Case," *Virginia Law Rev.* (1969), 55:1, p. 56.

29. Folk, "Civil Liabilities Under the Federal Securities Acts," p. 54; *Feit v. Leasco*, p. 581.

30. Comment, "BarChris: Due Diligence Refined," *Columbia Law Rev.* (1968), 68:1411–1423, p. 1421.

31. A good description of the traditional registration process of a public offering of securities is found in S. Pryor and R. Smith, "Significant Changes in Primary Stock Distributions Over the Last 25 Years," *National Law J.* (August 9, 1983), 21:39–41 ("Pryor and Smith I"). See also, A. Hovdesven and S. Wolfram, "Underwriter Liability in the Integrated Disclosure System," *National Law J.* (July 5, 1982), p. 13; and S. Forten-

baugh, "Underwriter's Due Diligence," *Rev. Securities Regulation* (1981), 14:799. The following description of the process is based, as well, on my personal experiences as a practicing securities lawyer and on conversations with other practitioners in this area.

32. Jennings and Marsh, *Securities Regulation*, p. 88.

33. Fortenbaugh, "Underwriter's Due Diligence," p. 805; Hovdesven and Wolfram, "Underwriter Liability in the Integrated Disclosure System," p. 13; and Pryor and Smith I, p. 21.

34. Fortenbaugh, "Underwriter's Due Diligence," p. 805; Hovdesven and Wolfram, "Underwriter Liability in the Integrated Disclosure System," p. 13; Pryor and Smith I, p. 21.

35. Nicholas, "The Integrated Disclosure System and Its Impact on Underwriter Due Diligence," *Securities Regulation Law J.* (1983), 11:1, pp. 15–17; Hovdesven and Wolfram, "Underwriter Liability in the Integrated Disclosure System," p. 13; and Pryor and Smith I, pp. 21, 29.

36. Nicholas, "The Integrated Disclosure System," pp. 15–17; and Pryor and Smith I, pp. 21, 29.

37. Fortenbaugh, "Underwriter's Due Diligence," pp. 805–806; and Pryor and Smith I, pp. 21, 29.

38. Hovdesven and Wolfram, "Underwriter Liability in the Integrated Disclosure System," p. 13; Nicholas, "The Integrated Disclosure System," p. 15.

39. Pryor and Smith, "Disclosure and Capital Formation Policies," *National Law J.*, August 16, 1982, p. 15 ("Pryor and Smith II"); Hovdesven and Wolfram, "Underwriter Liability in the Integrated Disclosure System," p. 13; Securities Act Release 6423 (Thomas, Comm'r, dissenting), reprinted in CCH Fed. Sec. L. Rep. ¶85,285–286 (1982 Transfer Binder); Nicholas, "The Integrated Disclosure System," p. 3.

40. SEC chairman Shad predicted that the savings in fees paid to printers, attorneys, and accountants resulting from the shelf registration component of the integrated disclosure program would be $300 million per year. *Shelf Registration: Strategies, Techniques, Pitfalls, Case Studies* (Washington, D.C.: The Committee of Publicly Owned Companies 1983), p. 16. No data is currently available to test this assertion, however.

41. Securities Act Release No. 6383.

42. To be eligible to use Form S-3 the registrant must not be delinquent in its financial obligations. The aggregate market value of the voting stock held by nonaffiliates of the registrant must be at least $150 million, or $100 million with an annual trading volume of at least three million shares. Louis Loss estimates that 2,000 firms are eligible to use Form S-3. *Fundamentals of Securities Regulation*, p. 144. Thus, firms that qualify are responsible for more, probably considerably more, than 75% of all real investment in the economy. See chapter 2, section B 3.1.

43. *SEC News Digest*, November 17, 1980.

44. Nicholas, "The Integrated Disclosure System," p. 21.

45. *Ibid.*, p. 6.

46. Pryor and Smith II, p. 15; Hovdesven and Wolfram, "Underwriter Liability in the Integrated Disclosure System," p. 13.

47. SEC Securities Act Release No. 6335 (August 6, 1981).

48. Hovdesven and Wolfram, "Underwriter Liability in the Integrated Disclosure System," p. 15; Nicholas, "The Integrated Disclosure System," p. 34.

49. Nicholas, "The Integrated Disclosure System," pp. 33–34, n.92.

50. *Ibid.*

51. *Ibid.*

52. Security Act Release No. 6335.

53. See Greene, "Determining the Responsibility of Underwriters," p. 789. To the extent that firms are risk neutral, the increased volatility of the market should make no difference to firms, since at any one point in time interest rates are as likely to decrease as increase.

54. Stone, *Where the Law Ends: The Social Control of Corporate Behavior* (New York: Harper and Row, 1975), pp. 42–46. See also, Stone, "The Place of Enterprise Liability in the Control of Corporate Conduct," *Yale Law J.* (1980), 90:1–77, pp. 15, 19–24.

55. See Loss, *Fundamentals of Securities Regulation*, p. 1040; and Greene, "Determining the Responsibility of Underwriters," p. 770.

56. Nicholas, "The Integrated Disclosure System," pp. 33–34, n.92.

57. The language of 11(c) reflects an amendment to the Securities Act one year after the Act's passage. The amendment substituted the accepted common law definition of fiduciary duty for the term "fiduciary relationship," because the latter term had been "terrifyingly portrayed." 78 Cong. Rec. 8669 (1934). See Greene, "Determining the Responsibility of Underwriters," pp. 767–770, 794.

58. Greene makes such an argument. "Determining the Responsibility of Underwriters," pp. 775–778, 794–800.

59. SEC Securities Act Release No. 5998 (1978).

60. An SEC rule of this sort, which in essence interprets a provision of a statute, is not binding on the courts, but courts, out of deference to agency expertise, give them considerable weight. *International Bhd. of Teamsters, Chauffeurs, Warehousemen, and Helpers of America v. Daniel*, 439 U.S. 551, 566 n.20 (1979). In that case, the Court, after stating the principle, went on to reject the SEC's interpretation because of "the clear meaning of a statute." But the Court has cited SEC interpretations as authority in support of the Court's positions in other cases. See, e.g., *United States v. National Association of Sec. Dealers*, 422 U.S. 694, 717–719 (1975).

61. The concepts of a "reasonable investigation" and a "reasonable ground to believe" under Section 11(b) have as their common law origins the concept of nonnegligence in tort, conduct which does not involve an unreasonably great risk of causing damage. L. Loss, *Securities Regulation*, pp. 1729–1730. (2d. ed. 1961). Behavior by a defendant that comports with the usual and customary behavior of others is evidence of nonnegligence. Prosser, *Law of Torts* 4th ed., (St. Paul: West, 1971), p. 166; C. Morris, "Custom and Negligence," *Columbia Law Rev.* (1942), 42:1147–1168.

62. See chapter 1, section C 2.22 and chapter 2, sections B 3.222 and B 3.3. There is also a body of empirical literature concerning whether the Securities Act and the Exchange Act have had a meaningful effect on the level of corporate disclosure. Compare Benston, "Required Disclosure and the Stock Market: An Evaluation of the Securities Exchange Act of 1934," *Am. Econ. Rev.* (1973), 63:132–155; Stigler, "Public Regulation of the Securities Markets," *J. Business* (1964), 37:117–142 (suggesting they have not); with Friend and Herman, "The SEC Through a Glass Darkly," *J. Business* (1964), 37:382–405 (suggesting they have). A survey of both bodies of literature is found in Seligman, "The Historical Need for a Mandatory Corporate Disclosure System" *J. Corp. Law* (1983), 9:1–61.

63. This statement is accurate from the point of view of static analysis, but a dynamic analysis suggests that there are competing considerations. The extra profits from keeping some kinds of information from competitors can be viewed as an incentive to develop the information. In such a situation, as with patents and copyrights, there is a conflict between the need for these incentives and the benefits of competition once the information is developed. But the kind of information elicited by a

traditional Securities Act registration process is far from the types—patents, copyrights, trade secrets—that the legal system has consciously granted monopoly rights with respect to.

For a fuller discussion of the benefits to society of corporate information disclosed as the result of underwriter due diligence, see M. Fox, "Shelf Registration, Integrated Disclosure, and Underwriter Due Diligence," *Virginia Law Rev.* (1984), 70:1105–1134, pp. 1109–1125.

The SEC is in fact more sympathetic to the concerns of issuers about the release of information that might be helpful to suppliers, customers, or competitors than this discussion suggests it should be. For a general review of SEC policy, see V.G. Comizio "Keeping Corporate Information Secret: Confidential Treatment Under the Securities Act of 1933 and the Securities Exchange Act of 1934," *New England Law Rev.* (1983), 18:787–806.

64. Under contract law, a mutual mistake by the parties may make a contract voidable if the mistake relates to a material fact upon which the parties based their transaction. See *Sherwood v. Walker*, 66 Mich. 568, 577–78, 33 N.W. 919, 923–924 (1887). Because the cow, Rose 2d, who was sold on the assumption that she was sterile, was found to be with calf, the court held that the contract was voidable on the theory that the "mistake was not of the mere quality of the animal, but went to the very nature of the thing." However, where there is conscious uncertainty in a transaction, each party risks an unfavorable resolution of that uncertainty. See J. Calamari and J. Perillo, *The Law of Contracts* 2d ed. (St. Paul: West, 1977) § 9–26. Hence, in *Riviere v. Berla* the court refused to rescind a sale of stock between two shareholders who had both relied on an erroneous auditor's report as to the value of the stock. 106 A. 455, 89 N.J. Eq. 596 (1918). See also, *Coachella Valle Lumber & Supply Co. v. Hollenbeck*, 303 P.2d 98, 103 (Cal. Dist. Ct. App. 1956).

65. See Fischel, "The Law and Economics of Dividend Policy," *Virginia Law Rev.* (1981), 67:699–726, p. 702.

66. Section 11(f) of the Securities Act provides "every person who becomes liable to make any payment under [Section 11] may recover contribution as in cases of contract from any person who, if sued separately, would have been liable to make the same payment, unless the person who has become liable was, and the other was not, guilty of fraudulent misrepresentation." This provision was intended to avoid the traditional common law policy against contribution among joint tort-feasors. L. Loss, *Securities Regulation*, p. 1737.

Although some commentators and claimants have interpreted the language in Section 11(f) "as in cases of contract" to require a pro-rata distribution, this strict interpretation is generally rejected. See Note, "The Role of Contribution in Determining Underwriters' Liability Under Section 11 of the Securities Act of 1933," *Virginia Law Rev.* (1970), 63:79–104, pp. 93–95. Instead the amount of contribution required is determined according to comparative fault or benefit received. *Gould v. American-Hawaiian Steamship Co.*, 387 F. Supp. 163, 170 (D. Del. 1974), *remanded on other grounds*, 535 F.2d 761 (3d Cir. 1976). See also the 1978 Proposed Official Draft of the Federal Securities Code, Section 1724(f).

67. For a general discussion of the effect of subsequent events on a registered public offering, see Bloomenthal, *Securities and Federal Corporate Law*, vol. 3A, section 7.22; and *SEC v. Manor Nursing Centers, Inc.*, 458 F.2d 1082 (2d Cir. 1972). The question is not settled whether or not an issuer that is considered a seller of a security would be liable for damages under Section 12(1) if it is unaware of the change in circumstances and in the exercise of reasonable care could not have known of the change. At least

one court has concluded it would not. *Jeffries and Co. v. United Missouri Bank*, CCH Fed. Sec. L. Rep. ¶99,257 (D.C. W. Mo. 1983).

68. In *Smolowe v. Delendo Corp.*, a 16(b) case, the court affirmed an allowance for "substantial" attorneys' fees, noting that "in many cases such as this the possibility of recovering attorney's fees will provide the sole stimulus for the enforcement of §16(b)." 136 F.2d 231, 241 (2d Cir. 1943).

69. The SEC considers indemnification by a registrant of its directors, officers, controlling persons, and underwriter for liabilities arising under the Securities Act "against public policy as expressed in the act and . . . therefore, unenforceable." Items 510 and 512(i) of Regulation S-K. This anti-indemnification policy stems from the theory that indemnification frustrates the *in terrorem* purpose of individual liability under the Securities Act. Loss, *Fundamentals of Securities Regulation*, p. 1201. See also, D. Oesterle, "Limits on a Corporation's Protection of Its Directors and Officers from Personal Liability," *Wisconsin Law Rev.* (1983), 1983: 513, 560.

Many state statutes, on the other hand, expressly sanction corporate indemnification of, and insurance for, directors and officers. The underlying rationale for this indemnification and insurance is that these practices attract competent persons to serve as officers and directors, discourage "strike" litigation by shareholders, and encourage innocent directors to defend themselves against "unjust charges." Cary and Eisenberg, *Cases and Materials on Corporations* (New York: Foundation Press, 1980), p. 960; also see Oesterle, "Limits on a Corporation's Protection," pp. 513–516.

70. Under the proposed Federal Securities Code an individual defendant's damages for fraud or manipulation-type liability would be limited to the *greater* of: $100,000 or defendant's profit, as calculated under the relevant statutory provision. See Sections 1708(e)(2) and 1710(d), Proposed Official Draft 1978. For a measure of damages tied in some cases to a defendant's compensation from the corporation in the context of certain corporate law liabilities, see section 7.17 of the ALI *Principles of Corporate Governance and Structure*, Tent. Draft No. 6 (1986).

71. It is true that corporations pay no taxes on 85% of their dividend income, but even with this break the tax regime discourages long-term corporate ownership of shares of other unconsolidated corporations because the gains are subject to triple taxation instead of just double. See Modigliani and Miller, "Dividend Policy, Growth, and the Valuation of Shares," *J. Business* (1961), 34:411, pp. 431–432; F. Black and M. Scholes, "The Effects on Dividend Yield and Dividend Policy on Common Stock Prices and Returns," *J. Fin. Econ.* (1974), 1:1–22.

72. See breakdown of holders of equity investment in figure 2.3, which shows that 81% of all shares, by market value, are held by investors that pay at least some taxes on dividend income (or pass the tax obligation on to their investors). Miller and Scholes demonstrate that it is theoretically possible for individuals, by borrowing and investing the proceeds in life insurance or a Keogh plan that pays risk-free, tax-deferred interest, to shelter dividend income from current taxation. "Dividends and Taxes," *J. Fin. Econ.* (1978), 5:333–364. However, given the transaction costs involved, limits on the amount of dividends the tax laws permit to be sheltered by this technique and the fact that Treasury statistics show that most individuals pay taxes on dividends, it is likely that, despite this technique, the size of the clientele that would prefer capital gains to dividends is still very substantial. See D. Feenberg, "Does the Investment Interest Limitation Explain the Existence of Dividends?" *J. Fin. Econ.* (1981), 9:265–269; Gordon and Malkiel, "Taxation and Corporate Finance," in Aaron and Pechman, eds., *How Taxes Affect Economic Behavior* (Washington, D.C.: Brookings Institution, 1981), pp. 131–132. E. Elton and M. Gruber, by examining the average price decline

when a stock goes ex-dividend, estimate that the marginal tax bracket of the average equity investor was 36.4%, which is well above the capital gains rate. *Rev. Econ. and Statistics* (1970), "Marginal Stockholder Tax Rates and the Clientele Effect" 52:68–74.

73. For an empirical study suggesting that the current regime has a substantial impact on corporate earnings retention, see M. Feldstein, "Corporate Taxation and Dividend Behavior," *Rev. of Econ. Studies* (1970), 37:57–72. In this regard, see also Organization for Economic Cooperation and Development, *Theoretical and Empirical Aspects of Corporate Taxation* (Paris: OECD, 1974).

74. Miller, "Debt and Taxes," *J. Finance* (1977), 32:261–275.

75. See a summary of the empirical evidence in Van Horne, *Financial Management and Policy*, 6th ed. (Englewood Cliffs, N.J.: Prentice-Hall, 1983), pp. 257–260.

76. For a summary of the arguments in favor of integrated taxation, see C. Mc-Clure, *Must Corporate Income Be Taxed Twice* (Washington, D.C.: Brookings Institution, 1979), pp. 19–27, 38–42.

77. *Ibid.*, pp. 24–25.

78. *Ibid.*, pp. 27–38.

79. S. Surrey, "Reflections on 'Integration' of Corporate and Individual Income Taxes," *National Tax J.* (1975), 28:335–340.

80. For a more detailed consideration of the effect on retention rates, see M. Blume, J. Crockett, and I. Friend, *Financial Effects of Capital Tax Reforms* (New York: New York University, Salomon Brothers Center, 1978).

81. Staff of Joint Committee on Taxation, *Study of 1982 Effective Tax Rates of Selected Large U.S. Corporations* (Washington, D.C.: GPO, 1983) pp. 1–2, 11–12.

82. Cary and Eisenberg state, "The odds that a court would compel a publicly held corporation to declare a dividend are exceedingly poor." *Corporations: Cases and Materials*, 5th ed. (Mineola, N.Y.: Foundation Press, 1980), p. 1415. See Brudney, "Dividends, Discretion, and Disclosure," *Virginia Law Rev.* (1980), 66:85–129, for a critical review of the current law of dividends; and a response by Daniel Fischel, "The Law and Economics of Dividend Policy," *Virginia Law Rev.* (1981), 67:699–726.

83. See, for example, *Dodge v. Ford*, 204 Mich. 459, 500, 170 N.W. 668, 682. The corporation had on hand $54 million in cash out of total assets of $132 million. The firm was making large profits and could easily have made more by raising the price of its cars. The corporation had expansion plans that would require about $24 million. The Michigan Supreme Court found that given the remaining cash balance of $30 million, the board was under a duty to make a large distribution to shareholders, and affirmed a lower court order to pay a dividend of $19 million. See also Fletcher, *Cyclopedia of Corporations* (Wilmette, Ill.: Callaghan, 1983), vol. 11, section 5325.

84. The Michigan Supreme Court in *Dodge v. Ford* sets out this burden by stating that "courts of equity will not interfere in the management of directors [with respect to the dividend decision] unless it is clearly made to appear that they are guilty of" behaving in the prohibited fashion. 204 Mich. at 500, 170 N.W. 131, 134 (citing *Hunter v. Roberts, Throp and Co.*, 83 Mich. 63, 71 (1890)).

85. Cf. *Dodge v. Ford*, 204 Mich. 507–508, 170 N.W. 684; Fletcher, *Cyclopedia of Corporations*, vol. 3A, section 1039.

86. For a discussion of this potential conflict of interest, see chapter 2, section B 3.221. For an argument that, because of the conflicts involved, it is inappropriate to apply the business judgment rule to the review of dividend decisions, see Note, "The Business Judgment Rule and the Declaration of Corporate Dividends: A Reappraisal," *Hofstra Law Rev.* (1976), 4:73–100, pp. 98–100.

87. See, for example, the Model Business Corporation Act, section 41, drafted by

the ABA, and their annotation thereto in the *M.B.C.A. Annotated* (St. Paul: West Publishing, 1971), pp. 841–844. Accord, *Gottlieb v. Heyden Chemical Corp.*, 91 A.2d 57, 58–59 (Del. 1952).

88. See generally, *M.B.C.A. Annotated*, p. 844, and Marsh, "Are Directors Trustees? Conflict of Interest and Corporate Morality," *Business Lawyer* (1966), 22:35–76, pp. 48–50.

89. Where no member of management is a defendant in the suit or is otherwise personally interested in the suit's dismissal, the plaintiff under the laws of most states would be required to make a demand on the directors to bring the action directly on behalf of the corporation. If the directors decide not to proceed on the grounds that the suit is not in the best interests of the corporation, the plaintiff may not proceed. See, for example, *Klotz v. Consolidated Edison Co. of New York, Inc.*, 386 F. Supp. 577, 581–582 (S.D.N.Y. 1974). The plaintiff can challenge the decision, but the board is entitled in such a challenge to the protection of the business judgment rule. See G. Dent, "The Power of Directors To Terminate Shareholder Litigation: The Death of the Derivative Suit?" *Northwestern University Law Rev.* (1980), 75:96–146, pp. 100–101, nn.24–25.

90. Where one or more members of management are defendants in a derivative suit or are otherwise interested in its dismissal, the shareholder would be excused from making a demand on the directors on the grounds that such a demand would be "futile." The action can commence without any board approval. The issue then is whether a committee of formally independent board members can seek dismissal of the action. Courts of different jurisdictions differ as to how much respect to pay to the determination of the committee that dismissal would be in the best interests of the corporation. Some courts are willing to apply the business judgment rule to that determination, conditioned upon a court finding that the members of the committee are genuinely independent, acted in good faith, and used adequate procedures to investigate the claim raised by the plaintiff. *Auerbach v. Bennett*, 47 N.Y.2d 619, 393 N.E.2d 944 (1979); *Maldonado v. Flynn*, 597 F.2d 789 (S.D.N.Y. 1979). The Delaware Supreme Court, on the other hand, suggests that even after these findings are made, the court should go through a second step where it should apply its "own independent business judgment, whether the motion should be granted." While this language sounds like the court is placing upon the judiciary the making of a complex business decision, the court's real concern appears to be where the action to dismiss "meet[s] the criteria of step one, but the result does not appear to satisfy its spirit." *Zapata Corp. v. Maldonado*, 430 A.2d 779, 789 (1981). If the court were really suggesting that judges should conduct a *de novo* review of whether dismissal is in the best interests of the corporation and substitute their judgment entirely for that of the committee, there would be no point in requiring the first step. For an opinion that suggests that such a *de novo* review is appropriate, at least where the committee is appointed by a board the majority of which were interested in dismissing the suit, see *Joy v. North*, 692 F.2d 880 (2d Cir. 1982) *cert denied*, 460 U.S. 1051 (1983). Even if the court makes such a *de novo* review, most of the factors it must consider are closer to those typically considered by judges (for example, considering how probable it is that the plaintiff will succeed on his substantive claim) than those typically considered by businessmen, such as whether a given investment opportunity holds out sufficient promise to be worth taking.

91. See R. Gelfond and S. Sebastian, "Reevaluating the Duties of Target Management in a Hostile Tender Offer," *Boston University Law Rev.* (1980), 60:403–472, pp. 435–437. Gelfond and Sebastian conclude that "hostile tender offers inevitably create

a conflict of interest" and that the business judgment rule should not apply to board decisions made in connection with such offers. Their view is cited favorably by the dissents in *Johnson v. Trueblood*, 629 F.2d 287, 300 (1980) *cert. denied* 450 U.S. 999 (1981); and *Panter v. Marshall Field Co.*, 646 F.2d 271, 300 (7th Cir. 1981) *cert. denied* 454 U.S. 1092 (1981).

92. See Bebchuk, "The Case for Facilitating Competing Tender Offers," *Harvard Law Rev.* (1982), 95:1028–1056; and R. Gilson, "A Structural Approach to Corporations: The Case Against Defensive Tactics in Tender Offers," *Stanford Law Rev.* (1981), 33:819–891. Bebchuk and Gilson each feels that it is desirable for tender offers to be delayed sufficiently to permit an "auction" to develop for the firm's shares so that the firm has the chance to be sold to the highest bidder rather than inevitably to the first bidder. They would rely primarily on regulatory devices to create the needed delay. They would allow management to seek alternative acquirors and to transmit information about the firm to them but do not view such management actions as "defenses." Not all commentators agree with this approach. Some feel in essence that any management action in response to any offer is inappropriate. See, for example, Easterbrook and Fischel, "The Proper Role of a Target's Management in Responding to a Tender Offer," *Harvard Law Rev.* (1981), 94:1161–1204. Others think that some measures that make a corporation permanently more difficult to take over are appropriate. See Lipton, "Takeover Bids in the Target's Boardroom," *Business Lawyer* (1979), 35:101–134. None of these three schools of thought cast the courts in the position of making business judgments about whether a particular offer is good for the corporation or its shareholders.

93. This influence on outsider voting is referred to by some commentators as "groupthink." See, for example, Dent, "The Power of Directors to Terminate Shareholder Litigation," pp. 111–112; and Note, "The Propriety of Judicial Deference to Corporate Boards of Directors," *Harvard Law Rev.* (1983), 96:1894–1913, pp. 1896–1897. For a more general discussion of the effectiveness of outside directors in representing shareholder interests, see chapter 2, section B 3.3.

94. A rule requiring cash distributions to shareholders in excess of accounting profits (i.e., paying out of some or all of the portion of cash flow allocated to depreciation) would, for any firm, eventually require a change in the legal capital rules applicable to it under state corporation laws. These rules currently prohibit a dividend payment not made out of earned surplus.

Kingman Brewster suggested a universal payout rule twenty-five years ago, but the idea has never received much attention. "The Corporation and Economic Federalism," in E. Mason, ed., *The Corporation in Modern Society* (Cambridge: Harvard University Press, 1959), pp. 77–84, 81–83. Brudney briefly considers the idea but concludes that it is probably impractical. "Dividends, Discretion, and Disclosure," pp. 105–107. He is concerned with, among other things, whether the rule should apply to all earnings or some percentage and the lack of any theory to give an answer to that question. The discussion that follows suggests that the theory developed in this book provides a way of approaching the question that concerns Brudney.

95. Dividends averaged 58% of after-tax profits in the decade of the 1970s. This calculation is based on figures in table B-82 in *The Economic Report of the President* (1984).

96. Domestic undistributed profits constituted an average of 33% total internal sources of finance of U.S. nonfarm, nonfinancial businesses for the period 1975–1980. Table 938, *Statistical Abstract of the United States: 1981*.

97. The cost estimate also assumes that the funds the saver receives are, directly

or indirectly, invested in a new issue of equity. If the corporate sector as a whole maintains its current debt/equity ratio after imposition of a universal payout rule, this assumption is the right one to make.

Income tax data indicates that the top 1% of returns by income received 52% of all dividend income. Blum, Crockett, and Friend, "Stockownership in the United States: Characteristics and Trends," *Survey of Current Business* (November 1974), 54:16–40, p. 27. Given an estimate of total corporate dividends of almost $75 billion for 1983 (*The Economic Report of the President*, 1984, table B-82) and an estimate of approximately ninety-three million individual returns, the average annual receipt of dividends for persons in this group is over $4,000.

98. E. F. Denison, *Accounting for United States Growth, 1929–1969* (Washington, D.C.: Brookings Institution, 1974), p. 130; R. Solow, "Technical Change and the Aggregate Production Function," *Rev. Econ. and Statistics* (1957) 39:121–143.

99. See chapter 1, section C 2.23. A more detailed survey of the benefits to the economy of more accurate security prices is found in Fox, "Shelf Registration, Integrated Disclosure, and Underwriter Due Diligence," pp. 1015–1022.

100. M. Miller, "Debt and Taxes," pp. 262–264; Warner, "Bankruptcy Costs: Some Evidence," J. *Finance* (1977), 32:337–347.

101. See unpublished 1981 study of S. Titman described in T. Copeland and J. F. Weston, *Financial Theory and Corporate Policy*, 2d ed. (Reading, Mass: Addison-Wesley, 1983), p. 446.

102. M. Jensen and W. Meckling, "Theory of the Firm: Managerial Behavior, Agency Costs, and Ownership Structure," *J. Fin. Econ.* (1976), 3:305–360. For a general discussion of agency theory, see chapter 2, section B 3.3.

103. J. H. Scott, "A Theory of Optimal Capital Structure," *Bell J. Econ.* (1976), 7:33–54.

104. T. Copeland and J. F. Weston, *Financial Theory and Corporate Policy*, pp. 440, 445.

105. See, for example, Public Laws and Resolutions of the State of North Carolina (1901), ch. 2, section 52 (100% payout after reservation for working capital, determined by shareholders or directors, but to be no more than two-thirds of total assets); as amended in General Statutes of North Carolina (1949), section 55–115 (no two-thirds ceiling); General Statutes of New Jersey (1895), P.L. 1891, p. 176 (ceiling of reservation for working capital put at one-half of capital stock; profits invested in realty and merchandise necessary to business not included in payout formula), as amended in New Jersey Corporations Law, section 47 (1896 Sessions Laws), p. 293, 1901 Sessions Laws, p. 246 (where proviso for directors being able to determine working capital was eliminated); New Mexico Statutes Annotated (1953), 451–3–16 (like New Jersey 1901 provisions).

106. Cary and Eisenberg, *Corporations: Cases and Materials*, p. 1419; Brudney, "Dividends, Discretion, and Disclosure," p. 106.

107. For cases construing this term according to state dividend payout statutes, see *Cannon v. Wiscassett Mills Co.*, 195 N.C. 119, 141 S.E. 344 (1928) (accumulated profits defined by the increase during the year in the "true cash value" of the firm's assets, not in their book value); *Amick v. Coble*, 222 N.C. 484, 23 S.E.2d 854 (1943) (accumulated profits cannot be reduced by provision for bad debts, future taxes, and inventory adjustments); *Stevens v. United States Steel Corp.*, 68 N.J.Ex. 373, 59 A. 905, 908, 912 (1905).

108. Concerning the decline in the doctrine, see Fordham and Leach, "Interpretation of Statutes in Derogation of Common Law," *Vanderbilt Law Rev.* (1950), 3:438–455.

109. See *Stevens v. United States Steel Corp.*, 59 A. 905, 908.

110. Such fact situations and corresponding judicial restraint are found in *Gottfried v. Gottfried*, 73 N.Y.S.2d 692 (1947).

111. *Raynolds v. Diamond Mills Paper Co.*, 69 N.J.Ex. 29, 60 A. 941, 942–943.

112. Cf. statutes cited in note 105.

113. Victor Brudney, for example, recognizes that institutional arrangements may operate to tempt management systematically to make dividend decisions in its own interest rather than that of the shareholders, but the finds a universal payout rule in part impractical because he can find no theory to answer the questions whether the payout should be total or partial and, if partial, what the percentage should be. "Dividends, Discretion, and Disclosure," pp. 105–107. Frank Easterbrook recognizes that payment of dividends by firms that as a consequence go on to seek outside finance starts up a monitoring process that causes their managers to act more in shareholders' best interests than do the managers of firms that do not regularly seek outside finance. However, rather than apply this observation normatively to suggest that the second group of firms should be required to subject themselves to such monitoring if they wish to make real investments, he uses it positively, as discussed in chapter 2, Section B 3.222, to construct an agency cost explanation of why there exist firms that both seek outside finance regularly and pay dividends.

Author Index

Subject Index